José Martí's Liberative Political Theology

José Martí's Liberative Political Theology

MIGUEL A. DE LA TORRE

Vanderbilt University Press
Nashville, Tennessee

Library of Congress Cataloging-in-Publication Data

Names: De La Torre, Miguel A., author.
Title: José Martí's liberative political theology / Miguel A. De La
    Torre.
Description: Nashville : Vanderbilt University Press, 2021. | Includes
    bibliographical references and index.
Identifiers: LCCN 2020055787 (print) | LCCN 2020055788 (ebook) | ISBN
    9780826501684 (hardcover) | ISBN 9780826501677 (paperback) | ISBN
    9780826501691 (epub) | ISBN 9780826501707 (pdf)
Subjects: LCSH: Martí, José, 1853-1895—Political and social views. |
    Martí, José, 1853-1895—Views on religion. | Nationalism—Cuba. |
    Liberation theology.
Classification: LCC F1783.M38 D37 2021 (print) | LCC F1783.M38 (ebook) |
    DDC 972.91/05092—dc23

LC record available at https://lccn.loc.gov/2020055787
LC ebook record available at https://lccn.loc.gov/2020055788

To my parents,
Mirta y Miguel—
may they rest in peace
so far from the land that
witnessed their birth

CONTENTS

The problem of independence [is] not a change of form,
but a change of spirit.   JOSÉ MARTÍ

PREFACE

JOSÉ MARTÍ NEEDS little introduction really in the Western Hemisphere, with the exception of the United States. Ironically, not many Euro-Americans are cognizant of his writings, even though he is among the first responsible for introducing the Américas to the everyday idiosyncrasies of U.S. life, shaping the ideas and attitudes of América Latina of the late nineteenth century toward her northern neighbor. He lived a life of incarceration, deportation, expatriation, and migration—he was a figure who did not belong exclusively to Cubans or solely to Latinoamérica. Because his writings were among the first in the Western Hemisphere to capture the dream of a postcolonial existence, he is among the few in history who philosophically transcended regional and national borders, thus belonging to all of humanity. Martí was among that breed of writer-activists who attempted to create *patria* through a lifelong dedication to praxis. And yet few within the nation where he spent the last fifteen years of his life are familiar with his intellectual contributions.

Decades before European philosophers began recognizing a postcolonial discourse, Martí was already developing his own form of *modernismo* that attempted to move beyond the Eurocentric modernity of his time, even though he still relied on modernist concepts like liberation and the importance of rational thought. Before postcolonialism became fashionable among Eurocentric intellectuals, Martí was among the first colonized persons to create a space in his writings for a worldview apart and separate from the declining Spanish colonizer and the emerging U.S. empire, a space apart and separate from the Eurocentric way of thinking that normalized, legitimized, and justified their place in the world.

For the Cuban theologian Reinerio Arce, the development of Cuban theological and philosophical reflection cannot be located within European systematics. Instead, it is developed in Cuban literature, in Cuban music, in Cuban art, in Cuban political discussions, in Cuban cultural manifestations, and in Cuban national symbols.[1] An examination of Martí's political theology is crucial because this revolutionary figure, venerated as "the apostle of Cuba," serves as the primary symbol, a cultural manifestation that communicates a moral way of being capable of shaping a political vision for the future. No other Cuban writer or political leader, before or since, skillfully blended the religious, scientific, and artistic views of América Latina, Africa, Asia, and Europe to create an image of *patria* that can encompass the multidimensional aspects of a complex and diverse Cuban people. Hence, it is not surprising Martí constitutes a common sacred space shared by all Cubans, regardless of religious or political views—or lack thereof.

According to Mircea Eliade, anything profane (a river, stone, star, animal, human being) can be transformed into something sacred, a marker pointing to something greater than itself.[2] The radically religious, whether prophets, apostles, or *el apóstol* himself, are not the only supreme forms of expression. Anything can reveal aspects of the Divine. Cubans, as all other finite beings, struggle to construct the concept of an infinite God; therefore, symbols become the means by which they access aspects of the Divine created in the image of humans. As such, Martí represents more than a set of political symbols inducing symbolic behaviors; he is a sacred space, even though all too often a kerygmatic Martí is created who does not coincide with the historical Martí.

Martí is significant to our research today because he serves as an important and potent symbol of Cuban identity—regardless of whether his works are known, studied, or faithfully adhered to by self-proclaimed disciples. Scholars of semiotics, such as Paul Tillich, proposed that symbols are fastened to reality, becoming the only way people are able to grasp the metaphysical. Because of the metaphysical transcendent nature and the existential dilemma of humanity, any and every expression of otherworldliness can be made only through symbolic words, actions, objects, images, and ideas. Unlike a sign pointing solely to the Divine, the symbol incorporates the people's attempt to grasp the Absolute while creating the space for an encounter with the Divine. Tillich lists at least four characteristics of symbols: the symbol points beyond itself toward the Divine; symbols proactively engage in the praxis of what they point toward; they "unlock" aspects of the Divine otherwise hidden; and they reveal a greater depth of human reality.[3] For our purposes, Tillich's understanding of the significance of symbols is useful as we explore the importance of Martí not only as symbol but as what, as symbol himself, he signifies.

Like some unknown and unknowable deity, Martí has become one of the most powerful examples of a Cuban symbol for transcendence. He stands among the most used symbols, communicating to all Cubans a hope in establishing a just society. And yet, this symbol of transcendence has successfully been confined in an ideological straitjacket so as to tame his words, which are then manipulated by those seeking power and privilege or by those opposing them. The anthropologist João Felipe Gonçalves argues that Martí as myth "functions in national communities as totem do in certain 'primitive' societies. They provide a material symbol to a group's cohesiveness and thus help in the very constitution of the group they represent. Both totems and national heroes help to create the group they represent."[4] As such, Martí the symbol reinforces whichever hierarchy masks itself as the legitimate heir of *el apóstol*.

But in spite of this abusive use of Martí as symbol, he still can be utilized as a crucial Cuban marker. The mythification of Martí, as the historian Lillian Guerra argues, was inextricably linked to the process of nation building, which explains how different interpretations of his works represent conflicting interpretations of nation.[5] This book argues that as a Cuban symbol, Martí provides more than just a model for political development; he is also a model for living a moral, ethical life indigenous to the Cuban context. Although not divine (in spite of some of the apotheosized biographies written about him), he nonetheless points to a moral theology allowing Cubans, and all other seekers of liberation, to tackle the wider political world from their own social location.

Unfortunately, many have overlooked his theological grounding in favor of emphasizing his poetics or spiritualities (as if anyone could ever truly understand the spirituality of another human being). And although much has also been written concerning his political world-view, little attention has been given to the moral and ethical theological underpinnings of those political views—his political theology. So rather than focusing on the political or the spiritual, this book seeks to explore the moral, the ethical, and the religious aspects to Martí's work and how those have contributed to a political theology that predates the rise of the liberation theological movement of the late 1960s in Latinoamérica.

The book you hold in your hands took me a lifetime to write. Only now, after six decades since my birth, living in exile, can I look back six decades before my birth to attempt an understanding of why I, like my intellectual mentor José Martí, have lived in what he called in an 1894 letter to a childhood friend "the monster whose entrails I know, my slingshot is the one of David."[6] As a child growing up in the exilic Cuban community, I lived in the shadow of the Cuban apostle, embracing a figure who was a metaphysical apotheosis. Even though he authored a trove of publications, Martí was someone to venerate, not rigorously investigate. My commitment to approach my hero with the eyes of a critical scholar is the most respectful manner by which I can move from fawning rhetoric to intellectual appreciation. Regardless of the years spent to bring this particular volume to fruition, I confess nevertheless that I publish this book with a certain degree of trepidation.

Attempting to master Martí's works is as ambitious as attempting to master the Talmud. Just as multiple conflicting interpretations arise from sacred text, so too, in spite of his call for unity, are there multiple elucidations of his words. And even though contradictions exist in his writings, a careful reading still reveals consistent thoughts expressed throughout his brief adult life. This book attempts to systematize the diversity of his religious thoughts, offering the reader more than one possible interpretation. Still, I'm left wondering, What if I failed to read some letter he wrote or a fragment in his notebook that can easily refute a point I am arguing? What if some forgotten suitcase in someone's attic contains some of his notebooks that contradict my propositions? Or maybe I simply misinterpreted one of his archaic and arduous phrases. After all, even though he was a master wordsmith, ever-changing etymology complicates accurate translations. Those, like myself, who claim Martí as an intellectual mentor can find themselves wrestling and arguing over his writings as ancient rabbis once did over Scripture, producing differentiated commentaries. Marti's writings, like Holy Writ, contain equivocations, incongruencies, and inconsistencies. And like Holy Scripture, those ambiguities become the basis for proof-texting his complex corpus to justify the action(s) any reader already decided in which to engage.

Complicating an understanding of Martí are his own writings, deliberately abstruse so as to unite a diverse and conflicted exilic community. Understanding his thoughts is complicated, too, when we consider that as a pragmatic political organizer of a revolutionary movement that comprised thousands of émigrés, he had to unite an unwieldy constituency of different races, economic classes, political persuasions, and conflicting ideas into what *patria* meant. As Lillian Guerra reminds us, Martí "carefully crafted and often circuitous discourse [was] as laden with overt messianic images at it was riddled with silences on the question of future government policies." As a result, he "avoided precision and practically in discussing just how a newly founded republic might mitigate the social, class, and racial extremes that defined colony."[7]

I thus publish this work recognizing that I join previous and current *martiano* and *martiana* scholars who have struggled with Martí's written words with a certain degree of humility. With a heavy dosage of hermeneutical suspicion I subjectively (like all scholars of Martí) interact with Martí's words while remaining cognizant of what Paul Ricoeur calls semantic autonomy, the disconnection between the author's mental intentions and the verbal meaning the reader gives to the text, which is exacerbated when the text spans generations.[8] Although I stand on the shoulders of the *martiano* and *martiana* scholars who have come before me, grateful for their contributions and

insights, I recognize that any interpretation of a text offered is influenced by the social location of the one who is doing the interpreting
(myself included). And while the bibliography demonstrates my reliance on multiple interpreters—of different political stripes—I nevertheless focused on reading Martí through my own lens as a scholar of
religion specializing in ethics, in the hope my reading resonates with
others. Still, despite these lingering concerns, I nonetheless offer up
this book with full confidence (not hubris) as a contribution to the
overall *martiano* discourse, realizing that it may not be the definitive
interpretation of his works concerning the influence of his religious
thought on his political philosophy, but none the same, it is a contribution I hope will further stimulate discussion.

This book would not have been possible without the generous grant
that the Louisville Institute provided for a summer sabbatical and
trips to Miami, New Orleans, and three Cuban expeditions to conduct
research. I am especially thankful to the institute's director, Edwin
David Aponte, whose encouragement throughout this project makes
him the *padrino* of this book. I am also grateful to the University of
Denver Latino Center for Community Engagement and Scholarship
(DULCCES), and its director Deb Ortega, which funded an additional
trip to Cuba for more extensive research. I give gratitude for the cour-
tesy and assistance offered by Dr. Hortensia Calvo, director of the Latin
American Library at Tulane University, as well as Rosa Monzón-Alvarez
and Gladys Gómez-Rossié, of the University of Miami's Cuban Heritage
Collection, for their assistance. I am deeply thankful to Dr. C. María
Elena Segura Suárez, director of El Centro de Estudios Martianos in
La Habana, Cuba, and the hours of critical conversation I had with
Pedro Pablo Rodríguez and Jorge Juan Lozano Ros discussing some
of my ideas. And of course, I continue to appreciate the assistance
extended to me by El Seminario Evangélico de Teología in Matanzas,
Cuba, especially the conversations with Reinerio Arce, the trip plan for
me to Caimito de la Hanábana by Ofelia Ortega Suárez, and the hospi-
tality extended to me by the rector Carlos Ham. Finally, to my beloved
and intellectual conversation partner Deborah De La Torre, who always
helps in sharpening my thoughts.

NOTES ON TRANSLATION

One should not write with letters, but with acts.

FATHER FÉLIX VARELA, an influencer of José Martí's political theology, in his monumental work *Miscelánea filosófica* (1827) titled one of the chapters "El arte de traducir es el arte de saber," or "The art of translating is the art of knowing." For Martí, translating becomes, according to the cultural historian Adriana Novoa, "a way of accessing knowledge that was not limited by one single reality placed in front of us. He understood the translator as the person who re-contextualized experience, opening a world of possibility and becoming."[1] There exists an art in translating the works of Martí; it is a process that enhances the knowledge of the one doing the translating. Consequently, translating Martí's works is much more than simply finding a particular English word that best corresponds with a Spanish word. The art of translation captures the colors, shapes, and forms of Martí's thoughts on a foreign canvas and must be aware of the pitfalls in faithfully capturing the original masterpiece.

The *martiano* scholar Manuel Pedro González asserted that Martí's prose is among the most difficult within Latinoamérica to translate into English.[2] I fully concur. His syntax and tenses follow their own rules. At times verbs or conjunctions are absent; other times he creates neologisms to specifically signify a particular idea lacking any linguistic sign capable of completely encompassing its meaning. The task of faithfully rendering the beauty of his words or the poesy of his sentence structures is arduous. His phonic style was more than an attempt to make his writing ornate. How he wrote was in and of itself a moral imperative. As the linguist Cathy Jrade observed, Martí's "longing for a fluid, responsive, musical language reflects a view of literature that reaches beyond the aesthetic into the realm of the epistemological and the political. Within this framework, the poet is able to claim both a moral and conceptual superiority."[3] Indeed, much can be lost in translation. Choosing the right word for Martí is a crucial responsibility when we consider that, for him, as he wrote in an 1889 poem: "Love triumphs. Only words, / that are just triumphs."[4] He took great care in choosing the best possible word to nuance his sentiment: "Language must be mathematical, geometric, sculptural. The idea has to fit exactly into the phrase, so exact it cannot be taken out of the phrase without removing that very idea," he jotted in his notebook when contemplating the Pythagorean theorem.[5] Martí is neither careless nor lazy when choosing his words. In another notebook he wrote, "Words should be as brilliant as gold, light as a feather, solid as marble."[6]

Besides attempting to choose the English word that best conveys his sentiments, the translator's task is further complicated by Martí's piquant prose and turns of phrases that fail to translate well into any language. He has a tendency to write paragraphs masquerading as a single sentence, indiscriminately sprinkling dashes and colons to force the reader to slow down and take a longer pause in an attempt to enhance the rhythmic style. Surely, I am not the first, nor will I be the last *martiano* scholar to secretly wish Martí would have been more liberal with the usage of periods, a desire shared by many of his newspaper editors. And yet Martí would argue that his writing was already succinct, and any attempts at its reduction would strip away the piece's color and ability to soar: "Is not the art of writing to reduce? Verbosity undoubtedly kills eloquence. There is much to be said, and it has to be said with the least number of words as possible. Of course, each word has wing and color."[7] Finally, even though his writings are at times a bit moralizing and overbearing, I tried my best to maintain his tone.

Like Muslims who argue that the Qur'an can be read and understood only in its original language (Arabic); some—myself included—wonder whether grasping Martí's significances can occur only in Spanish. Is the act of translating his words to a different language akin to an act of violence against his prose? Although Martí expressed in one of his notebooks that he did not want his works translated into English, I went against the *maestro*'s wishes and translated all his quotes from primary sources—unless I have otherwise noted.[8] Still, to appreciate Martí's virtuosity, one really must do so in his original tongue; hence, his quotes appear in Spanish in the footnotes while my humble attempt to capture their essence in English appears in the main text. I am grateful to Dr. Sergio Macías, who double-checked all my translations, offering corrections, suggestions, and alternative interpretations. Whenever the translation appears more poetic or crisp, it is due, no doubt, to his insights. I take full responsibility for any mistranslations where I did not incorporate his suggestions. I also appreciate my research assistant Grego Peña Camprubí, who provided a final proofreading of all my translations, greatly improving the finished rendering. Furthermore, the reader should be aware that any biblical passages, unless otherwise noted, were also translated by me from the original Classical Hebrew and Koine Greek, as were the passages in more modern languages like French, German, and especially Spanish.

The reader should also be aware of the male-gender-biased language, the legitimized—yet problematic—norm for Martí's time. Rather than translating his words to appear more gender neutral (a strong temptation to save Martí from his male-centeredness), I decided to purposely keep the masculine pronouns he used, even his usage of the generic *man* to refer to humanity. Translating Martí to sound more inclusive, I feared, would create a false understanding of his thoughts and mask the sexism reflected in his writings. Additionally, Martí refers to Black individuals as *negros*, which I translated as *Negro* in English. While I am aware of other terms, like *Afro-Cuban*, I chose to remain faithful to the original text (problematic, I know, for some English readers today) and use the Spanish word *negro* except occasionally for stylistic reasons. The same is true for the word *mulato*, which carries negative connotations among English readers, for the etymology of *mulatto* signifies the sterile product produced by a horse and a mule. Why not simply use the more neutral word *Afro-Cuban*? *Afro-Cuban* may appear neutral for some English speakers, but as the historian Ada Ferrer reminds us, it connotes a degree of exoticism in Spanish, blurring social and political distinctions between Black and biracial in the Cuban context.[9] Thus, I use the Spanish word to maintain the normative racism within the language, problematizing its usage rather than masking it through politically correct translation.

Finally, there are certain words I chose not to render into English for I feared they would have lost too much in the translation. Specifically, when referring to Latin America, I used *Latinoamérica*. When referring to all the nations of the Western Hemisphere, I chose to use *América* (with an accent) distinguishing *nuestra América* (our America) from *la otra América* (the other America)—the Anglo America. With more than forty countries comprising the Américas, it is problematic for one of those countries—the United States—to appropriate the word to refer to itself exclusively. Martí, I argue, was probably the first person to recognize how the United States had appropriated the entire name of the Western Hemisphere for itself. According to the *martiana* scholar Laura Lomas, Martí refused to refer to the United States as America while a delegate during the Pan-American Conference of 1889, and since 1891, he used the abbreviation "U.S." for *la otra América*.[10] I also have chosen not to translate the word *patria*, which is often rendered as *homeland*, *country*, *fatherland*, or *motherland*. Other words that I deemed lost too much in their rendition to English, include—but are not limited to—*nueva religión* (new religion), *nueva iglesia* (new church), *Jesús* (Jesus), and *sociabilidad* (sociability).

Introduction

The noble habit of examination destroys
the servile habit of belief.

AMONG DOÑA LEONOR'S prized possession was an 1884 prayer book
that her son, José Martí, lovingly gave her. The book, titled *Useful and
Profitable to Implore the Divine Clemency and Powerful Shelter of the Most
Holy Mary Our Lady Saint Anne*, consisted of devotional prayers vener-
ating St. Anne (mother of the Virgin Mary and grandmother of Jesús).
On the inside cover, Martí wrote these words: "For my mother Doña
Leonor Pérez from her son who does not forget her." A few words jotted in a religious book to his mother testify to the esteem in which
he held her, especially because exile forced their separation for most
of his adult life. More important, the gift signifies his unwillingness
to totally dismiss his Catholic upbringing. Martí may have been anticlerical and antidogmatic, but never antireligious or antispiritual. In
fact, he was a very spiritual man. A metaphysical dimension in Martí's
writings is easily detected in his argument for something more than
simply this material human existence. "Human life," he wrote in 1882,
"is not the totality of life! The grave is a way, not the end . . . Death is
joy, renewal, a new task. Human life would be a disgusting and bar-

baric invitation if it were limited to life on earth."[1] The metaphysical, for Martí, becomes a crucial component in the understanding and implementation of the political. While he held definite ideas concerning the metaphysical, there does not exist in his writings an advocacy for great religious absolutes.

Martí is recognized as a rebel—a rebel on the battlefield and a rebel whenever he put ink to paper. His overarching mission was the liberation of Cuba from the grasp of Spain's colonial control, and to that end he provided the moral justification for a "holy war," or as he would call it, *la guerra necesaria*. And while the theological thoughts employed to achieve this political goal are profound and mature, his religious conclusion remained fluid and hybrid. Still, certain religious themes can be ascertained if we look closely at his pronouncements concerning the spiritual that serve as guideposts indicating the boundaries of his thoughts rather than absolute truths. I am convinced that any serious scholar of Martí's work who fails to earnestly examine his pronouncements concerning the theological does so at the peril of failing to fully grasp a crucial underpinning of his political thoughts, for his concepts concerning political freedom were based on securing spiritual liberation.

Although it is clear he was an active political revolutionist, few in the English-speaking world have explored the theological underpinning of his works. But even among scholars who specialized in liberative theologies, Martí's contributions are all too often ignored. Even though twentieth-century liberative politics were highly influenced by Martí's writings, those grounding their liberative praxis in theological thought seldom look to him as a possible precursor to what would eventually come to be known as liberation theology. My task, therefore, is to explore the religious foundation of his political theology wearing the hat of a social ethicist. His spiritual response to political oppression is what we are calling political theology; and while all theologies are political (justifying or challenging the dominant cultural norms); liberative theologies make no attempt, unlike most Eurocentric theological paradigms, to mask their political leanings on deliberations. This book argues that some of José Martí's political writings resonate with the late 1960s liberation theological movement that crystalized almost three-quarters of a century after his death. Martí's overarching commitment to those seeking liberation requires us today to examine how his religious contributions had an impact on his political views. To that end, this book focuses on the genealogy of his religious thoughts and how they intersect with his political praxis to ascertain his contributions to the liberative discourse.

This book further argues that José Martí's political theology, which at first glance may appear outdated, remains relevant. He remains a transcendental figure not only for the further development of what it means to be Cuban but also for what it means to be a *latinoamericana o latinoamericano*. Wedged between the declining yet ironclad grip of colonial Spain and the emerging grasp of U.S. imperial expansion, Martí is recognized as the intellectual and organizational founder of the revolutionary movement that led to Cuba's rebellion against Spain. He was a recognized professor, translator, storyteller, first-class propagandist, art critic, ethnographer, journalist, revolutionary strategist, scholar-activist, and diplomat representing Argentina, Uruguay, and Paraguay, and through his works *Ismaelillo* (1882) and *Versos sencillos* (1891), he was an established international poet and founder of the genre *modernismo* in Spanish letters. He wrote with confidence and authority on history, politics, sociology, economics, anthropology, art, science, philosophy, and of course, religion. His journalistic articles found in daily newspapers throughout Latinoamérica read more as literary essays than reports on actual events. Fluent in four languages, Martí, through his writings, raised consciousness on how *latinoamericanos* and *latinoamericanas* incorporated modernity.

While *martiana* and *martiano* scholars argue over whether he should be considered a philosopher, he defined in one of his notebooks what he does, writing: "Philosophy is the knowledge of the cause of beings, their distinctions, their analogies and their relationships."[2] Elsewhere he noted: "Philosophy is no more than the secret concerning the relationship of various forms of existence."[3] If we accept his organic definitions of philosophy as accurate, then without a doubt he was among the greatest moral philosophical thinkers to have emerged from the Américas. True, he never systemized his philosophical thoughts and ideas in book form; although he did plan, according to the *martiano* scholar Félix Lizaso, to write a volume containing his major philosophical thoughts and ideas, to be titled *El concepto de la vida* (*The Concept of Life*).[4] Although no book self-systemizing his philosophy was ever published, he did disseminate his moral thoughts through newspaper articles, letters to companions, notebooks, and poetry. Some dismiss his philosophical and theological contributions because they do not appear synthesized in some comprehensive opus, or because articles, letters to companions, notebooks, and poetry are not necessarily viewed as mediums conducive for in-depth philosophical contemplations; nevertheless, a careful reading of his complete oeuvre does provide a philosophical and, more important, theological foundation to his thoughts that undergirded his political actions. If the task of thinkers is to have their work be useful, capable of spiritually transforming the reader, and creating a moral groundwork upon which to construct *patria*, then dismissing Martí's political-theological contributions because he did not systematize or synthesize his philosophical deliberations would be a grave error.

Predating the coinage of the term *axiology* by a couple of decades,[5] Martí was interested in this branch of practical philosophy that explored the moral foundation upon which ethical practices were based. Axiology studies value and how value is established within society by exploring the intersection of ethics (the values associated with the social conduct in which to engage) and aesthetics (the study of beauty and harmony), especially in relationship to religion. If indeed Martí was a philosopher—specifically a moral philosopher—then he was no doubt an axiologist who aesthetically used words, specifically theological words and spiritual imagery, as tools capable of initiating praxis designed to bring about political change that could lead to a more just social order. Not interested in employing words to engage in abstract speculative philosophical thinking, his pronouncements focused on how the metaphysical served as foundational in creating *patria*. As the *martiana* scholar Susana Rotker observed, "Martí attempts to reconcile transcendentalism with social life by insisting on a type of writing that would serve as a tool for human improvement."[6] As a pragmatic axiologist, as I argue, he understood philosophy as "the science of causes, of causality."[7] He sought to connect his writings with *lo cotidiano* (the everyday), which encompasses the mundane and the spiritual—not lofty metaphysical notions that simply tickle the mind but do nothing to liberate the people. Rather than trying to understand Martí as a philosopher, we might be more successful if we see him as a philosophical ethicist who wrestled with bringing forth justice.

The challenge of interpreting Martí's political theology, or anything he wrote, is the tendency of so-called admirers to make him into whatever they wished him to be. Many hagiographies have been written, especially by those advancing their own grip on political power. He has been propagandized and politicized by caudillos from both the Right (Fulgencio Batista) and the Left (Fidel Castro) who constantly claimed him as the intellectual basis of their diverse political movements. As the *martiano* scholar John Kirk observed, "Because so many different administrations since the War of Independence have used Martí as their source of inspiration, it is generally concluded that his writings must necessarily have been of an essentially bland, general nature."[8] While politically dissimilar *políticos* assert that they were enacting Martí's basic tenets concerning independence, they all are guilty of distortion.

I have no intention of molding Martí into some liberation theological thinker, for obviously he was not. Attempting to determine the political theology of Martí forces me to ask whether I am simply repeating the errors of many others by reading my own views, political inclinations, and biases into his writings. Am I seeking to wrestle and understand his thoughts, or am I simply seeking to re-create him in my own image? Am I appropriating his writings simply to prove what I predetermined he said or should have said? Any engagement with Martí's writings requires a healthy dosage of one's own hermeneutical suspicion. Nevertheless, there do exist commonalities between his writings and what would eventually come to be known as liberation theology. The attempt of this project is not to read liberation theology into Martí; nor is it to read from his writings a liberation theology. Instead, this book attempts to focus on those areas in his work that resonate with what would become liberation theology as a means of moving the latter's discourse forward. As crucial as liberation theology may have been during the latter half of the twentieth century, new ways of reimaging the discipline are required if it is to have an impactful voice during the twenty-first century.

Cognizant of the pitfalls of reading Martí through one set of political lenses, I have attempted to engage scholarship emerging from contradictory perspectives. I have studied the works of authors who would be considered pro-Castro as well as those who would be considered anti-Castro, always seeking to discard those sections in their presentations where I felt their political posturing adulterated Martí's thoughts. I have engaged in conversations with *martiano* and *martiana* scholars on the island and in *el exilio*, with scholars who spouted diametrically opposed political opinions derived from Martí's writings, some of whom attempted to aggressively seduce me in embracing the Martí they envisioned. I found both sides of the political spectrum's interpretation of Martí's work problematic; nevertheless, I did attempt to mine the insights they offered. No doubt scholars from the Right and Left will find the analyses I propose objectionable. So, I leave it to the reader to determine whether I succeeded in my task of attempting to read as objectively (a near-impossible task) as possible.

ONE

A Catholic Spiritual Foundation

It cannot be that God gives man reason, and an archbishop, who is not much like God, forbids him to express it.

HUMANS, FOR JOSÉ Martí, are transcendent beings, possessing an immortal soul and occupying, with certain duties and responsibilities, a central space in creation. The social location of humans within the cosmos fosters spiritual liberation, a freedom that is desired as long as it does not advocate hatred toward fellow humans or attempt to subjugate the political apparatus. Spiritual freedom is crucial and important because it is foundational for good governance and free societies. As Martí reminds us in his 1882 prologue to Pérez Bonalde's *Poema del Niágara*: "Neither literary originality is conceivable nor political liberation subsistent as long as spiritual freedom is not assured."[1] Spiritual and religious freedom were to be an integral dimension of the Cuban existence. Although he rejected the power of the Christian church—specifically the Catholic Church—because it abandoned the ethical principles it taught, Martí nevertheless used Christian-based concepts as an underpinning for establishing liberation. But achieving spiritual and political liberation was an arduous charge. The sociologist Pavón Torres has referred to Martí's attempt to lift people from the reign of material needs into the reign of spiritual necessity as a Cyclopean task.[2] How Martí sets out to accomplish this task through his intellectual writings and pragmatic actions is the focus of this book.

Martí's contribution to the revolutionary political discourse was his establishing of a Cuban-based philosophical ideology rooted in the spiritual by merging reason with universal metaphysically based ethics. The spiritual, for Martí, became the means by which he understood the material. To that end, he strove to create a spiritual way of being, manifested as a *nueva religión* (new religion) and *nueva iglesia* (new church), wherein emerge political ideals upon which *patria* could be organized. Although he was a metaphysical mentor for Cubans, and by extension Latinoamérica, determining what exactly his spirituality was is at times difficult to ascertain. Thus, this chapter begins by exploring his views and understanding of the dominant religious milieu of his time, Christianity, and specifically Catholicism. But first, we will attempt to situate Martí within the major physical-metaphysical philosophical debate of his time. Studying Martí's metaphysical perspectives is crucial because as he wrote in his notebook, "Metaphysics is the set of absolute truths which serve as explanatory and fundamental to all human knowledge."[3] As this book will argue, Martí's political theory, as an outgrowth of human reason, is rooted in the metaphysical.

The Physical-Metaphysical Divide

According to the cultural historian Adriana Novoa, "The nineteenth century was characterized as materialistic, mechanistic, and deprived of old metaphysic conceptions."[4] Through the Américas (and Europe), a debate between materialist (i.e., the works of Karl Marx, Charles Darwin, and Herbert Spencer) and spiritualist over the concept of human progress was unfolding, a debate in which Martí partook. Many thinkers flocked to some form of materialist positivist worldview, considering it modern, progressive, and scientific, over and against what was considered an outdated spiritualism, deemed superstitious by materialists. Rather than accepting this clear philosophical dichotomy, Martí insisted that the physical and metaphysical were united. While religious churches and organizations were up in arms over the evolutionary pronouncements of Charles Darwin, Martí saw unity. In an 1884 book review for *La América*, a New York newspaper where he served as editor in chief, he wrote: "The doctrine of evolution, yet important to explain all the mystery of life, is not opposed to the existence of a supreme power; instead, it limits itself to teach the works by natural law, and not miracles."[5] Martí insisted elsewhere that "the world was not produced through creation, but by continuous development."[6]

Martí feared that a full embrace of solely the materialist position meant erasure of the spiritual and rejection of God, the supernatural, and the purpose for existence. In an outline concerning his philosophical musings, he argued for the need of both the tangible and the invisible. For him: "All philosophical schools could be concertized in two schools. Aristotle provided the scientific means which has lifted much, twice already in the great history of the worlds, to the school of the physical. Plato, and the divine Jesús, had the purest spirit and faith in another life made poetic, durable, the school of the metaphysical. The two united are the truth: each isolated is only part of the truth, which fails when they do not help each other."[7] To solely rely on materialism while ignoring the metaphysical, as so many of his contemporaries were doing, endangered the individual and, by extension, the society, for such an approached denied a soul to both. Witnessing all around him the justification of economic oppression through the embrace of materialism, à la Spencer, Martí argued that possessing a soul was crucial for the well-being of the individual and for *patria*—for the soul "is the power to observe, judge, and transmit."[8]

Harmonizing the divide between extreme materialism based on a dogmatic science with an antirational superstitious spiritualism was a continuation of the foundation laid by Martí's pedagogical mentors José Agustín Caballero, Félix Varela, and José de la Luz (to be explored in greater detail later). Maintaining fidelity to these mentors and continuing his usual tendency for neat dichotomies, Martí divides reality as the tangible and the intangible, reducing all philosophical schools into one of the two categories; materialists follow the ancient lead of

Aristotle and spiritualists continue the thoughts of Plato and Jesús. True, Martí places much emphasis on Aristotle's scientific observation of nature, claiming, "The observable nature is the only philosophical source. The observer is the sole agent of Philosophy."[9] He argued that through the senses, humans received impressions, and through reason, reality was communicated.[10] Nevertheless, he balanced the scientific with the "dreamer" Plato, "the unrealistic—heir of the fakir [Hindu religious ascetic who lives solely on alms]."[11] He believed that the universal spirit already knows all that science can ever discover: "When the season of the sciences is complete, and they know all that there is to know, they will not know more than what the spirit knows today."[12]

In typical dichotomous fashion, Martí observed, "There are two kinds of beings: those who can be touched and those who cannot be touched."[13] God, as invisible, can be reached through the sciences; not the God constructed by humans but instead the God who is "an immense sea of spirits where all the arrogant nonconformities of men are to go to be confused."[14] Martí embraced the body-soul platonic duality in which the existence of an immortal substance, which he calls soul or spirit, is trapped within a corruptible body: "It is true! From my vile flesh this hand, / impotent truth! It does not reach Heaven; / but within the corpus human / being there is another being without form or measure / that touches and sees, after and before life."[15] One can almost hear the echo of St. Paul's anguished dualistic cry "O wretched man that I am! Who will rescue me from this body of death?" (Romans 7:24). A two-world dualism implies a dualism of existence. This dualism involves a material inferior and corruptible world that can be scientifically understood through observation and also a spiritually superior and incorruptible world. The world without substance that feels and sees exists before corporal human life and will exist afterward resembles reincarnation, a reincarnation not of the body, but of the soul, closer to Hinduism than to Platonism. He declared: "If all earthly things were to be turned into ashes, / These would rebirth more luxuriant and livelier: / And the soul is resurrected. I have seen it / Nailed to the cross as the immense Christ, / And later in the sun of peaceful love. / Flap the wings and taste the flowers!"[16]

First Spiritual Utterances

In previous publications, I have argued for an "ethics of place," insisting on the role of the geographical space a person inhabits in forming their sociopolitical thoughts. An ethics of place recognizes the physical location where oppression resides as crucial in understanding the lives, the hardships, the pains, and the concerns of those forced to exist on the margins of power and privilege, and how this milieu influences the construction of theological and philosophical thought for those occupying said space.[17] To engage in political and/or theological reflection requires being *¡presente!* To be present moves away from simply theorizing on people's actions and thoughts by recognizing that the physical location of oppression also makes a contribution to the analysis. To ignore physical location questions whether we can truly comprehend whatever is under investigation. Paying attention to geographical space occupied by the subject(s) of our investigation and how the everyday manifests in thoughts, opinions, norms, and traditions provides a better understanding of what is being investigated. To consider an ethics of place when it comes to Martí is to pay close attention to the disenfranchised physical spaces he occupied.

The young Martí was a child living in the colonial capital at the start of a major colonial rebellion. Rather than embracing his father's royalist views, he opted for the more revolutionary, if not seditious, views of his teacher and mentor Rafael María de Mendive. As a sixteen-year-old teenager, he published a poem in the school newspaper celebrating the call to war against the "oppressive barbarian."[18] Decades later, in an 1891 letter to Enrique Trujillo, editor of New York's *El Porvenir*, Martí recalled discussing Céspedes's uprising at Mendive's home, following his march through "swampy scrubland." Ironically, his fateful clash with the colonial authorities occurred on 4 October 1869 over laughter, not revolutionary activities. As *voluntarios* paraded outside the home of Fermín Valdés Domínguez in honor of Queen Isabella's birthday, they overheard the boys, including the young Martí, laughing—as teenage boys often do. Thinking that the boys were mocking them, they entered the residences and conducted a search. Five days later, while reviewing the documents confiscated from Valdés Domínguez's home, the authorities found a letter cosigned by the young Martí and Fermín, accusing a former friend and classmate of "apostasy" for enlisting in the army of Spain. The letter, written to Carlos de Castro y de Castro, was brief, just a few lines; nevertheless, it was a decisive moment that had an impact on the remaining course of his life. The letter simply stated: "Companion: Have you ever dreamed about the glory of the apostates? Do you know how they use to punish apostasy in ancient times? We hope that a disciple of Mr. Rafael María de Mendive would not leave unanswered this letter."[19] The young Martí was arrested twelve days later on 21 October, accused of treason because of the offending letter.

The physical "space" that the young Martí occupied, shaping his future spirituality and having a momentous lifelong impact upon him, was San Lázaro Quarry where he toiled under forced labor from 14 April until 13 October 1870, condemned as a youth to hard labor. As the *martiano* scholar Carlos Alberto Montaner romantically observed: "He entered as a young man and left as an Apostle. The seed which Mendive, while in the classroom, throws into the farrow, gave birth in the prison."[20] Although he served only six months, in his occupation of this hellish geographical space, the cruelty and brutality of colonialism scarred his body and spirit for life. He was required to hack out stone blocks and cart them to the top of the quarry while wearing shackles from ankle to waist. He was forced to walk four miles to the quarry, work twelve hours there, and walk back wearing these heavy chains, always under threat of the whip.

Martí's father, Don Mariano, upon seeing his son's broken body, "disconsolately wept." Recounting the event, Martí writes how his father clumsily tried to bind his wounds with bandages, weeping uncontrolledly, as Don Mariano's tears fell and mixed with his son's bloody wounds. The father was left alone with his tears on his knees in a puddle of his son's blood once the bell rang to drag the young lad away.[21] The *martiana* scholar Laura Lomas shows how Don Mariano's frustration, disappointment, and helplessness upon gazing his son led to bitter tears. The salty tears of his father, who worked as a police officer and enforcer of the colonial order, fell open festering wounds and stung the young Martí, serving as a reminder of how his father's complicity with the colonial powers was responsible for his imprison-ment. According to Lomas: "This image of the stooped father contrasts with the brutal anonymity of the prison, which forces the prisoner to labor by beating and pulling him with inanimate objects. A bell, a stick, and a rough arm drive the prisoner back to work and away from father who remains kneeling in the mud of his tears, the Cuban soil, and his son's blood."[22]

During his imprisonment, Martí experienced upon his flesh scars inflicted for the audacity of possessing his own thoughts. Although he served only a few months in the quarry, the experience wrecked his health and created physical ailments that lasted the rest of his life. The shackles worn led to lesions on his groin, which lead to lifelong fevers, pain, and swelling in his right testicle. It eventually had to be removed, and a sore on his right ankle never healed.[23] The labor in the quarries under the bright Cuban sun left him half-blind, while the strenuous work left him with a hernia. These physical wounds were injuries shared by other inmates, with whom Martí found solidarity.

As soon as he arrived in Spain after his release and expatriation, Martí began to write a pamphlet denouncing political imprisonment in Cuba and advocating for independence. Rather than focusing on himself and his sufferings, he turned his gaze to other inmates. *El presidio político en Cuba*, published in 1871, when he was eighteen years old, introduced the reader to a twelve-year-old child named Lino Figueredo who was working at the quarry, sentenced to ten years without know-ing why. The quarry's stone tore into Lino's hands, and he faced daily beatings and eventually contracted smallpox.[24] He related stories of cruel and sadistic punishments for nonexistent crimes, like that of a Chinese man left to die of cholera; the induced insanity of the Black prisoner Juan de Dios; the seventy-six-year-old man named Nicolás del Gatillo, whose back was reduced to a rotting wound leading to a fifteen-day coma; and the suicide attempt of the twenty-year-old Del-gado.[25] Martí's incarceration reinforced a lifelong commitment to priv-ileging the experiences of the world's oppressed and marginalized. With these individual stories, Martí attempted to raise consciousness among the Spaniards. "Prison," according to Martí, "was the prison of Cuba, the institution of the Government, the act, repeated a thousand times by the Government sanctioned by the representatives here [in Spain]."[26] By retelling prison testimonies to those he believed were uninformed, he hoped they might be horrified by what was being done in their name; he hoped to wake them from their dream state to face reality. He hoped to raise consciousness among them by appealing to their humanity and spirituality: "Oh! Your dream is neither beautiful nor heroic, because there is no doubt your dreaming. Look, look at the portrait I'm going to paint for you, and if you do not tremble in terror over the evil you have done, and do not curse in horror this façade of national integrity which I present you with, I will turn my eyes in shame from this Spain which has no heart."[27]

His brutal six months of hard labor changed the young man forever. From romanticizing about *patria*, Martí began a maturing process that eventually led to becoming a man of action, seeking to make his anticolonial ideals a reality. Prior to his imprisonment, in his epic play *Abdala*, he wrote of establishing *patria* so as to achieve fame and glory. But after his imprisonment, he sought *patria* as a duty and sacrifice. Although he is often portrayed as a dreamer and idealist, the fact remains that he carried on his body the stigmata of colonialism, which led to his responsibility to prevent other bodies from obtaining similar wounds. This cruel and brutal experience began the process that would eventually lead to an intellectual maturity for Martí that would become the basis from which future thoughts and writings evolved, specifically when it came to spirituality.

Most people might have turned bitter or angry. Many might have simply given into hatred toward those responsible for inflicting sadistic pain upon the old, the young, the infirm. But Martí chose a different response: "And I still do not know how to hate."[28] Rather than hatred, Martí felt God's presence leading him to express pity toward his abusers: "I feel in me this God, I have in me this God; this God in me pities you, more pity than horror and contempt."[29] Martí discovered early in life that there is an essential goodness to humans because their soul contains the teardrop of God: "God exists in the idea of the good, who watches over the birth of each being, and leaves in the soul which is framed in the soul as a pure teardrop. The good is God. The teardrop is the source of eternal feeling."[30] What is amazing about this quote—

seeing the good as God and humans as containing that good—is that he penned it shortly after experiencing unimaginable, coldhearted evil and inhumanity.

As a mere teenager experiencing humanity's viciousness, Martí developed a foundational understanding of the deity that was based on the goodness not only of God but also on the goodness within those who were persecuting him. When Martí gazed upon the scarred back of fellow seventy-six-year-old inmate Don Nicolás del Castillo, he expressed compassion for those who whirl the whip. He pitied them for not being able to listen to their consciousness.[31] With these fellow prisoners, who postcolonialist thinker Frantz Fanon would one day call "the wretched of the earth," Martí cast his lot. His solidarity with the oppressed was more than simply a concept he arrived at intellectually; it was a physical solidarity achieved by sharing the pain of persecution. In spite of the physical danger faced, he had the audacity to continue writing against repressive regimes, for as he elegiacally wrote in one of his poems, "The shame / Of man is my shame: my cheeks / Suffer from the evil of the Universe."[32]

He did not leave prison cynical or contemptuous of human nature, which would have been expected, having suffered atrocious human punishments; rather, he seems to have left prison morally fortified. The love toward his enemies learned at San Lázaro Quarry, mixed with a fervor for Cuban independence, became a lifelong obsession for Martí. Within this successful political tract, he proclaimed God's existence and presented himself as a messenger of the Divine: "God exists, and I come in God's name to break the cold vessel which encloses the Spanish souls in tears."[33] But he rejected the God of organized religions by claiming that followers are responsible for the death of God. Predating Friedrich Nietzsche's famous (and often misunderstood) quote "God is dead. God remains dead. And we killed him,"[34] Martí claims: "How wretched are the people when they kill God! . . . And how much will they weep when they make God cry!"[35] But unlike Nietzsche's accusation of us killing God by replacing revelation (spiritualism) with science (materialism) in our desire to better understand the world, Martí's claim is based on our refusal to follow God's teachings on love and justice, which will lead to the liberation of humanity.

While Nietzsche looks toward abstract thoughts to understand the killing of God, Martí turns toward physical acts in relationship to the oppressed. Rejecting the purely materialist path, he embraced Christianity's spiritual contribution to humanity: the moral obligation to stand in solidarity with those marginalized by the secular and ecclesiastical social structures of his day.

Martí's Religiosity

While his time at San Lázaro Quarry helps us better understand the genesis of Martí's spirituality, for the purposes of this book, we need to focus on how this early experience developed into his broader understanding of religiosity. Because "the world is religious,"[36] religion serves a crucial purpose in society. Contrary to the Eurocentric "Enlightenment" that exclusively moved philosophical thought toward reason and science at the expense of faith and spirituality, Martí advocated for a rationally based faith and spirituality. He was not in favor of dismissing religion as irrelevant, as were those during the so-called Age of Reason. He instead argued for its necessity and usefulness, even insisting that if no religion existed, one would need to be created:

> All people need to be religious. Not only is it essential, but for its own usefulness it needs to be. The reflection of the spirit of a superior being is innate. Even if there were no religion, every man would be able to invent one, because every man feels it. It is useful to conceive of a great high being . . . Morality is the basis of a good religion. Religion is the form of natural belief in God and the natural tendency to investigate and venerate God. The religious being is intertwined with the human being. An irreligious people will perish, because there exists nothing to nourish virtue. Human injustices dislike her. It is necessary that the celestial justice guarantees it.[37]

Martí held no animosity toward the basic tenets of Christianity as taught by its founder, Jesucristo. Jesús, he believed, should not be held responsible for the atrocities committed by those who come later in his name. Christianity, like all religions, was simply marred by sectarianism: "Exaggerations are committed when the Christian religion, like all other religions, has been disfigured by her bad sectarians . . . The founder of the family is not responsible for the offenses commit-ted by the children of his children."[38]

Succinctly stated, José Martí's religiosity appears to be an innate, practical, dualistic unitarianism that leads to the good and dismisses those acts that are useless in accomplishing one's duty as the bad. His religious worldview comes into focus when he attempts to provide us with a brief explanation for, and definition of, religion:

> There is in man an intimate, vague, but constant and imposing knowl-edge of a great creator. This knowledge is the religious feeling—and its form, its expression, the manner by which each group of men con-ceives and worship this God is what is called religion. This is why, in ancient times, there were as many religions as there were original peoples; but not one solitary group of people stopped feeling God nor offer worship. Religion, therefore, is within the essence of our nature. Although forms vary, the great feeling of love, of firm belief and respect, is always the same. God exists and is worshipped. Among the numerous religions, the one of Christ has occupied more time than any other peoples and centuries. This is explained by the purity of its moral doctrine, the open-handedness of its evangelists of the first five centuries, for the strength of its martyrs, for the extraordinary superiority of the celestial man who founded it. But the first reason is the simplicity of his preaching which greatly contrasted with the indignant sophistry, petty gods and childish arguments with which pagan reason of that time was entertained; furthermore, in the pure severity of his morality already so forgotten, and yet so necessary to contain the unworthy debaucheries to which the passions in Rome and their domains had been given.[39]

His views toward religion and spirituality were positive as long as they supported the good by opposing oppression while being under-girded by the preeminence of reason: "The spiritual life is a science, like the physical life."[40] Martí argued that the salvation of religion was linked to the deploying of reason. He wrote: "Worship is a necessity for the people. Love is no more than the need for belief: there is a secret power which always longs for something to respect and in what to believe. Fortunate to extinguish irrational worship, the worship of reason begins now. Do not believe in the images of religion anymore, the people now believe in the images of *patria*."[41] But when religion clings to superstition or negatively interferes in the political realm, then his critique becomes quite scathing: "Treacherous assassin, ingrate to God and an enemy of men, is the one who, under the pretext of directing the new generations, teaches them an isolated and absolute cluster of doctrines, and preaches for their ears, before the sweet conversation of love, the gospel of hatred."[42]

We simply do not know Martí's personal religious identity. What we do know is that he was baptized a Roman Catholic on 12 February 1853 at the Iglesia de Santo Ángel Custodio de la Habana. We can assume he accompanied his parents to church, at least until his adolescence, as was the custom of the day. He partook in at least two of the Catholic Church's sacraments during his adult life, the sacrament of marriage (a half hour after a civil service), during which he wed Carmen Zayas Bazán at Sagrario Metropolitano in Mexico City, just to the right of the main cathedral, and the baptism of his son, José Francisco, at the church of Nuestra Señora de Monserrate in La Habana, along with serving as María Mantilla's godfather during her baptism at St. Patrick's Church in Brooklyn. As he wrote in one of his notebooks, sacraments "are simply religious conventions, Catholic conventions. I partake in Marriage because I comprehend it the natural order as a just moral law, and in the civil order as a needed social institution. I respect Extreme Unction, because in the human sphere of charity, it is compassion toward the sick, and it respects death, which holds for me so many beautiful things."[43] What is missing from his writings is any indication that he frequented any particular church, signifying a lack of consistent religious participation. Although in his poetry, he refers to his relationship with the sacred sacrament of the Eucharist by writing: "I continue in my work as a believer / Who anoints the priest in the temple / Of smooth face and white robes / I practice: at the divine altar which I share / With nature: my Eucharist is the human soul."[44]

Martí believes, but not in the institutionalized church; rather, he claims his own way of believing, his own way of doing church. It is a church where he, not some priest, does the anointing, placing himself—as a representative of a liberative movement above the representatives of the church aligned with the repression of the colonizer. The anointing is done on the greatest of altars—nature—created by God, for the sake of a young priest, not some old corruptible mainstay of the church who wears white vestments of purity, not shadowy ones from some dark age. In this church he partakes in communion, where the bread represents the soul of humanity containing the *imago Dei*, God's presence, that is not exclusive to Catholics but inclusive of all humanity regardless of beliefs professed, or lack thereof. With this imagery Martí indicates the need for a new way of doing church that is not limited just to himself.[45]

Although he grew up within the Roman Catholic tradition, he did not adhere to it as some "true" faith or dismiss all others as false. He concludes:

> Religions are all the same: placed one against the other: all cut from the same cloth. One needs to be an ignorant cabal, like the many from universities and academies, not to recognize the world's identity. All religions are born from the same roots, worship the same images, have prospered by the same virtues, and been corrupted by the same vices. All religions, which in their first stage are necessary to weak people, later endure as an anticipation, in which man enjoys himself, of the final poetic well-being that he confuses and tenaciously desires. Religions, which they possess as durable and pure, are forms of poetry which man senses; outside of life, they are the poetry of the world to come. The worlds are liked by dreams and wings! The worlds rotate in united space, like a chorus of maidens, by these wings. Thus, religion does not die, but widens and purify, is enlarged and explains with the truth of nature and tends to its final state of colossal poetry.[46]

There was for Martí a certain poetry to religion: "Oh! Religion, always false as dogma in the light of high judgment, is eternally true as poetry."[47]

Martí's religious "calling" started early, as we have seen. As an eighteen-year-old he clearly stated what he considered his mission to be in the pamphlet *El presidio político en Cuba*, where he mentions God more than in any other of his publications. Besides being a political tract, it can also be read as his first public profession of faith. This "religious" calling is done apart from the Catholic Church, which supported the political repression of Cubans. In a May 1894 letter to General Máximo Gómez, written while planning the launch of the revolution, Martí commits to whatever consequences arise from his "fanatical" calling based on "respect for liberty, and foreign thoughts, even among the most miserable is my fanaticism. If I die, or am killed, it will be for this."[48] Anything that attempted to limit liberation and freedom of thought, especially the church, was considered oppressive: "Within religion, what there is essential in everything, without repressing anyone. No one has the right to compel anyone. Neither freethinkers to Catholics, nor Catholics to freethinkers."[49] Any religion that supports oppression can be understood as satanic, even if the religion proclaims Jesucristo: "As with humans, all progress is perhaps to return to the point of departure, it is returning to Christ, the crucified Christ, forgiving, captivating, the one with bare feet and open arms, not a nefarious and satanic Christ, malevolent, hater, bitter, criticizer, executer, godless."[50]

Martí recognizes something went wrong with the original message of Jesús. Christianity originally was the antidote to colonialism, but instead it became its defender. According to Martí, "the product of empire of the Caesars is Christianity!"[51] Over the centuries, the original faith of rebellion became an apologist for colonialism. Suspicious alliances were made with the powerful, placing greater interest in protecting their earthly treasures than in the oppressive political and economic circumstances of their congregants. Martí never shied away from holding the church accountable for this deceptive alliance with the powerful, who "offered to protect their worldly goods, and [the alliance with] the politicians, satisfying their need for the Catholic vote."[52] The Church, as a political party in religious garb, was destroying the faith of the people, which led Martí to conclude: "Christianity has died at the hands of Catholicism. To love Christ, it is necessary to tear him from the clumsy hands of his children. He is extracted in crude form in which the ambition of progenies converted defenses and vagueness they needed so as to speak of a mythological age of Jesús and propagate their doctrine."[53]

Catholicism

Regardless of the sincerity of Martí's belief or the depths of his faith, he probably was at the very least culturally Catholic, like most white Cubans of the nineteenth century. Cuba may officially have been considered a Catholic nation, but it hardly was. By the early nineteenth century, as the predominately Catholic Spanish clergy committed themselves evermore to colonial rule, as they failed to provide the sacraments in rural areas, the majority of the population was at best apathetic toward the church; at worst, anticlerical.[54] According to the historian Calixto Masó y Vázquez, the religious feelings of the Cuban population during the early twentieth century "always gave little importance to religious problems, being neither atheist nor fanatical, nonetheless their religiosity, above all else the practice of their religious duty, almost bordered on indifference."[55] Throughout Cuba's history, under colonial rule and the Republic of the first half of the twentieth century, the Catholic milieu allowed most Cubans to refer to themselves as Catholic even if they seldom attended services or partook in the sacraments. One could dabble in African orisha rituals or consult an *espiritista* and still be considered Catholic.

Cuban spirituality has always been fluid. So, having been baptized in the Catholic Church or participating in its rituals cannot be construed as obedience or support for the institutionalized church. And yet some Catholics do depict Martí as a faithful son of the church. Take, for example, his portrayal in the mural behind the altar of the tentlike Catholic shrine to La Virgen de la Caridad, built in 1973 on Biscayne Bay in Miami, Florida. The mural, titled *The History of Cuba at a Glance*, was painted by the exiled Cuban Teok Carrasco, who attempted to merge religious and patriotic emotions in retelling the history of the island from Cristóbal Colón (its history begins with European penetration) and ending with the Exile (ignoring the events that took place on the island since). In addition to ignoring the Other (native Taínos and Cubans who did not expatriate), it also ignores the effects of Spanish colonialism and North American imperialism (the Statue of Liberty appears as a symbol of hope). The image of La Virgen occupies the central spot, and Cuban history swerves around her. Martí also occupies a prominent position (directly to the right of the La Virgen), reinforcing the bond between the sacred and nationalism, the Virgin and *el apóstol*. In this, Martí is reimagined as a child of the church. The presence of Cuba's patroness and patron, side by side in the exilic imagination, indicates that they, too, went into exile as refugees.

In his 1941 book *Martí y las religiones*, written decades before the mural was painted, the *martiano* scholar Emilio Roig de Leuchsenring begins with a scathing indictment of the Catholic Church's appropriation of Martí: "The Catholic Church and the Catholics of Cuba, national and foreign, have hypocritically taken the name and words of Martí, and used them to wage their last battle for the reconquest of colonial privileges, threatened with total loss, they try to subjugate new consciences, thereby dominate the State itself, through invocations to freedom, equality and democracy, which they previously mocked and trampled upon."[56] Often missing from the construct of Martí as a faithful son of the church, though, is his very critical analysis of the slave-owning religious institution that consistently stood on the wrong side of history. He openly wondered in a July 1887 newspaper editorial whether one could simultaneously be a Catholic and a "man," writing: "At last, the battle is being fought. Liberty is before the Church. The Church does not fight its enemies, but instead their best children. Can one be a man and a Catholic? For to be a Catholic, must one have the soul of a lackey. If the sun does not sin for shining, how than can I sin for thinking?"[57] As incongruent and ironic as it may appear to find Martí so prominently displayed within the Catholic shrine on Biscayne Bay, there remains a metaphysical dimension to his thoughts that requires fuller exploration.

Before analyzing Martí's critique of the Catholic Church, it behooves us to begin with exploring how Roman Catholicism developed in Cuba, specifically its relationship to the Spanish Crown, to better grasp the context within which Martí writes. The Catholic Church established on Cuban soil was brought to the so-called New World by conquistadores from Spain. These Caribbean invaders were a product of a seven-hundred-year religious struggle to re-Christianize the Iberian Peninsula by expelling "foreign" Muslim invaders. Since the Moorish conquest of Iberia in 711 CE, Spain was a land where the worldviews of Muslims, Jews, and Christians collided, cohabitated, commingled, and communed. But by 1492, Christians had reconquered the land in the name of their faith and church, expelling those they called infidels (Muslims and Jews). This same church, which arrived in Cuba before the Protestant Reformation led by Martin Luther, had enjoyed its own reformation in 1493, one that established the power and privilege of being the sole interpreter of reality in coexistence with a tradition of Spanish folklore and mythology.

While Queen Isabella and her court advanced Christianity through reform and scholarship, the church showed no tolerance for doctrinal diversity. Even before initiating the Spanish Reformation, on 1 November 1478, Queen Isabella and King Ferdinand secured from Pope Sixtus IV the authority to implement the Inquisition as a tool to protect the faith from heretics. Persecution of Jews and Conversos (Jews who converted under threat of duress) was instituted. Concurrently, Granada, the last Moorish stronghold, fell to Christian hands on 2 January 1492, in the same year that Spain became aware of the existence of the Western Hemisphere. A few months later, on 31 March, a royal decree was issued expelling all Jews from Spain. And by 1501, Muslims were given a choice to convert, become slaves, or leave. The seven-hundred-year struggle to reclaim the land and vanquish the crescent by way of the cross succeeded in merging the church with nationalism, together signifying colonialism. To be Christian meant to fight enemies of both faith and nation.

As the last religious crusade in Spain came to an end, a new, vaster crusade opened in the West. This Reconquista spirit, in which Catholic orthodoxy and Spanish identity became synonymous, did not cease with vanquishing Jews and Moors from Spain's domain; instead, it journeyed across the sea with Colón. His "discovery" became more than the political conquest of the land of Others to expand an emerging colonial power; it was an act ordained and prophesized by God in Isaiah 60:9: "The coasts shall await for me, vessels of Tarshish [understood as Spain] in front, to bring your sons from far away, and their silver and gold with them, to the name of Yahweh your God, and to the Holy One of Israel for he has made you glorious."

The conquest of the Western Hemisphere acquired apocalyptic proportions, for the Spaniards saw an opportunity to usher in the

Second Coming of Christ by fulfilling the great commission of Matthew 28:19: "In your goings, then, disciple all the nations, baptizing them in the name of the Father and of the Son and of the Holy Spirit." The evangelization and domestication of Indians meant that Spain was standing on the threshold of the eschatological consummation of human history. By subduing the new "promised land" by sword and cross, Christ's messianic kingdom would be installed on the earth. Two years after Cuba's "discovery," Pope Alexander VI (the corrupt and controversial Rodrigo de Borja, with origins in Catalonia) negotiated the Treaty of Tordesillas, dividing the New World between Spain and Portugal. All ecclesiastical powers operating in what was called New Spain became subservient to the Crown. Through *patronato real* (royal patronage), the Crown was given the right to appoint the high ecclesiastical offices (including bishops) of the churches in the Américas. Also, the Crown took the responsibility of administering the *diezmo* (tithes) and church expenses. In effect, queen and king became vice-popes. The dependence of the church—the earthly representative of Christ—upon the Crown, which was bent on enriching Spain at the expense of the New World, led to a merging of religious and political goals.[58] Church and state worked hand in hand to preserve and expand Spain's presence in Latinoamérica. Because the church in Cuba (as well as all the Américas) was intertwined with colonialism, it bore the stamps of slavery, underdevelopment, and dependency. The church safeguarded its presence and expanded its own power by manipulating state power. With the exception of a few outstanding clerics, the mission of the colonial church of Cuba was to sustain and maintain the status quo while defending the interests of *la madre patria*. Christendom became a space carved out through royal power, providing religious justification and legitimacy to the existing political structures.

Historically, all Catholic priests were *peninsulares*, conservative Spain-born foreigners who usually aligned themselves politically with the colonizer during the wars of independence. Most considered an assignment to Cuba a terrible post, reserved for those priests who were far less than the best and brightest. Because few anointed priests were born in Cuba, the *peninsulares* failed to connect with the masses, instead serving the privileged in La Habana and Santiago, leaving the rural countryside devoid of churches and priests. The metropolis developed at the expense of the economically declining countryside. Through tithes, the church purchased property and became a major landholder, a process augmented by lands it had already received through donations and left to it in wills and estates. The church had slaves working its land and rented out parcels to poor peasant farmers to bring in additional income.

The early 1800s saw the rise of Latinoamérica's nationalistic fervor that would lead to wars of independence, thanks in part to Napoleon's 1807 occupation of Spain. These emerging nations sought to preserve the same control over the church previously held by the Crown. Not surprisingly, when local elites participated in the wars of independence, the church—usually the largest landholder and the main conservative political force—was perceived to be an enemy of the liberation movement. Most local bishops sided with the Spanish Crown, and popes made proclamations against revolutionaries both in 1816 and in 1823. The poor and dispossessed took up arms in their struggle for independence against crown and church, hating both equally. As Martí noted: "In the U.S. they are more religious because they are freer. That is why the atheist poet has not appeared here. But in the locals where religion has always been hostile to what is natural and the expansion of man's faculties, hatred of religion has been one of the natural manifestations of the love for freedom."[59] For Martí, one cannot serve two masters, loving liberation and also loving the institutional church that has stood against liberation.

No doubt Martí would have agreed with the Chilean liberation theologian Pablo Richard, who, a century after Martí, called for the death of Christendom in order to bring about the birth of the church.[60] In a jotted-down thought in his notebook, Martí observed: "Catholicism had a social reasoning. When that society was annihilated, and another new society created, the social reasoning needs to be different. Catholicism must die . . . Catholicism dies, just as mythology died, as paganism died, as what a human genius creates or discovers and another genius destroys or replaces."[61] Richard and Martí saw the Catholic Church in an unholy alliance with Spain, defending its power in civil society by means of the state.

Clergy, who do the bidding of colonial masters for political or financial reward in this world, promise riches in the next life as a reward for the oppressive suffering that people endure in the here and now. The submission of the church to political authorities is, of course, not exclusive to Catholicism. Referring to the civilizations of the Greeks and Hebrews, but probably also thinking of Cuba, Martí explains in his children's book *La edad de oro* how priests and kings conspire for power at the expense of the people: "Because men are proud, and they do not want to confess that another man might be stronger or more intelligent, they say that when a strong man or smarter man made himself king due to his power, it was because he was a child of the gods. The kings rejoiced when the people believed this. The priest would say this was true so that the kings would be grateful and assist them. That is how the priests and the kings ruled together."[62] The Catholic clergy's decision to side with Spain left freedom fighters no alternative but to battle the church. Even when Spain lost the war, the bishop of La Habana, fearing a Protestant invasion, wrote a pastoral letter "for civilization, against barbarism," that is, for colonial rule instead of independence.[63]

By the time Martí was born, the Catholic Church was fully colonized, ruling with the monarchy and growing rich and powerful in the process. Centuries of a Cuban colonial church had put it at odds with the goals and aspirations of those like Martí who sought independence from Spain, as clergy followed the lead of the then Pope Leo XIII, who supported Spain in its conflicts with Cuban insurgents. For Martí, in dualistic fashion, there were two Catholicisms, one of supernatural origins and one that was political. In an early writing he claimed: "The Catholic religion has two phases that each deserve special consideration. It is a religious doctrine, and it is a form of government. If it is wrong, it is not necessary to combat it. When error is not sustained by the dominant force and ignorance, the error by itself is undone and falls."[64] While embracing the teachings of Jesús, Martí condemns the Catholic Church for its "devil's bargain" with the state. In Martí's play *Patria y libertad (drama indio)*, commissioned by the Guatemalan government in 1877, the character Pedro succinctly summarizes the colonial unholy trinity: "The doctor, the Marquis, and Father Antonio have an air of distrustful people; an air of night vultures when from the clear east the sun arises. Noble, priest and doctor: the three serpents that nested in our bosom the colony. The cunning law kills justice, those who preach Jesús dishonor him and that race of servants with dress coat, that with our infamy, they purchased a noble title."[65]

Commenting on the 1857 Mexican Constitution for *Revista Universal*, Martí expressed how that unholy alliance was detrimental to freedom-seeking people: "Who does not know the many open wounds, the many throbbing evils, the many harmful elements in the Constitution of our people due to the domination and absorbing zeal of Catholic doctrine?"[66] For this reason he calls for the death of Christendom in another editorial with the same paper: "It does well the dead doctrine in fearing a living *patria*."[67] Any future hope of a liberated society requires the people to kill the oppression-inducing doctrines of Catholicism (and I would add the doctrines of any religion). According to the *martiano* scholar Rafael Cepeda, the Roman Catholic Church is guilty of two unpardonable sins: a dogma that blinds and hardens, and an abuse of power that degrades humans.[68] Martí would agree, as he saw the Catholic Church as simply corrupt, apostate, and devoid of the virtues it preached in its rhetoric. His pen unmercifully savaged the church. There is absolutely no way for a casual reader of Martí's works to miss his anticlericalism and antidogmatism, but this does not make him anti-Christian. In fact, worship—he believed—was important for the people. His attack on the church was mainly due to its complicity with the wealthy to oppress the poor.

The *martiano* scholar Cintio Vitier maintained that Martí underwent a mystical awakening during his travels through Latinoamérica, rejecting Spanish scholasticism when he rediscovered his roots.[69] While in Guatemala, Martí appears to have planned to write a book concerning true Christian teachings that he found incompatible with the church's doctrines. His hope was to make the book available, at no cost, to *campesinos* so as to raise their consciousness.[70] According to his notes, Martí hoped to focus on the church's pursuit of profits and its imposition of ignorance:

He [the priest] charges you to pour water upon your child's head, or proclaim you are the husband of your wife, which you already know since you started loving her and she loves you. Because he charges for you to be born, for you to receive unction, for you to marry, to pray for your soul, for you to die, and even denies you the right to burial if you don't give him money, he will never want you to know all you have thus done was unnecessary, for on that day he would cease to be able to charge money. This is an injustice which exploits your ignorance. I, who do not charge you anything for my book, want to speak with you, the *campesino*, to tell you the truth. I do not demand you believe as I believe. Read what I say and believe if what I say seems just. The first duty of man is to think for himself. This is why I don't want you wanting a priest, because he does not let you think.[71]

Martí held the church accountable for its abuse of power, stating in an 1887 editorial on the New York schism among Catholics that "the degrading aspect of Catholicism is the abuse of authority within the Church's hierarchies, and the confusion where they knowingly mix self-serving malicious advice with the simple commands of the faith."[72] He was concerned with the overall hypocrisy of priests, who are "almost always vicious, obligating you to have a wife while he has lovers, wanting your children to be legitimate, while his are not, and telling you that you must give your children your surname while not giving his surname to his children."[73] Such a church and such priests cannot be messengers of the true God. There must be another God they do not know, recognize, or follow.

The Catholic press, for him, was the church's propaganda arm. He asks in an early 1875 editorial, "What is it that Catholic newspapers do? What they have done in all times, to cloak themselves in piety, to bring down to earth those human eyes that were made to see everything that is in front. Beneath his black robes his irascible heartbeat is disguised. And hides in the shadow of his habit the smile drawn, before the wicked who desolate a fertile region, contorted on his lips by satisfaction and silence."[74] Yes, Martí was anticlerical; nevertheless, he was interested in the ethical teachings of Christianity, interested in the God of justice—a justice that cries out for liberation, equality, peace, and truth—as foundational for any civilized society. This leads him to be less concerned with doctrines and more concerned with praxis—specifically revolutionary praxis based on love and justice. Here it might be helpful to ask, as the theologian Reinerio Arce does, how Martí's anticlericalism is being defined. He was not opposed to all clergy at all times. Arce argues that he was opposed to a particular church and particular clergy.[75] Specifically, Martí's anticlericalism was limited to those who ignored the liberative message of their faith and had an allegiance to oppressive and repressive political structures that reinforced the colonization of the mind and the subjugation of the body. This explains why he did not advocate for the anticlerical fervor sweeping Mexico during his time there despite his ferocious critique of the church.

Martí's anticlericalism was a response to the corruption of the Catholic Church, its pursuit of profits, its imposition of ignorance, its overall hypocrisy, and its abuse of power. "The Catholic priesthood is necessarily immoral," he reminds us.[76] These views were formed early in his life, jotting these sentiments in his first notebook shortly after being released from San Lázaro Quarry. He envisioned a *patria* free of the papacy: "I want to educate a people who save whoever is going to intercede and who never go to Mass."[77] Not only does he envision a spirituality and morality not based on corrupt clergy; more important, he envisions a *patria* based on the goodness of humans: "There is in the human being an invisible and extraordinary force of secrets, good sense and reason. And if the Catholic religion distrusts its strength, in spite of its supernatural origin, yes, despite being divine, then it is afraid of men. If to give man self-consciousness, it wants to take the means of conscience, if the religion of sweetness converts to the courtesan of ambition and force, then this being what we want to dispossess ourselves of, this being which has free thought that rises up wounded, does not want his will to be hypocritical."[78]

Even though Christianity, for Martí, died under Catholicism and needs saving from the priests, he still desired to retain her moral teachings that were foundational in his writings and remained foundational in the development of his political praxis. A liberative Christian ethical thinking frames his moral views, even though he chooses not to adhere to any particular Christian doctrine (I address this later in this book as well). Still, we can speak of Martí possessing a political theology based on the liberative praxis that emerges from a faith tradition—in his case, the Christian tradition—that he otherwise despises for its stunting of reason and negative interference in people's establishing of a political structure based on justice.

Martí confesses to be captivated by the life of the Nazarene, not the doctrines of the church claiming to represent the Christ whose teachings it distorted for future generations. Jesús, and his teachings, are not liable for the perverted doctrines his followers devised. Martí saw Christ as a poor carpenter who preached the message of love. And whenever clergy follow Christ's example, they deserve praise. As already mentioned, Martí did not paint all priests and clergy with a board anticlerical brush. There were those, like Father Edward McGlynn, whose life he lifted up as one to emulate. The Irish priest Father McGlynn was, since 1865, the head minister of the largest parish in New York City—St. Stephen's Church on Twenty-Eighth Street. McGlynn is celebrated for being a priest of the poor who "said what Jesús has said."[79] McGlynn found honor with Martí because he was a "'priest of the poor' who he advised without belittling them for twenty-two years, who distributed his inheritance and salary among the unfortunate, who had not seduced their wives nor initiated their daughters in stupidity, who has raised in their poor neighborhood a church which always has open arms, who never used the influence of faith to intimidate souls, nor obscure thoughts, nor reduce its free spirit to the bind service of the worldly and impure interests of the Church."[80]

In 1882, McGlynn ignored a direct order from the archbishop of New York, Cardinal John McCloskey, not to speak in Cleveland, Ohio, at the Land League, an organization concerned with comprehensive land reform. McGlynn, contrary to teaching of the First Vatican Council, opposed parish schools in favor of the public school system. He held economic goals similar to those of Henry George, a U.S. economist and social philosopher who rooted a doctrine of land in ethics rather than economics. During George's run for mayor of New York City in 1886, McGlynn played an active role in his campaign. Ignoring the direct orders of another archbishop, Michael Corrigan, he delivered a pro-George address on 1 October 1886 to a crowd of more than two thousand. Corrigan suspended McGlynn and referred the matter to Pope Leo XIII, who in turn summoned McGlynn to Rome that December. McGlynn refused, citing personal reasons.

Martí shows little patience for religious individuals who rely more on rhetoric, tenets, and dogma than on praxis. Contrary to the historical role of the Catholic Church, Martí called on the clergy to follow the example of this renegade priest who, against the archbishop's orders, supported George's social programs and campaigned for him over the more conservative candidate favored by the church. By March of 1887, McGlynn and George had cofounded the Anti-Poverty Society. A few months later, in May, McGlynn was again summoned to Rome, and again he refused. This time, Pope Leo XIII excommunicated McGlynn on 4 July. Years later, on 15 May 1891, the same pope would release the encyclical *Rerum novarum*, which became a foundational text for what would later be called the "social teachings" of the church. And although he does not mention McGlynn by name in the encyclical, it is clear to those familiar with the episode that the pope was refuting the wayward priest, especially through his reaffirmation of private property. Tired of the controversy, the pope reinstated McGlynn in 1892, allowing him to celebrate Mass on Christmas Day. The good priest died on 7 January 1900 of kidney disease.

There is something fundamentally wrong, Martí thought, with the church using its spiritual influence to pressure the faithful to vote against their interests. Although Martí showed no qualms when individual clergy like Father McGlynn engaged in the political arena in solidarity with the poor, he did criticize other clergy for meddling in political matters and silencing those within the church who protested the church's political views and candidates: "[That] those (priests in politics) enter houses with indisputable and infallible authority concerning the essential and eternal thing of God to influence political things . . . is a theft worse than any other, they are usurpers of souls."[81]

Father McGlynn was a real Christian, a true priest in Martí's eyes, because Rome had censured him for defending and standing with the poor over and against politicians supported by the church and determined to economically repress them. Martí opposed any church's attempt to silence dissidents among the ranks who thought for themselves and followed their conscience. In his 1887 essay "La excomunión del padre McGlynn" (The Excommunication of Father McGlynn), Martí condemns the Catholic Church for misusing its authority to protect power: "Where do you have it written, Archbishop? Where, Pope, are your credentials written which entitle you to a soul? We no longer wear ticking tunics, we read history, we have good priests who explain a true theology! We know bishops do not come from Heaven, and know by which human means, by which conveniences of mere administrations, by which guilty binds to princes, by which means unclean contacts and shameful indulgences raise, all from the hands of men, all as a simple form of governance, that impure edifice of the Papacy!"[82]

Catholic Influences

Yes, Martí was anticlerical. Yes, Martí was suspicious of the Catholic Church, wondering whether one could simultaneously be Catholic and human—for to be Catholic meant having the soul of a lackey.[83] Nevertheless, as we have seen, Martí celebrates Catholics like Father McGlynn who, through reason, understood their faith and, regardless of the cost, were willing to stand in solidarity with the disenfranchised. Father McGlynn was not the only example. Cuban theological history consists of several devoted Catholics who left a profound mark upon the nation's consciousness, which in turn had an impact on Martí's own thinking. Specifically, he was deeply influenced by his schoolteacher and intellectual father, Rafael María de Mendive. But Mendive was himself the product of a Cuban intellectual genealogy. Specifically, he was a student of José de la Luz, who taught at the college he attended.

Father Félix Varela, a teacher and colleague of Luz, is probably the second most popular figure of Cuban history after Martí, or as the philosophical theorist Medardo Vitier said, "Varela came to this world with a mission to innovate."[84] Reading Varela, who was under the ecclesial supervision of Bishop Juan José Díaz de Espada y Landa, reveals his great indebtedness to his intellectual mentor Father Caballero, probably the first in Cuba to be and think apart from Spanish colonialization, a perspective Varela took to its highest level.[85] To understand

Martí's political theology, we must explore this Catholic pedagogical pedigree that broke with the domesticating Peninsular philosophies of their time. A thorough exploration of these Catholics' philosophical contributions would be beneficial, but such an analysis remains, unfortunately, beyond the scope of this book; thus, we instead focus on how their individual works created the intellectual milieu that influenced and shaped Martí's own thinking, regardless as to when he actually discovered or read their works.

According to the *martiano* scholar Jorge Juan Lozano Ros, Cuban philosophy, since its inception, chose to be integrated with social reality.[86] The generations of Catholic Cuban thinkers who laid the groundwork for an indigenous Cuban way of doing philosophy moved away from the normative abstract debates of their times to focus instead on how theological thoughts interacted with the everyday—what U.S. Latinx religious scholars today refer to as *lo cotidiano*. *Lo cotidiano* can be understood as what occurs every day among ordinary people, encompassing all particularities of existence. This social context, specifically a *criollo* social context, becomes the interpretive lens through which this genealogy of Catholic thinkers interacted with abstract philosophical thought. By focusing on the daily existence of the average person, *lo cotidiano* became a methodology for critically analyzing the good and bad that shaped and formed *criollo* Cubans' yearning to be liberated from Spain's dominion. More than just a form of analysis, *lo cotidiano* held the potential to become a catalyst for structural changes, serving as the foundation upon which all ethical political praxis could be determined and implemented.

These Catholic thinkers made relevant the political for Cubans, contextualizing *lo cotidiano* in what is understood as morality. Such an ethical paradigm incorporates hermeneutics of the self, a methodology that collapses the dichotomy between abstract theory and praxis. Hence, the writings of these Catholic thinkers, foundational for Martí's own political-theological thinking, developed a way of being and doing that avoided lifeless political understandings of moral dilemmas. Including *lo cotidiano* in their analysis provided heart to what was at the time a Eurocentric tendency to solely emphasize reason within philosophical thought regardless as to how important the implementation of logic was to these Catholics.

The Cuban social context, as opposed to the Eurocentric norm, of struggling for humanity, dignity, and liberation became the starting point for a new framework for theological and philosophical analysis. Grounding Cuban thought in *lo cotidiano* subverted the normalized direction of the discourse from the colonial Spaniard center toward the Cuban periphery. The everyday brought the Cuban margins to the center and, in the process, challenged Spain, which had grown accustomed to setting the parameters of the ethical discourse that morally justified colonial subjugation. But regardless as to how important *lo cotidiano* was to this thinking, it was nonetheless held in check by a preferential option for the least of these. For example, in an era where slavery was the everyday, supported by the colonizers and colonized alike, these thinkers distinguished themselves as abolitionists.

The Cuban Catholic Church to which men like Caballero, Varela, and Luz belonged was, of course, colonized. Still, they contributed to the nascent stirs of nationalism that would simmer up later in the eighteenth century as they, and clerics like them, began to define faith apart from the colonizing Spaniard church. But these stirrings did not develop in a vacuum. The Cuban Catholic theological thought developed by these thinkers like Caballero, Varela, and Luz became a breath of fresh air in a wasteland of mainly Spaniard instructors, most of whom were not among the brightest and the best. Spanish priests who were incompetent or had angered some ecclesiastical superior in Spain were usually shipped to the most unpopular post at the farthest reaches of the empire. Cuba was definitely such an undesirable post. Clerics shipped to Cuba were usually united in their support of Spanish dominion. Anti-independence sentiments strengthened throughout the island following the wars of independence throughout Latinoamérica, as many of the clerics assigned to the empire's outposts lost their influence in the newly created republics. Displaced clergy then migrated to the *siempre fiel*, Cuba. The influx of these clerics contributed to a predominant Cuban Catholic Church hostile to liberalism while friendly to Spanish rule, as well as a populace who maintained superficial piety while ignoring private or public morality.[87]

Among the important religious events of the latter part of the eighteenth century, after the 1767 expulsion of the Jesuits, was the 1774 inauguration of the new building housing El Colegio Seminario San Carlos y San Ambrosio (founded in 1689) in La Habana. Known as St. Carlos and St. Ambrosio Royal School Seminary, it gained a reputation as the best school in Cuba.[88] The school catered to the children of the elite, who received an education that exposed them to the liberalism of Latinoamérica, the same ideological trend that would spur independence movements throughout the Américas. And while the elite favored scientific economic development, committed to new techniques responsible for increasing productivity, pro-colonial sentiments continued. In spite of these intellectual stifling conditions, a golden age was starting to emerge. Even though within the walls of the new seminary the Catholic Church was identified with the Crown, there nonetheless arose a nationalist consciousness, a few priests and scholars who sought not only the reformation of the state but also the reformation of theology and philosophy. In short, a cornerstone was laid there for an emerging Cuban political theology.

Toward the last quarter of the eighteenth century, nearly half of the ninety churches on the island were led by native Cuban priests. After three centuries of Spanish rule, a Cuban native, Santiago José de Hechavarría (1724–1790), was appointed bishop (1770–1788). This era was also marked by economic growth and progressive governors.[89] As nationalist sentiments took root within the seminary, the teachings and writings of Caballero, Varela, and Luz arose to stroke the nationalist embers by focusing on morality, specifically the virtues of integrity, honesty, and decency. They concluded that the pursuit of morality was incongruent with subservience to Spain. Their theological and philosophical contributions were driven with the idea of a liberated and just *patria* and the importance that all humans complete their duty to humanity. Rather than engaging in by-the-by celestial theories, they were grounded in the problems faced by everyday humans in the here and now, in *lo cotidiano*. As we will see, Martí was not only the heir of this new way of thinking; he expanded these thoughts and implemented them as revolutionary praxis.

Bishop Espada and Father Caballero

Bishop Juan José Díaz Espada y Landa (1756–1832) is probably the first Catholic cleric in Cuba who sought a break with Spain. He served the see of La Habana from 1802 to 1832, condemning the practice of slavery, criticizing Spain's extensive landholdings, and calling for a more modern and liberal approach to the city's lax clerics.[90] He held views of the Jansenists,[91] a mid-seventeenth-century theology of predestination that emphasized original sin and human depravity, thus facilitating the need for divine grace. Furthermore, as bishop, he patronized public welfare projects, using the bishopric's revenues for the benefit of public health and education. For example, he helped fund a new smallpox vaccine, provided for cemeteries, sought new educational innovations, and drained marshes.[92] Martí referred to him as "that Spaniard bishop who carried on his heart all Cubans."[93]

José Agustín Caballero y Rodríguez (1762–1835) was a contemporary of Bishop Espada. José Martí would come to recognize the "sublime" Caballero as "father of the poor and of our philosophy, [who] declared, more through the advice of his mind than the example of encyclopedists, the proper field and foundation of world science, the study of natural laws."[94] Caballero began his studies at the age of twelve at the San Carlos y San Ambrosio Seminary, going on to become a foundational thinker in the study of philosophy. He sought the decolonization of his mind and can be credited with ushering in a Cuban reformation that rebelled against the uncritical dogma of the Catholic Church and the oppressive colonization by Spain. Prior to him, Cuban thought was but an appendix to the dominant theological discourses of Spain and, by extension, Europe. Frustrated with a backward education system, Caballero set out to create an indigenous Cuban way of thinking, marking the creation of a self-aware people. He is recognized for his efforts to bring free primary education to the island (for girls and boys); for his belief that education was the best means of modifying human behavior; for his criticism of the institution of slavery; for his commitment to the poor (he donated all his financial resources to those devastated by the Napoleonic invasion of Spain); and for his pursuit of autonomy through a reformed, free, and patriotic society across the Américas, not limited to Cuba. His student Varela would go on to say, "[Caballero] always was first in the sanctuary of letters and the sanctuary of patriotism."[95]

Caballero made three major contributions to the philosophical discourse that influenced Martí's own thinking. First, he critiqued Aristotelian-Thomistic scholasticism, which attempted to provide a rational explanation for God's self-revelatory truths derived from the Bible and nature. As the philosophy chair at the seminary from 1785 to 1805, he is probably the first thinker on the island who systematically rejected scholasticism, which until then had been accepted as doctrinal truth.[96] Having little desire to simply link Cuban thought to the scholasticism predominate on the peninsula, which parroted the debates in the hallowed halls of Spain's prestigious universities, he initiated an incipient Cuban philosophical conversation with the broader universal, Eurocentric thinking of the Enlightenment. For Caballero, "philosophy is defined as what is certain and evident knowledge of things by their most high causes, arrived at solely by means of natural light."[97] Within the walls of the seminary where he taught, he attempted to construct the first major philosophical contribution originating from the island by creating the foundation upon which a Cuban consciousness would rise.

Second, Caballero embraced Cartesian doubt and introduced modern thought based on reason. According to the Cuban philosopher Isabel Monal, he was a sincere believer and faithful son of the church; but faith had its place, and that place was in neither philosophy nor science.[98] As a Christian humanist, he rejected revelation as a means of knowing, taking an antidogmatic religious stance and calling for reason to serve as the way to arrive at true knowledge; as Caballero wrote, "Understanding, in possession of the rules of Logic, is sufficiently apt to distinguish what is truth from what is false."[99] He insisted on basing his philosophical contributions on the intersection of religion, humanism, hard sciences, and patriotism, believing that philosophy and science could be sustained only through reason.[100] He placed his faith in human reason and the capacity of humans to grasp reality by way of philosophy and science.

Finally, he adopted Francis Bacon's experimentation and supported the advancement of scientific exploration, specifically Bacon's dismissal of scholasticism: "Scholasticism bore somewhat the same relation to modern metaphysics that Alchemy did to Chemistry."[101] Caballero's nephew Luz would later call him the first Cuban thinker who "made resonate in [his] classrooms the doctrines" of the political theorist John Locke, the epistemologist Étienne Bonnot de Condillac, the empiricism of Francis Bacon, and the physics of Isaac Newton.[102] Not surprisingly, Caballero strived to defend the independence of philosophy and science from the encroachments of religion and theology. And yet when faced with a contradiction between philosophy and theology, he took an Averroist leaning toward the latter.[103]

Caballero's importance rests on the influence that his thinking would have on his students and, more important, on future generations of intellectuals like Martí. Varela said, "All of Caballero's disciples were eclectic."[104] While he may not have necessarily been all that radical, especially considering the limitations in the eighteenth century of an intellectual scene stifled by an authoritarian pedagogical principle, his philosophical contributions were nonetheless fundamental to the development of an indigenous Cuban way of thinking, serving as a crucial first step in creating that firm foundation upon which those who followed would construct a more radical philosophy.[105] The pragmatic contributions Caballero made to the philosophical discourse were developed in his only publication, the 1797 manuscript *Philosophia electiva*, written in Latin for the course he taught and appearing in book form in 1944. Martí would eventually be influenced by Caballero's *philosophia electiva*, by way of his teacher and mentor Rafael María de Mendive who in turn was a student of Varela and Luz, themselves students of Caballero.[106] Caballero, and all those who followed his *philosophia electiva*, engaged with major historical philosophical trends, willing to integrate their insights into the lived reality, *lo cotidiano*, of the Cuban people without adopting the entire systematic Eurocentric philosophical model, selectively electing outstanding contributions made while recognizing and discarding their fundamental limitations. Caballero advised them to "seek truth without swearing to the words of any one teacher."[107] Not interested with abstract logic-based arguments, he instead looked to analyze data produced from observation and experimentation in an attempt to harmonize faith with reason.

The rise of the Liberals in Spain during the 1830s and their anti-clerical measures had great impact on the Cuban Catholic community, dashing the hopes of presbyters like Bishop Espada and thinkers like Caballero who had witnessed the expulsion of priests and the confiscation of church properties. The Cuban church lost a significant portion of its clergy as religious orders were suppressed, thereby hampering educational programs and social ministries. Complicating the situation were the vacancies of the see of La Habana, from 1832 to 1846 after Espada's death, and the see of Santiago de Cuba, from 1836 to 1851. The unwillingness of Spanish authorities to fill these two important ecclesiastical posts revealed a church deemed irrelevant to the general masses and unimportant to the Crown. Left deprived of leadership and common support, the church, as a means of survival, drew closer to Spain, supporting Spanish interests over and against those of *criollo* Cubans. Part of the strategy adopted by the Catholic Church to reestablish its prominence, specifically in La Habana and to the neglect of rural areas, included avoiding any confrontation with Spain by ignoring injustices like slavery and colonialism.[108] Spurred by the French Revolution, the elite, the educated, and the affluent of Cuban society adopted a revolution's ideology and its anticlericalism. In reaction to these anticlerical and liberal attacks, church leaders strengthened their ties with groups they deemed sympathetic, specifically conservative parties, landowners, and the old aristocracy.[109] Still, within this anticlerical shift, two of Caballero's students sought a different response.

Fathers Varela and Luz

Félix Varela and José de la Luz y Caballero are responsible for building a uniquely Cuban philosophical structure upon the foundation originally laid by their teacher and mentor Caballero, radicalizing *philosophia electiva* and establishing it as the main methodology for creating Cuban thought. They understood that Cuba would never develop a useful philosophical base until scholasticism was totally rejected and eradicated. Continuing the philosophical work begun by Caballero, they ushered in a Cuban form of modernity that favored a Cuban social consciousness based on principles of liberty, reason, and Christian faith. They endeavored to overcome the existing dichotomy between the anticlerical liberal modernity with its democratic ideals and conservatives within the church who were clinging to absolutism and still recovering from the horrors of the French Revolution. Varela and Luz attempted to overcome this dichotomy by making a serious call for Cuban liberation. Although both were crucial in the development of an indigenous Cuban philosophical way of being, Varela's contributions are considered more evident, even though Luz's contributions had a more direct influence on Martí.[110]

Father Félix Varela (1788–1853) was one of Bishop Espada and Father Caballero's globally renowned students, an interculturalist thinker, Cuba's first philosopher-revolutionary whose gnoseology was rooted in what it means to be Cuban. He is considered the father of Cuban independence thought and the architect of Cuban nationalism. José de la Luz, a contemporary and student of Father Varela, remarked that he was "the first to teach us to think."[111] The historian Medardo Vitier claimed Varela was "the one who removed the foundation of colony."[112] And when Pope John Paul II much later gave his address at Universidad de La Habana on 23 January 1998, he referred to the priest as "the pre-eminent son of this land . . . the foundation stone of Cuban national identity" who incorporated "the best synthesis one could find of Christian faith and Cuban culture."[113]

By 2012, Varela was venerated by the Catholic Church, and as of this publication was awaiting beatification in the process of becoming canonized. Although he was the first to call for Cuba's political liberation, his importance was not limited to the island. In 1997, the U.S. Postal Service issued a thirty-two-cent stamp honoring the Cuban priest for his work among the poor in the United States, specifically while exiled in Manhattan, where he founded two parishes among the poor of the city (Transfiguration and St. James). The Church of the Transfiguration on Chambers Street is still in operation today; a plaque there describes him as a "forerunner in the field of social welfare." Martí fervently admired Father Varela, whom he probably fully discovered after leaving Cuba, since Varela's writings were banned on the island. Even though Varela was in New York for twenty-five years as a missionary, lines of communication were kept open with his followers on the island.[114] His short-lived but revolutionary newspaper *El Haba-nero*, published entirely in Spanish, was smuggled into La Habana for clandestine distribution.[115] While visiting his tomb at St. Augustine, Florida, in 1892 while planning the upcoming revolution, Martí vener-ated "the remains of that complete patriot," "a Cuban saint." He went on to note that when Varela saw the incongruence between Spain's government with the character and needs of the Cuban people, he articulated what he saw without fear.[116] For Martí, like Varela before him, political liberty could never be achieved apart from spiritual lib-erty. Through Luz's student and Martí's tutor Rafael Mendive, Varela's overarching commitments to dignity, equality, justice, and indepen-dence were no doubt transmitted to the young student.[117]

Father Varela, born in La Habana to a Castilian military family, was raised in St. Augustine, Florida, where his father served as a lieutenant in the Spanish regiment. He was orphaned at the age of six, and by four-teen had returned to La Habana to attend the Seminary of San Carlos and San Ambrosio, as student and mentee of Bishop Espada. The first philosophy class Varela ever took was taught by Caballero. Later, in 1811 at the age of twenty-three, he was ordained a priest by Bishop Espada and joined his alma mater as chair of philosophy (1811–1821), Caba-llero's former post. He gave his lectures not in the traditional Latin, but in the Spanish vernacular, believing that teaching in a "dead lan-guage" was an obstacle to learning.[118] In an 1884 editorial, Martí would agree: "May man live in accord with the universe, and with his era, for which Latin and Greek are useless."[119] Varela also rejected the tradi-tional pedagogy of memorizing preformulated Thomists Scholastics syllogisms as useless;[120] he instead insisted on observational reasoning, even to the point of establishing a laboratory to teach courses in physi-cal and chemical science.[121] For Varela, "experience and reason are the only sources or rules of knowledge in science."[122] Again, Martí would agree, auguring in a much earlier 1875 editorial that understanding the metaphysical is rooted in a reality understood through senses. Martí wrote: "Experience is the firmest basis of knowledge . . . I do not have the right to establish a metaphysical system about imaginations."[123]

Varela's writings are clearly influenced by Lockean, Condillacian, and Cartesian thought. And while he was cognizant of the limitations of Cartesian thought, aware that sensual perceptions can at times fool the observer, he nevertheless constructed an epistemology based on data collection through observation and experimentation. Moving away from theistic revelation, he looked to nature for the bases of egalitarian learning, writing: "Those who teach are but companions of the ones who learn, for having previously traverse the path, they can guard none separate from the direction analysis prescribes. The true teacher of men is nature."[124] In effect, Varela introduced a science-based philosophy to Cuba that centralized reason as the guide to living a moral life.

Varela taught during a time of revolutions across Latinoamérica and added his voice, providing probably the most intellectually advanced analysis of the credo of independence. In 1822 he left Cuba—never to return—when elected delegate to the Cortes de España, where he served for two years and distinguished himself by opposing colonialism and slavery. In an age of empire, he argued before the Cortes for nationalism, insisting that "the remedy of evils must be proposed by the people who suffer under them."[125] He optimistically believed that humans by nature leaned toward the good and avoided evil, explaining the existence of evil as a consequence of ignorance.[126] His belief in the dignity and liberty of every human being led him to the conclusion that the goal of social justice was irreconcilable with Spanish imperial rule.

Independence, unfortunately, was intolerable, for it threatened Spain's hold on the lucrative island, whose revenues were desperately needed to pay for Spain's public officials and the interest on loans taken from British banks.[127] Varela's opposition to the colonizer earned him a death sentence and the life of a refugee when he proposed two legislative bills: one that abolished slavery and a second that called for Cuba's autonomy. Persecution forced him to seek political exile in the United States. He arrived on 17 December 1823 and went on to work with the poor as a priest ministering to New York's Irish immigrants. A would-be assassin, "One-Eyed Morejón," was hired by Marqués de Vives, the governor of Cuba, and sent to New York, but Varela supposedly talked the would-be assailant out of committing the deed.[128] In the face of such hardships and danger, Varela wrote that "a son of liberty with a soul of América does not know fear."[129]

Exile was difficult for the priest who did not speak English and found the brutal cold winters detrimental to his already-frail health. Even so, besides founding churches, he published a magazine dedicated to science, literature, politics, and faith called *El Habanero* in which he attempted to reconcile the Catholic Church with liberalism manifested as rationalism, ecumenicalism, and modernism. *El Habanero*, which was the first newspaper ever written by a Cuban fully committed to the independence movement, was officially banned from the island but smuggled into wide circulation. In one of the final issues of the paper, he made clear his overarching goal: "We want to be liberated, which has been said since the start, because we do not believe that God created us to serve another country."[130] For the following thirty years, most of his life, he lived in exile serving the Catholic community as the vicar general of the archdiocese. Not only did Varela intellectually influence Martí; his irreproachable life of praxis served as a model for Martí's own life. Through his Church of the Transfiguration, he provided shelter for the widowed, orphaned, and unemployed; he worked with the poor and infirm, especially during the 1832 cholera epidemic; he provided relief for the incursion of the hungry and destitute from Ireland and Northern and Central Europe—all this made him the type of leader Martí could emulate. Varela did not only write about justice; he was engaged in justice work, specifically as pastor of the Irish parish where he fought for immigrant rights. Less than a month after José Martí's birth, Varela died poor and abandoned in St. Augustine, Florida, on 25 February 1853.

Through his writings and pastoral work, Varela struggled for liberation, specifically while a delegate to the Cortes de España. He raised awareness of widespread injustice, holding those with power and privilege responsible for colonial abuses and calling for justified rebellion against abusive governments. He criticized the Cuban elite for thinking more about sugar and coffee sacks then patriotism, human rights, or fidelity to God. Varela equated liberation with equality and constitutional rule, hence repudiating any form of inequality and calling all

Cubans to revolutionary change by creating a society governed by reason and justice. He contended that to assume responsibility for their existence, Cubans must learn to think with their own mind, apart from how Spaniards taught Cubans to think. He saw the need to awaken the oppressed from a traditional lethargy reinforced by colonialism: "Liberation and religion have one same origin, and never will it contradict because there cannot be contradiction in its author. The oppression of a people is not distinguished by injustice, and injustice cannot be the work of God. The people are only truly liberated if they are truly religious, and I assure you that to be made a slave is precisely to begin by making one a fanatical. So far away is true religion from being the foundation of tyranny!"[131]

Humans require self-analysis, an examination of self as if the individual were just another object of nature requiring study. Varela's theory of self-understanding recognized the immortal soul and the *imago Dei* (the imprint of the image of God on each individual) ensured the dignity of all humans and their divine right to exist as free, regardless of race or class. Human dignity created a responsibility for the church to advocate liberation (specifically from Spain) and endowed each Christian with a duty to construct a social order incarnated with the principles of Christ. Divinity, for him, provides the greatest good and the greatest utility. To love God is necessary because it best expresses the love for other humans.[132] Recognizing the Benthamite utilitarian formula (X is good = X is useful), Varela sought a new way of thinking that was both useful and good for the Cuban people, who sought dignity through liberation, for that which is good and useful can never be achieved when subjugated to a foreign power. Unlike many other Cuban clerics of the time, Varela's thoughts attempted to find a balance between liberal democrats, who included the church as part of the antidemocratic problem to be swept away, and the traditional elements of the church, which maintained its privilege through sovereign power. Thus, Varela contended that liberation required that the people learn how to synthesize themes from liberalism (i.e., democracy) with transcendental divine truth—a faith in truth based on reason. This enables a duty-based society to emerge, a society keen to ensure that opportunities are available for the people to perform.

Varela wrote against charlatanism and pseudoscience, suspicious of a church steeped in superstition, fanaticism, and injustice, specifically a medieval type of Christianity that stifles rational thought. He wrote about "overcom[ing] the insensible impiety, the dismal superstition, the cruel fanaticism, which travels by various paths but go to the same end, which is the destruction of the human race."[133] He argued elsewhere that "we have natural rights which the order of justice demands. Yes, we have rights to better our physical, political, and moral state. We want our nation to be all it can be."[134] Committed to the natural rights of equality, liberty, and private property, he attempted to redefine a Catholicism that prioritized piety, defended diverse perspectives, celebrated a liberated humanism, sought a utilitarian solution, and was rooted in the rational. He sought an equilibrium between such a faith with societal laws committed to similar priorities. The state, to be just, required a moral philosophy and an ethical religion. But when faith or state falls short of the utilitarian formula of securing the good and useful through suppression of the natural rights of equality, liberty, and private property, then the moral and ethical recourse is to rebel. As Varela claimed, "For if you call everyone who works to alter an order contrary to the good of the people revolutionaries, then I glory to count myself among these revolutionaries."[135]

A student of Father Varela and nephew of Caballero, José de la Luz y Caballero (1800–1862) was a major influencer of Martí's political theology by way of Martí's own teacher and mentor Rafael Mendive. Luz replaced José Antonio Saco as chair of philosophy at the seminary (1824–1828), the same chair previously held by Varela and Caballero. Later, Luz would assume the chair of philosophy at the Convento de San Francisco (1839–1843). Martí, in an 1892 editorial for *Patria*—the official newspaper for the coming revolution—refers to Luz as "the loving father of the Cuban soul."[136] Mendive may have been Martí's teacher and father figure, but it was Luz who Martí considered his intellectual mentor.[137] In a January 1892 letter to Ángel Peláez, Martí expressed gratitude for a book by Luz that Peláez gave him, sharing how much it influenced his thinking. He concludes by admitting, "For two men I have trembled and wept at the knowledge of their death, without knowing them, without knowing an iota about their life—don José de la Luz and Lincoln."[138]

Although Luz, according to Martí, could have been a successful attorney with a rich clientele, he chose to have only one client, *patria*, to whom he conveyed what he knew. In short, "he planted men."[139] No doubt Martí was referring to Luz's work at the Colegio del Salvador, the school founded by Luz in 1848, where he served as director and that later became home to Cuban spiritual culture. Many of the patriots who launched the Ten Years' War for Cuba's independence studied at Luz's school or fell under its influence. Luz may have been excommunicated by the pope, but that did not stop him from laying the foundations of an indigenous Cuban spirituality,[140] a Cuban spirituality openly sympathetic to liberal Protestantism, more so than his contemporary Cuban clergy.[141]

Luz struggled with the question of methodology, as illustrated in his 1839 article "Cuestión de método." Influenced more by Aristotelian observation and classification, as opposed to Platonic ideals and forms, Luz gravitated more toward Locke's empiricism than Kantian apriorism or Condillac's extreme empiricism. "Experience," Luz wrote, "is the point of departure of all types of knowledge."[142] He was more inclined to ground his philosophical ideas in the scientific methodology of empirical observation, hypothesis, experimentation, conclusion, and verification than in Cartesian mathematical formulas. This approach furthered the concept introduced by Caballero concerning an *electiva cubana*. He sought a Cuba-based morality as a result of observation and experimentation over and against the bankruptcy of Spanish colonialism, rejecting any and all aspects of Eurocentric philosophical thought that justified the colonial venture. As he put it: "We resolve to establish a philosophical school in our country. A school of ideas and sentiments, and of methods. A school of virtues, thoughts and actions, not of expectants of higher office nor scholars, but activists and thinkers."[143] Faith and science were not incongruent, thus he sought to eliminate contradictions between materialism and spiritualism. Although he sought to balance faith with science, for him, nature still was one, and all of what constitutes it subjected to its laws and principles, decipherable only through rational scientific thought.[144] An expert in physics, chemistry, and philosophy, Luz employed the scientific method as leading to God or, as he would say, "The sciences are the rivers which takes us to the fathomless sea of divinity."[145]

To achieve a new philosophical school, Luz sought a new ethical political model for society, independent from Spain or any other empire, and philosophically independent from the scholastic tradition. Repudiating metaphysical explanations for scientific naturalism, he sought a unitary understanding of the material, seeking to ground and harmonize moral and philosophical thought on the sciences.[146] Not surprisingly, he was critical of absolute revelatory truths. The idea of God was arrived at experientially, through an analytical and inductive rational contemplation of phenomena conducted in relationship with nature. Proposing a new philosophical school and new method implied a rejection of and confrontation with colonial rule. Rather than fidelity to Spain, the call was to love *patria*, understood as a task to unite Cubans. This new ethical model was based on social justice. As Luz often stated, "Justice is the Sun of the moral world."[147] This is a social justice more interested with a way of being than with maintaining a personal piety, more interested with integrating praxis to human intellect (for example, struggling to abolish slavery rather than just arguing for its demise), and characterized by human dignity achieved through the liberation of thought.

Martí's formative years occurred within a revolutionary social context of ripe philosophical and political independentist trends. When as a young lad Martí began his studies with Rafael Mendive, he was learning from a mentor who had been formed and shaped by the philosophical contributions of Caballero, Varela, and Luz—lovers of justice and patriots to a fault who sought to reconcile their faith with science, material with metaphysical. Not surprisingly, with such a pedigree, Martí noted that God could be reached through the sciences;[148] he placed philosophical emphasis on praxis rather than abstract thought; and he advocated for a theological preference for rational thought as opposed to doctrinal truths. He was thus intellectually raised within the very best indigenous Cuban philosophical tradition, a way of thinking that stood over and against the legitimized and normalized traditional scholasticism emanating from Spain. Caballero, Varela, and Luz found their fullest manifestation in Martí, who, rather than being a faithful disciple, stood upon their shoulders to reach a higher plane of Cuban thought.

La Santa Biblia

After his release from serving time at the San Lázaro Quarry, and before boarding the steamer *Guipúzcoa* on 15 January 1871, which would take him into exile, he recuperated for about three months at El Abra, the farm owned by José María Sardá. Martí—it is believed—was first introduced to the Bible during this time.[149] That he comes across the Bible for the first time in early adulthood is not as strange as it might sound, considering that before the Second Vatican Council, the biblical text was not as available among Roman Catholics as it was in Protestant circles. In fact, it wasn't until 1837 that the famous distributor of the Bible throughout Latinoamérica, James Thompson, began to pass out copies in different parts of Cuba.[150] Martí's introduction to the Bible seemed to have had an immediate impact upon him, as demonstrated a year later in his first major political publication denouncing Spain's atrocities in Cuba.

A high opinion of the Bible, specifically its inspirational verses, was evident in Martí's writings. He exclaimed in an 1884 editorial, "What beautiful poetry does the Bible have!"[151] Although he admired its poetic beauty, he wrote little about the text being literally true, being a Truth upon which doctrines and absolutes can be constructed. In an earlier 1883 editorial on why the Bible should not be used as a text in schools, he referred to it as "basic and erroneous."[152] This did not invalidate lowercase-*t* truths that could be gleaned from the book. He even claimed in another editorial for the same paper, some four months earlier, that the Bible "in truth is a book that on the matter of the soul has said everything."[153]

Although he described the "eloquence" of the Bible,[154] and referred to the text as "fragrant,"[155] the poetic beauty he found did not excuse him from conducting a critical analysis, indicating that he not only studied the Bible but also took it seriously, especially its moral imperatives. He wrote an 1884 article about the Episcopal priest Richard Heber Newton, a leader of the social gospel movement and a supporter of higher biblical criticism (also known as the historical-critical method, which sought the original meaning of the text as penned in a particular culture during a particular time). Conservative Christians, many of whom were involved in what would become an emerging fundamentalism, were contemptuous of higher biblical criticism because the approach attempted an interpretation in harmony with the non-supernatural. In 1883, Newton was accused of heresy for his book *The Right and Wrong Uses of the Bible*. Among his distractors was Rector Alfred G. Mortimer of St. Mary's in Staten Island, a critic of higher biblical criticism. Mortimer's type of faith must make way, Martí believed, for the critical analysis that marked the coming age: "After the age of faith comes that of criticism. After those capricious synthesis, that of scrupulous analysis. The more confident faith was, the more suspicious is the analysis."[156]

Newton's response to Mortimer served Martí as a guide on how to read and interpret the biblical text. Martí embraced higher criticism, utilizing the methodology as the means to understand faith. For both Newton and Martí, "the only way to salvage religion is to apply reason to the Bible."[157] For both men, "the only legitimate and definitive authority for establishment of truth is reason."[158] The only thing standing in the way of establishing truth, in Martí's opinion, was the church: "For Churches become irritated and are against the [critical] examination of the Bible because it requires what is not pleasing to them, the exercise of freedom. This is the secret which angers them, the discovery that this book which supposedly fell from the heavens like a meteorite, in reality belongs to 'human letters,' and thus is not the 'infallible despot of understanding and conscience.'"[159]

To summarize, pigeonholing José Martí as a faithful son of the Catholic Church does violence to his personhood. When Christian faith traditions utilized reason, Martí was quick to admire them. But when they preached intolerance, authoritarianism, superstition, or dogma, he was quicker still to unmercifully savage them. An eclectic thinker, he sought to incorporate the best they had to offer while rejecting what he understood to be their religious folly. In so doing, he rethought what Christianity should be and set out to create a Cuban indigenous way of being Christian. In the process, he came to be known as the apostle for a *nueva religión*

TWO

Apostle to a New Religion

The exercise of liberation leads to *la nueva religión*.

JOSÉ MARTÍ WAS a Catholic—in his own way. Catholicism, *a su manera*, led him to become an apostle for a new religion indigenous to the Cuban context. He believed in God but not clergy. He was a cultural Catholic—quick to critique the church when it sided with political authorities bent on protecting its privileged space and quicker still to praise those ministers who stood in solidarity with the oppressed and disenfranchised. There was a clear Christian philosophical genealogy shaping his political theology, and this requires further exploration. Moving away from solely a traditional Catholic perspective, this chapter seeks to understand other Christian influences to his thoughts.

A Positivist Age

Before exploring *la nueva religión* envisioned by Martí, it behooves us to first examine the milieu in which he wrote. With his migration to the United States on 2 January 1880, Martí found himself in New York City, the heart of an emerging economic empire. His arrival corresponded with radical transformative economic changes in the United

States. Although the economy had fully recovered from the devastating bloody Civil War fought twenty years earlier, it remained predominately rural, with an emphasis on mining, cattle raising, timber, and railroad building. A hunger for devouring land out West that was already inhabited by indigenous people remained unquenchable. Not yet an industrial or military superpower, the United States was beginning to come into its own, finding its place on the world stage as it sought new markets for its increasing production of manufactured goods. New York City, during his stay, was marked by national economic turmoil that negatively affected the average laborer. These years after Ulysses S. Grant's presidency were a time when big business controlled much of the government through bribery and graft. Regardless of partisan affiliation, the country's political apparatus embraced plutocracy and a nascent imperialism. Scandalous and corrupt political structures were the norm, giving rise to what came to be known as the Gilded Age (1870s–1900).

This was a nativist time of rampant industrialization fueled by technological advances that led to rapid economic growth. And yet the period is noticeable for its tremendous economic disparity: on one extreme lived an opulent and oblivious minority feasting off millions of workers being paid practically nothing, mainly immigrant labor who were fueling the economy but relegated, nonetheless, to abject poverty.[1] Although the nation had recovered from the 1873–1879 depression by the time Martí arrived, from 1882 to 1885 he witnessed and wrote about another economic downturn that gripped the country, placing millions out of work and causing strikes and labor unrest. This would be followed with a deeper depression in 1893 and 1894. These economic developments influenced Martí, leading to his apprehension about and concern with the emergence of unrestricted capitalism, as witnessed in his writings during this time.

The economic materialism that dominated and gripped the nation by 1880 stood over and against the spiritually based selflessness to which Martí leaned. As the *martiano* scholar Manuel Pedro González observed, Martí abhorred the U.S. propensity to elevate the tenacious pursuit of profit to the dignity of a national ideal at the expense of spiritual and cultural values.[2] This prevailing U.S. positivist ethos of "the survival of the fittest" was based on the works of Herbert Spencer, who appropriated the phrase after reading the works of Charles Darwin on natural selection. Spencer extended Darwin's biological insights to sociology and ethics. By the 1880s, the term social Darwinism emerged, providing justification to a Christianized capitalist exploitation, which led to a wealth gap by the end of the nineteenth century that prevented domestic markets from absorbing different product surpluses. Capitalist and industrialist thus needed foreign markets to dump their surplus products. Martí was probably among the first to see this economic transformation occurring from local competitive markets to a monopolist capitalism responsible for increasing poverty and spawning imperialism, specifically in its relationship with América Latina, a threat he called the "giant with seven-league boots who can crush [*nuestra América*] underfoot."[3]

This positivism was prevalent during Martí's time, and it justified greed and the exploitation of those who had the least, giving rise to the Gilded Age and its corrupt business and political structures. Advocates of positivism insisted that its implementation ensured free enterprise and promoted progress; those lacking intelligence and/or will would simply reap what they sowed. Yet Martí was troubled by the incongruence of a nation that claimed the Christian virtues of placing the needs of others first and a positivist philosophy that advocated dog-eat-dog social ethics. Spencer philosophically defended capitalists from the encroachment of governments attempting to create a more equitable society, an equity upon which Martí's *nueva religión* was to rest. Economic marginalization for the social Darwinist was the fault of the poor, whom Spencer referred to as "simply good-for-nothings," "vagrants and slots, criminals" who sought prostitutes.[4] He demonized socialist movements, critiquing the English Parliament's legislative attempts to improve the living conditions of the poorest of the poor by suggesting policies like the Industrial Dwelling Acts that would lead to "State-Socialism." For Spencer, "all socialism involves slavery."[5] Equating chattel slavery to social slavery, he argued that Parliament's reforms, which allowed the community to appropriate a capitalist's profits without consent, were akin to reducing the capitalist to a slave of society.

Martí responded to Spencer in two essays for *La América* in April 1884, the first titled "Herbert Spencer" and the second "The Future of Slavery." He ends the first essay by analyzing the conclusion of Spencer's ideas thus: "People who do not believe in the perpetuation and universal sense, in the priesthood and glorious accent of human life. They will crumble like a crust of bread gnawed by rats."[6] But Martí's rejection of positivism does not necessarily make him a socialist. He seems to find some common ground with Spencer's antisocialist views. While not denying the need to provide relief from economic oppression to the poor, Martí remains concerned about the danger of thwarting self-reliance:

> How will socialism come to be, or how will this not be a new slavery? Spencer judges as growing victories of socialist ideas, and weak concessions of popularity seekers, that noble tendency, precisely to make socialism unnecessary, born from all generous thinkers who see that the mere discontent of lower classes leads them to desire radical and violent improvements, and have no other alternative but to go to the root of the problem to remove the motive for discontent. But this must be done in a matter that the relief of the poor is not bartered for promoting loafers; and to this we need to direct laws which deal with relief, and not leave the humble with all their reasons to revolt.[7]

States have a responsibility to elevate the misery of the poor. While agreeing that laziness should not be rewarded, Martí, unlike Spencer, is not willing to view social measures that provide relief to the poor as fostering dependency:

> If the poor habitually ask the State for everything, they will cease to make little effort for their subsistence . . . [But] all those interventions of the State as judged by Herbert Spencer are caused by the rising tide, and imposed by the people who ask for it, as if great and sensible desire to give the poor a clean house, which simultaneously heals the body and mind, would not have been born within the ranks of cultured people, without the indignant idea of courting popular wills; as if this other attempt of giving the railroads to the State, with various inconveniences, high moralizing aims; such as leaving the

corrupting games of the stock market, and not being fed in various countries, at the same time, among people who are not, by the way, in taverns nor slums.[8]

Rejecting how Europe constructed socialist doctrines, Martí, though not a socialist, nonetheless advocated some socialist concepts. Cognizant of the risks associated with socialism, such as the danger to individual freedom, Martí believed they could be overcome. "The socialist idea," he wrote in an 1894 letter to his childhood friend Fermín Valdés Domínguez, "like many others, has two dangers: foreign, confused, and incomplete interpretations; and the arrogance and hidden rage of the ambitious, that in order to rise up in society begin by pretending to be frantic defenders of the helpless so as to have shoulders upon which to rise . . . But in our nation, this is not so great a risk, as in more wrathful societies, and of less natural clarity."[9]

Although it is true that Martí was no economist, few were during his time. The neoclassical economics that were developing as a way of thought during the 1870s is what we today consider mainstream economic thinking (along with Keynesian economics of the 1930s). Social writers of the time, motivated by pursuing political liberation, simply considered the economic reasons the poor remained impoverished as they sought an economically based praxis to bring about political liberation. Martí, in his pursuit of human liberation, envisioned the Américas as possessing a more equitable distribution of wealth. "The republic, in Puerto Rico as in Cuba, will not become the unjust dominance of one class of Cubans over the other," he wrote in 1893, "but the open and sincere equilibrium of all the real powers of the country, and the free thoughts and desire of all Cubans."[10] And yet Martí does not subscribe to the concept of class warfare, à la Marx. He simply recognized the existence of classes as a social construct and the dangers of a government under the control of one economic class. Regardless of the class to which one belonged, the moral and spiritual imperative of all people was to love one another. He saw the hypocrisy of those in the United States who imagined themselves philanthropists while making their riches on the backs of the poor. What men like Vanderbilt, Rockefeller, Drew, Duke, and Morgan—to name a few—had in common was what they did with some of the riches horded through monopolistic exploitation. They built Christian churches and seminaries (several of which still carry their names today), even though the men themselves adhered to a savage, anti-Christian capitalist ethos.

Economic liberation from the positivism of the emerging U.S. empire and political independence from the declining Spanish Empire would remain unobtainable if devoid of the spiritual. Liberation, for Martí, also comes through spiritual revival. One of the notes he jotted down was this: "Political freedom will not be assured as long as spiritual freedom is not secured."[11] Martí believed economic and political liberation would fail unless the Cuban national character was reformed, restructured, and reshaped. He visualized the construction of *la nueva religión*, a new ethics, even a new "man," capable of grounding an independent *patria*. This *nueva religión*, he wrote in an 1886 editorial, is to be a "scientific theism which each day would become clearer . . . each time with more spirit of the scientific knowledge of the world."[12] This *nueva religión* Martí called for was to be based on reason, not dogma, congruent with—not in rebellion against—the truth that can be discovered in nature.

La nueva religión

Martí came in the name of the Lord, like some Hebrew prophet, calling the people of Spain to repent from their sins, specifically their support for colonialism. He thundered like Amos, the prophet of doom, against the Spaniards for their complicity with oppression. But for Cubans, he inspired like Deutero-Isaiah with messianic visions of establishing national independence. He sought and demanded more than simply the political independence of one island in the Caribbean; he was attempting to construct a new way of being and believing, pursuing the creation of a new religion—a *nueva religión*—for and by liberated individuals committed to the task of seeking political and economic freedom for others through an unconditional, active love that rejects hatred and vengeance. This is a faith "which is essential in all without oppressing any."[13] For him, "liberation is the definitive religion. And the poetry of liberty the new worship."[14]

The *martiano* scholar Rafael Cepeda claimed that Martí never set out to write a thesis on some new religion, yet a thread of his theological understanding of what encompasses this *nueva religión* can be found in multiple texts written over the entirety of his career.[15] Central to his thought is the realization that political liberation could not be achieved as long as spiritual liberation was denied. Martí observed other countries throughout Latinoamérica that broke with Spain's colonial grip during the earlier decades of the nineteenth century. Lacking a moral compass, they eventually betrayed the ideals of liberation by succumbing to the rule of opportunist caudillos. He realized that political independence was insufficient to forge a nation rooted in principles of justice. Not all of Cuba's ills could be blamed solely on the Spaniards. It was not enough to simply raise the Cuban flag; the human spirit also needed to be raised. The goals for which independence was fought would fall short if society itself did not spiritually transform. To that end, Martí sought a *nueva religión* for a new age rooted not in coercion, but in a patriotism that leaned toward sacrificial duty. This *nueva religión* is "not virtue through punishment and duty; [but] virtue for patriotism, conviction and work."[16]

For Martí, "nothing more effectively helps than liberation to the true religion."[17] As the fin de siècle approached, Martí believed this new religiosity was dawning, a religiosity where reason and mystery embraced; a religiosity that was not sectarian, dogmatic, or institutional; a religiosity that harmonized materialism and spiritualism. He attempted to describe this *nueva religión*, what we might call a spiritual liberationist humanism, in romanticized imagery:

> Thus, we propose nothing less than a *nueva religión* and new priests! We are painting nothing less than the mission with which we will soon spread this religion in a new era! The world is changing; and so are cardinal purple robes and chasubles, necessary in the mystic times of men, lie stretched out on the bed of agony. Religion has not disappeared, but it has been transformed. Beyond the grief which joins together the observers of the study of details with the slow involvement of human history, we can see the growth of men, and that they

already ascended half of Jacob's ladder (what beautiful poems has the Bible!). If huddled up on a summit one suddenly cast one's eyes on the human march, one will see people have never loved each other as much as they love each other now. And despite the painful disorder and abominable egoism, with the momentary absence of final beliefs and faith in the truth of the Eternal, that is brought to the inhabitants of this transitory epoch; never worry for today the benevolence and impetus of expansion of human beings now burns in all men. They have stood up, like friends who know each other, and wanted to know each other, mutually march to a happy encounter.[18]

This idealistic quest was not unlatched from reason but rooted in it, or, as he would confess: "I do not know if I am crazy, since I am a complete idealist. The wonderful holy miraculous realism is the logic of nature."[19] He may have been a dreamer, but as he wrote in one of the poems to his son in his 1882 book titled *Ismaelillo*, "I dream with my eyes / open."[20] His idealism was moored to the piers of reality and reason.

When Martí envisioned *patria*, it was not simply a nation endowed by some Creator; nor was it based on some dying religion like Christianity. *Patria* in and of itself is divine, and Martí referred to it as deity, as "God *Patria*."[21] He embraced religion not because of some firm belief in its doctrine, but because of a vague innate understanding of its mysteries, coupled with a practical usefulness in creating a virtuous and just social order. "Temples?" he writes, "Now more than ever there is a need for temples of love and humanity which unleash all generosity within man and restrains all that is cruel and vile within him."[22] Martí thus advocates for what the *martiano* scholar Carlos Alberto Montaner calls "the religion of patriotism."[23]

Patria becomes the means by which humans fulfill their cosmic duty to humanity, and Martí becomes the evangelist, the apostle bearing this good news. In his famous tract from early 1873, *The Spanish Republic before the Cuban Revolution*, Martí wrote: "*Patria* is something more than oppression, something more than pieces of land without liberty nor life, something more than the right to possess strength. *Patria* is a community of people sharing interests, unity of traditions, unity of aims, a sweet consolatory fusion of love and hope."[24] Love of country and a community of people merge to become a foundational entity of an anticolonialist and anti-imperialist way of being and thinking. For Martí, *patria* should not be confused with nationalism, restricted by geographical boundaries, for it has a metaphysical dimension that unites all who seek love, peace, and justice as a way of being.

By 1885, Martí had expanded his description of *patria* as "that tight community of the spirits bounded by the deep roots of the people linked by their baptism of penetrating common pains, by the most delicious wine of patriotic glories, by a national soul which looms in the air, breathed and lodged in the gut, and by the subtle and formable strands which tied them to history, as the skin to the flesh."[25] *Patria* ceases to be limited to just one village, one people, one nation. In a sense, *patria* encompasses all of humanity, or as Martí succinctly proclaimed: "*Patria* is humanity."[26] Although Martí normatively possessed a very dualistic mind-set, a religious and political dichotomy is not revealed in his thoughts. "Patriotism is a holy duty," he wrote, "when one fights to place *patria* in a condition where men can live happier."[27] *Patria* has a divine essence because the humans who compose *patria* contains souls that encompass the essence of heaven. To establish *patria* is a spiritual act. When he reflects on the start of the Ten Years' War, he lifts up that day, 10 October 1868, as a holy day, "a day which is for Cubans religious."[28] As he worked to unify patriotic political clubs into a national movement, he preferred clubs with a spiritual foundation. As he proclaimed in an 1891 speech in New York City commemorating 10 October: "Spirit clubs is what we want!"[29]

What was important for Martí is that the God within, our consciousness, is synonymous with *patria*, and as such becomes the path to both liberation and justice. The merging of the God Consciousness created by the ultimate supreme being—the God who creates—is based on the human consciousness, which is itself divine. God Consciousness, God *Patria*, either understanding of how Martí understands God is worthy of our praise, our devotion, our worship, and our self-sacrifice. There is no Nietzschean call for an end of God as understood by Martí's contemporaries, but an emphasis on the moral imperatives that flow from said understanding. Martí, in his early notebook, concludes:

Catholicism dies, as mythology dies, as paganism dies, as what a human genius creates dies, or the reason of another genius destroys or replaces. Only one thing should not die. The God Consciousness, the sublime duality of love and honor, the inspiring thought of all religions, the eternal germ of all beliefs, the irreformable law, the fixed law, always sovereign over souls, always obeyed with pleasure, always noble, always the same. Here lies the Powerful and fertile Idea that must not perish, because it is identically born again with every soul which rises to the light. Here is the only true thing because it is the only thing recognized by all. Here is the axis of the moral world. Here is our omnipotent and omniscient God. The God Conscious who is the son of the God who created, which is the only visible bond unanimously received, unanimously adored, who unites a driven humanity with the driving divinity. Adored, but not reminiscent of Catholic education. This God, and the God *Patria*, are in our society and in our life the only adorable things.[30]

Patria as divine cannot be created out of hatred, discrimination, or self-interest. The creation of *patria* is a holy act sanctioned by the heavens, a spiritual quest for a morality requiring sacrifice for the betterment of self and others. According to the historian Armando García de la Torre (no relationship to me), "The *patria* to Martí was a living, spiritual entity, divine in nature, and composed of a large community of individuals that loved and identified with Cuba's well-being. In fact, Martí's concept of nation resonates with that of a later nationalist, India's Mahatma Gandhi. As Gandhi later would, Martí conceived of the *patria* as godly, and this divine conception of *patria* stems from Martí's personal views of the human soul as divine."[31] *Patria* becomes a humanistic spiritual project that seeks the liberation of land, individual, and soul and is rooted in the dignity of all.

Until Martí, no revolutionary organization existed that encompassed all the different émigré communities and patriotic clubs throughout the United States and Cuba.[32] Crucial to any liberative theological movement, as Chapter 4 explores in greater detail, is the concept of praxis. The praxis of creating an organization by which to bring about God *Patria* provides flesh to Martí's political-theological thought. On 5 January 1892, he, along with twenty-six other representatives, founded the Partido Revolucionario Cubano (PRC), a decentralized organization composed of independent clubs and incorporating a diverse group of Cubans. As committee chair, Martí strived to create a more liberative way of doing revolution based on patriotic passions and the moral theological compass he envisioned for a future Cuba. The mission of the PRC was to serve as the political wing of the armed struggle, or in Martí's words, "The Revolutionary Party was created for the democratic and judicious independence war, and it will not deviate from its purpose which is to democratically and judiciously create the war of independence."[33]

The creation of the PRC prevents dismissal of Martí as some intellectual dreamer, an idealist who constructed utopias in the clouds. How he organized the PRC provides clues as to the form of government Martí was envisioning, no small feat when we consider that some thirty-four clubs advocating Cuba's independence existed through the United States.[34] These clubs, besides being separated by great distances in an era dependent on written letters to coordinate cooperation, were also very diverse with respect to ideology (some leaned toward republicanism while others leaned toward anarchism), race (some memberships were mainly Black while others were entirely white), and class (come clubs comprised elite Cubans while others tobacco rollers). Complicating the diversity was gender—some clubs were entirely composed of women during a time when Cuban leadership, including Martí, held very patriarchal views.

Like the long-awaited Messiah, Martí accomplished the organizational feat of uniting such a diverse group of Cubans. Bringing these sundry factions together under the all-encompassing banner of *un Cuba libre* required a certain ambiguity with detail. The newspaper *Patria* became the PRC's means of communication, providing the Cuban populace the reasoning for the uprising. But discerning Martí's vision for the political structures of *un Cuba libre* through his articles in *Patria* is complicated. His writing style is designed to appeal to a large swath of patriots who could read their own visions into Martí's words; nevertheless, it is possible to deduce certain principles on which he hoped to construct Cuban governance. What the PRC demonstrated is that Martí was a shrewd strategist able not only to bring together diverse groups with competing interests under one tent for a common cause but also, and more important, he possessed the political leadership skills to raise funds and an army—in relative secrecy—to make his visions for Cuba a reality. And yet there is no governing apparatus in waiting to be implemented once the revolution proved successful. Still, dismissing Martí visions for a future Cuba because he failed to develop a concrete blueprint would be an error.

Martí's vision for the PRC, according to his comments in *Patria* concerning the 1892 reception in Philadelphia, was "to unite, with sufficient purpose and strength, all the necessary elements to accelerate, through a revolutionary organization which is spiritual with democratic methodology, the establishment of a republic where every citizen, Cuban or Spaniard, white or Black, American or European, can enjoy, in work and in peace, their human rights."[35] Although he can be praised for constructing a large tent, the participation of marginalized groups could be interpreted as symbolic in comparison to the authority held by their wealthier, whiter, and more educated counterparts. Not everyone thought the PRC was the most democratic way to organize the independence movement. A vocal minority existed. For example, Enrique Trujillo, editor of the New York paper *El Porvenir* objected to a structure that could be manipulated by a charismatic leader with mass appeal. He, along with Juan Calserón from Key West, expressed concern about too much power resting in the hands of the few; opportunities for questions or dissent were limited as decisions were rapidly made with little discussion.[36] Others, like General Enrique Collazo, publicly challenged Martí to a duel, accusing him of being a coward who lived off donations of tobacco workers. He wrote: "In the hour of sacrifice, we would not be able to extend a handshake on the Cuban battlefield."[37] With time, they would become allies.

This quest to create God *Patria* becomes a *nueva religión* that rejects creeds, doctrines, and dogma for a practical reason rooted in nature and influenced by an ecumenical universalist vision of different traditions coming together as one to tackle the challenges facing humanity. According to Martí: "Because it feels as if Christianity is dying at the threshold of *la nueva iglesia* where the heaven serves as the roof, where the Catholic Christ will sit side by side with the Hindu Christ, with

Confucius on one side and Wotan on the other, with no more clergy but the sense of duty, no more candelabras but the rays of the sun, no more censers but the chalices of flowers."[38] The fight for *Cuba libre* becomes a spiritual journey; and anything that impedes bringing forth *patria* must, like sin, be exorcised: "I will reply by finishing to cleanse my life, if it is not already well cleaned of all thoughts or guilts which impede me from the absolute service of *mi patria*."[39]

The spiritual and divine essence of *patria*, foundational to this *nueva religión*, is charged with reversing the Catholic dogma that replaced but did not fully vanquish reason: "The articles of faith have not disappeared. They changed form. Those of Catholic dogma have substituted the teaching of reason. Compulsory education is an article of faith of the new dogma."[40] This *nueva religión* converts normative dogmatic and mystical faiths into a religion recognizing reason and science and seeking justice and liberation in an independent Cuba. This *nueva religión* based on the duty to do justice, which is evangelized by Martí is a "religion, in short, of the new free men, grandiose, fraternal, humane, free like them."[41] This *nueva religión* rejects any form of an official colonizer's religion—be it Catholic or Protestant. Martí stood in opposition to how the colonial powers and the colonial Catholic Church coexisted to the detriment of subjugated people. Furthermore, he noted that in those countries that claimed independence, and which he had visited, the church simply made new alliances with wealthy landowners to maintain its privileged space within society.

Martí is clear as to his proposal: "a *nueva religión* and new priests!" He argues for "a faith that has to replace the one which has died and emerges with a radiant clarity of the arrogant peace of the redeemed man."[42] For him, the institutionalized religion of Christianity and the clergy must be swept away as relics because of their complicity with maintaining poverty, their spiritualizing of oppressive social structures. The church peddled visions of rewards in some heaven to preserve the domesticity of the people: "This is how the Church spoke: . . . To the rich: 'The masses are falling over each other, and it is necessary to face them. Only the Church promising justice in Heaven can contain them.' To the poor: 'Poverty is divine. What is more beautiful than a soul fortified by resignation? Over there in the heavens you will find your reward and your rest.'"[43] In other words, life, and life abundant, is for the hereafter, not the here and now. A spirituality is thus constructed that justifies oppressive social structures. In forming the counternarrative of the *nueva religión*, his writings tap into the depths of the inhuman conditions in which vast segments of the world's population are forced to live. He responds to their oppression by attempting to raise human consciousness so that the wretched can achieve their full potential as liberated beings. He reminds us in English, in the 1880 editorial for the New York newspaper *The Hour*, that "when the days of poverty may arrive—what richness, if not that of spiritual strength and intellectual comfort, will help this people in its colossal misfortune?"[44]

The major component of this *nueva religión* that Martí preaches is liberation—liberation from the oppression of declining colonial powers, from emerging empires, from dogmatic churches, and from the oppression of one's own egotistical, self-serving humanity. The *nueva religión* that Martí envisions is a spiritual humanist forerunner to what would eventually be referred to, some six decades after his death, as liberation theology, understood as a religious or spiritual countertradition of resistance rooted in the plight of the oppressed, a spiritual response to unexamined normalized and legitimized social structures responsible for privileging a powerful minority at the expense of the disenfranchised majority. If liberation theology is a theological analysis of the social, economic, cultural, and political causes of oppression from the perspective of the oppressed, then it is not difficult to view Martí as a conversation partner. Probably the first *martiano* scholar to do so, calling Martí "a prophet of liberation theology," was Rafael Cepeda.[45] While I, too, desire to make a connection between Martí and liberation theology, we must remain cautious of applying twentieth-century theological concepts to Martí's nineteenth-century political writings—such a move is at best problematic. Utilizing the modern nomenclature *liberation theology* to describe historical figures like José Martí runs the risk of simplistic analysis. To state that Martí was a liberation theologian would be an unscholarly stretch, a fall into a similar trap made by generations of scholars who have simply read their own particular political, religious, and/or spiritual convictions into a historical figure who predates the coagulation of the fluid theological

thoughts in question. All too often Martí's works have been uncritically used to justify diverse political positions, from the authoritarianism of Fulgencio Batista to the Marxism of Fidel Castro. I, for one,
have no intention of continuing this normative approach. This is why
I find myself agreeing more with the theologian Reinerio Arce; without
identifying Martí as a liberation theologian, he has no qualms identifying him as a precursor of the religious movement.[46]

Even though Martí's thoughts bear the marks of his own time (e.g.,
unbinding optimism for the coming century, unfounded hope in the
progressive goodness of humanity), many of his core ideas resonate
with what has come to be known as liberative theological thought,
providing a foundation on which we can construct a political theology.
This *nueva religión* as precursor to liberation theology, is an active
love rooted in an ethical duty deeply concerned with fostering and
enriching life, as opposed to the ethics of the dominant culture, which
remains complicit with hate-based social structures causing marginalization. The goal of liberation is to break with death-dealing structures
by committing to life, a process achieved through consciousness raising, learning how structures of oppression prevent abundant life from
unfolding. Thus, the "evangelical" goal is not to convince nonbelievers
to believe doctrinal Catholic or Protestant tenets but to convince those
upon whom society gazes as nonpersons that they, in reality, possess
infinite worth. Liberative political theology does not create, expand,
or sustain doctrinal beliefs; rather, it physically (not just intellectually) responds to the inhuman conditions to which the vast majority of
humanity is relegated. Such a response is costly, as Martí reminds us
in an 1880 lecture shortly after he emigrated to New York: "Liberation
costs dearly, but it is necessary, or else resign oneself to live without
it, or decide to purchase it at its price."[47] Liberative political theology
becomes a costly spiritual call to action whose goal is the rescue and
deliverance of all who face sociocultural and economic oppression.

La nueva iglesia

The church is called not only to signify liberation but also to be an
instrument by which liberation is achieved. José Martí understood this

principle and called for a church that separates the clergy who are more concerned with maintaining the dominance of their tenets from those who actually "do" their faith. To do one's faith is to raise the consciousness of those unaware of how power relationships shape oppressive structures, as well as those committed to working in and with disenfranchised communities during their struggle for liberation. Martí, as an evangelist of *la nueva religión*, was more concerned with "doing" his faith and calling others to also engage in praxis than with simply writing soaring poesy to tickle the ears of those duplicitous with soul crushing dogma. Unfortunately, the church was too corrupt and complicit in oppression to be part of any liberative answer, he thought. In his commentary on the excommunication of Father McGlynn he asked: "Is that so? Whoever serves liberation cannot serve the Church? Is that true? The Church turns against the poor who support it, and the priests who study its evils . . . ? Really? The Church does not learn history, does not learn freedom, does not learn political economy?"[48]

The established church—in Martí's case, the Catholic Church— ceased being a religious organization following the teachings of Jesús; instead, it made a Faustian bargain for the sake of political influence and expediency. In another editorial written six months earlier on the schism caused by Father McGlynn, Martí wrote: "So, the Church buys influence and sells votes? So, holiness angers her? So, it allies with the rich of enemy sects? So, it prohibits its parish priests from exercising their political rights, unless they exert them to be in favor of those trafficking in favors for the Church? With what intent to ruin and degrade those who offend their authoritarian politics, who quietly follow what sweet Jesús taught? Why can't you be a man and a Catholic? But see how you can, as these new fishermen teach us! Oh Jesús! Which side would you have taken in this fight?"[49]

Christendom, ever since becoming the official religion of the Roman Empire in 323 CE, a decade after Emperor Constantine issued the Edict of Milan, has remained closely linked to the dominant political establishment, designed to protect the interests of the privileged ruling few. As such, Christianity, especially in its Eurocentric manifestation, has operated as the spiritual justifier of politically oppressive structures; from the Crusades, to the Inquisition, to slavery, to genocide, to the colonial venture. But whenever spiritual coercion dominates the political arena, a spiritual resistance arises as a counternarrative.

Martí personifies this spiritual resistance to the organized religious authorities of his day. Recognizing that the church, more often than not, aligned itself with the interests of the ruling and economically privileged classes, he searched within his religious tradition to formulate a practical and spiritual response to the consequences of colonialism and oppression, a response rooted in rational thought. Liberative theological thought, throughout the ages, has focused on human needs rather than on ecclesiastical dogma, maintaining that the church can never be neutral in the face of injustices. Whenever the church stood in solidarity with the marginalized, it ceased being an extension of Christendom and became a co-laborer with the oppressed. God, if such a deity exists, would never be found in towering cathedrals whose ornate steeples serve as monuments to those who reached the pinnacle of wealth on the backs of the poor and disenfranchised. God is found among the gathering of the "least of these."

What is needed, in Martí's view, was a new church—a *nueva iglesia*. What, then, is the *nueva iglesia* that will house *la nueva religión*? Certainly not the established church in league with Christendom! For him, the ideal church was one "without dogmatic creed, but rather that great and firm creed which is the majesty of the Universe and is the good immortal soul which inspires what a great church would be! And dignifies the discredited religion!"[50] The minister of this *nueva iglesia* will be "a knight of men, worker of a future world, a cantor of the dawn, a priest of a new church."[51] He is quick to lift up individuals who are already doing their faith, engaged in what they say they believe, as opposed to simply spouting pietistic platitudes.

For example, among Catholics, he looks to Father Miguel Hidalgo, a leader of the Mexican War for Independence whom he exalted in his 1889 children's book *La edad de oro* as "a village priest who much loved the Indians."[52] Among Protestants, he looks to the U.S. abolitionist John Brown as an individual imitating Christ as opposed to simply claiming belief. John Brown advocated armed insurrection as the only way to abolish the oppressive institution of slavery. He led a raid on a federal armory in 1859 for which he was caught, convicted, and hung for treason. Martí wrote: "The heavens have stars, but the earth has, like a shining star, the scaffold of John Brown. Jesús died on the cross, and this one on the gallows. Later, the men were dead, hallowed out, without flesh nor consciousness of their memory in the universal existence. They arise from whirlpools, walk on the path to the Sun, happily sail forth; but if men, which are not be found, are found after death, Jesús and John Brown would go hand in hand."[53] Martí attacks all religions and political structures that contribute to poverty and are complicit with the repression of liberation, believing that faith communities have the ability to rectify social problems. Consequently, Martí welcomes the religious, regardless of tradition, who are willing to practice their faith in the construction of liberty and *patria*. Before examining non-Christian religious traditions in the next chapter, first we will turn our attention to Protestantism.

Protestantism

Martí may have exhibited in his writing an appreciation and admiration for Martin Luther; still, he never converted to Protestantism. And yet Cuban Protestants are at times quick to quote the many harsh and savage condemnations he expressed toward the Catholic Church, as if he somehow saw Protestantism as a viable alternative. But as the *martiano* scholar Rafael Cepeda confesses, "We Cuban Protestants have been dishonest for years and years in using [Martí's] quote[s]."[54] Cuban Protestants have uncritically used Martí's analytical pronouncements concerning the Catholic Church to present their own faith tradition as a desirable substitute, more in line with the apostle's thinking, ignoring concerns he also raised about Protestants. And while Martí did admire some aspects of Protestantism, he was nonetheless just as critical of it as of Catholicism.

Protestantism was almost nonexistent on the island until the nineteenth century; although, as the Cuban historian Marco Ramos reminds us, "since the sixteenth century the country had been constantly visited by pirates, corsairs, and filibusters, many of whom were Protestants—Huguenots, Dutch Reformed, Anglicans."[55] The welcomed contraband they brought that circumvented Spain's economic restraints no doubt included Protestant Bibles. The first Protestant service held on the island was probably officiated by the French corsair Jacques de Sores in 1555, responsible for also attacking and setting La Habana on fire. By 1741, with the British occupation of the Guantánamo Valley under the command of Admiral Edward Vernon, Anglican clergy aboard the warships held regular services until the end of occupation in 1763. But it wasn't until the beginning of the nineteenth century, as North American and British Protestants settled on the island in search of economic opportunities that Protestantism developed a more permanent presence.[56]

During Martí's lifetime, Protestantism had little influence on an island where the official religion was Catholicism and where Protestants were disenfranchised from political power. According to Cuban law, "no public ceremonies or demonstrations other than those of the State religion, that is Roman Catholicism, will be permitted." Revival meetings and church services were regularly banned and Protestant pastors faced detention and/or incarceration. Cuba's hostility toward Protestantism made evangelism difficult. In spite of the zeal of missionaries, there were few converts for their efforts throughout the nineteenth century.[57] Still, Protestants did experience minor successes prior to the 1895 War of Independence because of the Catholic Church's close ties to colonial rule, leading some Cubans, especially those with strong independence or annexation sentiments, to abandon the Catholic Church and make a preferential option for Protestantism. Hatred toward the colonial structures included both the political and the ecclesiastical authorities on the island. For some Cubans, being Protestant meant rebelling against the established colonial order, an act of defiance. The increasing acceptance of Protestantism was further fueled as the elite sought U.S. citizenship and sent their children to U.S. schools to be educated. Protestantism, in their minds, represented the future better than a medieval church clinging to Old World structures. Unlike Catholicism, Protestantism signified progress, modernity, democracy, and economic success. Although Euro-Americans had few successes during the nineteenth century in spreading the Protestant good news, Cuban Protestants experienced some successes in planting churches and establishing congregations. As a result of their efforts, Protestant communities were established. Unlike other countries in Latinoamérica, Cuba was the first where permanent Protestant congregations were founded by nationals, not Europeans.[58]

As one-tenth of the Cuban population—one hundred thousand refugees—streamed to the United States fleeing wars and rebellions, starting with the outbreak of the Ten Years' War in 1868, seeking jobs— especially in Key West, Tampa, Jacksonville, and Ocala—missionaries awaited them. Protestants set up social services, resettlement and relief programs, and English classes as a means of converting Cubans to Protestantism. Martí even praised these Protestants for their commitment to poor Cubans. Many of the Cuban converts in New York, Tampa, and Key West returned to the island after the signing of the Treaty of Zanjón (1878), which ended the first war for Cuba's independence. Returning Cuban exiles like Díaz and de la Cova (Southern Baptist); Moreno, Duarte, Báez, and Peña (Episcopal); Someillán and Silvera (Methodists); and Collazo (Presbyterian) are but a few of the individuals who formed churches with an entirely Cuban membership. But while Cuban Protestants proudly claimed that their first congregations were founded by Cubans, 95 percent of the resources needed to build and maintain these congregations came from their U.S. counterparts.[59]

While Martí was aware of Protestant groups while he was living in Spain, Mexico, and Guatemala, he does not appear to make any direct references to them.[60] Not until 1880, with his move to New York City where Protestant groups represented the majority of the population, did he begin to write about them. As Rafael Cepeda noted, after living in countries where the Catholic Church was complicit with autocratic rule, Martí found Protestantism refreshing, a religion for a democratic people.[61] There is no question that Martí was sympathetic to Protestantism, as demonstrated in his turn to the Protestant Church as a seed of liberty condemning the oppressive political corruption of Tammany Hall: "[Rebellion against this political boss] first arose in Brooklyn, home of the Protestant Church, which in spite of its narrowness— and why not say it—is the seed of human freedom."[62] His admiration for the Protestant commitment to liberty was such that he suggested,

"All free men should hang upon their walls, like that of a redeemer, the portrait of Luther."[63] He praised Bishop Phillips Brooks, the Episcopalian minister, as a brother, not an official of the church, "who does not want to know about this dogma or that one; but of the essentials of faith in God."[64] Even when praising a sermon by the Catholic Father McGlynn in 1887, he used imagery of Protestant rebellion: "He began his discourse slow and grave, with words which involuntarily recalled the hammer blows with which Luther stuck his thesis upon the Wittenberg Church's door."[65]

Many Protestants were among Martí's friends, men he admired for their religious convictions and their commitment to *patria*. One such Protestant, a Methodist, was Manuel Deulofeu, whom Martí described as "full of Creole fire with a soul rich in goodness."[66] During his stay in Key West from December 1891 until January 1892, Martí spent time at Deulofeu's Methodist home church, receiving from his daughter Julia a copy of the New Testament. Deulofeu, a refugee who fled Cuba in December 1886, was an author, abolitionist, and friend of Martí who collaborated with him in forming the Partido Revolucionario Cubano. Just as important, Deulofeu organized a *cocina económica*, a kitchen that provided two hundred thousand food rations to striking cigar workers from 1893 through 1894.[67] Other Protestants who Martí considered patriots were José Joaquín Palma, the first Cuban ordained in a U.S. Protestant church—Episcopal.[68] There was also José Victoriano de la Cova and Pedro Duarte, cofounders of the Partido Revolucionario Cubano in Matanzas (1892); Enrique Benito Someillán, who served as Martí's secretary in Key West; and Clemente Moya. Church commitment to charity, regardless of faith tradition, was consistently attractive to Martí.

There was much to praise Protestants for, and yet Martí was still just as critical of them as he was of Catholics. When writing the essay "Religious Liberty in the United States," he praised Presbyterians for their willingness during an assembly to reform some of John Calvin's more "unnatural and violent dogma," like the absolute authority of the church or a predestination that condemns newborns to "eternal flames." He lifted up the assembly as an example of how a Christian sect sets out to place religion on a more rational foundation.[69] He praised in his 1888 studies on North America the passengers of the *Mayflower*, who with "their plows, shotguns, and Bibles," signed a compact agreeing "in the things concerning the soul there is no more guide or authority than reason"; even though there were those "strong-jawed, musket-shouldered Puritans" who "burned witches and riddled Quakers with bullets."[70] In an 1890 essay for *La Nación*, Martí sings the praises of a particular Methodist church that he felt modeled a modern approach to presenting the Christian gospels:

> The Methodist Church, which has fallen elsewhere, flourishes in Chautauqua because it stands in solidarity with the humble and opens itself to the times. They do not want blue laws nor closed doors. Nor are they interested in running around in the dark and in circles like a mole due to too much or too little creed, but instead ask nature for her secrets, finding in intelligent and free communion a more dignified and penetrating pleasure—more humane and religious than the one who, because the church has a steeple or has three, leans toward detesting and destroying men. The Churches here, so as not to perish in the world, accompany him.[71]

What is interesting about this passage is Martí's revelation that Protestantism, while containing some admirable churches, remains cognizant of the many others failing elsewhere.

His main complaint about the church—Catholic and Protestant—was its lifting of ignorant dogma above rational thought and the preferential option of the clergy for the wealthy elite and the governments that represent them. Martí wrote: "And the people of the city, if religious are ultramontane, and if they are not religious, have advance too far in their faith in free thinking to return to the timid denials and incomplete concepts of Protestantism."[72] After witnessing a performance by the well-known nineteenth-century evangelist Dwight L. Moody in 1890, Martí described him as "another evangelist in a lesser church, making the Bible a joke, and converting the reluctant with anecdotes. He invites them with simplicity, he holds them with pleasantness, he suddenly moves them with a vehement and desperate exhortation, he wipes away the tears of their eyes with a story."[73]

Elsewhere, he referred to Moody as a "grotesque, frenzied" preacher.[74] Martí had no qualms writing about the *estrecheces*—narrowness—of Protestant churches,[75] rejecting "a creed that breeds churches, like Protestantism."[76]

In 1889, writing on his studies on North America, he describes a gathering of pastors who wonder among themselves why their churches fail to attract the bustle they see at the theater. Martí is quick to provide a response: "Because the teaching is false, their nature harsh, the rich proud, the poor distrusted, and the era of complete change and reincarnation, which asks for something more than churches favorably linked to the well off against the miserable—guidance in the judgment and consolation of the soul. They are reduced to be used as an instrument of the government in defense of castes and fall to the ground nail rammed."[77] Martí was quick to see the link between New York's gilded "nobility" marching along with Protestant bishops.[78] "And it can be said outspokenly," he wrote, "that the official clergy today serve the rich."[79]

Protestants sold their souls, Martí argued, for fortune: "In this way it can be seen that in this [U.S.] Protestant stronghold, the Protestants, who still represent the rich and educated class here are the tacit and tenacious friends, and grateful accomplices of the religion which roasted them at the stake but who they caress today because it helps them save their unjust excess of fortune! Pharisees all, and augurs!"[80] He extensively quoted a Methodist preacher's condemnation of his own church to remind readers that Protestantism, like Catholicism, ran the risk of justifying injustice:

The bishop of the Methodist Church, a robust Church protected by the wealthy, sends to the temples of his creed a pastor who lifts great passions in the country. "Enough" he says, "this building where we live is a building of injustice. This is not what Jesús taught, nor what men should do. Our civilization is unjust. Our structures concerning wages, asylums, and hospitals have been tested and failed. The order of reason is repugnant, with some having too much and others lack the basics. What is constructed like this, must be undone, for it is done wrong. Let us amicably encounter justice if we do not want justice to collapse upon us. For Christ and for reason. This unjust factory has to be changed. You who are rich have too much land! You who are poor must have your part of the land!" These condense words of the pastor have shaken the people's attention because they do not come from discredited philanthropists, nor for folks of odes and books, but from a great minister of deep intelligence and thought. He has a granite church with stained glass windows which has enjoyed a majestic life in service and affection for the wealthy. Blessed are the hands downwardly extended to the poor![81]

For Martí, both Catholicism and Protestantism made a preferential option for the rich, referring to them as "those leagues of the rich in all the [religious] sects, with that audacity to speak of the poverty of Jesús and yet live on pheasant with golden wine in the pomp of palace, slipping on the purple, smooth among high class ladies who like the clerics to be wusses."[82]

Protestants may have agreed with Martí's goal of rupturing relationship with Spain, but their motives for doing so were radically different and self-serving. Protestant support for Cuba to sever ties was driven by the prospects of obtaining new converts. If the United States represented the new Jerusalem, politically expressed as Manifest Destiny, then its mission was to spread the Protestant Gospel to overcome the "heresy" of Roman Catholicism. Protestant Christian magazines, at the turn of the century, described the military intervention in Cuba as an "act of providence," a response to a "Macedonian Call." A call to participate in the 1895 Cuban War of Independence took on religious significance. "The struggle for religious freedom is inseparably linked with that of political deliverance," wrote a Baptist weekly in 1896.[83] The *American Missionary*, which began publication in 1846 as a Protestant-based abolitionist magazine, seemed to ignore that Catholics were Christians, as indicated in the title of a September 1898 article, "Shall Cuba Be Taken for Christ?"[84] In the eyes of most Protestants of the era, the papacy was the anti-Christ and Catholicism represented the apostate church.

Hopes of turning Cuba into a successful Protestant mission field were directly tied to annexation desires, as expressed by Richard B. Kimball, who in 1850 wrote: "In short, the principal reason given by the serious and reflecting Cubans for desiring annexation to the United States, is derived from the present condition of religious and moral degradation of the island . . . With annexation to the United States will come the free Bible, the free Pulpit, and the free Press; the healthful and stimulating influence of Protestant competition in the labors of the spiritual harvest; the infusion of a new spirit, a renovated vitality, into the moral being of the population of Cuba, now corrupt with disease and palsied well-nigh beyond recovery."[85] Early, before Cubans rebelled against Spanish colonialism, Protestants in the United States already coveted the land, ripe for civilization and Christianization. This was the "white man's burden," which was much in play within the Euro-American imagination at the time. Euro-American missionaries arrived in Cuba with the U.S. occupation during the transition from Spanish colonialism to U.S. imperialism. They served the important role of confronting the Cubans with their supposedly defective character by offering redemption in normative Eurocentric structures.[86] While they originally limited themselves to economically assisting the efforts of local Cubans, after 1898, they took over the Protestant movement, relegating Cubans, who until then had led the movement, to secondary positions. While Cubans may have maintained some influence over missionaries, Euro-Americans had the last word.[87]

Protestantism was not the religious panacea some Cubans hoped for, especially Black Cubans. Martí noted how Protestants used their faith to justify U.S. slavery: "Slavery had its priests, just as it later had its martyrs, had its psalms, its prayers, and its interpreters of the Bible. From the start, the same men from the South called it a 'necessary evil.' But when later swept away by the frantic pace of controversy, the justification of trafficking was raised to dogma . . . The Southerner believed in slavery as belief in God."[88] When we consider that many of the missionaries coming to Cuba were Southerners, it should not be surprising that the Jim and Jane Crow racism of U.S. Southern states reinforced the racism already prevalent in Cuba. Setting up private schools and segregated churches during the early Republic years only strengthened Black Cuban disenfranchisement.

The best evidence of the failure of U.S.-based Protestantism in Cuba was revealed about fifty years after the invasion of the island.

Months after the 1959 revolution, Protestant missionaries returned to the United States, followed by many Cuban pastors and their middle-class congregations. Entire congregations disappeared. Those congregations held close ties with their U.S. counterparts and tended to reject the revolution. Those Protestants who remained felt abandoned.[89]

Krausismo

Martí's Christianity was highly influenced by the thought of Karl Krause (1781–1832). Krause, almost unknown in Anglo-Saxon philosophical thought, was a German humanist and contemporary of Hegel who attempted to update Immanuel Kant's thinking; a deliberative project that developed moral and ethical principles on rational thought rather than revelation. Krause studied at the University of Jena when Johann Gottlieb Fichte and Friedrich Schelling, proponents of German idealism, taught there. The thoughts of Krause, a Mason, resonated with and were highly influenced by the ideas of progress and humanism prevalent in Masonic lodges throughout the European continent. During the eighteenth and nineteenth centuries, Freemason lodges were centers of cultivation and social propagation of Enlightenment ideas rooted in the deliberative (rationalistic) thoughts of Kant. Krause gain popularity among Spain's Freemason lodges, where a metaphysical, panentheistic understanding of the Supreme Being took root over the materialist view or Kant's potent rationalist approach.[90]

Krause, attempting to distinguish himself from the pantheists (all-is-God) of his day, coined the term *panentheist* (all-in-God). For him, the Supreme Being is separate from the universe (a divine organism)—all is not God, with God understood not as an individual proper name but as a signifier of single reality, a principle of existence and essence of the world. There is a *Wesen* (German for "essence") to the transcendent God. God, which he calls *Urwesen*, or primordial essence, is apart from, outside, and above the world existing beyond Godself in how much its essence also contains the world. Where the world is in God, not outside, nor above, nor on, is what he calls *Orwesen*, the highest principle in virtue.[91] In other words, everything within the universe extending beyond any limited time or space is identified with and found in God.[92]

Yet God cannot be reduced to any particular essentiality that composes God's being.[93] Unlike pantheism, in which God and the universe are identical, in panentheism God pervades and encompasses the universe more as its soul—not a person but an essence—which is greater than what was created. As such, this is a scientific God of Universal Religion that is built upon and surpasses all institutionalized religions.[94] Krause sought to reconcile the monotheistic God of faith, which as ultimate harmony can be understood through reason with an empirical panentheistic understanding of reality. Martí as a man of his times embraced panentheism, writing: "You love a God who penetrates and prevails everything. It seems desecration to give the Creator of all beings and all that has to be, the form of only one of the beings."[95] Panentheistic thoughts such as those of Krause were congruent with the popular spiritual currents during the fin de siècle such as transcendentalism, theosophy, and spiritism.

Humans are meant to live in harmony with themselves, with nature, and with their God. According to the Spanish philosopher José Ferrater Mora, Krause rejects Hegelian absolute theories concerning the state, emphasizing universal associations of family and nation—the bases for morality—as opposed to limited associations as church and state. Humanity cannot be restricted to the dominion of one state over others; rather, there exists a call for a federation of universal associations where the peculiarity of none is sacrificed.[96] Such familial values, rooted in Christian thought (or any other religious tradition for that matter), are presented through a deliberative motif of moral analysis where rational enlightenment paradigms—specifically those of Kant—are employed to create a positivist understanding of what it means to be human. An anthropological approach is constructed that can objectively observe and classify phenomena based on natural sciences. Thus, humans are meant to live in harmony in accordance with a Christian value system based on reason minus the dogmatic. But Krause deviates from Kant. While Kant believed that through speculative reason humans can know phenomena (what can be perceived or observed), not noumenon (*das Ding an sich*—the thing-in-itself); Krause argued that human reason could perceive ultimate harmony, *Wesen*.

The ego or proto-I as the subjective and original I (*Urich*) consists as a whole human being living above body and soul, and as ultimate unity that includes the corporal and the intellectual.[97] As component elements, the body (*Leib*) and mind (*Geist*) are finite essences comprising the whole human, which as part of humanity is where the unity of nature and spirit can be found.[98] The *Urich* recognizes that the only metaphysical entity that exists is God who as the highest principle is the whole of reality. All that exists constitutes two elements, reason and nature and their union; humanity whose essence consists in the divine infinite consciousness transcends the universe, which comprises nature, spirit, humanity, and reason. Humans are to be free because they are in God, and as such, God is free.[99] The fact that nature and the spirit war against each other within humans who are not free indicates the failure of constructing an organic society reflecting the universal associations of family and nation.

Because evil cannot be the ultimate reality, Martí relegates the concept to what ignorant people think and do. Reason leads humanity to the ultimate harmony of God; thus, humans must learn morality through the raising of consciousness. Seeking and implementing the greatest good through the scientific spirit, as per Kant's categorical imperative, becomes for Martí the foundation of his theological ethics. The doing of ethics gradually leads humanity to discover unity with the divine *Wesen*. Not surprisingly, Martí's religiosity resonates with nature-based spirituality, in which the essence of moral character can be found throughout all elements of nature, which is in God, or panentheistic. In his 1882 eulogy to Ralph Waldo Emerson, Martí wrote: "For one to be good, you need no more than to see the beautiful . . . See that the spectacle of nature inspires faith, love, and respect . . . Nature inspires, heals, comforts, strengthens, and prepares man for virtue. And man is not complete, nor reveals himself, nor sees the invisible, but in his intimate relationship with nature."[100]

Martí was deeply influenced by Krause, recognizing him as "greater [than Hegel]" who "studies [philosophy] in the Subject, the Object, and in the individual subjective manner by which the Relationship leads the subject who examines the examined object. I had great pleasure when in Krause I found that intermediate philosophy, the secret of the two extremes, which I thought of calling a Philosophy of relationship."[101] Martí studied Krause during his graduate education in Spain (1868–1874), also visiting and participating in discussions concerning his thoughts at the Ateneo de Madrid, a private cultural institution founded in 1835. Still, this might not have been the first time he had contact with Krause's ideas. From 1829 through 1831, José de la Luz was the first Cuban to ever translate German thought on the island into Spanish in 1819. He traveled throughout Europe spending time in Germany, and upon his return to Cuba, he taught a course between 1834 and 1835 on formative German philosophers, among which he included Krause.[102] But as the historian Medardo Vitier reminds us, Luz's empirically based philosophy is profoundly different from Krause's metaphysical teachings, even though common ground can be found in their analysis of social ethics.[103] It is quite feasible that Martí was introduced to Krause's thoughts by way of Luz's student and Martí's teacher: Mendive.

Regardless as to when Martí first encountered Krause's thoughts, while in Spain he was introduced to a Krausism influenced by the social location of Spain, a manifestation known as *krausismo*. During Martí's time at the university, and until the 1936 Spanish Civil War, *krausismo* became more prevalent throughout Spain than in Germany. Condemned by the Catholic Church, *krausismo* was embraced by many liberals and masons, and many followers chose to dress in black.[104] While a student at the University of Madrid studying philosophy and law, Martí discovered the works of Julián Sanz del Río (1814–1869), one of Krause's most avid intellectual disciples, who died a few years prior to Martí's arrival to Madrid. Sanz del Río, professor of the history of philosophy, came in contact with Krause's thoughts while a student in Heidelberg. Sanz del Río adopted Krause ideas to the realities and idiosyncrasies of Spain, ushering in the *krausismo* era. *Krausismo* advocated for a moralistic idealism understood through a positivist Christianity filtered by a neo-Kantian lens. Sanz del Río introduced, translated, and advocated the works of the German philosopher throughout the peninsula, attempting to merge Krause's emphasis on the rational with the liberal commitment to liberative ideas, specifically in its opposition to power and privilege prevalent in Christianity.

When in 1860 Sanz del Río introduced a summary and adaptation of Krause's 1811 book, *Das Urbild der Menschheit*, into Spanish as *Ideal de la humanidad para la vida*, he incorporated ethical-philosophical thoughts that resonated with Freemasonry, specifically concepts of liberty, tolerance, universal fraternity, freethinking, democracy, predilection of reason, equality before the law, and ethical perfectibility.[105] He transformed a philosophical movement attentive to the ideas of Krause into a spiritual and educational renewal that at its foundation was metaphysical and ethical.[106] The Masonic panentheism that emerged developed strong mystic overtones, elevating moral purpose rather than utility.[107] Hence in Spain, Krause's thoughts became less philosophical and more ethical. This Spanish-based *krausismo* could be understood as a passion for knowledge; a faith in reason and science as a means of knowing God; a rejection of dogma, revelation, and miracles; a rejection of reason as an absolute replacing of faith; an acceptance of Christianity as the most evolved level of religious thought; an embrace of a rational Christianity; an ethical way of being; a call for a separation of church and state; a call from oppressive religious and political structures; and beauty expressed as good and truth. According to Martí, Sanz del Río, along with other more contemporary scholars, "Germanize the spirit. They explain the abstract hardness of positive intelligence to a people of generalizing imagination. They Krausify rights; but they are strict, clean, clear spirits—truly legitimate children of the grave mother science."[108] This renewal led to an evolution of *krausismo* that not only include Freemasonry influences but also made Masonic thought and principles its backbone.

Although he was influenced by Krause, Martí was not a faithful disciple, for he was persuaded more by its Spanish interpretation as defined by Sanz del Río. This is why Martí can never be pigeonholed as a disciple of any particular school of thought. Deeply influenced by Luz and Krause, he harmonized those aspects of their works concerning social ethics, eclectically taking differentiating strands of thought to weave an asystematic poetic-metaphysical political theology. What *krausismo* did was provide Martí with a formula by which he could express his ideas and concepts. He wrote in his notebook: "Krause is not all true. This is simply a simplifying, dividing, Spanish language which I stock and use because to me it seems more appropriate in bringing out (expressing) my ideas."[109] Martí, as we saw earlier, became disillusioned with positivist thought, especially after seeing how it unfolded in the United States, advocating instead for an antipositivist rationalism. Although rejecting *krausisto* positivism (idealist realism, by way of Herbert Spencer and Karl Marx), *krausismo*'s philosophy concerning "harmony rationalism" continued to resonate with Martí's own thoughts on the harmony and balance of the universe and humanity's familial relationship. This organic pan-harmony, according to Rodríguez Carro, brought together and balanced the religious with the political, the economic, the scientific, and the artistic—all animated by a Masonic universalism.[110] For Martí, there existed a universal harmony between nature and the spirit found in God that he rationally understood as the basis for an ethical, moral foundation on which to build *patria*.

Masonic Influences

During the nineteenth century, Masonic lodges were centers of revolutionary activities. Freemasons in the United States and Britain were committed to promoting public education and what they called "the religion of reason," while holding decisive anti-Catholic, anti-Spanish, and antimonarchist views. These North American and British lodges were committed to liberating Latinoamérica from the "ignorance and superstition" of the Catholic Church and the "despotism" of Spain.[111] An anti-church, pro-reason attitude also existed among Freemasons in Spain, while a stronger commitment to revolutionary change existed among Spain's colonies. The lodges' secrecy, quasi-religious rituals, and social networking made them ideal spaces for those critical of colonialism and its religious ally, the Catholic Church. Not surprisingly, membership in the Freemasons in Spain and its colonies posed an existential danger, hence the heightened secrecy and controversy surrounding Martí's own membership.

During the British capture of La Habana in 1762, Freemasonry was first introduced to Cuba as a Military Lodge No. 218 ascribed to the Regiment of Infantry No. 48. With the departure of the British in 1763 (after eleven months of occupation), no record exists of any Masonic activity until 1804, with the establishment of Las Virtudes Teologales (The Theological Virtues) Lodge No. 103, the first chartered in La Habana, by the Grand Lodge of Pennsylvania.[112] Martí celebrated the introduction of Freemasonry to the island: "I believe in that first Freemasonry in Cuba, children of the immortal mistletoe [Druid sacred plant used in rituals], sworn to extinguish servitude, foreign or domestic."[113]

By 1818, three lodges in La Habana organized the Spanish Grand Lodge of the Rite of York. By the 1820s, there were sixty-six lodges in the city with a population of ninety thousand. Besides the Grand Lodge of Pennsylvania, groups from Louisiana and South Carolina also established lodges throughout the island. Almost simultaneously, the Masonic lodges La Perseverance and La Concorde were established in Santiago de Cuba by French immigrants fleeing the Haitian Revolution in 1805 and 1806.[114] Thus, Masonic lodges were well established in Cuba before the Ten Years' War (1868), especially in Bayamo on the eastern part of the island, where armed hostility against Spain first broke out. From the first pro-independence conspiracy in 1809, forged by the Masonic brotherhood, through the 1895 War of Independence, Freemasonry played a critical role in Cuba's liberation.[115] Lodges, as already mentioned, became a space for rebellion. Even the Cuban flag was based on the Masonic symbols of triangle and star. Designed by Miguel Teurbe Tolón in 1848, the flag's five-point star—according to the 2017 president of Cuba's Academy of High Masonic Studies, Ramón Viñas Pérez—"means the perfection of the master mason: strength, beauty, wisdom, virtue and charity."[116] The star is centered within a triangle, each side of which represents liberty, equality, and fraternity.[117] This flag, designed in New Orleans, flew on Cuban soil when the Mason Narciso López brought it in 1848 during his invasion of the island.

The rebellion that launched the Ten Years' War was organized at the Masonic lodges Antilles and Grand Orient of Cuba. Carlos Manuel de Céspedes, who launched the Ten Years' War, served as venerable master of the Buena Fe (Good Faith) Lodge in Manzanillo. In Puerto Príncipe, seventy-two of the seventy-six rebels who rose up in the town of Las Clavellinas belonged to the Tinima Lodge.[118] Because of the Masons' revolutionary activities, their assembly had been forbidden by

Spanish authorities since 1812, although it was tolerated because several Spanish officers who were administrators on the island themselves were Masons. Still, some members were compelled to carry out their activities in inviolable secrecy, even to the point of adopting aliases, lest their true identities be discovered, forcing them to incur grievous penalties.[119] In 1869, eighteen Masons were captured in Santiago de Cuba without warrant and immediately shot for being Freemasons; others were arrested and imprisoned for similar offenses.[120]

Some of the leading revolutionary organizers and military leaders seeking independence from Spain during the war in 1895 were Masons. Members included Antonio Maceo, Máximo Gómez, Calixto García, Guillermón Moncada, José Maceo, Quintín Banderas, and Juan Gualberto Gómez. Organizationally, Masonic alliances provided revolutionaries like Martí an already-established secret national and international society through which they could forge transnational connections and conduct clandestine meetings. When Martí later established the newspaper *Patria* in 1892, he founded it in a multiracial Caribbean lodge in New York.[121] Freemasonry lodges became crucial spaces where local leaders could rise to national recognition. But what about José Martí? Was he a mason? I believe he was. We know through his writing that he was well connected with Freemasonry and sympathetic to the Masons' mission. He sang the praises of the Manhattan Masonic Lodge No. 387, Fraternidad, founded in 1852, believing that it would have many more years of active service because "what is born of patriotic fire endures."[122] The lodge is still in existence today.

Martí lists Masonic lodges among organizations in which Cubans could participate in "all the virtues necessary for peaceful enjoyment of liberty,"[123] particularly through their activities of providing aid to the poor and needy.[124] In his praise for a Cuban Mason who died far from his beloved island, Martí compared the rites of the Masonic brotherhood with *patria* because it is impossible to establish either "without free and indulgent treatment of those who live there as brothers, [so he did not] fall alone, or between cold breast, but surrounded by heads uncovered."[125] Probably the greatest influence Freemasonry had on Martí was *krausismo*, as mentioned earlier. He seems to indicate that Masonic membership is part of what it means to be Cuban:

"And over there in Cuba, will the Cuban be seen as they are here, col-
laborating to grow, from death defending the hunt, teaching at night
after working during the day, creating from the workers stool a *nueva
religión* of active love among men, Saturday at the lodge, Sunday in his
chairmanship or in is treasury, the night between newspapers and the
book?"[126] "Saturday at the lodge" but, interesting enough, Sunday is
not spent at church. In his affectionate tributes to those lodge brothers who had gone on to their final resting place, Martí described the
earthly Masonic lodge as a reflection of the "perfect lodge, the heav-
enly lodge."[127]

Early in life, during his time in Mexico (February 1875–January 1877),
Martí engaged in a public dispute with the Masons of the city because
he divulged the names of some members in an editorial. In an article
dated 25 March 1876, titled "Masonic Feast," he praised the Masonic
commitment to morality, freedom, and civic duty. However, this
defense was based on an earlier column he wrote in 1875 for *Revista Universal* in which he named several Mexican socialites who were Masons.
The incensed editor of *El Federalista* responded by accusing Martí of
breaking his Masonic oath to not divulge members' names, which he
had sworn to keep "on penalty of death." In "Masonic Feast," Martí
defended sharing the names of other members by distinguishing his
goals from the rules of Freemasonry.[128] In another article written in
April, he continued his critique of Masonic secrecy, arguing that while
in some recent past it required secrecy as a means of self-preservation,
it continued to maintain secrecy out of habit. Martí goes on to say:
"Freemasonry cannot be a secret society in a free country, because their
work is the same work of the general advancement . . . Freemasonry is
nothing more than an active form of liberal thought."[129]

Martí's criticism of the Spanish government and Catholic Church
made him an ideal Mason, and although many scholars have denied
he was one, an archival find by the historian Manuel Sánchez Gálvez at
the Fernandina de Jugua Lodge in Cienfuegos seems to put to rest the
question of his membership. Sánchez discovered a diploma on which
Martí's signature and a rubric he used appear. Also, a letter bearing
his pseudonym, Anáhuac, was discovered.[130] Apparently, Martí had
been a member of the Masons since the age of eighteen, although

his name does not appear in the records. Nevertheless, the Nahuátl pseudonym, which he had used for some of his revolutionary activities and writings (e.g., the charter of the Central Revolutionary Club), also appeared in an 1871 document used to identified Martí as grand secretary of the Madrid lodge, thus suggesting he had been invited by the Masons after his first arrival in Spain, shortly after his exile from Cuba.[131] Considering that the lodge of his supposed initiation, Caballeros Cruzados (Gentlemen of the Cross) was a Peninsular lodge, choosing Anáhuac was an act of rebellion, for the name signified the ancient indigenous (Nahuátl) name for Mexico from before Spain's colonization.[132] On display at the National Masonic Museum in La Habana are his corresponding Masonic jewels.[133]

Martí is alleged to have joined the local Freemason group in 1871, highly influenced by his mentor Mendive, who was also a Mason.[134] His childhood friend and companion in Spain, Fermín Valdés Domínguez, in his article "Ofrenda de hermano" that appeared in a May 1908 article in the newspaper *El Triunfo*, confirmed Martí's participation in the Armonía Masonic lodge. There he found a home among freethinkers who reconciled a respect for reason with the experience of religion, emphasizing human God Consciousness over Divine revelation. Among Freemasons, faith tradition is less important than rationalism: "Masons, Protestant and Catholics chanted together at the foot of the monument of freethinking, the anthem 'América.'"[135] While living in New York City, Martí apparently belonged to Lodge No. 39, Sol de Cuba, or Cuba's Sun.[136] Several of his writings reveals contact with the Freemasons of New York City. For example, he referred to a procession of six hundred Cubans that originated from a Masonic lodge and gave several speeches in 1887 and 1888 at a Masonic temple on the anniversaries of Cuba's first call for independence on 10 October 1868.[137]

More important than Martí being a Mason is the influence of Masonic views from Latinoamérica on his thoughts. According to the cultural studies scholar Jossianna Arroyo, Martí's critiques of race and empire owe much to the earlier political language of Freemasonry. The republic Martí envisioned was a political manifestation of the universal fraternity of the lodge, thus he constructed *patria* on the Masonic principles of brotherhood and equal citizenship.[138] Men who were drawn to rationalism and fraternity were also drawn to the lodges, especially those who saw Catholicism as the religious domain of women. The *martiana* scholar Carolina Gutiérrez Marroquín agrees, arguing that Masonic records of the time are democratic, republican, and laic.[139] Upon his death, the Spanish general José Jiménez de Sandoval ensured that Martí's body was not desecrated and instead received Masonic honors; the general recognized Martí as a fellow Mason. Martí would eventually become disillusioned with the Masons, but even so, he maintained his affiliation so as to advance *Cuba libre*.[140]

Strands of Christianity, whether Catholic genealogy, Protestant influence, *krausismo*, or Freemasonry, became foundational to the creation of Martí's vision for a *nueva religión* and *nueva iglesia*. However, it would be a grave error to relegate Martí's political theology to a Christian-only influence. Just as important and foundational were non-Christian thoughts and beliefs. It is to these pluralistic strands of Martí's thought that we now turn our attention.

THREE

Pluralist Spiritual Foundation

The spirit foreshadows, the beliefs ratify.

TO ASSUME THAT José Martí's political theology was solely influenced by Christian or quasi-Christian thought would be an error. He cannot be reduced to a faithful student of one theological or philosophical school. As we have seen, he was an eclectic thinker, appropriating the best any particular tradition had to offer while remaining severely critical when followers of the faith failed to live up to lofty rhetoric. His hunger for knowledge that could assist him in achieving his life goal of *un Cuba libre*, was never limited to just one religious perspective. He devoured other traditions, always seeking what was true, specifically metaphysical truth, wherever he found wisdom, even if that particular tradition was not Christian. "I am insufficiently educated in all of the religions to be able to reasonably say that I belong to any of them. It's enough for me—indeed—an absurdity to distance my sympathy from them," he wrote in an early notebook.[1] True, Martí's religious worldview and ethical foundation remain unsurprisingly

Christian in orientation. But one would be hard pressed to find in his writing any claims of exclusivity to a belief system. Although his ethical and moral views mainly remain Christian, he does not dismiss other faith traditions as false, for all contain the presence of the metaphysical as manifested in nature. Martí agreed with the sentiments of Peter Cooper, designer of the first steam locomotive: "the only religion worthy of men is the one which does not exclude man from his heart."[2]

We find in Martí a celebration of religious pluralism and a disdain for the empty trappings of rituals. To his mind, religions are free to flourish and humans have a right to be wrong about what they believe. As he wrote in 1894 in *Patria*, the official paper of the revolution: "Venerate the men of religion, whether they be Catholics or Rarámuri. The whole world, whether they have straight or wooly hair, has a right to their conscience. The Catholic who places themselves over a Hindu is a tyrant, as is the Methodist who hisses at a Catholic . . . The sincere man has the right to make mistakes."[3] This freedom of religion that Martí advocated does not encompass the imposition of particular doctrines and dogmas on people of different beliefs. He found reprehensible any religious system that subjugated people to oppressive structures or inhibited their ability to apply reason and think for themselves. Religious freedom was to be a fundamental component of any future *patria*, and these religions would be welcomed to critique the state whenever it strayed from liberative policies. The faithful, regardless of their faith tradition, were encouraged to participate in the building of *patria* as long as they employed their faith and beliefs to solve the social problems facing the emerging nation. Before concentrating on aspects of Martí's political theology, it behooves us to first investigate the contributions made to his thinking that emanated from non-Christian sources. To that task we now turn.

Spiritualism

Martí partook in the physical-metaphysical and philosophical debate that undergirded the nineteenth century, seeking harmony within this dichotomy. Important to ponder is his understanding of the metaphysical, which he sought to reconcile with the material. According to the historian Adriana Novoa, Martí, while in New York City, "came in contact with theosophy. He liked this doctrine for the same reasons that he also liked the Knights of Labor, [Henry] George, [Edward] Bellamy, [Oscar] Wilde, and [Eduard von] Hartmann; it was another way to defend metaphysical/spiritual principles that were under siege because of the popularity of the new materialism."[4] Foundational to Martí's religious thought is an abhorrence of this new materialism that dismissed or ignored the spiritual. After all, faithful to his panentheistic leanings, he wrote, "Every grain of matter brings within itself a grain of the spirit."[5] To ignore the spiritual, he thought, would rob social-political structures of their humanity, leading to mechanical states that would themselves lead to a coldhearted society. Embracing the spiritual within the midst of the material ensured that the *patria* he envisioned would have a soul.

In 1939, the *martiana* scholar Raquel Catalá asked whether Martí was a theosophist.[6] Theosophy is a nondogmatic philosophy—not a religion—whose roots can be traced to Neoplatonism and Gnosticism. This philosophical movement of the late nineteenth century maintained that the impersonal God could be reached by humans, who are but sparks of the divine imprisoned in the material world. One grasped this transcendent God by way of spiritual ecstasy or direct mystical intuition. There are many manifestations of theosophy, but generally all embrace pantheism and reincarnation, as well as a radical equality and fraternity among all humans, because every human has the same physical and spiritual origin. Theosophists sought to understand the unknown laws of nature; it was a Brahmanic or Buddhist quest for inherent divine wisdom through an enlightened Eurocentric methodology.

Martí wrote in an article for the Mexican paper *El Partido Liberal* about hearing the British theosophist Annie Besant—a socialist and women's rights activist—give a talk in 1891; he called her "a humanitarian orator."[7] For him, Besant would "educate what is superior of men, so that he may, with a brighter vision, achieve solace, advance in the mystery yet unknown, and explore the highness of the spiritual orbit."[8] He was also familiar with Helena Blavatsky, the Russian aristocrat and occultist who claimed to have psychic powers including telepathy and clairaudience. In 1875, Blavatsky and Besant cofounded the movement, establishing the Theosophical Society in New York City. Blavatsky argued that all the world's religions stemmed from an original source, the esoteric Ancient Wisdom, in an attempt to synthetize spiritualism with an evolutionary materialism in hopes of encouraging fraternity among humans, the highest evolved species. Martí celebrated this recently departed "high priestess" who, like "any other scientist," helped "discover and clarify the acts of the spirit" like "hypnotism and mesmerism, dream [interpretation] and clairvoyance, [and] the genius and power to read minds."[9] Although he was never a member of the Theosophical Society, the society's spiritual views influenced his work and may have sparked his interest in Eastern religious traditions.

Theosophy was not the only metaphysical movement that Martí encountered. Among the different manifestations of spiritualist thought during his time in New York, Kardecism was among the most popular, a spiritist practice that came to the Américas around the mid-nineteenth century.[10] A French engineer named Hippolyte Léon Denizard Rivail, writing under the pseudonym Allan Kardec, was among the first to codify spiritualistic philosophy, launching a movement that immediately spread throughout Europe. He developed what can be called a spiritualistic science based on the relationship and communication between humans and incorporeal entities (spirits). There is a God, and there exist the spirits of the departed, who can interact and interfere in the lives of physical humans. Kardec saw his work as countering the prevailing materialist understanding of humans "as only matter, only a *machine organisée*."[11] Kardec believed he was proposing "the death-blow to materialism."[12] For him, "Spiritism neither discovered nor invented [the necessity of the union between the spiritual and material elements]; but was the first to demonstrate it through undeniable proofs."[13] The spiritual and material elements are the two living principles or forces of the universe, and as such they are regulated by natural laws that make them accessible to scientific observation and experimentation.[14] Kardec sought to study the origins, nature, and destiny of spirits and their impact on the physical world as a *science expérimentale*,[15] not as supernaturalism, for he denied the existence of miracles and relegated them to the realm of ignorance.[16]

Kardec attempted to use human observation and experimentation as the bases for explaining and subjugating the spirit world. Since the 1850s, he had subjected mediumistic experiences to rigid scientific investigation. And although he recognized the existence of charlatans who seized on his principles for the purpose of turning a profit,[17] he nonetheless maintained that his scientific investigations showed the personalities of the deceased survived death and became the source through which the medium communicated; that is, the spirit communicated through the medium in a language that the medium could neither speak nor write.[18]

Originally, spiritism was not considered a religious movement and was perceived instead as a positive science that combined progressivist ideology, Christian morality, scientism, and mysticism. Soon, many who had difficulty with a Catholicism hostile to modernity found spiritism to be a suitable substitute, given its anticlerical tenets and denunciation of institutionalized Christianity. As the movement spread, small groups of mediums assisted individuals in communicating with the spirits of the dead. After the bloody U.S. Civil War, these séances became very popular as bereaved families sought comforting final words from loved ones they lost in faraway battlefields. The séances usually consisted of a group sitting around a table with a medium, who fell into a trance to bridge the spiritual with the physical world. Some of these practitioners found a connection with a pre-Christian past in which ancestral spirits were part of everyday reality, not yet repressed by the official Christian church.[19] In the Spanish Caribbean, specifically in Cuba and Puerto Rico, freedom fighters found spiritism to be an alternative to the Catholic Church and perceived it as in league with the Spanish Crown. Spiritism served as a political space for liberal ideas to flourish despite the suppression of all political organizations that challenged Spain's colonial authority. Not surprisingly, many spiritists, who shared with Catholics a belief in the Supreme Being and practiced esoteric rituals, found a home in the Freemasonry movement; membership in both organizations often overlapped.[20]

Spiritism as advocated by Kardec gained popularity in Mexico in the 1870s, the time during which Martí resided there. Among the first attracted to this movement were the European white middle and upper classes. Participants found in spiritism a progressive ideology that they believed advanced and advocated the sciences, modernity, and democracy. By the time Martí was living in New York, groups of different races with less power and economic privilege had turned to spiritism for help and guidance with the struggles of daily life. For those occupying the lower rungs of society, specifically the rural poor who still considered themselves Catholic, participation in spiritism was not, to their minds, incongruent with their nominal Christian worldviews. For those who participated in the African orisha traditions, spiritism proved important with the demise during slavery of African ancestor worship. Ancestor worship was conducted within a particular extended family; however, slavery destroyed the family unit, making it impossible to continue ancestor veneration. Fragmented family members were thus unable to come together to carry out their religious rituals without a spiritual guide. The introduction of spiritism in Cuba, though, reintroduced African ancestral worship to Cuba.[21]

Spiritists believed in the immortality of the soul or spirit, arguing for the capability of consciousness to survive the death of the body and the ability of the disincarnated spirit to communicate, without magic or the supernatural, through a medium with the incarnated. This spirit would traverse numerous incarnations until it achieves perfect knowledge and morality through spiritual evolution. This knowledge and morality, empirically investigated, would become the foundation for a new ethics based on science and reason rather than revelation. Martí agreed with what Kardec called the law of spiritual progress, an evolution of the soul achievable through good works. He asserted in an early notebook that the soul was universal and eternal: "The soul post-exists. And if it is post-existent, and we are not born equal, it then pre-exists, it has passed through different forms—here or there? It is useless to ponder, but it has happened."[22] Because human suffering can be explained as the consequences of cause and effect from previous lives, spirits or souls, from the moment they cease being material entities, seek advancement in the hierarchy in which they exist. They can achieve perfection through light (enlightenment), which facilitates their reincarnation. The spiritist learns how to provide light, assisting the spirit of the deceased in moving to the next higher spiritual plane of existence. In this view, for spiritists, Jesucristo, who achieved the highest plane of spiritual incarnation, becomes the archetype for the supreme virtue of love. The practice of any morality based on love ensures a higher spiritual level of incarnation.[23]

One can see why a person like Martí would have been attracted to some of the ideas of spiritism. And while Martí may have agreed with the spiritists' embrace of the immortality of the soul, he was not convinced that spiritual phenomena could materially be reproduced—specifically that the spirits of the dead could communicate with the living through a medium. He wrote in his notebook: "The spirit departed from human form is not human. The medium does not speak for it. How can the spirit speak a human language when it is not human? How can it always speak the language of the medium? Two mediums in identical conditions consult the same spirit on the same subject. But the two answers are different."[24] He was well aware of mediums who fed off of the gullible: "A drum that beats because of electricity invites the unemployed of Broadway to enter the theater of the minstrels to see how the magicians like [Harry] Kellar, the rival of Hernian, replicate and explain all the noises, writings, and appearances with which the professional spiritists, like a certain Dr. [Henry] Slade [a well-known fraudulent medium], deceive the sad and decent souls whom they unbalance with their disconsolation of the earth and the need for the marvelous."[25]

Although we have no indication Martí ever visited a medium or participated in a séance, we do know that he was an active participant in the physical-metaphysical debate of his time. In April and May 1875, while in Mexico, Martí attended Monday discussions at the Liceo Hidalgo titled "Materialism and Spiritualism." Sponsored by the Sociedad Espírita Mexicana, discussions covered the relationship among spiritualism, materialism, science, and positivism. This is probably the first time Martí dealt with positivism, to which he would become a lifelong critic of its methodology as he hesitated to totally repudiate the metaphysical. Martí took upon himself, through his writings, an active role in defending spiritualist concepts, if not Kardec spiritism. During the physical-metaphysical debate at Liceo Hidalgo on 5 April 1875, Martí situated himself as a centrist in the debate while addressing the question of what the spirit is:

I come to this discussion with a spirit of conciliation which rules all of my life's acts. I am between materialism, which is the exaggeration of matter, and spiritism, which is the exaggeration of the spirit. [Sensation.] What is the spirit? Mr. Baz asks us. The spirit is that which he thinks, what induces us to acts independent of or corporeal needs, is what strengthens us, encourages us, fulfills us in life. [Applause.] Does not Mr. Baz remember when he placed a chaste and pure kiss upon his mother's forehead, [bravo, bravo] when he has loved with the passion of a poet, when he has written with miserable ink on miserable paper something which was not miserable? [Bravo, good, good.] There is something which properly gives us the conviction of our immortality, which reveals to us our preexistence and our existence. [Resounding applause.] On the other hand, gentlemen, I believe this conversation is useless, if we do not altercate Mr. Baz's proposition, because we do not first find out if spiritism is true or not, for from a false thing a truth cannot result. [Applause.] . . . With my nonconformity in life, with my need for something better, with the impossibility of achieving it here, I demonstrate it: the abstract is demonstrated with the abstract, I have an immortal spirit, because I feel it, because I believe it, because I want it. [Great applause.][26]

Martí clearly attempted to reconcile the principles of materialism with spiritualism, avoiding the extremes of both positions. This led him to embrace an immortal spirit in which he could feel and believe, convinced of humans' pre- and supraexistence. For Martí, the spiritual realm is accepted; he argued "that the Universe was formed by slow, methodical, and analogous procedures, neither announces the end of nature, nor contradicts the existence of spiritual facts."[27]

Unitarianism and Transcendentalism

Unitarianism is a Christian tradition whose application of reason led its followers to reject long-established Christian doctrines, specifically the concepts of the Trinity (hence the name), predestination, original sin, atonement, eternal damnation, and the infallibility of the Bible.

More important for our purposes, Unitarians emphasized the usage of reason to determine morality. Martí's methodology of employing reason to establish religious truths found common ground with the Unitarians. His own thoughts resonated with several of their conclusions, especially rejection of the divinity of Christ. This explains the lack of Trinitarian dogma and concepts in his faith vocabulary—though once in his notebooks he referred to the "divine Jesús."[28] For Martí, reason led him to ground concepts like liberty and tolerance in religious thought. He refused to embrace official doctrines that reason could not substantiate, although he advocated for tenets that created stronger societal bonds, like love of God and neighbor, the fatherhood of God, the fraternity of humans, the victory of the good, the reign of God, and eternal life. He may not have been a Unitarian; nevertheless, one can see how his thoughts resonated with those of prominent Unitarian thinkers. This is obvious in his praise and admiration for leading figures like William E. Channing, Henry W. Longfellow, Theodore Parker, and especially Ralph Waldo Emerson, who eventually rejected Unitarianism and originated the transcendentalist movement in 1841.

Transcendentalism was a reaction against the Unitarian church and all religious institutions that embraced dogmatic tenets. The transcendentalists rebelled against Unitarians for moving away from the spiritual, placing too much reliance on the rational. Morality was more than a simple mathematical equation (the greatest amount of good for the greatest number of people), it encompassed a complex spiritual dimension that the Unitarians' exclusive embrace of materialism ignored. Transcendentalism also rebelled against oppressive political structures of the day, like slavery and patriarchy, actively seeking to bring about social change through direct action, like civil disobedience. Many transcendentalists remained Unitarians, for transcendentalism never organized as its own religious sect, even though its followers moved away from the exclusive use of reason, the Bible, and church teaching as guide for determining what is moral, relying instead on personal spiritual experience.

Transcendentalism, whose concepts eventually began to merge with those of theosophy, supported an antimaterialist worldview. Many, like

Martí, who lived in New York City during the latter nineteenth century experienced an age of rapid industrialization that reduced humans to cogs in a profit-generating machinery. The *martiano* thinker Rafael Rojas reminds us that the transcendentalists of the city sought to abandon urban life, taking a theological cue from St. Augustine, who saw the city as originally being established by Cain after being punished by God for his fratricide. As such, the city was conceived in sin, alienated from God's family-oriented will.[29] Transcendentalists romantically pined for a return to nature, and those who were financially able sought liberation from the consequences of urbanization. The popularity at the time of transcendental thought as it merged with theosophical tendencies would serve as a corrective to the Industrial Revolution unfolding in the United States. Martí lived among the dehumanized poor; Emerson had sufficient class privilege to create a retreat for pondering his transcendentalist thoughts at Walden Pond.[30]

Martí admired Emerson as personifying the philosophical romanticism of the age: "the grandiose Emerson . . . one of the most powerful and original thinkers of these time, [is] an exalted man and . . . [one of] the greatest of poets of América."[31] Elsewhere he described Emerson's poetry as able to "purify and exalt."[32] Through his newspaper articles published throughout Latinoamérica, Martí introduced the Spanish-speaking world to the North American philosopher and poet, probably the first exposure of Emerson in Spanish. Holding Emerson in high regard, Martí devoted more space to him in his writings than to any other U.S. author. It seems that Martí took pleasure in Emerson's thoughts; he noted: "I have journeyed enough through life and have tasted its various delicacies. But the greatest pleasure, the only absolutely pure pleasure that I have enjoyed to this day was of that afternoon, from my room half-naked I saw the prostrated city, and envision the future thinking of Emerson."[33] Martí, in another undated notebook, scribbled under the heading "The Supreme Moments": "The afternoon of Emerson."[34] He is not known to have ever met Emerson in person, so this note is somewhat cryptic. In another notebook, he shed light on what he might have meant: "The imperfect of this existence is known in that within all of it there hardly are a few moments of absolute joy, which are those of full disinterest, those of man's confusion with nature. (Emerson. The afternoon of Emerson: when man loses his sense of self and transfuses himself in the world)."[35] A reference to an afternoon when Martí rigorously studied Emerson's philosophy? Perhaps—surely this was not the first time he had come across Emerson, as he may have encountered him while a student of Mendive.

Regardless as to what Martí was alluding to, throughout his writings, he praised Emerson's philosophy, referring to him as a "seer" and his writings as "prophetic."[36] Emerson, according to Martí, "was a priest of nature . . . He saw beyond himself the creative Spirit which through him spoke to nature."[37] Holding him in high regard, Martí wrote: "He was one of those to whom nature reveals herself, opening herself up with extended multiple arms as to enfold with them the entire body of her son."[38] Elsewhere, he called Emerson "an affectionate Dante, who lived on the earth, rather than in it—for he saw it with all fullness and certainty, and wrote the human Bible."[39] He translated into Spanish Emerson's poem "Good-Bye Proud World,"[40] and wrote his own poem in Emerson's honor titled "Each One to His Trade: New Fable of the North American Philosopher Emerson."[41]

Some scholars of Martí look to Emerson as foundational to the construction of Martí's thinking. No doubt Emerson was influential, but I wonder whether instead Martí, who already had a firm foundation upon which to build his ideas, found in Emerson a kindred spirit. Emerson and Martí find common ground in concepts concerning the purity of the individual person, that the inherent goodness of humanity was corrupted by society, and specifically by organized religion. Both Martí and Emerson sought a way back to the purity of the human soul through radical freedom and self-reliance. Religion must thus move away from clergy-made doctrinal "truths" and toward the truth found in nature. While maintaining a respect for Christianity and the spiritual experiences of individuals; both Emerson and Martí separately developed an organic relationship between nature and humans, a mysticism that remained pragmatic even though the spiritual was emphasized at the expense of the material.

Martí's thought resonated with Emerson's understanding of God's soul as one with nature and humanity, as Emerson explains in his essay "The Over-Soul": "Within man is the soul of the whole; the wise silence; the universal beauty, to which every part and particle is equally related; the eternal one. And this deep power in which we exist, and whose beatitude is all accessible to us, is not only self-sufficing and perfect in every hour, but the act of seeing and the thing seen, the seer and the spectacle, the subject and the object, are one."[42] Or, as Martí would eulogize Emerson: "All that is within [nature] is a symbol of man, and all that is within man exists in nature."[43] In their minds, the Spirit and Nature were one; "God does not have to be defended; nature will defend Him."[44] Emerson's understanding of the eternal soul would lead Martí to say that he "is trampling on the mud of dialectics."[45] As did Emerson, Martí turned to the spirituality of nature, not of the church, for it is nature "which inspires faith, love, and respect."[46] Nature is the moral mirror of the soul: "Nature inspires, heals, comforts, fortifies, and prepares virtue for man. And man is not complete, nor reveals himself to self, nor sees the invisible, if not through his intimate relation with nature."[47]

"Emerson does not argue, he establishes," Martí contended. "What nature teaches him seems preferable to what man teaches him. For him a tree knows more than a book; and a star teaches more than a university; and a ranch is a gospel; and a farm-boy is closer to universal truth than an antiquarian. For him there are no candles like the stars, nor altars like the mountains, nor preachers like the throbbing and deep nights."[48] What is nature for Martí? Nature is the great educator of humans. He moves away from a Hegelian dialectic in which distinct thesis and antithesis create new synthesis, instead embracing an Aristotelian understanding that organically unites spirit and matter. In his own notes on philosophy, he provides his understanding of nature:

> What is nature? The rugged pine, the old oak, the brave sea, the rivers that go to the sea as we men go to Eternity: Nature is the ray of light which penetrates the clouds and becomes rainbow; the human spirit which approaches and raises with the [illegible word] clouds of the soul, and becomes blessed. Nature is everything that exists, in all forms,—spirits and bodies; enslave currents to its channel; enslave roots in the earth; feet, slaves like the roots; souls, less enslaved than the feet. The mysterious intimate world, the marvelous external world,

whatever it is, deformed or luminous or dark, close or far, vast or paltry, liquefied or earthy, regulate everything, measured everything except the sky and the soul of men [unintelligible word] is Nature.[49]

Religion remains a childlike step toward more complex answers about the harmony of nature (physics) and God (metaphysics). "In summary," Martí wrote, "what are religious dogmas if not the infancy of natural truths?"[50] Nature does not contradict truth because "there are no contradictions in nature, but in the men, who do not know how to discover analogies. [Nature] does not disdain science as false, but slow. Open its books, and they overflow with scientific truths."[51] And although there are no contradictions in nature, there are contradictions in religion, which remains incongruent with the laws of nature. Nature, according to a Martí notebook, "has prescribed a law, unavoidable like all her others. The Catholic religion imposes on its apostles the necessity of not observing a law. If religion is the clear manifestation of God on earth, if it is God who creates and rules while man adores and obeys, naturally, how is it religion commands man to rebel against the precepts of his God? Or to be clearer: How is legitimate religion against the law?"[52]

The *martiano* scholar Félix Lizaso concluded that if Martí had not been a *latinoamericano* and had written in English, he no doubt would have been hailed in the North as the last of the transcendentalists.[53] He was more than simply an interpreter of Emerson; he made his own contributions to the conversation. An eclectic thinker, Martí did not solely engage in dialogue with Emerson; he went beyond to allow his understanding of nature to be further influenced by the sixteenth-century French humanist philosopher Michel de Montaigne.[54] And although Martí did not elucidate how Montaigne specifically influenced him, one can speculate that Montaigne's understanding of nature might have had the greater impact on him. In Montaigne's latter essays in the third book of *Essais*, the dichotomy he originally set up between human reason and divine reason, between nature and God (with the latter being superior), are collapsed when he begins to use *nature* and *God* synonymously.[55] Montaigne was not necessarily advocating pantheism, but we are left to wonder whether Martí read him as though he were, or as though he should?

Not only is Martí influenced by other thinkers when interpreting Emerson; his thoughts, with time, evolved beyond Emerson. Emerson, after all, was trapped in privileging Eurocentrism, specifically the pre-eminence of the Anglo-Saxon race over the *mestizaje* of other groups. In his oddly titled book *English Traits*, he extols the superiority and virtues of the Anglo-Saxons. Emerson was attempting to create a mystical Anglo-Saxon commitment to freedom as a counter to the slavery prevalent in the Southern states, but his description of Anglo-Saxon superiority is, at best, troublesome:

> The English at the present day have great vigor of body and endurance. Other countrymen look slight and undersized beside them, and invalids . . . in all ages they are a handsome race . . . please [*sic*] by beauty of the same character, an expression blending good-nature, valor and refinement, and mainly by that uncorrupt youth in the face of manhood, which is daily seen in the streets of London . . . When it is considered what humanity, what resources of mental and moral power the traits of the blond race betoken, its accession to empire marks a new and finer epoch . . . The fair Saxon man, with open front and honest meaning, domestic, affectionate, is not the wood out of which cannibal, or inquisitor, or assassin is made, but is moulded for law, lawful trade, civility, marriage, the nurture of children, for colleges, churches, charities and colonies . . . If in every efficient man there is first a fine animal, in the English race it is of the best breed.[56]

Martí had a different vision of modernity, one based on *nuestra América* that, unlike Emerson, did not privilege Anglo-Saxon "traits." Reducing Martí to a student of Emerson is problematic because of the difficulty in reconciling the apostle's attempt in creating a postcolonial space with Emerson's sense of imperial destiny.

Eastern Traditions

For Martí "the East invades the West."[57] Not surprisingly, he was well versed in Eastern religious traditions, and he introduced a young audience, through his children's book *La edad de oro*, to the Buddha in a sophisticated manner that celebrated Buddhist meditation.[58] When describing Theravada Buddhist doctrine, written in fifth-century Sri Lanka by Buddhaghosa, Martí concentrates on Visuddhimagga (path of purification) meditation exercises. Concerning these he wrote: "Such a certain and rational method of discovering the truth! To gaze one's attention on an object, in order to fully investigate the parts which constitute it, the start of its origin, its existence, and its final destruction; the nature of the parts which compose it—what is essential and accidental in it."[59] He was also influenced by the forty calming subjects of Samatha (the practice of single-pointed meditation) known as Kammatthāna, which suppress the five hindrances: *kāmacchanda* (physical desire), *vyāpāda* (ill will), *thīna-middha* (sloth and inertia), *uddhacca-kukkucca* (worriedness), and *vicikicchā* (faithlessness).

Martí had more than simply an intellectual understanding of Buddhist thought; he incorporated its traditions into his thinking. For example, in *La edad de oro* he lifts up the importance of nirvana for our lives:

> That sweet nirvana, which is the beauty like the light which gives the soul disinterestedness, is not achieved by living as an insane person or glutton for the pleasures of the material. One should not accumulate authority and fortune by the force of hatred and humiliation without understanding one should not live for vanity, nor want what others have, nor hold grudges, nor doubt the harmony of the world or ignore nothing in it or be bothered by the offenses and envy of others. One should not rest until the soul is like a dawn light which fills the world with clarity and beauty; and weeps and suffers for all the sadness within it, seeing oneself as a doctor and father to all who have reason to suffer. Is it like living in a blue which doesn't end? With a pleasure so pure it should be called glory, with arms always open. This is how Buddha lived.[60]

Martí was fascinated with the East, and he verged on what we might today call Orientalism. But while he appreciated Eastern thought in the construction of his religious views, he did not romanticize the East by ignoring how Eastern religious traditions also have a history of complicity with oppression. For example, he explored how some of Buddha's disciples employed Buddhist thought to reinforce the privilege of the rulers by repressing the people.[61]

Martí also incorporated Hindu thought, specifically the divine worth of all living creatures. Even "animals," he concludes in a notebook, "have souls."[62] I concur with García de la Torre who argues that Hindu thought nurtured Martí's spiritual views. Martí was probably first exposed to Hinduism during his first exile to Spain in 1871. At the time, students like Martí who debated *krausismo* tended to integrate the thoughts of the German philosopher with Hindu philosophy. Although his writings reveal no direct quote from a Hindu text such as the Bhagavad-Gita,[63] he praised Emerson for owning the Mahabharata. He writes that Emerson "at times dazzled by those brilliant books of the Hindus for whom human beings, after being purified by virtue, flies like a butterfly from the fire, from their earthly scum to the bosom of Brahma, settles to do what he has censured. And to see nature through the eyes of others, because he has found those eyes conforming to his own, he sees darkly and starkly his own visions. Indian philosophy intoxicates like a forest of orange blossoms or watching birds fly, which sparks the desire to fly."[64]

Martí believed in the Hindu concept of reincarnation, that life is an uninterrupted circle of death and renewal. In his poem "Yugo y estrella" ("Yoke and Star"), he traced the soul as it travels through different species: "When I was born, without sun, my mother said: / 'Flower of my breast, generous Homagno [*Homo magnus*], / Sum up and reflect of Creation and me, / Fish that turns into bird, then horse, then man.'"[65] For Martí, a body-spirit dichotomy existed, with the body being a subservient vessel for the spirit: "Actually," he wrote in his notebook, "the body is no more than a servant of the spirit."[66] According to the Hindu concept of reincarnation, the soul journeys through different bodily manifestations before reaching *moksha*, the cessation of rebirth. In some of his writings, Martí seems to hint at *moksha* and the spiritual dimension of the end of the material body: "Death is a victory, and when one has lived well, the coffin is a chariot of triumph . . . The death of the just is a feast, in which the whole earth sits to see the heavens open . . . The one who gave all of themselves, and did good unto others, goes to

their rest. The one who did bad works in this life, goes to labor anew
. . . the one who deserve to be immortal shall be: to die is to return the
finite to the infinite."[67]

How we live determines the reincarnated form: "The one who works
the most is the one who is less depraved, the one who lives in love with
his wife and children. Man is not a beast created to enjoy oneself, like
a bull or a pig. Man is a creature of superior nature who if he does not
cultivate the land, love his wife, and educate his children, will undoubtedly return to live as a pig or as a bull."[68] Martí linked reincarnation
with the role of cause and effect (*karma*), viewing his current exile as
punishment for what he must have done to his country of origin in
some previous life: "Over there are other worlds, in previous worlds,
in which I firmly believe, as I believe in the worlds to come. Because
of them we have an amazing intuition based on a prior knowledge of
life which reveals a former life . . . I must have committed to what was
then my country some grave wrong. Hence, I now live in reprimand,
live perpetually banished from my natural country which I know not
where it is—from what was so beautiful when I was born, to where
now there are only poisonous flowers."[69]

Another concept from Martí that resonates with Hinduism is the
duality that is foundation to most of his discourses. He is guilty of
expressing essentializing dichotomies, especially when discussing so-
called human nature, explaining complex human interactions through
a narrow lens of good versus bad. In an 1892 *Patria* article, he divided
humanity into just two groups: "those who love and create, those who
hate and destroy."[70] Yet ironically, he does not look to Christianity to
justify this simple duality of those who are saved and those who are
destined to damnation. Instead, he looks to Hinduism; the very next
sentence reads: "The world's fight comes to be that of Hindu dualism:
good versus evil."[71]

García de la Torre asserts that Hinduism, as interpreted through
the Bhagavad-Gita, was a significant influence in Martí's philosophical
worldview, specifically the inherently divine nature of all humans and
the essential unity of everyone. He goes on to list several concepts in
Martí's writings that seem to have been influenced by Hindu thought.
I do not necessarily agree with all of his interpretations, but I do con-

cur with at least three. First, the idea of salvation as lying in sacrificial acts geared for the welfare of others, with altruism as a means by which the soul is purified to facilitate union with the divine. Second, by acting selflessly and sacrificing for the sake of others, the *ātman*, the inner true self where the spiritual essence signifying the deepest level of existence is found, becomes outwardly realized. For Martí, heaven exists within humans. Third, one of the foundational goals of the Gita is the concept of *moksha*, which as previously noted is the release from the cycle of rebirth to achieve enlightenment and emancipation. For Christians, *moksha* can be misinterpreted as a concept of salvation and redemption linked to personal sacrifice. But for Martí, any idea of salvation or redemption required engagement in liberative praxis without regard for personal benefits, desires, or ambitions.[72]

A final Eastern worldview that seems to have resonated with Martí is the Chinese philosophy of Taoism, which he mentioned in an 1888 newspaper article concerning the funeral of the Taoist Li-In-Du.[73] Martí had more than simplistic familiarity; he incorporated Taoist thought into his own worldview, best illustrated by the concept of yin and yang, in which all things exist as independent yet inseparable, contradictory yet complementary, and is found in dichotomies such as male and female, light and darkness, white and black, negative and positive, young and old. Such dichotomies illustrated by the yin-yang symbol of the dark yin swirl contrasted with the light yang swirl; neither side of the circle is superior to the other. Each swirl contains at its core a spot representing the essence of the other. Humans, for Martí, existed along this yin-yang construct: "This is me," he jotted in a notebook: "A personality which is vigorous and impotent, free and enslave, noble and miserable, Divine and very human, refine and crude, darkness and light. This is me. This is every soul. This is every man."[74]

While Martí's exploration of Eastern religious traditions had an impact on his own spiritual views, his curiosity about the East was probably due more to his interest in the anticolonial struggles of the time, especially in Vietnam and India. In current affairs, he criticized the so-called enlightened French, who expounded "Liberty, Equality, Fraternity," for the oppression they maintained in the colony of Indochine.[75] Martí was also critical of the English for the oppressive colo-

nial ventures in India.[76] He introduced their social contexts as teleo-
logical examples of the human quest for liberation in his *La edad de
oro* children's narratives, thus eluding the Spanish censor of his time.
Martí's methodology predated postcolonial writers who would eventually lift up as equal the narratives of the globe's disenfranchised, those
whom Europeans had relegated to inferiority. As the historian García
de la Torre observes, "The implicit message strengthening nationalist sentiment against imperialism and illegitimate authority are not
plainly visible. They are encoded in a large global narrative that aggran-
dizes the political mission of decolonization."[77]

Martí recognized that all who are colonized face the same global
foe, which is dispersed among different Eurocentric nations. Cubans,
as well as all from América Latina, had much in common with the
world's colonized in places like Vietnam and India, joining them as
an oppressed people at the hands of those who loudly expound high-
minded words like *liberty*, *egalitarianism*, and *fraternity*. In an insight-
ful twist, Martí insisted that Cubans were one with the Vietnamese, a
proud people with the ability and fortitude to fight foreign powers for
their freedom (although his characterization of the Vietnamese is, at
best, disturbing): "We wear pigtail, pointed leaf hat and wide pants,
and colored shirts. We are yellow, pug-nose, puny and ugly. But we
work both with bronze and silk. And when the French came to take
away our Hanoi, our Hue, our cities of wooden palaces, our ports full
of bamboo houses and junk boats, our warehouses of fish and rice;
with our almond eyes, we have known how to die, thousands upon
thousands, so as to close their path. Now they are our masters; but as
for tomorrow: Who knows?"[78] Drawn to the anticolonial struggles in
the East as an example for Cubans, he explored Eastern spiritualities
for clues that would inform his own.

African Traditions

I have elsewhere argued for an "ethics of place," insisting on the importance of the geographical space a person inhabits in forming their
sociopolitical thoughts. Doing so enhances an investigation, focusing us on how norms and traditions of the everyday might manifest in

one's thoughts and opinions, thus providing a better understanding of Martí's own thinking and actions. Probably no other space contributes more to the formation of an individual than the neighborhood(s) of their childhood. And yet little attention has been given to the physical characteristics of the neighborhoods Martí occupied during his formative years. Because of this, my analysis, while speculative, is based on circumstantial evidence, what can be reasonably ascertained in the absence of documentation. The philologist Alexander Welsh contends that "narrative consisting of carefully managed circumstantial evidence, highly conclusive in itself and often scornful of direct testimony, flourished nearly everywhere—not only in literature but in criminal jurisprudence, natural science, natural religion, and history writing itself."[79] Welsh's usage of inference in the absence of documented evidence to elucidate history (among other disciplines) serves us as a point of departure for better grasping Martí's historical relationship, or lack thereof, with African traditions.

Although it may be true that openly participating in African traditional rituals was against the law in a nation firmly rooted in Catholic norms and laws, such laws nonetheless were routinely flaunted wherever there were large concentrations of Africans, especially in rural areas. Because Catholic priests were mainly concentrated in the more profitable urban centers, proper catechism was often lacking among the poor in those urban areas and rural plantations. For example, in the rural agricultural areas, years and decades would pass without contact with a priest. Sugar mills would hire poor priests (usually not among the church's brightest) to attend to the spiritual needs of their family and slaves. As the years progressed, the influence of the church would decline as clerics continued to find richer urban centers more profitable. A spiritual vacuum developed that the orishas would fill as a way of meeting adversity and medical needs.[80]

No doubt his parents, *peninsulares*, would have been horrified at what they probably perceived to be the primitive and superstitious faith practices of their Black, "backward" neighbors. But what about Martí? In an 1877 letter to the Guatemalan minister of foreign relations he confessed: "I write everyday about what I see every day."[81] And yet he seldom wrote about what he probably saw everyday growing up—the religious practices taking place among his Black neighbors. One is left perplexed by attempting to reconcile the great observer of humanity who captured from whichever culture in which he happened to be immersed but commented little on the religious, ethical, and moral foundations of those who would have lived next to him during his youth and those to whom he considered co-laborers in the cause of *patria* during his adult years. Curious indeed that Martí jotted down in his notebook reference to Norse mythology, writing about Odin, Thor, and Valhalla yet ignored the mythology closer to the indigenous African Cuban experience of Obatalá, Changó, and Ile-Ife.[82] This is peculiar, especially considering that he sketched about ten pages of an outline for a proposed book on the religions of the Américas with the tentative title *Los milagros en América* (Miracles in the Américas).[83] Why the relative silence, then, concerning African religious traditions?

As did so many others during his time who wrote accounts of Cuba, Martí ignored the traditional role of African-based religions in the development of Cuban identity, seldom mentioning either their contributions or their philosophical worldview. In his mind, practitioners were paternalistically praised as *l'homme sauvage*, as indicated in the following 1886 newspaper passage:

> The *negro* has a great native goodness, which neither the martyrdom of slaver perverts, nor is it darkened by his manly bravery. He has, more than any other race, intimate communion with nature, which appears more apt than other men to tremble and delight in its changes. There is something supernatural and marvelous in his terror and joy which does not exist in other primitive races, and he remembers in his movements and looks the majesty of the lion. There is in his affection a loyalty so sweet that does not make you think of dogs, but of pigeons. And there is such clarity, tenacity, intensity in his passions, which resemble the rays of the sun.[84]

For Martí, Blacks were not inheritably inferior; they simply were stuck in a lower evolutionary stage than whites as a consequence of the prevailing suppressive structures.[85] Hence, he disregarded the veneration of the orishas, the quasi-deities of the Yoruba pantheon, as superstitious, a primitive religious expression, what he called "barbarian feasts from Africa."[86] Yet one can never truly understand Cuba, its people or history, without fully coming to terms with the religious traditions of the descendants of Africans, specifically the Yoruba people, and how the overall white Cuban culture was grafted onto this African vine.

The Yoruba are originally from northwestern Africa, in an area that is today southern Nigeria. These Africans were not ignorant savages, as usually depicted by white Cubans—including Martí; they were members of a society that had established property holdings, conducted long-distance trade, and maintained different commercial associations and transacted deep within the African continent. The only true disadvantage the Yoruba had when compared to European cultures was that the Europeans possessed technologically superior weapons of destruction. Since 1448 the Portuguese and later other Europeans stole African bodies for forced labor, mainly transporting them in slave ships to Cuba and Brazil. By 1553, the British and Dutch had taken over the trade routes to provide slave labor to the Spanish colonies. The demand for sugar in the late seventeenth century triggered a demographic revolution in the West Indies as more Africans were transported to work on the flourishing sugar plantations. It is conservatively estimated that between nine million and ten million Africans crossed the Atlantic. Of that number, 6.3 million are estimated to have been transported from West Africa, and of those, Cuba became the destination for about 750,000 to 1.3 million of them.

Torn in tragedy from their ordered religious life, there was perhaps no time for people sold into slavery to ponder a spiritual response to the calamity they faced. Although their gods had been in Cuba since 1517, when the first slave ship carrying human cargo disembarked, it wasn't until the nineteenth century when Africans firmly established their orisha religious traditions. The orishas accompanied them on their journey across the Atlantic and so they, too, could be with and provide ministry to their devotees. These enslaved Africans were compelled to adjust their belief system to the immediate challenges of their new social location, and that transition created the nascent religious worldview from which Santería would eventually emerge. The

Yoruba's religious ethos survived by manifesting itself in a medieval Spanish Catholicism.

Catholic Cuba was more conducive to preserving the faith of the orishas than the Protestant North was. Unlike the United States, which relied on breeding slaves, it was more cost effective for Cubans to import replacements for those who were worked to death. Even with the life expectancy of a slave arriving to Cuba being seven years, the plantation owner was still able to profit. A greater number of slaves were being sent to Cuba during the nineteenth century as a result of the Owu and Egba civil wars and the final 1840 conquest of the Oyo by the Muslim Fulani people. This latter forced migration of Africans to Cuba ensured a greater opportunity to preserve the orisha traditions. As late as the 1930s former slaves known as *negros de nación* were still alive, remembering the religious rituals and customs as practiced in their African birthplace. Hence, the African ethos and culture did not diminish as rapidly as in the United States, where African heritage was diluted with each ensuing generation of slaves born under Anglo rule, which was committed to breaking off slaves from their culture.

In Cuba the last official ship bringing African slaves to the island docked in 1865, although the practice unofficially continued until the early 1870s. Therefore, it is not surprising that at the close of the slave trade, when Martí was but a young lad, one-third of the Cuban population was of African descent, of which about 75 percent were born in Africa and many still practiced the religious beliefs of their homeland.[87] In contrast, at the close of the U.S. Civil War in 1865, the four million U.S. slaves in the country at the time was ten times the total number of slaves that had been imported from abroad. The 427,000 slaves imported to former British colonies (including the 28,000 brought to French and Spanish Louisiana), represented 4.5 percent of all Africans imported to the Américas. Cuba alone took in more slaves after 1808 (428,023) than the United States received in all.[88]

When Martí was born, La Habana was undergoing urbanization under the direction of Governor and Captain General Miguel Tacón y Rosique (1834–1838) and would emerge as a cosmopolitan city with centralized colonial power.[89] The city's power brokers consisted of an aristocratic group, whose privilege was due to their bloodline, and the nouveau riche, whose privilege was derived from wealth acquired through trade. These powerful citizens existed over and against a pre-dominately large population of illiterate *negros* (slaves and free), *mulatos*, and whites from the lower classes; the majority of La Habana's population comprised *negros* and *mulatos*.[90] City growth and urbanization forced the population during this time to inhabit space beyond the obsolete city walls.

Martí was born on the southern edge of La Habana, *intramuro*, a few blocks west of the docks and close to the old city wall. Well into the 1950s the neighborhood was considered among the less desirable, poorer parts of La Habana Vieja, occupied by what was described as "malefactors and lazy" residents. During Martí's time, the *criollo* aristocrats escaped the summer heat of the *intramuro* for more spacious homes located *extramuro* (outside the city wall), particularly to the Cerro neighborhood.[91] *Extramuro* neighborhoods were home to the white upper and middle classes, who left behind the urban poor of the of *intramuro*. By 1860 (when Martí was seven years old) the population of the *extramuro* neighborhoods had become larger than that within the city walls—by 122,730 to 46,445.[92] The Martí family would eventually move to the *extramuro*, but they tended to live in the poorer sectors of it notorious for criminality and a large Black population.[93]

These poorer neighborhoods were not racially segregated. *Peninsulares* like Martí's parents lived next to merchants, laborers, freed and enslaved Blacks, and seasonal workers. Born on the literal margin of whiteness—*intramuro*—as the Martí family suffered continuous financial setbacks, they moved to less desirable spaces *extramuro*. But Martí, an acute observer of the everyday, missed the African religious influences that surrounded his childhood—or did he? We know that on the side street where he was born, Avenida Ejidos, there were several *cabildos* where large religious festivals were held on Sundays and feast days in honor of the orishas, with loud *bembe* music and dancing until daybreak.[94] We also know that Martí was knowledgeable of these secret African societies, per the title of an April 1893 article in *Patria*: "Una oden secreta de africanos" (A secret African order). His childhood friend and roommate while in Zaragoza, Spain, Fermín Valdés Domínguez, speaks of a Black Cuban servant also residing in their guesthouse whom he described as carrying the "mark of ñáñigo," *ñáñigo* being an African religious male fraternity.[95]

According to Pedro Pablo Rodríguez, "[Martí] was not born in a neighborhood composed of wealthy people, but instead a poor neighborhood of the working class. . . with whom did he play and associate? Surely with the children from that neighborhood, who were white, *negro, mulatos*; playing with the son of the Spaniard who ran the corner *bodega*, with the son of the *negro* or *mulato* artisan who lived around the block, and probably with the son of some domestic slave."[96] If so, there is no way he could have missed the practices and rituals of those of African descent. It would have been impossible not to see the offering to Ellegúa left by the side of the road, to hear the *bembe* pulsing through the streets, to see the sacred amulets worn by the practitioners, or to come across the carcass of a sacrifice. Did the inquisitive child ask his playmates or their parents why they conducted certain rituals or what exactly they believed? Besides the presence of orisha followers, could this worldview have influenced Martí consciously or unconsciously?

The main purpose of the Africa-derived religion of Martí's childhood neighbors and several of those with whom he associated during his years in the United States is to assist anybody, regardless of faith tradition, to live in harmony with nature and their assigned destiny. The part about living in harmony with nature no doubt would have resonated with Martí. The faith derived from the African orishas begins with the obstacles faced by the individual, for such difficulties prevent reaching their full potential. Unlike Abrahamic faith traditions, whose starting point is an almighty and all-knowing being, the point of origin of the African faith is a frail, hurting person. "Where there is no human, there is no divinity" states a popular Yoruba proverb. The individual is the starting point, responsible for any and all actions taken—actions that produce positive or negative consequences. The basic mission of the faith becomes helping individuals with everyday trials and tribulations of life. To address material problems, followers of African religions in Cuba turn to the metaphysical world for answers and solutions. In a very real sense, the physical universe emerged from the invisible spiritual realm. When the two realities are aligned, harmony exists. The faithful who understand that a dichotomy does not exist between physical and spiritual and who are willing to pursue the mysteries of the spiritual realm will find answers and solutions within the orisha traditions to bring healing to life's difficulties.[97]

Harmony for Martí was a sacred methodology by which to establish a moral foundation upon which correct praxis can be determined. As he wrote in a newspaper article, "There is something sacred in the harmony of beautiful works."[98] The underlining concept holding Martí's philosophy together—harmony—was probably influenced by his Black neighbors, especially those living their Yoruba faith. Martí's diverse and at times contradictory concepts are held together by his commitment to harmony, specially a physical-metaphysical harmony. Unlike Hegelian dialectics, which depended on the clash of thesis and antithesis to produce a new synthesis, Martí sought what he called *equilibrio*, or equilibrium, among diverse perspectives.[99] The actions to which he commits his life, establishing *un Cuba libre*, is understood as an attempt to bring balance to the world. As he wrote in the official paper of the revolution, "It is a world which we are balancing; not just two islands which we are going to liberate."[100]

Many scholars attribute Martí's ideas concerning harmony—a crucial component of his thoughts—to Buddhist thinking; no doubt, it probably was a contributing factor. Nevertheless, harmony—between humans, destiny, and nature—is also the ethical foundation of Yoruba religiosity that surrounded him during his most formative years. Also, scholars are quick to pin Martí views concerning reincarnation on Hinduism, and this too is probably true. But reincarnation is also a major component of orisha religious thought. If Martí was exposed to Yoruba spirituality as a child, before he had ever heard of Buddhism or Hinduism, then given the circumstantial evidence concerning Martí's childhood experiences in a neighborhood where Yoruba spirituality was definitely in the air, these experiences with his Black neighbors probably affected his worldview in the same way that all of us are deeply influenced and shaped by the neighborhoods of our childhood. He did not read of the orishas in books, but he probably saw the rituals and practices around him; perhaps he was even scandalized by them. And although there is not yet a known written text in which Martí makes a clear connection, I nevertheless offer up the possibility. There exists no written proof that Martí was philosophically influenced by the Black laborers and slaves who lived and worked in his neighborhood, but still I propose that one of the foundational tenets of the Yoruba belief system—the concept of harmony—influenced Martí even if he was too young to notice.

Regardless of whether Martí's concepts of harmony—or reincarnation, for that matter—were influenced by the orishas or Buddhism or Hinduism or any combination thereof, the fact remains that his political theology cannot be understood without exploring what he meant by harmony. "The world is an equilibrium," he wrote, "and while there is time, balance the two weights on the scale."[101] Martí always embraced reason and the spiritual, and any religion (not necessarily Christian) that stressed pursuit of the harmony of the two, instead of dogma: "Man will seek outside of historical and purely human dogmas that harmony of the spirit of religion with the freedom of reason which is the religious form of the modern world where it should come to rest, like the river to the sea, the Christian idea."[102] If Martí's thoughts concerning harmony were influenced by sources such as Buddhism, transcendentalism, and *krausismo*, why not also the orishas?

Similar to Emerson, Martí equates the forces and laws of nature with the transmigration of human souls, and also a God who functions as a universal, neutral, and impersonal substance. He looks not to the Judeo-Christian supernatural God of miracles but to nature for moral guidance, writing in his 1882 eulogy to Emerson, "There is a moral character in all elements of nature, for all of them revive this character in man."[103] But before he had ever read Emerson, Martí was exposed to this worldview of his African neighbors who believed the physical elements of existence—air, fire, water, and earth—have a spiritual correspondence. When Martí wrote in his philosophy notebook that "nature is everything that exists, in all forms," it sounds like he is describing the spiritual concept of orisha traditions known as *ashé*.[104] *Ashé* can be understood as a neutral cosmic energy that undergirds every aspect of existence, a transcendent world energy that encompasses the power, grace, blood, and life force of all reality. The origin of all *ashé* emanates from the supreme being Olodumare as sacred energy that is neither seen nor personified, neither good nor bad. All that inhabits life or exhibits power has *ashé*. One can find *ashé* in the energy produced by the blood of living creatures being spilled or by the movement of water, wind, or fire. This spiritual concept of *ashé* resembles Martí's understanding that "everything leads to man, who embellishes everything with his mind; that through every creature all the currents of nature pass; that within every man dwells the Creator, and every created thing has something of the Creator within it, and everything will ultimately go to the bosom of the Spirit creator."[105]

Although I argue for a connection between Martí and concepts of the orisha traditions, an echo brought forth from a past neighborhood experience, I do not argue for an embrace. Martí saw as "backward" Africans who held on to their religious worldview, welcoming their eventual embrace of Western "civilized" culture. For example, he praised a seventy-year-old Black man—Tomás Surí of Key West—who belonged to a secret African society. Surí deserves Martí's acclamation for forgoing the playing of sacred drums during his African rituals and instead embracing a more "civilized" alternative, learning to read. And although learning to read at any age is noteworthy, to Martí's mind, for a Black man to learn how to read and forsake ritual drums (as if the two were mutually exclusive) is a means for evolutionary advancement.[106]

"*Patria* is humanity," he wrote.[107] Unlike any other *latinoamericano* at the close of the nineteenth century, Martí attempted to fuse the need for Black liberation with the task of creating *un Cuba libre*. His writings concerning African descendants consciously attempted to impose racial equality on an unwilling Cuban public. And although he no doubt deserves praise for his efforts, his argument was problematic, as it perpetuated a "racial equality myth" that asserted that equality was achieved in the military forces while fighting Spain. Martí, the mastermind of the War of Independence, argued in *Patria* that an integrated army forged a single Cuban consciousness. "In war facing, all barefoot and naked," he wrote. "Blacks and whites were equal: they embraced and have never since separated."[108] More *negros* and *negras* died in the struggle for independence than whites did, yet if they were indeed equal in military services, then overrepresentation in fighting for Cuba can be ignored and the proportional rewards of military victory denied.

In his groundbreaking article "Mi raza" (My race), Martí proposes that to be Cuban meant "más que blanco, más que mulato, más que negro" ("more than being white, more than being a mulatto, more than being Black").[109] There was no such thing as color—only Cubans. His color blindness also blinded him to depths of whites' hatred for all that fell short of the white ideal. By denying the existence of racial and ethnic groups, Martí preserved Cuba's racial hegemony by advancing a repackaged Cuban white supremacy that effectively masked structural inequalities and injustices under the rubrics that Cubans were *más que blanco, más que mulato, más que negro*. In spite of the omnipresence of white supremacy in Cuban life—then and now, on the island and in the exile—the dominant white culture was able to insist on a rhetoric that absolved them of culpability.

Racial injury, when it did exist, was thus reduced to the individual and not structural, rationalized as an expected outcome of individuals competing as equals. Racial reconciliation under the guise of *más que blanco, más que mulato, más que negro* created an antiracist national philosophy that miserably failed in fundamentally transforming the social structures that had historically maintained and sustained Cuban white supremacy. Martí's vision of a raceless *patria* allowed white Cubans to insist on the end of white supremacy even while those who were negatively affected continue to suffer under oppression. The historian Alejandro de la Fuente documents how Black intellectuals of the Cuban Republic ridiculed white rhetoric concerning a Cuba with all and for all; used by politicians as a cantilena for votes. *Patria* may have been made by all, but it benefited the few.[110]

Indigenous Traditions

The liberal Mexican government of Sebastián Lerdo de Tejada was overthrown in 1876 while Martí was living in Mexico and replaced with the dictator Porfirio Díaz. In response, Martí publicly rebuked Díaz in the newspaper *El Federalista* in a December 7 editorial titled "The Die Is Cast."[111] Soon, rumors spread that the lives of those loyal to the defeated regime, including liberal journalists, were endangered. At the start of the new year, with a forged passport, Martí fled to La Habana.[112]

But by 24 February, he had returned to the Yucatán port of El Progreso, from where he made his way to Guatemala—an arduous journey as per his letter of 28 February to his friend Manuel Mercado, "From here by canoe to Isla de Mujeres; later by cayuco [small local canoe] to Belize; by boat to Izabel [*sic*]; on horseback to Guatemala."[113] On this first journey to Guatemala, where he planned to prepare a home for his soon-to-be bride, he was distracted by what he described some three years later in English for the New York paper *The Hour*, with "a Crown Venus . . . a supple, slender but voluptuous Indian woman" whom he "loved and was beloved."[114] He eventually arrived in Guatemala in May, when he started teaching at the Escuela Normal Central of Guatemala as professor of French, English, Italian, German literature, and history of philosophy (he returned briefly to Mexico in December to marry Carmen Zayes).

Living in Mexico and Guatemala exposed Martí to the indigenous population, contributing to his vision of a political future free of racism and rooted in the incorporation and celebration of the contributions made by Indians. In an era when the norm consisted of the use, misuse, and abuse of Indians, Martí recognized the interconnectedness of Indian oppression with the normalization and legitimization of oppressive structures, and the importance of including native populations as equals in the construction of any future América: "How can we walk forward, with history before us, with this crime behind us, with this impediment."[115]

Martí sought to save the Indian, seeking to make them co-laborers in the construction of a new *latinoamericano* and *latinoamericana* identity, chastising those who expressed shame in possessing indigenous roots: "Those born in the Américas, who are ashamed because they wear the Indian loincloth of the mother who raised them; whom they disown. Rascals! For leaving the ill mother alone in her sickbed."[116] He went so far as insisting that Indians had no obligation to participate in white civilization. Speaking about Native Americans in the United States, he wrote a newspaper article titled "The Indian Problem in the United States." In the 1886 editorial he argues that "the Indian in his people's reservation, who barely has meat to eat or something to wear, has reason to resist paying the public burdens of a citizenship he does not enjoy, and laws written in a language he does not understand.[117] But in spite of his celebration of the potential contributions of indigenous people to Nuestra América, Martí nonetheless remained complicit with the broader cultural genocide, seeking—as with those of African descent—their erasure through assimilation. The literary scholar Susan Gillman explains, "Just as Martí's rhetorical invocation of the Indian elides the role of the African in 'our *mestizo* America,' so too, more broadly, does *mestizaje* assimilates by whitening the people of America; so too does *indigenismo* celebrate a mythic Indianness while destroying actual Indians and displacing black Africans."[118] *Blanqueamiento*, or whitening, became a prerequisite for nationalist advancement. *Blanqueamiento*, in short, was a home-grown Cuban eugenics strategy that encompassed both the African and Indian. The establishment of *patria* and the institution of racial reforms were based on whitening Indians and Africans.

Indian erasure begins with perpetuating Jean-Jacques Rousseau's "enlightened" myth of the noble savage: "The Indian is discreet, imaginative, intelligent, predisposed by nature to elegance and culture. Of all primitive men, he is the most beautiful and least repugnant. No savage people exist that are in such a hurry beautify themselves, nor do they do so with such grace, correction and abundance of colors."[119] Indians, for Martí, may have been noble and beautiful, but they still lacked fortitude to rise from the evolutionary stage in which they were stuck: "A noble and impatient race, like men who begin to read books from the back. They do not know the small things but are ready to tackle the big. They always love the dowry adornments of the children of the Américas, and for them they show off, and for them their movable character sins, the premature politics and the leafy literature of countries in the Américas."[120]

Regardless of Martí's best intentions, he contributed nonetheless to their whitening process. In his 1878 book on Guatemala, he concluded: "The indigenous race, accustomed, by unforgivable and barbaric teachings, to laziness and selfish possession, neither sow, nor let sow. And the energetic and patriotic [Guatemalan] Government obligates them to sow or obtains permission to sow. And what they, who are lazy, do not use, the [Government], anxious about the life of the *patria*, break-

down into lots and gives them away."[121] Lazy Indians lacking any vision
for a future, he thought, must be tutored in the ways of cultures farther along the evolutionary scale. "Savings is useless for those who do
not know the pleasures produced by capital—smart, honest and accumulated savings," Martí wrote. "[The Indian] has nothing because he
wants nothing. He does not work for his well-being because he does
not want a more loving home, a softer bed, a more valuable outfit, a
better stock table than he already has. The intelligent man is asleep
at the foundation of another beastly man. The [Indian] race sees no
further than today. He works for what he needs, he produces what he
thinks he will consume. His intelligence is narrow, for narrow is everything he conceives and does. The imbecile race, for here is our opinion explaining this miserable race."[122] For Martí, domesticating and
pacifying Indians occurred through their erasure. The answer to the
Indian question was assimilation through education and hard work so
that the Indian could move farther along the evolutionary scale and
enjoy the benefits of participating in a market economy and a superior
political and social order. Although Martí rejected the popular classifi-
cations of superior and inferior races as proposed by positivist thinkers of the time like Herbert Spencer, he nevertheless attributed certain
intrinsic characteristics to different racial and ethnic groups. Inferiority was not innate but taught and learned. Only education could restore
the natural harmony among equals.

Martí argued: "The [Latin] American intelligence is an indigenous
headdress. Can you not see how the same blow which paralyzed the
Indian, paralyzed América? And not until the Indian walks, América
will not begin to walk well."[123] Jeffrey Belnap, a scholar of fine arts,
takes issue with this passage. He proposes that Martí "goes so far as
to equate this act of affective cross-identification with the forging of a
fiction of kinship, an act of cross-identification in which the intelligent-
sia learns to don an 'Indian headdress' and imagine itself as descended
from Native American peoples 'by blood.'"[124] The pure Indian, as well
as the pure Black, the pure Spaniard (whatever the word *pure* connotes) must all be erased for Martí to create a liberative *patria* based
on his equality ideals, a Cuba that essentially would remain Eurocentric in culture, ethos, power and tradition while appropriating the cul-

tural "headdress" of all who fell short of whiteness. For the sake of constructing *patria*, whites—like Martí—engaged in identity cross-dressing, becoming Indian when beneficial to them.

With the disappearance of the Indian (and the African for that matter), all Cubans become Indian (and Black). An Indian problem cannot exist if a color-blind society is achieved so there is no *más blanco, mulato, o negro (o indio)*. All Cubans, regardless of DNA tests, are white, Black, mulatto, and Indian. For white Cubans, Indians have always been more useful dead, gone, and invisible, so the dream of a more just and inclusive society, which fondly remembers them, can be constructed. "Dead," according to the law professor Larry Catá Backer, "the Indian could be transformed, generalized, denatured, and repackage for the benefit of emerging elites . . . [I]ndigenous people supplied the foundations for a trope, both literary and political, which is essential for the construction of cultural, ethnic, racial, and political identities distinct from traditional colonial masters of emerging Latin American states, as well as from that great power to the north."[125] Indians worked for the colonized European descendants only if reduced to symbols, not flesh-and-blood entities; Indians as symbols enable colonized whites to inherit Europe's former possessions without the responsibility of dealing with their complicity in Indian genocide. In fact, because there is no *blanco o indio*, only Cubans, then Indians—as Cubans—are also guilty of the sin of genocide.

Yes, Martí wrote numerous essays to celebrate and honor Indians throughout Latinoamérica, a position that few other whites, if any, took during his time; nevertheless, his lofty rhetoric lacked substance. Because there were no races—only Cubans—he remained silent on what exactly society or government could do to create a more racially just *patria*. Rather than praxis, he relied on an overabundance of hope and political optimism. Racism would come to an end because of human good nature, specifically the good nature of whites. The implementation of Martí's color blindness moved the discourse from addressing deeply held Cuban institutionalized oppression to creating a political correctness that expunged collective complicity in genocide.

Because the Indian was "born again" as white, a symbol for all Cubans, then Martí too could claim to be Indian, finding stronger

kinship ties with those who hailed from the same geographical location. He wrote: "What does it matter if we descend from parents with
Moorish blood and white skin? The spirit of men floats on the land in
where they lived and still is drawn in with the air they breathe. It comes
from fathers from Valencia and mothers from the Canary Islands, but
in our veins flow the enraged blood of Tamanaco and Paracamon and
claiming as its own . . . the heroic and naked Caracas warriors!"[126] Jeffrey Belnap argues that for Martí geography trumped biology. His parents may have been born in Spain, but his identity was formed by his
social location as he found kinship not with the Spaniard colonizers
but with the indigenous warriors who fought them.[127] With the Indian
gone, assimilated into whiteness, Martí could claim his *indigenismo*,
even adopting the Indian name *Anáhuac* (Nahuátl for "close to water")
in his Mason membership and some of his revolutionary writings. If
the Indian could be erased, then a new one could be constructed with
which Martí and all other non-indigenous Cubans could claim affinity.

Judaism

Was Martí an anti-Semite? He wrote little concerning the Jews of his
time, and when he did, it was usually in passing. He acknowledged their
brutal persecution, especially at the time in Russia, which he recognized as the latest installment of centuries of persecution that forced
them to "wander as cursed men through Christian land."[128] His writing
insists on equal treatment and the right of Jews to practice their faith;
celebrates their establishment of great school of art and trade; and recognizes their capacity to accomplish extraordinary things, even an eventual return to Jerusalem.[129] He praises the ancient Hebrew writers of
the Talmud, keen observers of nature, for having similar modern ideas
as Darwin.[130] Nevertheless, Martí appears guilty of the anti-Semitic
sentiments common among intellectuals of his time. For example, he
compliments non-Jews by comparing them to Jews through the use of
"positive" stereotypes, which in reality reinforces certain caricature-like
"natural" traits that have historically proved deadly.

     When describing a particular group of people in a newspaper edi-
torial, he compared them to Jews, stating "they amass wealth like

the Jews";[131] or when comparing another group of workers to Jews, they were "assaulting with their eyes and gestures," the "same expression and gestures as the Jews of the Bowery, stationed at the doors of their shops, haggling with the rural buyer, who is unsteady and bewildered."[132] He praises a painter's business acumen "who sold one of his painting for more than what he gave for it, like a Jewish merchant."[133]

Still, in spite of these so-called positive stereotypes, there appears in Martí's mind a more sinister side to Jews. They are more prone to suicide than Protestants or Catholics, he claims without documentation.[134] Elsewhere, he attempts to excuse their selfishness: "We shouldn't think so badly of the Jews, even though in the depth of the most generous, one can see the anguish and misery of the race, because among the Hebrews there is much natural nobility, even though living without a country [*patria*] makes them selfish and egotistic"[135]—an interesting comment considering that Martí and his Cuban compatriots also were without a *patria*. Was he projecting? Elsewhere, in his notebook entry "The God of the Jews," he wrote about implacable Jews needing revenge to satisfy their anger and eventually becoming "rich and corrupt": "Jews: always persecuted, always oppressed . . . [God's attributes are] implacability and revenge, needed by the Jews to the tremendous satisfaction of their anger . . . Later, the Jew became rich and corrupted—despot, educated by means of terror—'do not smile at your daughter' Ecclesiastes. Beasts—they subjected the woman to an indecent test. They made the greatness of the woman and the nobility of matrimony consist in the vigor of the hymenic cloth!"[136]

Martí has no qualms in referring to them as having a "long nose" or a "piercing profile and greedy eyes."[137] In list of dualisms to describe a practical democracy, he contrasted something desirable and advanced with something backward: "As in every society there is the visionary and the unbeliever, the poet and the vulgar, the Messiah and the Hebrew, the one who announces the future and the one who believes only in the visible."[138] Not surprisingly, Martí fell into the common trap of his time (and ours): blaming the foolish Jews for being the accusers of Jesús: "After nineteen centuries which the world worshiped the divine innocence of Jesús, there has been men who are quite arrogant and mislead against the Divine Majesty by again formulating the accusations presented by the Jews."[139] Their accusation, Martí goes on, "confirms the confusion and perversity of the Jews."[140]

Liberative Christian Humanism

Only a fool would attempt to provide a label to Martí's religious or spiritual commitments. Because no theological or religious system-ization exists in his writings, one sees his spirituality as if through a kaleidoscope—rotate his writings, and a constantly changing spiri-tual pattern emerges. Some images are positive, others not so much. But this eclectic incorporation of diverse concepts does not lead to a deafening cacophony; instead, he weaves different philosophical and theological threads together to create a spiritual congruency among contradictory ideas that we might label a liberative Christian human-ism, probably in the vein of Erasmus. After all, for him, "Erasmus laid the egg and Luther incubated it."[141]

In his notebook, Martí self-described as a "Christian, pure and sim-ply Christian. A rigid observance of morals—improving myself, yearn-ing for the betterment of everyone, life for the good, my blood for the blood of others; this is the only religion."[142] Christian, yes—but more a cultural one than a theological one. Martí was certainly not a Christian in terms of how the term was used during his time, or even in our own. This was not a Christianity that unquestionably believed. Blind faith, as the *martiano* scholar Entralgo Cancio states, was for Martí "the rub-bish dump in the bonfire of reason. Only through studying and medita-tion can believing be achieved. There is no limitation on the ability to reason. All which can be defined as spiritual is guided by reason in the search for Truth a Truth upon which justice is based. Because God gave humanity free will, through reason, humanity can determine between right and wrong."[143] Martí was not a Christian who rejected science whenever it contradicted dogma; but by the same token, he was not a secular humanist who rejected a theistic source of human values. Both the spirituality of religion (in his case predominately Christian) and the scientific underpinning of secular humanism were required. Both the spirituality of the "divine Jesús" and the scientific method-ology of Aristotle unite to achieve and arrive at truth.[144] The physical and spiritual world intermingle in Martí's thoughts, finding unity and harmony within nature. He had, after all, a mystical awareness that was revealed especially in his poetry, a mystical awareness understood through reason.

Martí reconciled classical humanist principles on the basis of the primary importance of human beings with an understanding of Christianity in an attempt to move society and individuals away from an oppressive faith and toward a more justice-based existence:

> Who will we ask? Faith? Oh! No—enough! In the name of faith there has been many lies. One should have faith in higher existence, conformed to our internal irritable agitation,—in the immense powerful Creator, who consoles—in a love which saves and unites—in the life which begins with death. An internal and natural voice, the first voice heard by a primitive people, and which man always hears, cries out for all this. But mystical faith, faith in the cosmic word of the Brahmins, in the exclusivist word of the Magi, in the traditional, metaphysical, and immobile word of priests, the faith which opposes the movement on earth, says it moves in a different manner; the faith, which confronts the Valencia mechanic, oppresses and binds; the faith which condemns as witches Marquis of Villena, Bacon, and Galileo. Faith, which first denies what later sees itself obligated to accept; that faith is not a means to arrive at truth rather to obscure and stop it. It does not help man, but instead stops him. It does not respond, but instead punishes. It does not satisfy, but instead irritates. We free men already have a diverse faith. Their faith is eternal wisdom.[145]

The *martiano* scholar Julio Ramón Pita argues for a convergence of Christian ethical principles in Martí's thought that verges on a critical passionate evangelicalism, leaving little doubt that his moral identity was Christian.[146] I lean toward Pita's assessment, but the task before us is how to give nuance to this Christian moral identity. Presenting Martí as the mere paragon of Christian belief or as a secular humanist who rejects Christianity does violence to his writings. The temptation is to reduce Martí solely as a Christian critical of an apostate church. Such a reading, though, is too simplistic. If Christianity can be understood as placing God at the center of justice, morality, and ethics, then Martí falls short. For him, human beings, not God, occupied this central space. In his writings, he makes the case for being a Christian, but on the basis of these same writings he is also a humanist. Martí is closer to a Christian humanist, one who believes that rational thought, free will, and individual conscience are compatible in the truest sense with Christian faith. And while Martí acknowledged that "the spirit perceives and feels, and with it reaches the truth,"[147] he nevertheless recognized that "contrary to august reason there is nothing."[148]

With comments like these, I find myself agreeing with the literary critic Ezequiel Martínez Estrada, who described Martí's thoughts as "pre-Christian humanitarian."[149] Martí was influenced, as we have seen, by the philosophies of earlier Cuban Christian thinkers like Caballero, Varela and Luz, but he nonetheless embraced a panentheistic worldview in which humans occupy the apex of nature; humans unite the two components of nature, physical and spiritual. Martí's form of Christianity is laic, void of dogma, churches, and fanaticism. Questions concerning the specifics of his beliefs may abound, but there is no question of his spirituality. Although he rejected the dogmas of the clergy, he nonetheless embraced spirituality, a spirituality that, I argue, was nourished when in solidarity with the oppressed.

On the tension created in uniting the spiritual (Christianity) and the material (science) Martí constructed his Christian humanist understandings. But missing from a description of Martí's religious tendencies is his commitment to the oppressed, which, some seventy years after his death, would come to be expressed as liberation theology. Cognizant of the danger in imposing a twentieth-century theological perspective upon a nineteenth-century man—or reading oneself into Martí—I nonetheless gingerly argue in the final two chapters of this book that the concepts that would eventually come to be known as liberative theologies resonate with Martí's religious views, making him a possible precursor to liberation theology. The exploration conducted thus far is what leads me to conclude that Martí was a liberative Christian humanist. The rest of this book takes up the task of exploring why I insist on the word *liberative* as an adjective for Christianity in any description of Martí's religious thoughts.

FOUR

Precursor to
Liberation Theology

Every so often it is necessary to shake the
world, so that what is rotten falls to the
ground.

ARE THE THOUGHTS of a historical figure like José Martí to be relegated to a particular era that encompasses only the years in which he
lived? What can be speculated is that as a prolific writer throughout
the Américas, probably the best known and most read journalist of his
time, Martí toiled to develop the fertile soil from which some seventy
years later, the seeds of liberation theology could take root and blos-
som. But such an argument assumes a dialectical movement of history,
a proposition that appears somewhat dubious to those of us who view
the movement of time as nonlinear. And yet writings concerning the
liberation of humanity from political, social, religious, and intellectual
oppression are timeless. Can we argue that historical figures like Martí
who have expressed liberative concepts and ideals within the body of
their writings and the space of their era serve as better representatives
of liberative thought than the normative Eurocentric thinkers to whom
the academy normatively turns?

At best, throughout different moments of history, wherever oppression flourished, so too did resistance, and at times, such resistance has been understood spiritually. There have always been those who insisted on the concept of liberation through a spiritual paradigm: the second-century theologian and martyr Polycarp, who argued that ignoring poverty bordered on idolatry; the medieval bishop of Paris, Guillaume d'Auxerre, who during plague and famine insisted that the poor engage in "starvation theft"; the fourteenth-century Dominican nun Catherine of Siena, who wrote against the wealthy of her time and the social structures they created to enrich themselves. It would be unsophisticated and unscholarly to impose the modern term *liberation theologian* upon such historical figures. Some, with a more linear approach to history, have erroneously argued that liberation theology began in Latinoamérica and then spread to the rest of the world. But if liberation theology is a spiritual expression of how the oppressed theologically reflect on the liberative praxis in which to engage, then liberative movements have always existed throughout different spans of history. What we can say is that historical figures, including Martí, expressed politically liberative ideals rooted in the spiritual. Given their understanding of the metaphysical, a political moral obligation existed for them to seek the physical and spiritual liberation of those marginalized by secular and ecclesiastical structures. And here is the crucial note: it really doesn't matter whether Martí was or was not personally spiritual. What interests our exploration here is how his words, rooted in religious rhetoric, could have created fertile ground in América Latina to give rise in the late 1960s to the theological expression known as liberation theology.

Early thinkers of liberation theology throughout Latinoamérica have insisted on doing their analysis from the community's grass roots. To that end, a thinker like José Martí would naturally be pivotal in their analysis; but unfortunately, many instead have heavily relied on Eurocentric Catholic philosophy and thought, as indicated by who was quoted in the footnotes of the early published books on the topic (i.e., Gustavo Gutiérrez's 1971 *Teología de la liberación*). One would be hard pressed to find any of these early liberation thinkers quoting or referring to Martí—even so, his writings are foundational to the intellectual trajectory of liberation thought throughout the twentieth century in Latinoamérica. Most intellectuals south of the U.S. border have no doubt read Martí.

For example, the theologian Frei Betto, best known for his interviews with Fidel Castro that culminated in the 1985 book *Fidel y la religión*, is among the few liberationist thinkers who seriously considered Martí's influence on liberation theology. For Paul Borgeson, the poetry of Ernesto Cardenal derives from the prophetic tradition common among revolutionary intellectuals throughout the Américas; his verses are "authentic, profound, and popular," similar to those of Martí, who referred to his verses in the introduction to *Versos libres* (a collection of poetry he wrote between 1878 and 1882) as "mis guerrilleros."[1] The Puerto Rican theologian Luis N. Rivera-Pagán, commenting on Reinerio Arce's 1993 doctoral dissertation for the University of Tübingen (since published in book form), celebrates his liberationist endeavor, which opens "a whole new field of dialogue and discussion in the Cuban Martí studies, one that evades the dead-end of fruitless and sterile attempts to make Martí a Caribbean Marx." Rivera-Pagán goes on to wish that Gutiérrez in his book would have paid more attention to the "unexplored wealth of religious imagery and symbolism, which could be of inspiration for a new generation of Cuban and Latin American theologians."[2] I, too, for some time now, have argued that Martí, "[a]s an indigenous Cuban symbol . . . serves as a precursor to liberation theology."[3]

If liberation theology bases its analysis upon its own cultural symbols, then should not Martí's thoughts and writings serve as a counternarrative to the imposed influential Eurocentric foundations of the discourse? This is not to redefine or reimagine Martí as a liberationist theologian—he was not. But it is to say that his thoughts—especially through his journalistic writings—started to articulate throughout Latinoamérica what would eventually resonate with what has come to be known as liberation theology. And even if no direct link is ever found between Martí's writings and what eventually became liberative theological thought, we can still say that what today is understood as liberation theology deeply resonates with Martí's work, which can better ground the theology's way of thinking in *nuestra América*.

Liberation Theology

The religious movement known as liberation theology developed in Latinoamérica during the late 1960s. During an era when the church was aligned with the interests of the ruling and economically privileged classes, some searched deep within their spiritual traditions to formulate a response to the causes of oppression. In a very real sense, liberation is salvation. The Hebrew word *yāša'* and the Greek term *sōzō* appear in most English translations of the Bible as "to save," yet they also connote "to liberate." For those who claim to be liberationists, salvation is neither an abstract concept nor a personal feeling; rather, it is a state of being that encompasses rescue and deliverance. And although most religious are quick to connect deliverance with the concept of sin, those who are liberationist redefine sin to encompass oppressive social structures.

There does not exist one liberation theology upon which everyone agrees, because all theologies (including Eurocentric ones) are contextual, rooted in the social location of those who are seeking faith-based responses to their situation. However one defines liberation, it can be determined only by local communities that live under specific suppressive social structures. Rural Mexican Catholics understand the spiritual response to their oppressive predicament different from how Palestinian Muslims might. Different ethnicities, geographies, religious traditions, and oppressive structures lead to different conceptions of theology, even though congruence can be found around certain themes. Any attempt to create a uniform definition of liberation theology is therefore problematic, even though the theology itself provides a response to the reality faced by the dispossessed and disenfranchised. Although the common starting point of theological reflection is the existential experience of the marginalized, the ultimate goal remains liberation from the misery of society's oppressive structures.

Liberation theology, like all political-theological perspectives, was not created *ex nihilo*, or out of nothing. The historical trend of those resisting the powers and principalities of this world, since the first colonizers landed in the Western Hemisphere, became the antecedent to what would come to be known in Latinoamérica as liberation theology. Any movements, Christian or not, that spiritually seek the dismantling of social, political, and economic structures responsible for the creation of poverty and oppression can be understood as being liberative.[4] The liberation theology that arose in Latinoamérica was influenced by six major events—and I argue for a seventh. The first and most important occurred when Pope John XXIII (1958–1963) convened the Second Vatican Council (1962–1965) in order to "modernize" Catholicism. A major document that emerged from the council was the pastoral constitution *Gaudium et spes* (1965), which emphasized the responsibility of the church to "those who are poor or afflicted in any way."[5] The document declared that the church cannot tie itself to any particular economic or political system but instead must find its purpose for existence through solidarity with the most marginalized segments of society.

The second event that contributed to the development of liberation theology in Latinoamérica was the 1968 conference held in Medellín, Columbia. How does the local church implement the Vatican Council's attempt to modernize Catholicism germane to an oppressed people who were suffering during a time of right-wing dictatorships that served as guardians for the globalization of capitalism, an economic system that eventually came to be known as neoliberalism? What is the proper role of theology's seeking of fidelity to both the poor and the Gospel message? What becomes the moral foundation upon which political praxis are formulated? Specifically, the Vatican Council wrestled with how the church in Latinoamérica could complete its earthly mission in a context of poverty and death that was caused in good measure by the United States economic policies designed to profit multinational corporations.

The third event was the publication of Gustavo Gutiérrez's groundbreaking book *Teología de la liberación* (1971), translated into English in 1973. The book provided a reflection on what Gutiérrez believed was the proper role of theology in its attempt to be faithful to both the poor and the Gospel, and on how theology can be constructed by learning from the everyday struggle of the poor. Fourth was the spread throughout Latinoamérica of Christian Base Communities (CBCs), physical places where the dispossessed gathered to discover how to channel their religious convictions to bring about change within the realty of their marginalized lives. CBCs were often in rural locations where the dispossessed organized grassroots political action and received education or, as they called it, *concientización*, or awareness raising. Fifth was the example of the 1959 Cuban Revolution, which showed that nations in Latinoamérica could indeed break free of U.S. hegemony. And although Cuba was never accepted as a model to emulate by liberationists, it did prove that a nation need not be organized along a pro-U.S. capitalist paradigm. Finally, sixth is the example of the revolutionary Colombian priest Camilo Torres, who inspired a generation of religious leaders who politically leaned leftward. Torres came from a wealthy family and served the church as a university professor. Finding it difficult to carry out his duties within Christendom, he chose to align himself with the church of the poor. At first, he attempted to work within the system to bring about change, but he soon concluded reform was unattainable. Hanging up his holy vestments in 1965, he took to the hills and joined the revolutionary Columbian guerrilla forces. "I took off my cassock to be more truly a priest," he proclaimed.[6] In 1966, he died a violent death during a battle. His radicalization inspired other young revolutionaries; however, many within the liberation theological movement considered Torres to have been naïve. Even his friend and former classmate Gustavo Gutiérrez did not believe "the decision of Camilo to join the guerrilla movement was a wise one."[7]

Liberation theology clearly emerged as a spiritual response to political and economic oppression in Latinoamérica, a specific theological perspective geared toward answering questions arising from a particular historical moment in a specific geographical area that occurred almost seventy-five years after Martí's death on the battlefield in Dos Ríos.[8] Still, Martí can be understood as having influenced what would become liberation theology in Latinoamérica. He was a historical figure who during a time of political oppression turned to the spiritual to imagine a *liberative* response to the oppression of his people. To engage in liberative theological thought is to wrestle with forging a justice-based social order focused on the political and spiritual liberation of those whose humanity is denied and those whose humanity is lost as they pursue power and privilege at the expense of the disenfranchised. Hence, Martí is not a liberation theologian per se, but he was a precursor to a movement whose tenets at times resonate with Martí's thoughts and writings. To prove this thesis, the rest of this chapter and the next consider some of the overarching tenets of liberation theology to demonstrate the similarities and differences with *martiano* thought.

Gustavo Gutiérrez, one of the first to articulate liberation theology, stressed the importance of a theology that communicates in terms of the significant symbols of the culture: "If we see theology as knowledge shot through with the 'savored' experience first of God but then also of the people and culture to which we belong. [The use of national thinkers] has had the purpose precisely of communicating some of this 'savor.' These [national individuals] have experienced their own time in depth; they have been deeply involved in the sufferings and hopes of our people and have been able to express, as few others have, the soul of the nation."[9] Martí, for Cubans, became the ultimate symbol upon which Cubans can seek the "flavor" of God, and that "flavor," I would argue, is liberative.

The young Martí found himself as a teenager condemned to hard labor, which began his quest for physical liberation. Martí was not interested in copying, imitating, or reproducing Eurocentric religious thought or dogmas; he was interested in creating something new and apart from it. He feared that Eurocentric theological thought was philosophically constructed to justify colonial and imperial oppression through its use of liberty-based language. By making theological thought abstract and supporting a faith devoid of social justice, the violence of disinheriting and dispossessing the colonized is obscured. Martí was among the first to question the political and spiritual normalization and legitimization of a particular Eurocentric religious way of thinking that enslaves minds inasmuch as it seeks to free bodies, for if the mind remains colonized, then those for whom society is constructed to benefit need not worry about resistance to oppression. Once those privileged by society determine what the colonized should think, they need not be anxious about what they would do. To counter this trend, Martí attempted to introduce those seeking their own liberation with *una nueva religión*—a new religion that was liberative.

Liberative Message of Love

The foundation of Christianity is love. "For God so loved the world that God gave us God's only begotten son," declares the Evangelist (John 3:16). And: "Anyone who loves is born of God and knows God. Anyone who does not love does not know God, because God is love" (1 John 4:7–8). If God is love, then God is incapable of hatred. Martí echoes this core Christian message concerning love, calling us to also love our neighbor as ourself (Luke 10:27), a love best demonstrated by how Jesús loved, even his enemies, whom he willingly forgave as they were crucifying him. In his struggle for *un Cuba libre*, Martí faced several attempts on his life. He once met behind closed doors with a would-be assassin who attempted to poison him. Martí, who never divulged the would-be poisoner's name, made a friend out of an enemy, so much so that the would-be assassin later became a member of the National Liberation Army.[10] Loving the enemy committed to one's crucifixion, for Martí, was the path to liberation for both oppressed and oppressor.

Martí's concept of love, as per the *martiano* scholar Rafael Cepeda, was rooted in the life of Jesucristo, which deeply influenced Martí's thinking.[11] As an eclectic thinker, he was also influenced by Eastern traditions, where love moves beyond androcentric relationships: "Embrace the living in ineffable love. Love the grass, the animal, the air, the sea, the pain, the death, for suffering is less for the souls which love possess."[12] Love of all that exists, as the bases for moral and ethical praxis, became his supreme absolute, the motivation behind all his political decisions. He declared: "The only truth of this life, and the only power, is love. In it is salvation, and in it the command. Patriotism is nothing but love. Friendship is nothing but love."[13] This love advocated by Martí should never be confused with sentimental emotion or paternalistic intention. For Martí, according to the theologian Reinerio Arce, love was not an abstract concept or feeling; rather, love manifest in concrete praxis, actions that lead to precise results—only then can we know whether love is true.[14] For Martí, *love* is a self-sacrificing verb, an act that places the needs of the other first, an action defined as service to others for the greater good of liberation: "It is necessary that in order to be serviced by all, one must serve everyone."[15] Elsewhere he wrote: "Serving is our glory, and not serving ourselves."[16]

Unfortunately, Martí's tendency to create neat dichotomies lacked some nuance in dealing with the conflicting emotions of those abused who may show pity for the oppressor yet still feel the pangs of hatred emanating from their scars. Martí simply divided people between those who chose to love and those who chose to hate. Agreeing with St. Teresa de Ávila, Martí harshly describes those who "do not know how to love" as demons.[17] He refused to distinguish humans according to race, culture, or social class. Instead, he differentiated them by the ability or inability to love. Regardless as to how others may choose to react to their enemies, Martí chose to love by rejecting hatred, and he called others to do likewise. "I only know of love," he writes. "I tremble in terror / When like snakes, the passions / Of man stubbornly engulf my knee."[18] The *martiana* scholar Gutiérrez Marroquín succinctly summarizes Martí's lifelong philosophy: "All his works is a song to love, a call to improve humanity, an invitation to only puff out one's chest for the best of humans, to live a life for good."[19]

For Martí, the love he called for was based on righteous indignation for the cruelty he witnessed, especially during his time at the quarry: "I do not hate those who do not think like us. It is a petty quality, fatal among the masses, and rickety and unbelievable in true statesman, for they neither know the times nor the consistent work and intention of those who with goodwill differ in methods from them."[20] Speaking about the abuse he witnessed in prison, he notes that those being abused are God in the flesh—"They forgot that in that [abused] man was God!"[21]—reminiscent of Jesús pronouncement that whatever is done to the least is done unto him as well (Matthew 25:40). But Martí's love message was never limited to those who suffered cruelty at the hands of others. Reminiscent of the theological notion of *imago Dei*— the image of God—all, as he would say, "have God within themselves."[22] Because all possess the image of God within them, love is also to be showered upon the abuser, for within even them God exists. One cannot love a God who cannot be seen while hating a fellow human who can be seen, as the apostle John reminds us (1 John 4:20). Such a love was so powerful that it sought the abuser's salvation, hoping to turn enemies into friends. "Love is the bonds of men," Martí wrote, "the way of teaching and the center of the world."[23] In short, Martí modeled a radical love that did not waste a word denigrating another human being. In a September 1890 letter to Rafael Serra, fellow journalist and revolutionary, Martí confessed, "I am a sinner, but not in my own way of love for men."[24]

Most political liberators throughout Latinoamérica advocated hatred for their adversaries. Those from the Right and the Left—before, during, and after Martí's life—were united in their desire to punish their opponents. But not Martí. Love, love, love, and then more love—always do love. In another letter to Serra, written in January 1895, Martí continued with this same theme: "Do not tire of loving."[25] While he was exiled in Spain, Martí wrote a poem to commemorate the execution by firing squad on 27 November 1872 of Cuban medical students, giving Cuban rebels their first popular rallying point. Martí refused to hate the oppressors responsible for their assassination and instead imagined the martyrs giving him advice on how to respond in love: "They are the ones! They are the ones! They tell me / To suspend my wrathful rage, / And they show me their pierced chest, / And their wounds with love they bless, / And their bodies tightly embraced, / And they implore favor for the despots! / . . . Forgive! That's what they said / For those whom they abandoned on earth / Their remains scattered."[26] Neither life nor humanity can exist void of love, for love is the only truth capable of moving beyond the petty quality of hate and the only force capable of constructing community. Maintaining mutual hatred only advocates a praxis of destruction. "Only love," Martí argues, "constructs."[27]

A methodology of axiological analysis can be derived by Martí's radical call to love, which can best be understood as relational, a morality of imitation that emphasizes casuistry. For Martí, Jesús is to be imitated more than doctrinally accepted. Imitating Jesús creates for Martí an ethical foundation upon which the greatest commandment, love, can be implemented. But as important and crucial as Christ may be as a moral claim, he is not *the* only moral claim. Although Martí (to the best of my knowledge) never referenced Søren Kierkegaard, the Danish philosopher of a generation previous, Kierkegaard also called people to be followers seeking to imitate Christ, not be Christ admirers. In more modern parlance, one would say, "Don't talk about Jesús; be Jesús." To understand Martí's axiological foundation is to understand love as a moral duty: "My duty will therefore be very simple—die for what I love."[28] Death is never to be feared if it is the consequence of duty. Duty, service, and utility are the virtues derived from the love that led Martí to commit to lifelong acts of justice and liberation. A year before his death, he explained in the newspaper for the revolution: "Only in the sad and rough fulfillment of duty is there true glory. And it must be the duty fulfilled for the benefits of others, because if it contains hope for its own good, as legitimate as it may appear or is, it will already be tarnished and will lose moral force. The focus is in the sacrifice."[29]

But how did Martí reconcile his radical call for love with planning a revolutionary rebellion that would no doubt lead to violence, death, misery, and destruction? A call for war based on the example of Jesús can be perceived as blasphemous. What happens when love of the "enemy" intersects with the enemy's determination in preventing one's liberation? While the love Martí advocates seems to be based on the biblical concept of *agape*, a Greek word that connotes unconditional love, for Martí conditions nonetheless exist. Rather than turning the other cheek, he advocated violence in the form of war against political oppressors, even though he called for the revolution to be carried out as an act of love, not hatred or anger. In preparing Cubans for the coming war, he declared, "Let our motto be: liberty without anger."[30] Although he organized a war of violence to be carried out against Spaniards, he refused to hate them simply because they were Spaniards. In the 25 March 1895 Manifesto of Montecristi, the document that outlined the goals and hopes of the liberation movement days before Martí landed at La Playita to engage in the revolution, Martí wrote: "The war is not against the Spaniards, which is assured their children and in compliance with the *patria* will win, will be able to enjoy respect and love from the liberty which will only overwhelm those lacking foresight who come to the road."[31] Spaniards living on the island were to be neither hated nor mistreated.

He went on to offer a significant olive branch: "The Cubans started the war, and the Cubans and Spaniards will finish it. Do not mistreat us, and you will not be mistreated. Respect, and you will be respected. Steel answers to steel and friendship responds to friendship. There is no hatred in the Antillean's heart. The Cuban greets in death the (brave) Spaniard to whom the cruelty of the forced practice of being ripped from their house and homeland to come and kill in men's heart the liberty they too long for."[32] Former oppressors are welcomed with open arms. He understood his enemies on the battlefield were part of his identity because they shared the same humanity. In a notebook of fragmented thoughts, Martí jotted down: "And if I attack the Spaniards for being Spaniards, my father would rise from his grave, and say to me: parricide. But the bad government, the oppression, the ignorance in which we live, the moral misery to which we are condemned, this dear father! is not you, this is not Spain, but some other country; that is infamy and abomination, and wherever this is found must be extinguished."[33] Martí demonstrated in his words and praxis how to love the nation of one's enemies, inviting them to be part of constructing a new *patria* after the war.

Martí called for a violence tempered by love, a proposition some would argue is impossible to maintain. Failing to seriously take into account the depravity of humans would no doubt lead to disappointments. Martí however recognized this depravity: "I know humans, and I find them evil. / Perfect for igniting the eternal fire / Are those burned at the stake! / A bad apple spoils the bunch! The crucifixes / For the crucifiers! On wood / They nailed Jesús: among themselves / The men of these times are nailed."[34] In response, Martí's vision had to be more than simple political salvation; it also required spiritual redemption. No doubt he was calling for more than a political revolution to liberate the land. He called for a spiritual revolution rooted in love to liberate the soul. He took up the task of completing Jesús' work to create a new way of being that was a reflection and response to a God who is love. Martí sought to create not only *patria* but a new human to occupy the newly established political regime. If not, Cuba would dissolve into political fighting and civil wars, as he had witnessed firsthand in other countries throughout the Américas. Attempting to save Cuba from a similar fate, Martí sought a new way of being that was rooted in the spiritual, in the *nueva religión*.

Violence

Martí, advocate of love and rejecter of hatred, found no contradiction in calling for war, for he believed that any war for the liberation of the enslaved and disenfranchised is an act of love, not hatred. The quest for *patria libre* required the domestication and democratization of violence to avoid the temptation of hatred. He wrote: "By God, this is a legitimate war—the last essential and definitive which can liberate men. The war against hatred."[35] Although he did not believe in the use of violence to bring about economic reform or justice, he nonetheless saw violence as necessary in the pursuit of political justice, specifically the liberation of *patria*.[36] He shunned violence but still saw the need to pick up arms.

The etymologist Agnes Lugo-Ortiz has understood Martí's concept of *patria* as a space prefiguring a new civilian social order through its military preparation. In his call to arms, Martí legitimated violence by denouncing violence and elevating it into the orbit of reason. Language (writing) ceased to be an antagonistic mode of exercising violence by becoming its rational dimension, in effect institutionalizing violence.[37] The man who prized peace was uncompromising in his call for war. War to liberate Cuba was unavoidable—in a speech in Tampa on 26 November 1891, he called it "this sad and resolute desire for an inevitable war."[38] But this was more than simply an armed conflict; it was a holy and redemptive violent cause, what he called in that same speech, a "holy revolution" imported from abroad.[39] "Through the doors which we exiles open," Martí confessed, "will enter Cubans with the radical soul of the new *patria* . . . The war is prepared abroad for the redemption and benefit of all Cubans."[40] *Patria* created the means to domesticate and democratize the violence in what he foresaw as the necessary war. The democratization of violence rooted in reason created an alternative to military dictatorships by providing a democratic and civilian discourse that exercised control and discipline over *caudillo* elements.

Martí, who witnessed how tyrants arose throughout Latinoamérica, feared militaristic ventures that could lead to despotic political structures. *Caudillos* were to be avoided at all costs in Cuba. He feared wars led by charismatic leaders rallying around their cause. In a letter from 9 October 1885 responding to an invitation by J. A. Lucena to speak in Philadelphia, Martí wrote that "tyranny is the same in its various forms, even when dressed with pompous names and mighty deeds."[41] He was suspicious of the generals planning for Cuba's final war for independence, fearing that they might betray the ideal of liberation and impose a dictatorship. Such expeditions were doomed to fail if they lacked a national moral compass. Martí's vision did not include a war that exchanged repression of the colonizer for that of a *caudillo*. He instead sought a social revolution in which the very character of the people changed, united in mutual respect for duty, justice, and equality.

Unfortunately for him, the generals Máximo Gómez and Antonio Maceo, heroes of the Ten Years' War, remained cognizant of how civilian political disagreements and interference hamstrung the military. They opposed the Zanjón Pact that brought an end to the war and blamed civilian leaders for caving. For them, success rested with a military junta. Both generals were unwilling to operate under civilian leadership, a point on which Martí was unyielding. At first, both military heroes viewed Martí with scorn, an upstart lacking credibility or credentials who did not participate in the Ten Years' War, and also naïve concerning the problems associated with war making.[42] Furthermore, Gómez, who viewed civilian government as "effeminate,"[43] curtly dismissed Martí: "Look, Martí, limit yourself to what the instructions say, and as for the rest, General Maceo will do what he thinks should be done."[44] This impasse led to a break that lasted several years. In a letter to General Gómez from 20 October 1884, two days after being dismissed by him, Martí explained why he was withdrawing his support from revolutionary activities: "It is my determination not to contribute one iota, due to a blind love for an idea guiding my entire life, to bring to my country a regime of personal despotism, more shameful and baleful than the political despotism that now endures, and more severe and difficult to eradicate because it would be excused when it arrives as some virtues, established by the idea it embodies, and legitimized by its triumph. A nation is not founded, General, as a military camp is commanded."[45]

Some six years after this break with the generals, Martí began imagining in earnest how to bring about independence, still concerned with the threat of *caudillos*. The breach was eventually mended when Gómez relented and reconciled with the poet on 11 September 1892. A shaky reconciliation took place with Maceo the next year, in July 1893.

While he eventually won over the military heroes, tensions remained; one is left wondering whether Martí, who until launching the War for Independence never engaged in armed conflict, was romanticizing war, no matter how noble he may have thought it was. When musing on Odin's great hall Valhalla, site of the eschatological feast denied to those who die peaceful deaths, he wrote in his notebook: "How beautiful! Only those who have engaged in battle enter heaven and sit next to God!"[46] Whether he romanticized war or not, one thing is certain: he justified its pursuit as the necessary means. But to engage in armed struggle required a moral foundation. If praxis is revolutionary, then a certain violence must be accounted for, because "rights are taken, not asked for; they are seized, not begged for";[47] they are "conquered with sacrifices."[48] Martí understood that "great rights are not bought with tears, but with blood."[49]

"Every man of justice and honor," he wrote, "fights for liberty wherever he sees her offended, because this is the same as fighting for his integrity as a man. But he who sees liberty offended, and does not fight for her, or helps those who offend her,—is not a whole man."[50] Violence is an act of macho love, a means by which "men" become whole. Love for the other encompasses seeking the liberation of the other and defending the rights of the other by whatever means necessary. In a tribute to the Protestant minister Henry Ward Beecher, Martí claimed that "the best way to serve God is to be liberated and to ensure freedom is not impaired."[51] Ensuring that freedom for Cuba was not impaired meant, without a doubt, employing violence. But does this call for violence empower those who see themselves as Martí's legitimate heirs to use violence against their perceived enemies? After all, like the concept of love, a perfect dualism existed for Martí when it came to justifying violence. Sin and evil resided both in individual persons and in social structures: "On the rough stonework both hands, the white and the black. May God dry up the first hand that rises against the other!"[52]

Should Martí be held responsible for Cuba's bloody history since its 1895 War for Independence as his self-proclaimed disciples unleashed violence upon their compatriots? As the *martiano* scholar Rafael Tarragó argues, belittling recourse to law and political compromise can find legitimacy in Martí's works: "Cuban revolutionaries have found in [Martí's writings] a treasure trove of thoughts and words praising war and belittling political compromise, which they have interpreted as legitimizing their causes."[53] Tellingly, on the last page of his children's book *La edad de oro*, Martí ends: "Before everything was settled with fists. Now, strength is in knowledge, more so than in punches. There are always beastly people in the world, thus it is good to learn how to defend oneself, because strength makes one healthy, and because one needs to be ready to fight, for when a thievery person wants to steal our nation."[54] Having declared oneself heir to Martí's thoughts, as has every political regime since the start of the Republic, opponents fighting for power in Martí's name are then designated among the thieves wanting to steal the Cuban nation to justify the violence unleashed upon them—and vice versa.

Martí deserves praise for his commitment to liberation, yet one must wonder whether his dichotomies of just and unjust ignore the messiness of life. In an 1889 letter to his longtime friend Serafín Bello he advised him, "Yield to the just and the unjust will fall by itself."[55] And while he attempts to define what is just through consciousness raising, he seems to ignore that, all too often, the disenfranchised seldom have clear choices between just and unjust. The reality of the human condition usually leads to choices between what is unjust and what is more unjust. Maybe such clear dichotomies play well in rhetorical speeches geared toward unifying a diverse crowd behind a revolutionary act, but they seldom afford the philosophical wrestling required for the oppressed, who are relegated to a more ambiguous human existence and faced with the challenge of committing to the lesser unjust praxis in an embrace of the vain hope that one day justice will reign. For example, while Martí through sleight of hand justifies violence as necessary and just in the cause of liberation, it might be more honest to confess that violence is always unjust and wrong, but in life's complexities, the wrong act might be the least damning choice among a multitude of bad choices with no clear, right, or just act available. Missing from Martí's analysis is how to achieve justice when the simple right-wrong dichotomy fails.

Establishing Justice

Some have ignored Martí's commitment to justice by portraying him as an idealistic romantic. But we do him a disservice if we relegate him solely to the realm of a dreamer. Martí may very well have been a dreamer, but he dreamed with open eyes fixed on a future liberative point that he believed could be reached only through praxis, or as he said during an 1891 speech in Tampa, "We work for truths and not for dreams."[56] As a man of action—no matter how futile—Martí believed that "the times are for Sisyphus to push rocks to the peak of the mountain and not for Jeremiah to cry over lifeless ruins."[57] He believed a day of judgment was coming when the acts of our lives would rise up and give testimony for or against us. As he wrote in a 12 January 1892 letter to Enrique Collazo, who accused him of cowardliness and defrauding tobacco workers six days earlier in the Habana paper *La Lucha*: "If my life defends me, I cannot cite anything to protect me more than her. And if my life accuses me, I cannot say anything which lends credence. Defend me my life."[58] He understood that words were cheap, and all too often, people spoke and wrote against injustices in safety rather than participating in action, no matter how futile those acts might have been.

Martí noted that "when the book of the Hebrews wanted to name an admirable young man, they called him just."[59] If God is love, then God must be the God of justice. Martí struggled for liberation in the name of that God and in the name of justice, a concept he began to develop at the young age of eighteen, shortly after his imprisonment: "Not in the name of that integrity of the land which does not fit in a well-organized mind, nor in the name of that vision which has greatly change; but in the name of the integrity of true honor, the integrity of the bonds of protection and love which you [Spain] never should have broken. In the name of the good, supreme God, in the name of justice, supreme truth, I implore compassion for those who suffer in [political] prison."[60] But what was justice for Martí? How did he define and understand it?

"Justice," Martí argued when commenting on the 1877 New Codes initiated by Guatemalan president Justo Barrios limiting the power of the church and securing freedom of the press, "is and wants the accommodation of the positive Right to the natural."[61] In short, he sought actions oblige to natural rights (what today we might call social rights), such as to a family, to an education, to work, to a standard of living, to health, to social security, to a safe and healthy environment. For justice to flourish, a political component must exist for Martí in which justice manifests as natural rights and leads to the wholeness of humanity. The political rights necessary to ensure natural rights include the rights to a self-determined identity, to human freedom, to be protected from governmental repression of body or mind, to participate in civil discourse and the political life of the state, to organize, and to not be judged according to skin color—rights, unfortunately, never achieved in the *patria* Martí dreamed for. Justice and its pursuit have always undergirded his writings. "This is my dream, everyone's dream," he exclaimed during his 1891 speech in Tampa. "Palm trees are waiting brides, and we must establish justice as tall as the palms!"[62] In a eulogy to Ulysses S. Grant published shortly after his death, Martí noted: "One fights as long as there is a reason to, since Nature placed the need for justice in some souls, and in others to ignore and obey. As long as justice is not achieved, one fights."[63] This duty of establishing justice becomes a religious quest encompassing all of humanity, for "to do justice is to do it for all of us."[64] Or as he stated elsewhere: "Liberty is not for one's own pleasure, it is a duty to extend to others."[65]

But how did he arrive at what was just? According to Martí, we are guided by "the God within," which for him is consciousness, or what he calls in his notebook "the God Consciousness."[66] Possessing a God Consciousness is crucial in determining what is good or evil, especially when oppressive authorities, seeking to normalize and legitimize unjust powers and privileges, label good as evil. What is considered evil—money laundering, gun running, and violent acts to overthrow the established government—became for Martí acts of justice. He found comradeship with those whom the authorities called criminals. From a Haitian border town, prior to embarking to Cuba to fight for liberation, he noted in his diary: "When tariffs are unfair, or resent the law of the border, contraband is the right of insurrection. In the smuggler one sees bravery, one who takes risks; astute, who deceives the powerful; the rebel, in whom others see and admire. Contraband comes to be loved and defended, like true justice."[67] For Martí, pursuing justice provides its own strength: "All together we can . . . Being all together, it seems like we are more, we will have victory; but we will not succeed if we do not have justice on our side. Because a single man with justice is stronger than a multitude without it. In order to overcome in reality our enemies, we must overcome them morally. Whosoever convinces an enemy they are not right, has already won. Nothing is accomplished without the internal God."[68]

Economic Imperialism

Crucial to José Martí is a commitment to understanding the causes of poverty, a commitment that eventually would be shared by those who referred to themselves nearly a century later as liberation theologians. This commitment was not an attempt to encourage greater charity toward the poor; instead, the focus was on understanding why poverty exists. During the late 1880s, the United States—with its Manifest Destiny visions of unity—began in earnest to restructure its monetary relationship with América Latina, a blatant attempt to seize hemispheric economic power. With the 1878 presidential veto override, the Bland-Allison Compromise Silver Act required the U.S. Treasury to purchase and mint silver for circulation, a response to a worldwide movement to demonetize silver. The United States and France called a conference to fashion a ratio between silver and gold, establishing international bimetallism (the equalizing of gold and silver currency at a fixed rate of exchange). Fourteen nations met in Paris during April 1878 and again in 1881. While there existed sympathy for bimetallism, the inability of Germany and England to act led to the conference's failure. But failure in Europe motivated U.S. Secretary of State James G. Blaine to seek success elsewhere.[69]

Blaine, a dominant political figure of the time, was a former Speaker of the House (1869–1875) and senator (1876–1881) who distinguished himself as an advocate for the interests of big business. In 1876 he made a bid for the presidency but was derailed over accusations of influence peddling, for having sold worthless bonds to Union Pacific Railroad for $64,000. He went on to serve as secretary of state in both the Garfield administration and the Harrison administration, in which he positioned himself both times as spokesperson for U.S. imperialist designs. Between the two administrations, he garnered the 1884 Republican nomination for the presidency but lost to Grover Cleveland. Martí was quite critical of Blaine: "Blaine, who speaks the ruffian's slang, who stands with the Irish against England, and with the English against Ireland, . . . who abuses the great name of his people so that those who are belligerent can recognize his impure obligations; Blaine, versatile and unruly, perceptive and dreaded, never great; . . . Blaine, marketable, true to himself, buys and sells in the market of men."[70]

In 1889, Blaine organized the first Pan-American Conference, inviting seventeen nations from América Latina to Washington from 2 October through 19 August 1890. The U.S. bimetallism strategy, if adopted throughout the hemisphere, would greatly enrich the United States, the largest silver producer in the world at that time. Most of the Américas and Europe lacked silver—with the exception of Mexico and Peru. Thus, if the conference proved successful, América Latina would become dependent on the U.S. economy, contributing to its own impoverishment. Blaine envisioned imposing his economic designs on the Western Hemisphere as a first step before eventually springing back to Europe. He envisioned a *pax americana* in which the United States positioned itself as the sun around which all other Latin American countries revolved. Martí realized Blaine's designs.[71] Writing to his friend Gonzalo de Quesada, who served as assistant to the chief Argentine delegate to the conference, he succinctly exposed the hidden agenda of the conference when it came to Cuba: "Upon our land, Gonzalo, there is a shadier plan, which till now we know about. It is to force the island to precipitate a war, serving as a pretext for intervening, credited as a mediator and guarantor. There is nothing more cowardly found in the annals of free peoples, nor colder evil."[72]

Martí attempted to have influence indirectly through his friend de Quesada.[73] Furthermore, he sought to raise the consciousness of other countries of América Latina through articles in their newspapers. For example, he wrote in *La Nación*:

There has never been in América, from its independence to the present, a matter which requires more sensibility, or the highest vigilance, or demands a clearer and thorough analysis than the invitation by the powerful United States. This powerful country, glutted with unsellable products and determined to extend their domains in América, seek to make the less powerful nations in the Américas, bound by free and useful trade with European nations, to adjust their alliance against Europe, and stop trade with the rest of the world. Spanish América was saved from the tyranny of Spain. Now, after seeing with judicial eyes the antecedents, causes and factors of the [U.S.] invitation, it is urgent to say—because it is true—that the time has come for Spanish América to declare her second independence.[74]

Unfortunately for Blaine, the conference, like the one in Paris, ended without resolution, but this did not stop him from trying again. He organized and held a second international monetary conference in Washington from January to April 1891. Frustrated at the launching of a second attempt to impose economic colonialism upon América Latina, Martí wrote in the prologue of his *Versos sencillos*:

It was that winter of anguish, when, through ignorance, or fanatical faith, or fear, or civility, Spanish American nations met in Washington under the dreaded eagle. Who among us has forgotten that coat of arms bearing the eagle of Monterrey or Chapultepec [locations of Mexican defeat during the Mexican American War], the eagle of López [led an expedition to liberate Cuba in 1851], or Walker [invaded Nicaragua and set up a slavery-based empire], with the flags of the Américas clung to its talons? And the agony in which I lived until I could confirm the caution and determination of our nations? And the horror and shame in which I was had legitimate fear Cubans with parricidal hands aid the foolish plan to alienate Cuba, for the sole good of another crafty master, from the patria that claims her and perfects itself in her, from the Spanish American *patria*?—for forces depleted by unjust pains were taken away.[75]

The purpose of the second conference was twofold: to lobby delegates from the Américas in support of bimetallism and to pressure delegates to sever their economic ties with Europe and instead increase trade with the United States. Success of the conference would make América Latina only more dependent on the U.S. economy. Martí again played a pivotal role in frustrating Blaine's designs when several countries selected him as their representative. During the conference Martí served on both the credentials committee and on the committee tasked with debating the U.S. bimetallism proposal. He was, after all, well versed in economic theory, serving as editor of two journals that focused on commercial relations with the Américas.[76] Representing Uruguay, Argentina, and Paraguay, Martí distinguished himself as leader of the non-silver-producing nations.

Much depended on the conference's success. Success could boost Blaine's political aspirations, and maybe another run for the presidency. He might well have succeeded if not for the tenacity of Martí. Almost singlehandedly, Martí prevented Blaine's objectives from materializing. Although successful, the experience left Martí deeply troubled by the unapologetic attempt at U.S. hegemony. He became convinced the United States would stand as an obstacle in any future attempt to establish a free Cuba. In a report he wrote and presented to the conference on behalf of América Latina's delegation, Martí argued: "It is not the province of the American continent to disturb the world with new factors of rivalry and discord, nor to reestablish, with new methods and names, the imperial system through which republics come to corruption and death. It is not the province of the American continent to raise one world against another, nor to mass in haste elements of diverse nature . . . The hands of every nation must remain free for the untrammeled development of the country in accordance with its distinctive nature and with its individual elements."[77]

This would not be the last time the United States tried to control the fate of América Latina. Decades later, organizations formed like the International Monetary Fund (1944) and the World Bank (1944), organizations with a similar rhetoric of fraternity and a similar purpose of domination. As did Martí, liberation theologians have denounced the complicity that the policies of those organizations have had with the poverty of their countries.

Solidarity with the Oppressed

Solidarity with the oppressed in a major tenet of liberation theology. Standing with those who face injustice is a duty, regardless of personal cost. In May 1877, Martí, thanks to the efforts of his compatriot José María Izaguirre—director of the Escuela Normal Central of Guatemala— was offered a professorship in French, English, Italian, and German literature and history of philosophy. This was his first teaching post, and it provided him a livelihood that made his marriage to Carmen Zayas possible. But by April 1878, with the rise of right-wing elements in the increasing despotic regime of José Rufino Barrios, Izaguirre was fired on frivolous grounds. As an act of solidarity Martí, with no other prospects in hand, resigned his post in principle and left the country. According to Izaguirre, Martí told him, "I will resign, though my wife and I might die of hunger. I prefer this than being complicit with an injustice."[78]

"Those despisers of the poor," Martí wrote, "seems like maggots to me."[79] Martí was always quick to cast his lot with *los de abajo* (those from below), with *los humildes* (the humble) and *los pobres de la tierra* (the poor of the land): "With the oppressed, common cause has to be made, to strengthen the system opposed to the interests and habits of oppressors' rule."[80] Martí's writings advocated "a preferential option for the poor" decades before the term became foundational to liberative theological thought. Through his actions, he voluntarily lived a life on the economic margins, resisting the U.S. cult of conspicuous consumption. Among his more popular *Versos sencillos*, he wrote, "With the poor of the land / I want to cast my lot: / A mountain stream / Means more than does the sea. / Give to the vain the yielding gold / That burns and glistens in the crucible: / But give me the eternal forest / When the sun breaks through."[81]

In his mind, a link exited between those suffering and those necessarily unaware of the suffering of the oppressed: "As long as there is an unhappy man, there is a culpable man!"[82] With whom does divinity stand? With whom does God stand during the struggle for justice— with the unfortunate dispossessed or with those culpable of their disenfranchisement? Martí wrestled with these questions while observing the great personal cost suffered by Father McGlynn's decision to stand in solidarity with the oppressed of his parish (see Chapter 2). Martí ended his article on the schism McGlynn was causing by asking, "Oh Jesús! Where would you have stood in this struggle? Accompanied [as Bishop Ducey] by the rich [banker] thief to Canada, or in the little poor house where Father McGlynn waits and suffers?"[83] The bishop not only stood against the poor; he stood against a God who sides with the poor. In the same article Martí asked: "Who sins? Is it the one who abuses his authority in the things of dogma from the sacred chair to immorally favor those who sell the law in payment of the Vow which placed them in a condition to dictate it; or the one knowing that on the side of the poor there is nothing but bitterness, consoles them in the temple as priest, and assists them outside the temple as citizen?"[84]

The church often fails to stand in solidarity with the oppressed, instead siding with those who are powerful and successful;[85] this equals a preferential option for the privileged and wealthy: "Vanity and pomp continues in the work initiated by faith; disdaining humble people to whom they owe their establishment and abundance, raising royal Churches on the streets of the rich . . . so as to appear before the alarmed rich as the only power who with its subtle influence on the spirits can restrain the fearsome march of the poor."[86] Church power is maintained by keeping the humble of the earth ignorant, which is why Martí advised not bringing his writings to the priests: "Do not go and teach this book to the priest of your town, for he is interested in keeping you in the dark, so that all of you must go and ask of him."[87]

The God of churches who choose to stand in solidarity with the powerful and privileged worship a God who justifies their social location and fails to convict them of their complicity with oppressive structures. Such a God must be rejected: "That God [of the Catholic Church] who haggles, who sells salvation, who does everything in exchange for money, who sends people to Hell if they do not pay, and if they are paid, they are sent to Heaven, that God is a type of moneylender, usurer, discharger of debt for money. No, my friend, there is another God!"[88] The God of the church who watches over the reigning institutional violence that creates disenfranchisement, dispossession, and disinheritance for the benefit of ecclesial institutions and their wealthy patrons must be rejected in favor of the other God, the one in whom

Martí believed. Through faithfulness to the teachings (not doctrines) of Jesús and humanist reason, radical solidarity with those being crushed could be established in accordance with God's teachings.

For the liberationist, solidarity with the oppressed placed one in solidarity with God, for God resides among poor oppressed workers more so than in any cathedral or house of worship: "More, much more than entering a temple a hundred times, is the soul moved to enter, on a cold February dawn, one of the vehicles which transports from slums to factories artisans of cheated dresses, wholesome weather-beaten face with skillful hands, at that hour when a newspaper is idle. There is a great priest, a living priest: the worker."[89] For Martí, the disenfranchised, the true priests, possess the preferential option of God because they are closer to the truth of the Gospel: "As always, the humble, the barefoot, the needy, the fishermen band together shoulder to shoulder to fight iniquity and make the Gospel fly with its silver wings aflame! Truth is best revealed to the poor and the suffering! A piece of bread and a glass of water never cheat!"[90]

And while Martí was usually prone to clear dichotomies, he did not fall into the trap of describing the rich as always unjust and wrong and the poor as always just and right: "When the poor exaggerates their rights, they override their pretensions in good time. No one has a right to hurt another, but to repudiate as creatures that stain and shame to those whose patient and admirable virtues would not for a single day be capable to imitate those who repudiate them, such a vileness worthy of public punishment."[91] The theological task is not to reverse roles between those who are oppressed and those who are privileged, or to share the role of privileged at the expense of some other newer group upon which to take advantage, but to dismantle the very structures responsible for causing injustices—to create a new way of being, a revolutionary society, a *nueva iglesia*. These justice-based praxes, engaged in transforming society, bring individuals closer to understanding the spiritual.

Unlike the church, Martí's radical solidarity was not paternalistic. As he wrote in a Key West newspaper, "The lowering of a man reduces me."[92] By linking his status to how others were treated, he recognized the important role of the oppressed in creating a justice-based *patria*.

Such a *patria* was not just for the disenfranchised; for "if the Republic does not open its arms to all and advances with all, the Republic dies."[93] Past revolutions, Martí noted, were led by and for the upper class. But he saw a different type of revolution trajectory for the Américas: "In América, the revolution is in its initial stage. We have to finish it. The upper class's intellectual revolution has been done, it's all here. And from this has come more evils than goods."[94] His outreach to the economically struggling cigar workers throughout Florida was his attempt to create an economically and racially inclusive revolutionary movement.

Like most liberative thinkers, Martí had a preferential option for the oppressed; however, he did not necessarily center the call for solidarity on Christian thought or beliefs. What is moral is rooted in neither church dogmas nor enlightened universal truths but rather in the lives of those who sought the good for the marginalized. Since 1871, Martí focused a portion of his writing on biographical sketches, serving as an ethical methodology based on a relational motif of imitation. He embraced what today we would call narrative ethics, an approach similar to virtue ethics that relies on the life stories of individuals as the basis for moral reflection. By recounting fragments of biographies, specifically of those excluded and marginalized, he sought to provide examples of ethical behavior that should be emulated. What comes to represent ethical and moral behavior are the virtues narrated in the biographies Martí recounts, examples of what he expects would represent how to be citizens of the *patria* he envisioned.

Solidarity with the oppressed is an epistemological path by which to develop reason, by which to discover a way of thinking closer to truth. Martí wrote in his article "The Truth about the United States," "One must keep with the poor, weep with the destitute, abhor the brutality of wealth, live in both mansion and tenement, in the school's reception hall and in its vestibule, in the gilt and jasper theater box and in the cold, bare wings. In this way a man can form opinions, with glimmers of reason, about the authoritarian and envious Republic and the growing materialism of the United States."[95] This praxis of solidarity must be learned, lessons that should begin early in life. In his collection of children's stories, *La edad de oro*, is the poem titled "Los zapaticos de rosa" (The small pink shoes), among the most popular children's poem in Latinoamérica, memorized by generations of children. The poem is of a rich little girl in a feathered hat with pink shoes named Pilar who, while playing by the seashore, encounters a poor, frail, and shoeless little girl. She gives the girl her shoes, noting that she has many more at home.[96] Martí introduces class differences to children by making the teaching of Jesús concerning the giving of one's spare coat to the one who has none (Luke 3:11) accessible to children, lifting Pilar as an ethical example to imitate. An ethical relational motif that stresses imitation becomes the bases for teaching children (and adult compatriots) principles to create a more just society. The rich are not condemned simply because they are rich. What they do with their riches becomes the means of condemnation or redemption. His concern for the wealthy leads Martí to provide examples of solidarity with the poor, a praxis to be learned.

The focus of Martí's solidarity with the oppressed is praxis oriented. Action stands over and against doctrinal beliefs. The move to orthopraxis, or correct action, focuses on the goal of achieving liberation, spiritually as well as politically. He asks: "Would it not be better for the church's faithful to lift up these souls, clothing the naked and removing these bottles from [an alcoholic's] lips; rather than hearing commentaries about the beast of the Apocalypse, or rejoicing in the jabs exchanged by pastors of rival churches in their districts?"[97]

Praxis

As Martí prepared to sail to Cuba to engage in the final war for independence, he recognized the island as overrun by bandits who claimed allegiance to revolutionary movements, justifying their selfish actions as stealing from the rich to give to the poor. In spite of such rhetoric, few of the poor who supposedly benefited from their activities believed their motives.[98] When Martí was offered substantial financial support from one such bandit, Manuel García, known as "El Rey de los Campos," or King of the Countryside, who terrorized planters through robbery and kidnapping, Martí refused his money. He responded to the offer by exclaiming that "the tree must grow healthy from its roots."[99] Seeking justice, for Martí, led to a deontological methodology. He believed the ends to achieve liberation do not justify the means.

As important as education was for Martí, he had no patience for intellectuals who hid behind their diplomas, pontificating about the world's injustices without ever lifting a finger to tilt the scales toward liberation. In a tribute, written in English, to the Russian poet Alexander Pushkin, Martí wrote: "The hand must follow the inspiration of the intellect," and "It is not enough to write a patriotic strophe: you must live it."[100] Although a prolific writer, Martí insisted that "doing is the best way of saying."[101] He summed up the link between his words and praxis in a 1 April 1895 letter to his friend Gonzalo de Quesada, the day he took the schooner *Brothers* for the Bahamas, making his way to Cuba to launch the revolution: "You already know that serving is my best way to talk."[102] As a young man, in an 1882 letter to another friend, Manuel Mercado, Martí confessed that for months "whole editions [of writings] piled up because life thus far has not given me enough to demonstrate I am a poet in acts. I fear that releasing my verses to be known before my actions, the people will go to believe that I am just like so many others, a poet in verses."[103] Using the abolitionist John Brown as an example to emulate, mainly because Brown advocated armed insurrection as the means to eradicate slavery, Martí noted: "The fire of martyrs and apostles reignites. The ardor of the generous floats among the apathetic. John Brown offers himself in sacrifice and turns the idea into action."[104] "The duty of a man," Martí wrote to his mother in his final letter to her, "lies where he is most useful."[105]

For Martí, "justice does not bear children, but it is love who begets them!"[106] If love is indeed an action word, then justice-based praxis is the child of love. This is what Martí would call "love with explosions, not with words."[107] Throughout his writings and life, Martí denounced Spanish colonialism and U.S. imperialism as unjust, immoral, and un-Christian in both word and deed. But as important as his writing was, he always considered his actions paramount. The liberationist mantra of orthopraxis (correct action) over orthodoxy (correct doctrine) would have resonated with him. The praxis of establishing *patria*, understood as independent and justice based, was a holy duty, a faithfulness to a determined history in which the independence of the people is the destiny of the *patria*.

Rigorous engagement with philosophical thought was, for Martí, important only if linked to the act of transforming society. He showed little interest in or patience with pure speculative thinking, and less concern with developing a complete understanding of the metaphysical. Instead, he focused on developing knowledge to better humanity through the practical implementation of love-based justice. Doing, for Martí, was always more important than words, or even thought: "Before making a collection of my verses, I would like to make a collection of my deeds."[108] The *martiano* scholar Carlos Ripoll demonstrates how Martí's overriding desire to destroy oppressive structures led him to reduce abstract thoughts to concrete praxes, motivated by his religious commitment to duty.[109] The creation of liberation could simply not be reduced to political independence from Spain, because the struggle for political liberation was also a quest for spiritual liberation. A *Cuba libre* ceased being a parochial freedom movement.

Martí called for selfless actions as a duty, exhorting Cubans to place the needs and interest of *patria* before themselves. This is how one becomes, what he patriarchally calls, a man: "Man is an instrument of duty, this is how he becomes a man."[110] In an 1868 speech at Hardman Hall in New York, commemorating 10 October, he called for all Cubans to serve, subordinating their interests to the concerns of the overall society: "The true man does not look to see on which side one lives better, but on which side is duty."[111] *Sociabilidad* (sociability) becomes a spiritual duty associated with *la nueva religión*, which Martí sought to frame in a larger universal and humanitarian project. To shrug off one's duty and seek self-interest was to steal from *patria*: "The egotistical man is a thief. The self-interested politician is a thief."[112] In a 25 March 1895 letter to the Dominican journalist Federico Henríquez y Carvajal, sent less than a week before he embarked to Cuba to participate in the battle for political liberation, Martí considered it immoral to initiate duty for personal glorification: "For me, *patria* will never be a triumph, but agony and duty."[113] The responsibility to fulfill one's universal duty to *la nueva religión* superseded duties one might have to parent, spouse, or even children. For Martí, *patria* came before family.

The quest for liberation required, then, a fundamental change or conversion within the essence of human identity. Such a conversion could occur only if compatriots undertook their responsibilities and duties as a call from *la nueva religión* in creating a new social order. Consequently, Martí downplayed intellectualism in favor of the praxes undertaken to bring about liberation for all and for the good of all. In his *Versos sencillos* he poetically wrote: "Being still, I understand, / And I remove the versifier's pomp, / And hang upon a withered tree / My doctoral robes."[114] Martí's understanding of *patria*'s existence depended on a consciousness raising in which humans become ethically aware of and active in the establishment of liberation, or as he often stated, "To think is to serve."[115] Pity the person who dies without leaving the fruits of praxis behind.

Referring to Wendell Phillips, the abolitionist and Native American advocate, Martí wrote: "An orator shines for his speeches; but remains for what he does. If his sentences are not sustained with his acts, even before his death, his fame evaporates because he has been standing on a column of smoke."[116] Martí surely could never be accused of standing on a column of smoke. The mere fact that he was able to accomplish the Herculean feat of organizing and launching a revolution speaks to his practical organization skills of incarnating his moral philosophy. Besides organizing a rebellion, Martí also engaged in the praxis of raising consciousness, which was crucial to Martí's thinking, for not fulfilling the duty to educate "[was] a crime."[117] Educating the next generation was too important to leave to the care of religious institutions. Not only did public education carry an awesome responsibility; children had a responsibility from an early age to learn something new each and every day. In *La edad de oro*, Martí warned young readers of the importance of learning: "It is better to be useful than be a prince. Children should burst into tears if a day passes without them learning something new, without them being useful."[118]

Raising Consciousness

In one of his notebooks, Martí defined consciousness as "the science of ourselves," an understanding both individual and conceivable.[119] But what happens when a people's consciousness is underdeveloped, when a community is not taught how to think or, worse, is taught to think the thoughts of their oppressors? Centuries of Cuban colonization led

Martí to wonder whether the Cuban people were destined to perpetually suffer from an inferiority complex: "Is Cuba to be nothing more but a tavern, a lazy brewery in San Jerónimo, an inn of the Four Nations? Or is it to be its own country, an industrious nation of the Américas? This, and nothing less, is the work of Cuba."[120] For Martí, the greatest impediment to liberation was an uneducated, colonized mind whose subservience to the dominant culture bordered on keen dedication. Only an educated Cuban community could work effectively to create a new *patria*. So crucial was education that it took precedence over the state's responsibility to feed the people: "Bread cannot be given to all who are in need . . . In every street a kindergarten . . . A city is guilty as long as it is not a school in its in entirety. The street that is not a school is a strain on the city's forehead."[121] An educated people, Martí believed, would naturally create a liberated *patria*, a people composed of "subjects" determined to reconstruct their social reality.

The enemy of conscious raising has long been the church. The historical role of Christendom on behalf of the state has been to convince the masses that they are not the victims of unjust social structures. Rather than religion paternalistically encouraging lethargy and ignorance so people remain obedient and dependent on political, economic, and social dominance, Martí strived to raise critical awareness of the unholy causes of oppression. Hence, education can never be reduced to a privilege; it is a right. Upon the foundation of education, liberation is constructed. In detail, Martí explained the importance of education in establishing *patria*:

> I. Instruction is not the same as education . . . II. Popular education does not exclusively mean education of the poor class, but all the classes of the nation, all the people are to be educated . . . all are equal. III. Whoever knows more is worth more. To know is to have. Coins melt, to know does not . . . The rich need their coins to live, but they can be lost, and if so, they lose the means by which to live. An educated man lives off his knowledge, and because it is part of him, he is not lost, and his existence is easy and secured. IV. The happiest people are those with better educated children, in the instruction of their thoughts and the direction of their sentiments. And educated

people loves work and knows how to take advantage of it . . . V. Every man who comes to Earth has the right to be educated, then, in return, has the duty to contribute to the education of others. VI. An ignorant people can be deceived with superstition and made servile. An educated people will always be strong and free. An ignorant man is on his way in becoming a beast, while a man who is educated in science and in conscience is already on the path to become God. There is no doubt between a people composed of Gods and a people composed of beasts. The best way to defend our rights is to know them well . . . An educated society will always be a free society. Education is the only means of saving oneself from slavery.[122]

Education was also a safeguard against fanaticism, which all too often became the legitimized norm. Through education, he explained to his friend Miguel F. Viondi in an 1880 letter, "the impossible is possible. We lunatics are sane."[123] While one is called to act according to one's conscience, this can never become an excuse for fanaticism, a state of mind Martí abhorred: "He who believes they are entitled to give a reason, has the duty to hear the one who gives him a response."[124] Consciousness raising is the antidote to such blind faith, for which Martí had little patience. "Fanatics are evil," he writes in his notebook. "Everything in life has its song and poem. But the fanaticism poem is terrible. The Circus of Rome, the Saint Barthèlemy of France, the Inquisition of Spain—horrible songs. Nero, Catalina de Medici, Torquemada, barbarian singers."[125]

The worst form of occupation for Martí was not necessarily the land, but the mind, which can be liberated by raising consciousness through reason as an act of love. He argued that "the first to be liberated, the basis of all others, is that of the mind."[126] This is probably the main motivation behind Martí's prolificacy: his attempt to guide and teach future generations of citizens what it meant to live and practice the moral and civic virtues held by patriots who have learned to decolonize their minds. For Martí, "there is no greater delight than to see men battling with liberty and faith for what seems to be true. Just as there is no greater painful spectacle than submissive men, due to their ignorance or emotions or self-interest, to a foreign will."[127] The occupation of the mind was not limited to those whose lands were physically occupied by foreign powers. Martí recognized the danger of developing a colonized mind among those who were living in exile.

A hazard exists when the exiled learns to see reality through the eyes of a dominant culture, especially if said culture embraces white supremacy. The exiled soon learns to elevate the social context through the dominant culture's epistemology, a process that leads to a loss of identity, if not downright hostility toward one's own culture after long separation: "The education of son of a small country by a people of an opposite character and superior wealth, could lead the student to a fatal opposition to the native country where he must apply his education— or lead to the worst and most shameful human misfortune, the distain of his people."[128] Integral to consciousness raising must be the rejection of Eurocentric paradigms justifying the colonial venture and their methodologies designed to implement an educational system that normalizes and legitimizes said venture. This quest to decolonize one's mind is as much a spiritual as a political mission: "Neither literary originality is achieved, nor political freedom subsist until spiritual liberation is secured. The first task of man is to reconquer himself."[129]

Decades before European philosophers engaged in a postcolonial discourse, Martí had already developed his own form of thinking that attempted to move beyond Eurocentric modernity. Before postcolonialism became fashionable among Eurocentric intellectuals, Martí was among the first colonized persons to create a space in his writings for a worldview apart and separate from colony and empire, apart and separate from the Eurocentric worldview and the philosophy that normalized and legitimized that worldview, even though his Latinoamérica-focused *modernismo* still relied on the concept of liberation and the importance of rational thought. He elucidated an alternative to a Eurocentric colonialism that was accepted as the normative and legitimate prevailing discourse of his time, even by those also subjugated to the colonial venture. We can summarize Martí's call to action, his call to liberation, the root of all he attempted to create, in one of his best-known phrases: "Our wine from plantains; and if it turns out sour, it's our wine!"[130] Creating a new wine called *patria* was the means by which the mind could be decolonized.

Martí was prolific because through writing he contributed to the raising of his compatriots' consciousness. "Publish, publish," he wrote in a January 1892 letter to Ángel Peláez, a friend and organizer from Key West: "To Cuba through every opportunity. Wars advance on roads of paper. Let them not fear us but desire us. May they eventually have confidence in us. For it is easier to invade a country which stretches their arms, than a country which turns its back to us. To open arms by the force of love, and by the strength of reason open their judgment."[131] Writing, the form of labor in which scholar-activists like Martí engaged, provided an educational foundation of responsible citizens in need of learning how to think, to reason, to discern. If, as Martí wrote, "to read is to work," then the act of writing is a revolutionary activity.[132] Despots fear an educated constituency, a people who write, read, think. "Intelligence," Martí wrote, "produces goodness, justice and beauty. Like a wing, it raises the spirit. Like a crown, it makes the one wearing it a monarch."[133] Succinctly put, to think for oneself is a human right. "To think," Martí wrote, "is to foresee."[134]

Consciousness raising, through education, is the best defense against oppressors, foreign and domestic. Those who suffer deeper disenfranchisement, Martí believed, can become the source of their own liberation through education. Commenting on the disadvantage of workers who lacked educational opportunities, Martí wrote: "Not until laborers are educated will they be happy. At times passion makes justice odious. The reason is like a colossal arm, which raises Justice beyond the reach of greedy men. To the ignorant laborers, who want curt remedies to the evil they feel, but whose origins they do not grasp, will always be overcome by the interests of capitalist disguised in sheep's clothing for social convenience and prudence."[135] If liberation were truly a grassroots movement, fermenting and rising from the underside of power and privilege, then education would be the way to achieve it.

In a December 1882 letter to Bartolomé Mitre y Vedia, director of the Argentine newspaper *La Nación*, Martí advocated for "mak[ing] the eyes clean of prejudices in all fields."[136] Part of seeking knowledge requires a hermeneutical suspicion. Whatever truth might be; it can never contradict reason achieved experientially: "You cannot see something without looking at it. You cannot understand something without examining it. The examination is the eye of reason. We ourselves are the first means of knowing things, the means of natural investigation, the means of natural philosophy."[137] For Martí, all social reforms could be realized through education, an education that almost a century later, Paulo Freire would refer to as *conscientização*. Martí predated what Freire would eventually call the banking model of education, which treated students as empty vessels, like piggy banks, to be filled with knowledge.[138] Martí instead argued that "the professor should not be a vessel where students cast their intelligence and character, resulting in a wen and ruin; but an honest guide, who teaches in good faith what must be seen, and explains its pros as well as the opposing position, so that the student's character as a man is strengthened, which is the flower which should not dry up in the herbarium of universities."[139]

Liberation for Martí required self-actualization, a sociopolitical and historical awareness facilitated by education: "Every seed that is sown into the soul blooms and fructifies,"[140] he wrote in 1881 in a notebook. This education was not limited to the abstract. He called for night schools where workers could also be students, learning everything from the alphabet to critical thinking.[141] In 1890, he cofounded and served as a night instructor at La Liga de Instrucción in New York, a school dedicated to freely educating future revolutionaries, most of whom were Cuban Black laborers. Rather than participating in frivolous entertainment, Martí strived to bring about liberation through a commitment in raising the consciousness of people: "The best entertainment is to plant souls."[142]

Martí called for free kindergartens, especially in poor neighborhoods.[143] He also called for "a traveling body of teachers."[144] In his essay "Maestros Ambulantes" (Ambulatory Teachers), he rejected Eurocentric higher education models of situating education in centralized urban settings.[145] Instead, he envisioned a redistribution of educational opportunities by having teachers go to where education was most needed, among rural peasants and workers. "The cities are the minds of nations," he wrote, "but its heart, where it beats and distributes blood, is in the countryside. Men are still eating-machines, a reliquary of preoccupations. It is necessary to make of each man a torch."[146] Just as military service was obligatory, so too should there be an obligatory service for teachers to serve the poor.[147]

Martí's commitment to education has been shared by different political regimes since his death. The Sergeant's Revolt of 1933 led by Fulgencio Batista attempted to incarnate Martí's vision of *maestros ambulantes*. To that end, the Batista regime built education centers in rural areas and attempted to recruit *maestros cívicos rurales* (rural civic teachers). Unfortunately, these civic military projects bore little fruit. As the historian Alfonso Quiroz documents, regardless of the sums allocated to the national budget to make public education a priority, rampant corruption diverted crucial resources.[148] Corruption was obvious. When Batista fled the island on New Year's Eve in 1959, he had been able to accumulate a personal fortune of about US$300 million—already in foreign banks and representing one-quarter of all government expenditures.[149] Regardless of one's opinion concerning the 1959 Castro-led Revolution, there is no denying that no other Cuban government since 1898 has done more to bring about Martí's vision of an educated Cuba. Free education became a cornerstone of the 1959 Cuban Revolution. During the start of the 1961 literacy campaign, termed the "Year of Education," some one hundred thousand student teachers (many of whom were teenagers) donned uniforms, took up oil lanterns, and traveled the rural backroads to reach a million inhabitants in an effort to abolish illiteracy within a year. The campaign was a success by any measure; in 2018, Cuba boasted a 99.75% literacy rate.

Consciousness raising, commitment to praxis, solidarity with the oppressed, seeking justice, and the evangelism of love are but a few of the liberative commitments Martí made in his quest to establish *patria*. These components of his political theology, no doubt, resonate with what would come to be known as liberation theology. To complete the argument of Martí as precursor to liberation theology, we now turn to the last chapter, where we will explore the similarities and incongruities with some of the basic assumptions of Martí's liberative theological thought.

FIVE

Theological Assumptions

To die is nothing, to die is to live, to die is to plant. Whosoever dies, if they die where they should—serve.

THE FORTY-TWO-YEAR-OLD JOSÉ MARTÍ died in battle on 19 May
1895. Hours before his life was cut short by Spaniards' bullets, he gave a
speech to the troops, a speech that Colonel José Miró described as given
"with the fervor of an apostle."[1] According to a 19 May diary entry by
General Máximo Gómez, which became the official (though disputed)
record of that day, eight hundred Spanish forces under the command of
General José Jiménez de Sandoval led a surprise attack two hours after
Martí's speech on three hundred rebel soldiers—the combined forces
of Gómez and Masó at Dos Ríos. Gómez hastily organized a counter-
offensive and rushed into the fray after giving strict orders for Martí to
remain in the rear flank, where he would be relatively safe. Stubbornly
disobeying Gómez's orders, Martí saddled a white horse and followed
Gómez into battle, charging a Spanish position with a revolver in his
hand. Lacking any military experience, Martí died before his time, an
anticlimactic end to an extraordinary life. He was shot in the neck
and chest; his body captured by the Spaniards and taken to the town
of Remanganaguas, where it was initially buried in a common grave.[2]

On 23 May, under Spanish authorization, his body was exhumed and provided a proper Christian burial at the cemetery of Santa Ifigenia, which had been established in 1868 in the northwestern part of Santiago de Cuba to accommodate those who died during the first War for Independence. There his remains would stay. For over half a century, his tomb was too simple to house a giant, so a mausoleum worthy of his stature was constructed in 1951 in his honor. The architect Mario Santí, whose blueprints for a new construction won an open competition of 1946, designed the hundred-foot hexagonal tower so that a ray of sunshine always rested upon the coffin—so that Martí would lay "con cara al sol," or with his face to the sun. Built during the corrupt reign of Prío Socarrás (1948–1952), Santí faced constant budget cuts, which made the task of completing the mausoleum difficult.

His son, Enrico Mario Santí, would eventually break a promise made to his father and share a family secret concerning Martí's remains. According to the younger Santí, his father made a startling discovery when moving the remains from one part of the cemetery to the newly constructed mausoleum. While lifting the lead and concrete catafalque that contained Martí's remains from the ground with a crane, the senior Santí noticed water leaking from a wide, moldy hole on one of the corners. Fearing the catafalque was damaged by the crane, he ordered his assistant to set the structure down. When they opened the catafalque to ensure the remains were intact and undamaged, the two men made a startling discovery: the tomb was empty. They concluded that the crane was not responsible for the damage. The presence of mold around the hole led them to believe an underground stream, over the decades, drilled the hole from which the water drained. Santí's son, Enrico Mario, determined that "the remains that had rested there once had long since departed with the stream that had gotten inside the tomb, and had now become part of the Cuban soil."[3] The two men swore each other to secrecy as an empty tomb, if they are to be believed, was placed in a mausoleum designed to hold the earthly remains of Martí.

Santí's claim concerning his father's confession has been questioned and critiqued. But discussion of the tomb as empty or not is not the purpose of retelling this story. It would be a stretch to make a Chris-

FIGURE 1. Martí's mausoleum at the cemetery of Santa Ifigenia in Santiago de Cuba. Photograph by BluesyPete, licensed under CC BY-SA 3.0. Courtesy of Wikimedia Commons.

tological claim—for no one is arguing Martí's resurrection in the way Christians understands Jesús' empty tomb—but still, there is something poetic about Martí being resurrected in the soil of the country from which he was exiled for the majority of his life. More important than the beauty of having Martí's essence become one with the land for which he longed, for our purposes, is how his liberative thoughts can become one with the people who would inhabit the *patria* he envisioned. Is such a resurrection of his religious political thoughts even possible? If Martí was indeed a precursor to liberation theology, as I have argued, then it behooves us to explore some of his theological understandings—not to fit them into a neat liberative category but to explore their complexities, paying attention to areas of congruence and areas of real differences.

God

In a 26 November 1889 letter to his friend Manuel Mercado, Martí explained why *La edad de oro* had ceased publication. Originally released in monthly magazine form, only four issues were published, between July and October 1889. By 1921, the children's stories had taken on book form. A disagreement arose with the wealthy Brazilian publisher—d'Acosta Gómez—over the religious content of Martí's stories, specifically his representation of God. "The editor," Martí wrote, "wanted me to talk about the 'fear of God,' and the name of God to be in all the articles and stories, and not tolerance or the divine spirit."[4] Cowering before a fearsome God was an anathema for Martí, or as he explained: "Human race, lover of the servile! I can well conceive of God without feeling the need to be his slave."[5] Rather than compromise his understanding of God, he ceased contributing to the journal. Integrity concerning his understanding of God was more important than any financial setback. But what exactly was his understanding of God?

Martí rejected as false the God taught by Christianity in general, and Catholicism in particular: "Who can we ask? God? Oh! He does not respond because we have been taught to believe in a God who is not the true one. The true one imposes work as a means of reaching repose, research as a means of arriving at truth, honesty as a means of reaching purity."[6] Martí's God, as an impersonal God, differs from the God of Christians and from the traditional God understood by liberation theologians. For Martí, God is an element of nature uniting the material and spiritual worlds, a God who can be understood through reason: "It is not necessary to pretend in a God which can be proved. Through science, God is reached. Not God as a producer of men; but God as immense sea of spirits, where they must go to be confused, which results all arrogant disconformities of men."[7] Although Martí may have recognized the possibility of things existing beyond reason, he insisted that with time they could be reasonably understood, because "the only legitimate and definitive authority for the establishment of truth is reason."[8]

Martí embraced a God similar to the God presented by *krausismo*, a God who resembles that of the deists, as opposed to the anthropomorphous Christian God. His deist God was a supreme being whose existence is based on reason, responsible for creating all that exists but without interfering, intervening, or interacting with humans or their universe. "And with this scientific faith," he wrote, "you can be an excellent Christian, a deist lover, a perfect spiritualist."[9] Among the first *martiano* scholars to connect Martí and deist thought was Antonio Iraizoz, who argued that Martí never denied God or offered up any form of external worship.[10] Others, like the more contemporary theologian Reinerio Arce, have made a similar argument, noticing that on many occasions Martí appears sympathetic to deist thought.[11]

Whomever this God is, it is not a God of providence, a God who controls the fate of humans, a position Martí probably arrived at while in the quarry, where no theistic higher being saved the tortured from their forced death-dealing existence. Early in his life, probably while a student in Spain, Martí jotted down in his notebook: "There is no Providence. Providence is nothing more than the logical and precise result of our actions, favored or hindered by the actions of others. If we accepted Catholic Providence, God would be a very busy Bookkeeper."[12] Rejecting Providence is not a rejection of God: "I believe in God, because I understand God." But in the very next sentence he confessed: "I do not believe in Providence, because my reason does not make me see its effects, nor feel its need."[13] Martí's reason led him to understand that humans are not puppets to be manipulated by a Providence in the sky who pulls strings to test our faithfulness or resolve. Instead, humans have radical free will, and as such they must fulfill their own will, totally responsible for their acts of volition or omission: "Progress is fatal—but it is within us. We are our criterion; we are our laws; everything depends on us. Man is the logic and Providence of humanity."[14] Providence rests not with God, but with humans: "For men Providence is nothing more than the result of their own works. We do not live at the mercy of a foreign force."[15]

Martí wrote "[humans] turn their eyes to a Father which they do not see, but whose presence they are sure of," yet a careful reading of his works leaves the impression he is not absolutely convinced this Father exists.[16] Later in the same paragraph, he continues: "And this is how this gigantic man stirs the powerful mind, and searches with open eyes in the shadow of the divine brain and discovers it generous, invisible, uniform and beating in the light, in the earth, in the waters and in itself, and feels it knows what cannot be said. Man will spend his life eternally touching with his hands, without ever touching, the edges of the wings of the golden eagle, on which at last he must sit. This man has stood before the Universe and has not vanished. He has dared to analyze the synthesis and has strayed."[17]

It really doesn't seem to matter if there is a God, or if Martí is a deist, a theosophist, or a panentheist. What is important for Martí is the God within, which he calls our consciousness, which is synonymous with *patria* (see Chapter 2). He recognized that all too often, gods are created in the image of humans, a point he insists we should recognize early in life. In his writings for children, his observations of Greek gods can be applied to all gods: "The same things occur in the heavens than on earth because it is men who invent the gods in their image. Each nation imagines a different heaven with divinities who live and think as the people who created them, worshiping them in their temples. Because man views himself insignificant before the nature which creates and kills him, and feels the need to believe in something powerful which he can beg to treat him well in the world and not take his life."[18] While Martí's belief in a God as understood by the Judeo-Christian thought is questionable, he did maintain, as did Emerson, belief in the spiritual: "The eternal spirit divines what human science chases. This one sniffs like a dog, that one saves the abyss, where the naturalist wanders entertained, like an energetic condor."[19]

Martí recognized that begging to be treated well and not killed by a God is a simplistic way for humanity to recognize global oppression and the existence of marginalization, treating humanity poorly and devouring her children. The question asked by liberative thinkers standing in solidarity with the world's wretched is not, Is God created in the image of humans? Instead, it is, What is the character of this God professed to exist in the face of these global oppressive structures? What word does this God have to say to the world's oppressed who seek to be free? Martí, like most liberationists theologians since, struggled less with God's existence and more with God's character and how it guides humanity. Who is this God whom we profess? More important than God's existence for Martí is God's significance. Which God deserves our attention? These are the questions Martí struggles with as he attempts to move beyond the God that ecclesial authority legitimized and normalized. False gods who do not exemplify love require total rejection. Even after his horrific prison experience, he maintained, "If my God cursed, I would deny my God."[20]

Depending on how one reads Martí, he either understands God to be created in the image of humans, changing as they change, or he advocates for a process theism wherein God's attributes are affected by temporal processes, making the deity mutable and passible. I argue for the former. In his notebook, he jotted down impressions about God under the title "The God of the Jews":

[The Jews are] always persecuted, always oppressed, by power, are unable to expect their redemption if not by another superior power than the former. That is why the God of the Jews is potent. His attributes are fear. Implacability and revenge, needed by the Jews to the tremendous satisfaction of their anger; does not forgive, but punishes, announcing himself between thunder and lightning. Like all people, the Jews admit to God those things which they lack. They need a liberator, a powerful avenger, that can be greater than their oppressors; terrible as his grudge. Then comes Jeremiah, a loving man, and weeps.

Since then, the Jewish God cries, who like all the gods, develops and changes in form as his people unfold. Deduction: God changes with the changes of men. Later, Jesús came, the man of forgiveness, so he forgave. But, if he was God, he himself must have always been God. And there is something of revolution in Jeremiah, against something of caste. He says the same thing I say: Redemption will come to men by means of men: All will know who I am without needing Doctors.[21]

Martí seems less interested in whether one believes or not in God's existence and more concerned that people embrace the doctrine of love promulgated by Jesús. More important than faith, for Martí, was liberative ethics—the doing of one's faith. Yet this position does not necessarily negate God, or whatever God is for Martí: "God is the idea of *created substance* enveloped in itself the idea of *creative essence*. And as we are *creative substance*, we are governed by a *something* which we call *consciousness* which directs another something we call reason, made ready by another *something* we call *will*. Will, reason, conscience—essence in three forms. We, created life, have this—God, be creator, live creative, this you must have. God is then the supreme conscious, the supreme will, and the supreme reason."[22]

The psychologist Diego Jorge González Serra probably provides us with the best summary of how Martí understood God, and it is worth concluding this section with his list of eight characteristics:

1) God exists in the idea of the good. 2) The idea of God is either elaborated or conceived by humanity and society according to their circumstances; but responds to an innate and immanent need of human beings. 3) The idea of God responds to a moral need which grounds the moral. 4) Religion is the belief in God and the tendency to investigate and revere God. 5) God exists within humans and is expressed in their work, in the fulfillment of duty, in the love for *patria* and humanity, and in investigation which arrives at the truth. 6) Martí opposes the provident God of religions because God does not intervene in our lives, nor in the society. Everything which happens is because of humans. 7) God is not a producer of humans but an immense sea of spirits where the nonconformities of human beings

are resolved. 8) By way of science one reaches God and a spiritual-ism emerges pruned of superstitions and armored with facts. It also highlights the stock and profound faith in the utility and justice of nature. These criteria indicate the pantheistic character of Martí's philosophical ideas; which is, God is in nature and is expressed in the acts of nature.[23]

To González Serra's list, I would add that Martí's God is incarnated both in the human consciousness and in the concept of *patria*, both leading and demanding praxis for justice.

Humans

A unifying relationship exists between the human spirit and the spirit of the universe. Crucial to Martí's understanding of humans is the oneness they share with the divine, the universe, and one another. This oneness becomes the ethical and moral reasoning for how fellow humans are to be treated. Channeling the New England transcendentalist, himself influenced by the basic tenets of the *Bhagavad-Gita*, Martí wrote:

> [Ralph Waldo Emerson] maintains everything and everyone is the same, that all has the same objective, that all rests within man, which beautifies all with his mind. Through each creature all the currents of nature pass, every man has within the Creator, and everything created has something of the Creator, and all will end up on the bosom of the creative Spirit. There is a central unity in all deeds—in thoughts and in actions. The human soul, traveling through all nature, finds itself in all of it. The beauty of the Universe was created to inspire desire, console the pains of virtue, and encourages man to seek and find himself. [As per Emerson,] "within man is the soul of the whole; the wise silence; the universal beauty, to which every part and particle is equally related; the eternal One."[24]

The essential oneness of humanity with nature and the divine led him to proclaim: "I want the first law of our Republic to be the worship of the full dignity of man by all Cuban."[25] Even though humans remain a product of evolution—from "worm to man"[26]—in a panentheistic way, all of humanity lives in God as God, existing in all beings and humans.

The nation possesses a divine essence because it was composed of humans who housed in their souls the essence of heaven. When criticizing Buddhist monks who lied for the sake of serving the king for earthly treasures, he embraced their inherent divinity of humans: "And if Buddha had lived, he would have told the truth, that he did not descend from heaven but rather he came like all men who bring heaven within them."[27] Because all humans carry the essence of the divine, all humans have a divine mission to be free and an obligation to seek and obtain liberation when denied: "The best way to serve God is to be a liberated man and to ensure liberation is not undermined."[28] Liberation is the natural state for humans, a freedom maintained through virtues. Elsewhere he wrote: "By being men we bring to our lives the principle of freedom. And by being intelligent, we have the duty of its realization."[29]

And yet the self-aware are often dominated by those whose minds are less developed: "The intelligent man is asleep at the bottom of another beastly man."[30] This is not because those who are beastly are superior, but—as liberationist claim—the dominant culture is designed to privilege oppressors while expounding rhetorical phrases like liberty, equality, or fraternity. More effective than force are lullabies. As soon as humans enter the world, social structures, especially religious structures, begin to domesticate their minds. Humans cannot progress as long as they are denied their humanity through the denial of their liberty, especially by foreign powers. Martí wrote: "Under the pretext of completing the human being, they interrupt him. No sooner born, they already stand next to their crib with large and strong prepared bindings in their hands, philosophies, religions, parents' passions, political systems. They tie him up and girdle him, making man already, for his entire life on earth, a bridled horse."[31] The domestication of humans binds the divine essence and breaks their soaring spirit: "But what is man but a broken vessel from which fragrant and very rich smoldering essences break through. Each man is the prison of an eagle. It feels the blow of its wings, the moans which its captivity rips out of it, the pain in its breast and head caused by its clutches. Nature has not been able to formulate a question to which it has not been able to give at the end a response."[32]

The divinity found in humans can be understood as a "human spirit," an immense source shared by and connecting all individuals: "All peoples have in common something immensely majestic, vaster than the sky, larger than the earth, more luminous than the stars, and wider than the sea: the human spirit. This sympathetic spiritual force, binds and unites the chests of honorable men—essentially good, intuitive brothers, innately generous, who love each other more as they sympathize more with each other."[33] To live as human is a priesthood in which one's humanity is denied by selfishness. The lure of apostasy makes human life contradictory: "Life is undoubtedly a contradiction. We desire what we cannot obtain; we desire what we do not have; and there could not exist contradiction if there did not exist two different and opposite forces."[34]

Community becomes important in assisting humans to choose the good and take action against the bad; for when community is lacking, humans lack meaning: "Man is nothing in himself, and what he is, is what his community makes him. In vain Nature grants some of its children privileged qualities, because they will be dust and scourge unless they are part of their community."[35] Thus, a dichotomy exists between the goodness of human nature and the environment that can lead good humans astray. The divinity found in humans did not blind Martí with some romanticized thinking that they can do no wrong. Humans may basically be good, but the conditions of life teach us to be oppressive and/or vindictive: "Societies are not made of men as they should be, but of men as they are. And revolutions do not triumph, and societies do not improve if they wait for human nature to change. They must act according to human nature, struggle with men as they are, or against them."[36] Humans were not yet the way they should be; but that did not stop him from raising their consciousness so they could come closer to the ideal they were meant to be. He committed himself to the work of unbridling humans, recognizing that their dignity is found in their harmony with a just social order—a social order that is "with all, and for the good of all."[37] A new human and new world are possible, one in which individuals have a place and purpose within politics striving toward a moral good for all. He falls into the idea prevalent in the nineteenth century that humans and their universe are capable of regeneration. The duty to practice justice demonstrated in praxis that leads toward a liberated *patria* becomes the means by which the soul is purified. The old world may be crumbling; but in its wake, hope exists for the gestation of a new world in which humans can reach their full potential. Salvation is not obtained from a deity but realized in the doing of justice and bringing forth *patria*.

"This is everywhere a time of reencountering and remolding," Martí wrote. "The preceding century threw out, with sinister and vigorous anger, the elements of the old life. Clogged in its progress by the ruins, which at every moment are threatening it with a galvanic and animate life, this century, marked by detail and preparation, accumulates the durable elements of a new life."[38] Hence, Martí is not only concerned with the establishment of a liberative and revolutionary *patria*; he is equally concerned with the establishment of a liberated and revolutionary "man." In effect, "*Patria* is humanity, it is that portion of humanity which we see up close, and to which we had to be born."[39] A holy trinity develops for Martí of the divinity of the Creator of all, the divinity of the created humans, and the divinity of the *patria* they create, with humans being the link between the infinite Creator and the finite *patria*.

In the twentieth century, there is a need for a new human in harmony with the liberation of his political surroundings and centered in a transcendental rationalism. Rather than an anthropocentrism of the time that understood man as conqueror, Martí's anthropocentrism was based on a philosophy of harmony in which humans exist in unity with their being, their society, and nature. The human being is the only place where both portions of nature, spiritual and material, become indivisible. What is needed is balance, harmony. He does not provide a naturalist philosophy because humans, in his thinking, remain superior at the center of reality; the task is raising their consciousness so they can fulfill their duty to achieve their purpose of harmony and their destiny of independence. The essence of this revolutionary "man" is liberation, for self and for *patria*. Humans, who with radical free will choose to think for themselves, achieve fulfillment not through a personal relationship with God but through the implementation of ethics and the practice of virtues. The pursuit of freedom is more than a sacred duty; it is as essential as the air we breathe: "Without air, the earth dies. Without liberation, as without essential air itself, nothing lives. Like the bone to the human body, the axis to the wheel, the wing to the bird, and the air to the wing; so too liberty is the essence of life. How much is made imperfect without her. The more it is enjoyed, the more one lives among more flower and more fruit. It is the inescapable essence of all useful work."[40]

As with Emerson, Martí subscription to anthropocentrism, understood nature in terms of its value to humans, who are the most significant entity in the universe: "The Universe is the servant and king is to be human. The Universe has been created to teach, nourish, gratify, and educate man . . . [Emerson's] laws of life all revolve on the axis of this truth: 'All of nature trembles before the consciousness of a child.' Religion, destiny, power, wealth, illusions, grandness were for them as if by a chemist's hand, deconstructed and analyzed."[41] While most Christian-based ethical reasoning places Jesús (or God) at the center of any quest for justice, Martí places humans at the center in determining any type of just destiny: "We are the authors of our own good or bad, and to each author, themselves the complaint."[42] The privilege of being human hurts, and that pain is what defines humanity. But with the privilege comes responsibilities. Because humans are the center of the cosmic order and reason for creation, the burden of responsibility in bringing about justice rests on their shoulders, not on that of some celestial God. Still, humans can find guidance and inspiration from the Divine, specifically Jesús. A relational motif that undergirds ethical analysis seeks examples to emulate. He turns to Jesús less as Savior and more as a model to imitate:

Unhappy (to have to) recognize that the man of greatest ideal of the Universe, the Christ, probably has his countenance tarnished, tired, fallen, without that beauty or that glory which still rises in the countenances of the innocence and confidence of the untested mistress, in

the age of youth, ignorance, and fierceness. But the truth is life eats
and leaves dental marks as it passes; but for those who live intensely,
either for their sake or the sake of others, more is left. The truth is
that the countenance of the most moral beauty decays and loses much
light consistent with living, as eyes become fatigued and eclipsed, skin
discolors, the skull disrobed of hair, the forehead gaunt, the cheeks
hallowed out, and only in the divine hours of action or the supreme
discourse that the Glory of the soul comes to the countenance.[43]

Liberation for Martí is thus divinely revealed as harmonious order
with one's God, one's nature, and one's environment. Humans must
aspire to move away from the failures of Eurocentric modernity
imposed on them since childbirth as political and religious prejudices
and toward a liberation that is conducive to living, believing, and being
free. However, "the vast majority of men has spent their time asleep
upon the earth. They ate and drank but did not know themselves. The
crusade must now be undertaken to reveal to men their own nature,
and to provide them with plain and practical science, personal independence that strengthens goodness and fosters decorum and pride in
being an amiable creature and living thing within the great universe."[44]

While freedom may be an innate human principle, it does not
come about of its own volition. Humans must strive to bring forth
liberation, a task accomplished through the cultivation of civic virtues. According to the political scientist C. Neale Ronning, "Industry
and the capacity for hard work, generosity and sacrifice, compassion
and love; these were, for Martí, the elements of civic virtue that proved
beyond doubt that Cubans could and would progress under a just and
orderly government of their own making."[45] Martí believed with all
his heart that these virtues could be developed and a liberated *patria*
could be achieved. As he was planning for the eventual revolution in
1892, he declared: "What I have to say, before my voice fades and my
heart stops beating in this world, is that my *patria* possesses all the
necessary virtues for the conquest and maintenance of liberation."[46]

This concept of *patria* envisioned by Martí moves away from the
twentieth century's exclusive constructs of nationalism along racial
and ethnic lines. *Patria* becomes an inclusive manifestation of the

diversity of humanity; hence the focus is on calling for a political revolution while simultaneously calling for a social revolution that creates
a better human existence and leads to a new way of being virtuous.
Martí can be accused of having a high-Christian anthropology, a core
belief that humans are basically good: "One is always born good, evil
is created afterward . . . For every man is good; he only needs to be
produced in a good environment."[47] He began his 1882 book *Ismaelillo*,
written to his son, with the words "I have faith in human betterment,
in the future life, in the utility of virtue, and in you."[48] Any shortcoming can be blamed on a lack of education, a remedy rectified through
consciousness raising. "Man," he believed, "is noble, and leans to what
is best. The one who knows the beautiful, and the moral which come
from within, cannot live long without the moral and beauty."[49] Because
humans are basically good, he looks to them, not God, to bring about
a new humanity: "One need not lift their eyes to God, for God is in
them: the reason by which to understand oneself, the intelligence by
which to apply oneself, the active strength by which to fulfill the honest will."[50] In short, he looks to humans, who are divine, for redemption: "There is a God: man. There is a Divine force: everything. Man
is a piece of the infinite body, which creation sent to earth bandaged
and bound in search of his father, his own body."[51]

Jesucristo

Not all humans are equal. Some deserve our respect for what they do
and contribute; others do not and are better off forgotten. For example,
"Don Juan," Martí writes, "who for this poet symbolizes languishing
poetry, corrupting love, false brilliance, perverted laziness, should
be dead. Don Juan should die, and Jesús should live: Jesús, strength,
labor, truth, liberation, equality, justice, chaste love."[52] Christology is
a foundational concept of Christian liberative theologies and Martí's
own construction of God *Patria*. He approached Jesús with the same
respect he showed other great figures of history who struggled for the
liberation of humanity through a message of love and fraternity. He saw
Jesús as a fully evolved guide, a man of flesh and bone who achieved
full liberation even though he lived under Rome's colonialism. He is

truly a superior redeemer and a true revolutionary patriot who, motivated by love, offered up his life for the good of others: "With the words of a sublime rebel who with strength and patriotism gave impetus to humanity and reach to the Universe."[53]

But was Jesús God incarnate? After all, this is the foundational claim of Christianity, the doctrine that the Word became flesh (John 1:14). Here, Martí appears to be more influenced by unitarian thought than traditional Christianity. In his earliest notebook, he jotted down the following question: "If Jesús was God, why then this void of evangelical anointing from creation to him? Either he was not God, or God is capricious."[54] Of course, he wrote these words when he was young and his views might have changed as he grew older, although that does not seem to have been the case. Martí did not deny Jesús saw himself as having a divine mission, a calling from God. What is important for Martí is not if Jesús is God but who was Jesús? What was his character? According to Martí:

> [Jesús] was a very poor man, who wanted men to love each other; those who had means to help those who did not; that children respect their parents, as long as parents cared for their children; that everyone work, because no one has the right to that they have not to work for; to do good to everyone on earth and not desire to do anyone harm. Christ was full of love for men. And as he came to tell slaves they should be more than slaves of God, and as the people developed great affection for him following behind him wherever he spoke these things, the despots who governed in those places became afraid of him and made him die on a cross.[55]

As the *martiano* scholar Rafael Cepeda points out, this is probably the first time a political leader of the nineteenth century based theological thinking on Jesús' poverty.[56] If true, then Martí does predate liberation theologians' Christology by almost a century.

Whoever Jesús was, more important than any claims of divinity is the example he provided to humanity on how to live morally, proactively, and liberated. This crucified Galilean provided humanity with a sense of duty and purpose. Martí explained: "Jesús did not die in Palestine, but is alive in every man . . . The crusade must be undertaken to reveal to men their own nature (ethical and moral nature)."[57] Jesús' importance is what he did, how he lived in solidarity with the least of these, and how he suffered as a result of injustice. This is the Jesús whom Martí seeks and encourages readers to imitate, not the Christ of oppressors. Martí insists: "As in what is human, all progress perhaps consists in returning to the point of departure, in returning to Christ, the crucified Christ, forgiver, captivator, of bare feet and open arms, not an odious, satanic, malevolent, hating, bitter, harshly criticizing, punishing, ungodly Christ."[58] Just as there is the God of the oppressor and another God to whom the oppressed turn, so too is there the Christ that is satanic.[59] And just as the false God requires rejection, so does the false Jesús of those claiming to follow him, but through their actions, their praxis, give testimony of never having known him.

When in Martí's 1877 play *Patria y libertad* Father Antonio, the "false Christian," utters the name of Jesús, Martino retorts: "The name of the sublime seems to me blasphemy on your lips!—The one who maintains slaves, the priest feigning religious doctrines disfigures Jesús who diminished the landlord who searches in remote areas. He who denies the poor all the law, but who gives the rich the entire law; who rather than dying in its defense sacrifices an exploited race lies to Jesús and to the meek teaches a radiant stained and criminal face."[60] Belief in Jesús is more than an intellectual acknowledgment or a public profession of faith, it is an action which clearly delineates the tree by its fruit (Luke 6:44). For Martí the call of Jesús is to struggle with and for the oppressed, amenable to learning about God through them. The greatest culprits of preaching may well be the church. But as Cepeda reminds us, "Jesus, for Martí, is the great liberator of corrupt ecclesiologies."[61]

Jesús ceases to be an object of worship and becomes a model to emulate. Before setting off to fight in the Cuban Revolution, Martí wrote to his friend Gonzalo de Quesada on 1 April 1895: "A man died on the cross one day. But we must learn to die on the cross every day."[62] He identified with the one who was crucified, finding solidarity and fraternity with the rejected and abused Christ, even to the point of sometimes poetically referring to himself as the "broken Christ,"[63] or the "Christ without a cross."[64] Days before his death, de Quesada recounted an encounter between Martí, General Gómez, and other rebels. After recounting a life of hardship and struggle in preparing the launch for the war for independence, Martí concluded: "Let me be clear. For the cause of Cuba, I let myself be nailed to the cross. I will go to the sacrifice without uttering a single complaint."[65] Suffering at the hands of oppression was the cross carried by Martí, and by the Cuban people, not because it is to be sought for its own sake, but as the consequence of unjust and abusive governments; a suffering Jesús—in solidarity—understands.

Whatsoever is done to the least of these is done unto Jesús (Matthew 25:40), who is resurrected among those who are suffering oppression during Martí's time and in the present time. Whatever indignities suffered by the marginalized are also the sufferings of Jesús. Months after Martí's own suffering in the quarries, he wrote: "On the first page of history, men of hearts write of human suffering: *Jesús*. The children of Cuba must write on the first page of their history of pain: *Castillo*. All gran ideas have their great Nazarene, and don Nicolás del Castillo has been our unfortunate Nazarene. For him, as for Jesús, there was a Caiaphas [the high priest who condemned Christ]. For him, as for Jesús, there was a Longinos [the Roman soldier who, according to tradition, pierced Jesús' side]. Unfortunately for Spain, none has had for him the sad valor of at least being Pilate."[66]

Aesthetics

Martí's writings as a journalist were much like painting, as much a contribution to aesthetics as his poetry or playwriting: "The press is [Leonardo da] Vinci and Angelo [Michelangelo], creator of the new and magnificent temple, of which the pure and hardworking man is the brave priest."[67] Martí's search for beauty, according to the cultural historian Adriana Novoa, "opened the possibility to reconcile matter and spirit, since something beautiful was the result of matter given form by the Spirit."[68] Harmony, as we have seen, is foundational to Martí's ethics as it holds in tension the material and the spiritual. "Art," according to Martí, "is one form of harmony."[69] Beauty becomes the basis for spiritualism and a means to unify the people. His artistic expressions manifested through words become a space where matter and spirit can become one. Writing words was not purely for aesthetics; they encompassed revolutionary praxis: "In every word, an act must be involved. The word is an abominable dressing table when it is not placed at the service of honor and love."[70]

An obligation to society exists for the writer or anyone who creates art. The work is a sacred vehicle to teach, fulfilling a duty, an objective, a responsibility to raise consciousness. In almost everything he wrote, Martí explored the human condition to discover an ethical lesson. For Martí, according to the *martiana* scholar Susana Rotker, "art was not a means of escaping from life's worries, but rather a way to infect the population with a desire for knowledge and transcendental searches."[71] Martí spells the duty and obligation of the artist in his children's work *La edad de oro*, for even children's stories had a purpose in training the next generation in the ways of justice:

> What the poet has to do is to advise men to love each other, and to paint all the beauties of the world in a way that it can be seen in the verses as if it were painted with colors. And punish with poetry, as if a whip, those who want to take away men's liberty, or steal with rogue laws the money of the people or want the men of their country to obey like sheep and lick their hands like dogs. Verses should not be written to say one is happy or sad, but to be useful to the world, teaching that nature is beautiful, that life is a duty, that death is not ugly, that no one should be sad or cowering while there are bookstores full of books, and light in the heavens, and friends, and mothers.[72]

Aesthetics and ethics, for Martí, form the axiological foundation upon which social consciousness is constructed; therefore, artistic manifestations of aesthetics are crucial to establishing liberative moral philosophy for society. "To be good," according to Martí, "all you need is to see the beautiful."[73] Martí understood that a unity, a harmony, existed between aesthetics and ethics; "he who knows the beautiful, and the morality which comes from it, cannot live without morals and beauty."[74] The artist, therefore, symbolically expresses beauty, not to "fan [themselves] like the enormous peacock tail, but for the good of the neighbor."[75] Through different forms of art, humans are able to snatch a glimpse of the eternal and ethical: "Sad is the one who before a beautiful painting has not felt within them the growth of an outside force, or in their throat words of content and upheaval—piled up without exit! These are the laws of the eternal, which escape the legislators of the physical."[76] But more than a mystical glimpse, art becomes salvific and prophetic. Reflecting on his trips to Mexico, he wrote:

> Immoral peoples [of the United States] still have a salvation: art. Art is a form of the divine, the revelation of the extraordinary. The vengeance which man took to the Heavens for having created man, snatching the sounds of the harp, unraveling with golden light the heart of the cloud's colors. The rhythm of poetry, the echo of music, the beatific ecstasy which produces in the spirit the contemplation of a beautiful picture, the soft melancholy which takes over the spirit after these metaphysical contacts, are mystical vestments, and placid prophecy of a time which will become entirely clear. Oh, that this light of the centuries has been denied to the people of North America![77]

Through art, a space is created that allows the artist to construct utopias, not to escape to but as models to imitate. Art, as such, can become a method for creating new realities, a way to teach, a means of raising consciousness, a vehicle leading to salvation. "Do you want to raise up a temple?" Martí asked. "Build houses for the poor. Do you want to save souls? Then come down to this Hell, not with alms that devalue, but with arts of example. Since human nature, which is essentially good, seldom witnesses a noble model besides it, rises up to it."[78] For this reason, art is a necessity within a free society, and as such, it must be made available to citizens: "Free art, art in everything and at all times, is as necessary to the people as the air we breathe. A people without art, without much art, is a second-class people. The great educators, and the great governments, have always made art education obligatory."[79]

Martí demonstrated the relationship between ethics and the aesthetics in his review of the play *La hija de rey* (The daughter of the king) by José Peón Contreras in an 1876 article for *La Revista Universal*:

It is good that teaching occurs in the theater; for there is more a divine and humanizing form, to teach. The latter is left in charge of comedy, that one to the exaltation of fantasy, madness for those who fall short, but revelation and religion for those who caress and sense it. Who denies a mountain's summit because their weak eyes do not see the summit? Beauty and goodness appear in their works so united, that the one can never be realized without immediately producing the other. And if this is not true, what learning has occurred which has touched our spirit so profoundly as those of strange ecstasy, which leaves our hearts bigger and our bodies fatigued and overwhelmed? Because at times, joy is so fatiguing.[80]

Literature, like theatrical presentations, also points to the ethical. For example, Martí looks to Leo Tolstoy, as the exemplar priest of what Martí calls *la nueva religión*.[81] Tolstoy, who lived among the poor, as did the French novelist Marcel Proust, "belongs to the new humanity, and to that legion of aesthetic and high men . . . [who] write, as satisfaction for the drawn-out injustice for those who do so much."[82]

Martí demonstrated—in an article written for *La Nación* on an art exhibit by the Hungarian painter Mihály Munkácsy (1844–1900) that he attended in 1886—how aesthetics provides insight into the divine and contributes to the construction of ethical analysis. Munkácsy, known also as Michael Lieb, was a well-known, established painter conducting a U.S. tour of his works. Munkácsy's exhibition was linked to a then-current yearning among Hungarians for independence, a sentiment that resonated with Martí. Martí turned to the visual arts, specifically the depiction of Jesús, to aid in comprehending how believers and nonbelievers, powerful and marginalized alike, see a Christ in solidarity with the oppressed. Over a century before philosophical sociologist and anthropologist Pierre Bourdieu laid out his own methodology for aesthetics, Martí was already employing a similar analytical foundation of interpretation. For Bourdieu:

First, one must analyze the position of the [artistic] field within the field of power, and its evolution in time. Second, one must analyze the internal structure of the [artistic] field, a universe obeying its own laws of functioning and transforming, meaning the structure of objective relations between positions occupied by individuals and groups placed in a situation of competition for legitimacy. And finally, the analysis involves the genesis of habitus of occupants of these positions, that is, the systems of dispositions which, being the product of a social trajectory and of a position within the [artistic] field, find in this position a more or less favorable opportunity to be realized (the construction of the field is the logical preamble for the construction of the social trajectory as a series of positions successively occupied in this field).[83]

Martí was fascinated with one particular portrait, the 1882 masterpiece *Christ before Pilate*, which for our purposes demonstrates how he arrived at ethical praxis through aesthetics. In his review, Martí realized that masterpieces do more than simply inspire; they impose upon the viewer what interests the artist, interests based on the artist's worldview. Such interests exist as transhistorical, as intentional signs, as symptoms regulated by something or by what someone else does. The inherent social structures behind visual art are the product of the same social location in which artists find him or herself, for artists do not exist in a social vacuum; they are shaped by the sociohistorical space they occupy, a space that influences their works. This is why Martí spends so much time describing the difficult and death-dealing life of political oppression faced by Munkácsy, specifically war, massacre of his family, illness, and orphanage. Art reveals the pain of the artists, or as he commented in the prologue to his collection of poems titled *Versos libres*, his own contributions was "written not with academic ink, but with my own blood."[84] Similarly, the message of Munkácsy's artistic creation comes to be understood through the context of his lived experience, serving as historical document expressing *lo cotidiano*, which includes the hopes, struggles, disappointments, joys, and tragedies of his social location: "With what did Munkácsy paint if not with the sadness of his soul, with his gloomy memories, with the colors of those who do not know joy?"[85] Upon empty canvas, Munkácsy transformed blank space into liberative ideas as a response to a life of oppression and calamity.

Martí understood that art opened a path toward transcendental knowledge, capable of interrupting complicity that unites artist and observer in the same harmonious relation, a relationship that negates the reality expressed in the painting. Knowledge, illustrated by the painting *Christ before Pilate*, is revealed in a way that does not fully proclaim what the truth of Jesús is. This form of noncommunicated truth allows for the emergence of the deepest reality and the best-hidden structures of power, veiled so as to allow painter and observer to discern artistic expression while closing their eyes to it. Art becomes more than escaping from reality into imaginary worlds. A painting reflects the inability to take reality seriously, because it cannot appropriate the present in the way the present presents itself.[86] Thus, art becomes a document raising human consciousness by unmasking the false consciousness of utopias. A painting, as a sign, contains within it the meanings given to it by the particular culture from which it arises. The reality by which we measure a painting merely becomes the recognized referent of a shared illusion. Yet this illusion becomes a self-contained whole subordinate to its own order and structure. Through the artist's rendition, the inner structure of the work not only surpasses the power structures of reality but also transforms those structures by providing a vision, an illusion that challenges the prevailing normalized gaze and discourse. The success of the artist is in the ability to evoke the images of the dominant reality while subverting them. According to the art philosopher Clive Kronenberg, Martí's comments concerning Munkácsy's *Christ before Pilate* reinforce Martí's belief in a life rooted in virtue and honor where art, as a notion of ideas, can combat oppression and injustices.[87]

Munkácsy's *Christ before Pilate* further allowed Martí, an acclaimed art critic in his own right, to construct a Christology rooted in the painting and not some theological thesis buried in a book. Martí saw a depicted Jesús, insisting: "It is necessary, in order to fully understand Jesús, to have come into the world in a darkened manger with a pure and pious spirit, and have felt the dearth of love during life, the flowering of greed and the victory of hatred. It is necessary to have sawed wood and kneaded bread amidst the silence and offenses of men."[88] According to Martí, Munkácsy "sees Jesús as the most perfect incarnation of the invincible power of the idea. The idea consecrates, enlightens, attenuates, sublimates, purifies; it gives a stature that cannot be seen nor felt; it cleanses the spirit of scum, the way fire consumes the underbrush; it spreads a clear and secure beauty which reaches the soul, and felt by it. Munkácsy's Jesús is power of the pure idea."[89] In this reflection Martí moves away from Jesús as the incarnation of God to Jesús as the incarnation of pure idea, in a real sense, a more literal interpretation of "the Word becoming flesh" (John 1:14).

Martí contrasts Munkácsy's Jesús with the figure behind him with arms raised and who is yelling, creating again another neat dichotomy between "the virtuous man who loves and dies, and the bestial man who hates and kills."[90] And then there is the wealthy man observing the trial: "He is the hated rich man of every age! Wealth has filled him with brutal pride; it seems to him that humanity is his footstool; he is worshipped for his purse and its fullness."[91] Martí wrote of how Munkácsy depiction of a living, broken Christ without a halo—the human, rational, and fierce Christ[92]—signified the desire of the Hungarian people for independence from suffering under Russian oppression. Through aesthetics, Martí gazed upon Munkácsy's artistic rendition to construct a theological perspective for liberation linked to the national character of a politically oppressed people.

Sin

When Martí looked to humans, he saw the possibility for good: "Every human being has within him an ideal man."[93] But while humans have the potential of living into the ideal, he recognized that they also carry the undoing of the ideal. "We are all sinners," Martí wrote. "Those over there [in Cuba] and those over here [in the United States], and we are all heroes."[94] Both sinner and hero, bad and good, reside within all humans. Within each person there exists a yin-yang dichotomy—good and bad: "People are composed of hate and love, more hate than love. But only love, like the sun which scorches and melts everything, with natural following of oppressed souls cast down, with a shake and the indignation of pious souls, whole centuries of accumulated greed and privilege."[95] Martí's high-Christian anthropology led him to wonder:

"Why should the soul and body be enemies, what tends to escape and what tends to retain."[96] He sought to make room for the possibility of choosing not to lean toward the ideal human all possess. He sought the goodness of humans while recognizing human depravity; similar to St. Paul he sought deliverance from his wretched body (Romans 7:24): "I believe in the divinity of my essence, I touch and see and believe in the wretchedness of my existence—And yet at times, it is as if I involuntarily give way to my wretchedness."[97] The purest soul could still choose evil: "All crimes, all brutalities, all vileness is a germ within the most honest man. The most vile or bestial has appeared in the cleanest soul at some feasible or desirable instance."[98] For Christians, the wretchedness to which St. Paul refers was caused by original sin, a stain upon the human soul carried by all humans since Adam and Eve. But for Martí, original sin was caused by the first Darwinian act of standing on two hind legs, or politically by being Cuban within the Spanish Empire.[99]

Missing from Martí's analysis was an attempt to sociologically analyze, for example, the evil in which "good" humans engage, which he witnessed while a prisoner in the quarry. He presented depravity as rectifiable through education. Humans fall short of glory when they allow themselves to be negatively influenced by their environment, specifically because of a lack of education. "Men are products, expressions, reflexes," he exclaimed.[100] In dichotomic fashion, he creates a neat division of humanity between good humans and those who fall short of goodness. Although there are people who choose evil, humanity remains good by expressing the contradiction between humanity as a whole and the shortcoming of individuals: "Man is ugly; but humanity is beautiful. Humanity is joyful, patient, and good."[101]

Failing to seriously consider the causes of human depravity can lead Martí to utopian visions of a future political system. If consciousness could be raised, people would selflessly do what is right, what is best for humanity and *patria*. Failing to wrestle with why humans, including those who are educated and possess an already-raised consciousness, continue to participate in depraved acts like genocide led him to simplistic solutions. This becomes evident when he writes to the wealthy: "They're hungry, relieve their hunger. Let not the teachings of the Roman Senator be in vain: open the barns to the people when the people have no grain in their homes. Let each State remedy the grave wrongs of its region; let them create work for those without who would perish; and let those with surplus give to those who have an empty table and make their bed on the ground."[102]

For Martí, the wealthy should renounce their excessive wealth for the good of *patria*. Through science and education, humanity would be saved as people begin to realize the importance of crucifying self-interest for the good of society. Unfortunately, feeding the hungry, remedying wrongs by states, and the willing distribution of wealth by the rich will never occur despite all the consciousness raising offered. The rich will never agree to the distribution of their wealth no matter how much they would be convinced it is just. Those with power, as history seems to indicate, have never selflessly abdicated their privilege without a fight. Any liberative discussion requires a more sophisticated conversation about continuous human depravity, not its original cause. Regardless of the intractability of human depravity, Martí nonetheless looked to duty as the cure leading to the human potential of goodness for the benefit of all. "Virtue now is only the fulfillment of duty," Martí wrote, "no longer its heroic exaggerations."[103] To neglect one's duty to humanity was a sin, Martí explained in an 1888 letter to his friend Enrique Estrázulas: "He who does not do all he can do, sins against what is natural and pays the fault of his sin.[104] For example, in an earlier 1886 letter to insurgent leader Nicolás Domínguez Cowan, during the Ten Years-War, Martí wrote that not living to one's full potential "[because] you are made for something more than just to live in peace. You are being an egregious sinner for not making public all that is within you."[105]

Sin is more than simply an individual choice. For Martí and liberation theologians alike, sin is also and primarily understood as the ramifications of the prevailing social structures. Anything that reduces the quality of human life, short-circuits liberation, or reinforces the colonization of the mind was sin. Oppression and poverty, as expressions of sin, are mostly caused by societal structures that are designed to enrich the few at the expense of the many. Because the consequences of reigning socioeconomic structures during Martí's time (and ours) cause death, they are understood as sinful. The ultimate aim is to go beyond reform, for reform attempts to make sinful societal structures more bearable while maintaining power in the hands of the few. Martí called not for reform but for revolution. He understood the interconnectedness of sin, how one abhorrent act against one individual was a contemptible act against all of humanity: "A vile person is known to abuse the weak. The weak should be as the insane were for the Greeks: sacred. The man who enjoys humbling another is a pledge of infamy. There is an aristocracy of spirit: and it is formed by those who rejoice with the growth and affirmation of man. The human race has but one cheek: wherever a man receives a slap on his cheek, all other men receive it as well!"[106]

But what should the response be to the one who dealt the slap upon the cheek? Martí construct a revolutionary war upon the concept of forgiving sins, making the struggle for *un Cuba libre* more than simply a political venture, but also a spiritual journey: "For piety has the Cuban fought [and] not for revenge."[107] One of his most famous pose claims: "I cultivate a white rose / In January as in July / For the sincere friend / Who freely offers me his hand. / And for the brute who tears from me / The heart with which I live, / I nurture neither grubs nor thistles: / But cultivate a white rose."[108] This white rose symbolizing pure love is cultivated not only for those who offer friendship but also for cruel brutes who attempt to tear out the very heart beating in the one who has chosen to love. Cultivating white roses for those to whom hatred and vengeance are duties is not a performance enacted to call attention to one's virtues: "The good must be done without calling the universe to see it occur. The good is good because it is, and because within one feels pleasure when a good is done, or when something useful has been said to others. This is better than being a prince: to be useful."[109] The white rose is cultivated for the brute who sins against the innocent purely; it is cultivated for the sake of cultivating white roses regardless of the worth of those who will get to smell their aroma.

Martí does not hate the cruel brutes; he pities them. When Martí demanded justice after his time in Cuba's political prison, he decided pity was the proper response for those who refused to reconcile: "I demand compassion for those who suffer in [political] prison, relief for their undeserved, mocked, bloodied and vilified fate. If you provide relief, then you are just. If you do not provide relief, you are infamous. If you provide relief, I will respect you. If you do not provide relief, I pity your opprobrium and harrowing misery."[110] Pity is rooted in the understanding that for the oppressor there can never be peace of mind or wholeness: "It must be internally miserable the heart of those who help oppress men!"[111]

But pity is not enough. A responsibility exists to confront the oppressor in the hopes that he or she might be healed and saved: "Enablers want men that permits them to go on living with their appetites and vices; and not loving denouncers who forces them to face themselves, so as to shame them who rot and thus be healed."[112] Like that of Jesús, Martí's call to oppressors, for their own salvation, leads away from ignorant bliss. For both Jesús and Martí, the fight for liberation of body and soul may end with crucifixion; nonetheless, this call is not to simply theorize but to willingly offer up the ultimate sacrifice, and in so doing, paradoxically, life gains meaning and satisfaction: "How happy a martyr dies! How satisfied a wise man lives! He fulfills his duty, which, if it is not the end, is the means."[113] Jesús' suffering for others to be free is not only why Martí admires Jesús and calls us to emanate his fulfillment of duty regardless of the cost; it is also why he loves him: "Oh! Jesús, we who love you, keep quite out of guilt; and suffer. Oh brother! For what you have suffered, we ask our sore and exhausted soul like your body—which of us has been most heroic. If it's you, lifted on an object, died as you did, adored and hated by us, that without an object which doesn't guide, do not have the right to die."[114]

Although justice is eternal for Martí, it can come to an end: "Many things come to an end. Everything moves on. Eternal justice, unfathomable when eternal, also moves on, and someday will end!"[115] There is a limit to cultivating white roses. Love and forgiveness must be tied to justice. "Have you forgotten," Martí reminds us, "that there can be no forgiveness, when there has been no justice."[116] For forgiveness to be offered, commitment to justice, by all parties must exist. This is how this messenger of unconditional love can be reconciled with calling for a violent revolution. Of course, justice takes its toll on those who seek it, and Martí recognized the price. In an undated letter to his mother, Martí wrote: "Luck spares me much of its rewards. Oh, there is a plan for universal justice, which is only balanced at the end of the world, so what is just seems unfair in this world, or human life is the work of an evil lunatic: what is not possible is a thing so august and wonderful, so rich in pure joys and deep sorrows. For if the justice is limited to life on earth, there would be reason to believe, judgment for the part of prizes that touches me, that I am a great evil."[117]

He constructed a type of salvation history where the work for justice will never be vanquished. Eschatological hope, not in some Christian version of a heaven but of an eventual reign of justice, is what sustains and maintains Martí in the midst of setbacks and failures: "For me there is no defeat. Yes to prudence, sacrifice, and martyrdom. No to defeat."[118] Everything may not work out for the best in this life, but justice will one day reign as education raises consciousness. And for those who seek justice in the here and now, even if they fall short, they still triumph, for meaning and purpose come from the struggle. In an 1895 letter to Fernando Figueredo (the first mayor of West Tampa) and Teodoro Pérez (a wealthy Tampa cigar manufacturer) days before embarking to fight on the island, Martí wrote, "Pain is the only school which produces men. Blessed is he who is unhappy!"[119] Eschatological hope in a just society occupied by repentant, self-interested sinners led Martí to a radical grace foundational to his quickness to forgive: "The sin of the sinner is forgotten, it is discarded. Time is provided for them to come to their senses. The door is left open so they can return to love and honor without embarrassment."[120]

Suffering and Martyrdom

Suffering for Martí signified the abundance of life. "I am like the Siberian plains," he jotted in his notebook, "which give abundant fruit in the midst of cold. From suffering, flowers."[121] Suffering is not to be avoided but embraced, for through suffering, humans are prepared to face life's vicissitudes. The *martiano* scholar Félix Lizaso argued that Martí's stoicism was influenced by his readings of Marcus Aurelius and specifically Seneca; Rafael Cepeda reminds us that Martí absorbed and was influenced by the writings of St. Teresa of Ávila and St. Juan de la Cruz while a student in Salamanca and Madrid.[122] No doubt such intellectual influences were real; nevertheless, he was probably more swayed by his time imprisoned to hard labor, which resulted in life long physical scars. Reflecting on his experience in prison as a teenager, he wrote: "Prison, God: ideas as close to me as immense suffering and eternal good. Perhaps to suffer is to enjoy. To suffer is to die for the awkward life we created, and to be born to the life of the good, the only true life . . . To suffer is more than to enjoy; it is to truly live."[123] Suffering became for Martí an act that purifies and prepares humans to accomplish their duty, a duty—if need be—unto death.

On 18 May 1895, the day before Martí met his fate on the battlefield, he finished a letter to his friend Manuel Mercado, sharing the danger and suffering he faced: "Every day now, I am in danger of giving my life for my country and my duty."[124] A frail and delicate man, Martí, who spent most of 1894 living in poverty, infirm, and probably suffering from tuberculosis and ulcers, did not last long on the battlefield. On the day he was brought down by bullets from Spaniards in a skirmish at Dos Ríos, he gave a speech to the rebel troops informing them, "For the cause of Cuba I would be crucified."[125] Later that day he supposedly disobeyed a direct order from General Máximo Gómez and foolishly rode into battle, becoming an easy target. Some have argued that this final act was a romanticized attempt to embrace martyrdom. After all, a major theme coursing through the writings of Martí is martyrdom as a proper response to divine justice: "Death! Generous death! Death, friend! Colossal heart where all sublime mysteries are elaborated; fear of the weak; pleasure of the brave; satisfaction of my desires; dark path to the remaining episodes of life; immense mother, at whose feet we tend to gain new strength for the unknown way where heaven is wider, limitless horizons, where ignoble feet are dust, truth at last, wings; tempting mystery, breaker of powerful iron, nuncio of liberty."[126]

True, a romanticized embrace of martyrdom fascinated Martí since his youth. As early as sixteen years old, in his first written play, *Abdala*, the lead character serving as his alter ego is willing to die for the fictitious country of Nubia in the name of honor and God: "I am Nubio! To defend their freedom, all the people await me. A foreign nation has marked our lands, with vile slavery they threaten us, audaciously brandish their powerful spears. Honor dictates, and God dictates to die for the *patria* rather than to see it enslaved by a barbarous coward oppressor!"[127] To lay down one's life for others is a divine mandate expected by those committed to duty, service, and being useful. Ah, but to die for country uttering its name with one's last breath! In that same play the character Abdala assures readers: "We know how to die, we children of *patria*. For her we will die, and the last sigh from my lips will be for Nubia, for Nubia our strength and valor were created."[128]

His romanticization of a glorious death led to fantasies of dying in the Ten Years' War, which was raging on the eastern part of the island during his teenage years. On 4 April 1870 he wrote a poem to his mother: "I've enclosed in you my hours of joy / and bitter pain; / At least allow me in your hours to leave / My soul with my goodbyes. / I leave for an immense house where they have told me / Is life expired. / The *patria* takes me there. For *patria*, / Death is to greater joy."[129] No wonder his mother would warn of the martyrdom awaiting him if he continued on this path. In one of the early letters to Martí during his exile to Spain, Doña Leonor, upon discovering his political activism, prophetically forewarned that all who seek to be "redeemers end up crucified."[130]

With all his talk of dying for *patria*, one can mistakenly interpret Martí's views on death not just as romanticization, but also as simply morbid, especially with thoughts like "He does not know how to despise life, does not deserve it."[131] While earlier in life this might have been true, his thinking did mature, realizing martyrdom for its own sake would be selfish. Seeking death for its own sake ceased being the prize, rather the goal was ensuring death—through whose door all will pass—had meaning. "Even death gives a certain aurora of life," Martí wrote.[132] For death was not the opposite of life; rather, it was life's reward. Surprisingly, no dichotomy exists between life and death for the man prone to dichotomies. They exist as harmonious elements of a dual relationship according the theologian Arce.[133] The main characteristic of life, for Martí, is suffering mitigated by grief, which creates in his writings an all-consuming preoccupation with death.

Given his focus on mortality, some have erroneously concluded that his death was suicide. But contrary to some who have suggested that Martí sought martyrdom for the cause, I believe he held no death wish. He encouraged those listening to his 26 November 1891 speech in Tampa to "think of more than the beauty of dying on horseback, fighting for the *patria*, at the foot of a palm!"[134] Martyrdom as the consequence of liberative praxis in fulfilling one's duty can be embraced if it comes, even if it is not sought after. Fulfilling his duty to *patria libre* meant going to the battlefield, where he knew he would face death— he did not seek it out but expected it as a possible consequence. "I already know how I will die," he wrote in 1894 to fellow revolutionist José Dolores Poyo, but "what I want is to provide the public service I am able to provide at this time."[135] Such a death was not a morbid conclusion but a celebration of life's purpose. When the just do die, then "death is a victory, and when one has lived well, the coffin is the chariot of triumph. Crying is to please, not for mourning, because rose pedals now cover the wounds made by life on the hands and feet of the dead. The death of one who is just is a feast in which the whole world contemplates how heavens opens up."[136]

When the war hero of all three campaigns for independence, Serafín Sánchez, insisted that Martí stay in New York away from the danger of the battlefield, Martí replied: "Know that I will not unthinkingly expose myself to unnecessary danger; however, I will not neglect any need or action in combat to guard and protect myself as if I was some fragile relic."[137] Before he lost his life at Dos Ríos, he was planning to head to Camagüey to form a government, so such suicidal desires would appear counterproductive. In reality, his death is probably more a product of machismo and/or incompetence than any romanticized embrace of a glorious death. One can imagine soldiers returning to camp after risking their lives to find the poet scribbling verses. If he did not join in the battle, he would lose face before the "manly" troops. To gain their respect, he had to be willing to fearlessly ride into battle.

The truth is that in spite of his fascination with death, Martí embraced life: "This morning I opened a book, a book from a sane mind and read 'Life is a humbug!' But I here and see it is not true. Life is inspiration, life is fraternity, life is encouragement. Life is virtue!"[138] Life was a lie if one failed to complete his or her duty.[139] "Sad," he wrote, "is the one who dies without having accomplished their task!"[140] Yes, Martí embraced life, but he also did not fear death. To live embracing a transcendental political theology saves one from fear of death by providing the opportunity to fully live life cognizant that the end represents new beginnings. As such, he was not seeking martyrdom, but he wasn't afraid of sacrificing his life if required. He did have his eyes gazing toward eternity as a response to the oppression experience in this world—thus, an acceptance of some concept of eternity: "One walk, one cries, one's chest is oppressed; / and the gaze to the Heavens go astray: / Hope on earth is lost / and it is awaited for in the cycle that is to come. / And what if I die? If I conceive / The immense eternity which does not perish, / Then I will never die: eternally alive: / I know well where the sun never dusks."[141] This eternity is not for the chosen few but a call for all: "Eternity has Purity: / She is eternal, I am eternal, everything is eternal. / From the bolt of light which lid up in my head / To even the miserable atoms in the mud!"[142] Eternity encompassed complex thoughts (bolt of light in mind) and material substance (atoms in mud). This immortality could be achieved only in living a life for others. The fact that this book, like so many others, focuses on Martí might very well prove his immortality! Immortal because we continue to learn from his wisdom over a century after his death. He fulfilled his own prophecy: "Whoever lives for others, will continue to live in others, sweet prize!"[143]

Among Martí's most famous poetry from which we continue to learn is the verse "I wish to exit this world / Through nature's door: / In a carriage of green leaves / They must carry me off to die. / Do not put me in darkness / To die as a traitor: / I am good, and because I am good / [*Moriré de cara al sol*] I shall die with my face to the sun."[144] Only traitors and cowards die in the darkness of comfortable beds. But good revolutionaries, committed to transforming society toward justice, die on the battlefield facing the sun. Images illustrating Martí's death have him falling from his horse face forward, and with the last depleting ounce of strength, pushing himself over so as to die facing a beam of sunlight. Such Hollywood-type portrayals miss Martí's point. To *morir de cara al sol* is not to be taken literally; it is the ability to stare at truth in the face. Death was never intended to be a once-and-for-all event, but a way of living by facing truth, which requires daily dying. As he prepared to join the battle in Cuba, he wrote: "On the cross a man

died one day . . . but he had to learn to die on the cross every day."[145]
To die with one's face to the sun has more to do with living then with
how one physically dies; an authentic way of life does not hide one's
praxis, or actions, in the darkness as some traitor, but brings death in
the light for all to see a life struggling for the liberation of all: "Death
is not true when the work of life has been fulfilled."[146] Martí called
on patriots to follow him into the battle for the cause of liberation, to
be willing to lay down their lives if necessary so others could live with
justice. To live in such a way so one can die facing the sun becomes
the kernel of Martí political theology.

For the cause of justice, Martí called fellow revolutionaries to live
by joining him, to *morir de cara al sol*, reminiscent of an earlier trans-
former of society who called followers to pick up their cross and follow him. Central to Christian thinking is crucifixion, the laying down
of one's life so that others can live: "There is no greater love than this,
to lay down one's life for one's friends" (John 15:13). Or as Martí would
say: "Happy is he who for the good of man dies!"[147] Martí clearly has
Jesús in mind, not hesitating to identify with him. In writing of his
experiences in prison, Martí stated: "Martyrdom for *patria* is actually
God, as the good, as the ideas of spontaneous universal generosity.
Beat him, hurt him, bruise him. You are too vile for me to return blow
for blow and wound for wound. I feel this God within me, I have this
God within me. This God in me feels pity for you [Spaniards], more
pity than horror and contempt."[148] It is not difficult to see in Martí's
words a resemblance to Jesús' own words on the cross: "Father, forgive
them for they do not know what they do" (Luke 23:34). And like Jesús,
he was quick to turn the other cheek, even at the moment of his death.

To die a good death is to live, or as he would say, "to die well is
the only secure way to continue living."[149] For Martí, death is not the
end: "No! Human life is not all life! The grave is a way not an end."[150]
Because death is not the end, it is not morbid: "Death should not be
painful for those who have lived well, nor for those who knew virtue
up close. To die is to continue traveling."[151] Contemplating death is
thus not morbid, so neither is martyrdom—for there is a joy in facing
death with one's face to the sun when one fulfills one's duty: "Dying is
the same as living and better, if one has already done what was due."[152]

Before sailing to Cuba, Martí ended his manifesto with the words "La Victoria o el Sepulcro" (victory or the tomb). For Martí, there exists no greater glory, no greater exemplar to duty and service, than dying for one's country and struggling to liberate others from bondage: "We will die for true liberty; not for a liberty which serves as a pretext to keep some men in excessive pleasure, while others in unnecessary pain."[153]

A good death for Martí is defined through the lens of a good life, the lifelong struggle to faithfully, through praxis, accomplished one's duty: "The end of life is nothing more than the difficult achievement of compensation and conciliation of vital forces. Since we have free will, judgment, and imagination, we will be served by the three: the imagination to create, the judgment to discern, and free will to repress. Men are still fallen eagles and there must be some reason why our wings are not yet been given back."[154] Martí established a political way of being by creating a *patria* that discerns the goodness of humanity and represses the ignorance of the populace who is not willing to lean toward their better nature. Humans, thanks to education, which enhances the ability to reason, were like eagles soaring upward toward a higher level of consciousness. But achieving that was not enough if it was not tied to praxis: "I live for the strict fulfillment of my duties."[155]

Life is lived fully when it accomplishes its natural purpose of existing for the good of others: "It is the marvelous law of nature that only the one who is complete is the one who gives of themselves; and one does not begin to possess life until we empty ourselves without hesitation and without measure for the sake of our others."[156] What humans need is to be prodded to be better, and upon this nineteenth-century optimism, Martí attempted to create a *patria* based on moralism: "Let each one fulfill his duty as a man, and governments, where they are bad, should become better. Stop living as filthy limpets attached to State offices."[157] And while concepts of justice and equality are crucial to the foundation of any social order, relying on humans choosing self-sacrifice for the good of all has proved to fall short. We are left grappling with the realization of how practical his political theology is. Can he—can we today—truly construct a nation relying on a romantic quasi-religious nationalism of enlightened citizens who place the need of the *patria* before their own self-serving interests?

FIGURE 2. Martí's catafalque located in his mausoleum in Santiago de Cuba. Photograph by Princesschino, licensed under CC BY-SA 3.0. Courtesy of Wikimedia Commons.

If we define a fulfilled life as one in which a person witnessed the realization of hopes and aspirations, then without any argument, José Martí fell short. His vision for *un Cuba libre* was not realized during his lifetime, and some would argue (myself included) has never been realized on the island—period. "For me," he wrote weeks before his death, "*patria* will never be triumph, but agony and duty. The blood already burns."[158] A certain hopelessness seems to be present in his realization that a free Cuba may not be reached. So, if he realized the hopelessness of achieving his goals of liberation, why dedicate a life to its pursuit? Duty. Fulfilling one's duty, regardless of success, defines one's very humanity and manifests one's actual spiritual beliefs. Embracing the hopelessness of the circumstances should never be confused with embracing despair, defeatism, or martyrdom. In the construction of a political theology whose hopeless and unattainable goal is the construction of a liberated *patria*, Martí created meaning in life.

In Santiago de Cuba, at the Santa Ifigenia cemetery, situated between the graves of Fidel Castro and Carlos Manuel de Céspedes is Martí's mausoleum. Whether his remains occupy the sepulcher or not is immaterial. During a speech at the inauguration of Martí's mausoleum on 30 June 1951, then president Prío Socarrás correctly stated, "The colossal soul of José Martí does not fit in this mausoleum." He went on to argue that all the lands of the hemisphere were insufficient to house his soul.[159] This plot was designated as "sacred" space, signifying the summation of *cubanidad*. Here, Martí's catafalque is centered, draped with the Cuban flag and a bouquet of roses at the foot of the coffin, fulfilling his request, as spelled out in one of his poems: "I want when I die, / Without *patria* but no master, / To have on my tombstone a bouquet / Of flowers—and a flag!"[160]

NOTES

Book epigraph. El problema de la independencia: no era el cambio de formas, sino el cambio de espíritu (*El Partido Liberal*, 30 January 1891, in *Obras completas de José Martí*, 26 vols. (La Habana: Centro de Estudios Martianos, 2001) (hereafter *OC*), 6:19.

PREFACE

1. Reinerio Arce, Religión poesía del mundo venidero: Implicaciones thelógicas en la obra de José Martí (La Habana: Ediciones CLAI, 1996), 10.
2. Mircea Eliade, *Patterns in Comparative Religion*, trans. Rosemary Sheed (New York: Meridian Books, 1963), 11.
3. Paul Tillich, *Dynamics of Faith* (New York: Harper Colophon Books, 1957), 42–43.
4. João Felipe Gonçalves, "The 'Apostle' in Stone: Nationalism and Monuments in Honor of José Martí," in *The Cuban Republic and José Martí: Reception and Use of a National Symbol*, ed. Mauricio A. Font and Alfonso W. Quiroz (Lanham, MD: Lexington Books, 2006), 19.
5. Lillian Guerra, *The Myth of José Martí: Conflicting Nationalism in Early Twentieth-Century Cuba* (Chapel Hill: University of North Carolina Press, 2005), 3.
6. Viví en el monstruo y le conozco las entrañas; y mi Honda es la de David (*OC* 4:168).
7. Guerra, *The Myth of José Martí*, 26.
8. Paul Ricoeur, *Interpretation Theory: Discourse and the Surplus of Meaning* (Fort Worth: Texas Christian University Press, 1976), 29–30.

NOTES ON TRANSLATION

Epigraph. No se debiera escribir con letras, sino con actos (*La Nación*, 29 April 1888, *OC* 13:333).

1. Adriana Novoa, "'Transpensar': Materialism, Spiritualism, and Race in José Martí's Rejection of Socialism (1870–1890)" (paper presented at Cuban Research Institute, Florida International University, Miami, 2017), 28.
2. Manuel Pedro González, *José Martí: Epic Chronicler of the United States in the Eighties*, 2nd ed. (Chapel Hill: University of North Carolina, 1953), 28–29.
3. Cathy L. Jrade, "Martí Confronts Modernity," in *Re-Reading José Martí (1853–1895) One Hundred Years Later*, ed. Julio Rodríguez-Luis (Albany: State University of New York Press, 1999), 5.
4. Vence el amor. La palabra / Sólo cuando justa, vence (*A Néstor Ponce de León*, 1889, *OC* 16:357).
5. El lenguaje ha de ser matemático, geométrico, escultórico. La idea ha de encajar exactamente en la frase, tan exactamente que no pueda quitarse nada de la frase sin quitar eso mismo de la idea (Notebook #9, 1882, *OC* 21:255)
6. Las palabras han de ser brillantes como el oro, ligeras como el ala, sólidas como el mármol (Notebook #5, 1881, *OC* 21:164).
7. El arte de escribir ¿no es reducir? La verba mata sin duda la elocuencia. Hay tanto que decir, que ha de decirse en el menor número de palabras posible: eso si, que cada palabra lleve ala y color (*La Nación*, 28 July 1887, *OC* 11:196).
8. It should be noted that his quote—"Yo no quisiera tener mis obras traducidas al inglés o al francés, sino al . . ."—is an incomplete fragment; the remainder of the sentence is illegible (*OC* 21:360).
9. Ada Ferrer, *Insurgent Cuba: Race, Nation, and Revolution, 1868–1898* (Chapel Hill: University of North Carolina Press, 1999), 11.
10. Laura Lomas, *Translating Empire: José Martí, Migrant Latino Subjects, and American Modernities* (Durham, NC: Duke University Press, 2008), 281.

INTRODUCTION

Epigraph. El hábito noble de examen destruye el hábito servil de creencia (*El Progreso*, 22 April 1877, *OC* 7:98–99).

1. ¡La vida humana no es toda la vida! La tumba es vía y no término . . . La muerte es júbilo, reanudamiento, tarea nueva. La vida humana sería una invención repugnante y bárbara, si estuviera limitada a la vida en la tierra (prologue to Pérez Bonalde's *Poema del Niágara*, 1882, *OC* 7:236).

2. Filosofía es el conocimiento de las causas de los seres, de sus distinciones, de sus analogías y de sus relaciones (*Juicios filosofía, OC* 19:359).

3. La filosofía no es más que el secreto de la relación de las varias formas de existencia (prologue to Pérez Bonalde's *Poema del Niágara*, 1882, *OC* 7:232).

4. Félix Lizaso, *Posibilidades filosóficas en Martí* (La Habana: Molina y Cía, 1935), 7.

5. The term *axiology* was first used in the title of a philosophy book in 1908 by Eduard von Hartmann, *Grundriss der Axiologie*, although the concept concerning the theory of value can be traced to the eighteenth century in the political-economic work of thinkers like Adam Smith.

6. Susana Rotker, "José Martí and the United States: On the Margins of the Gaze," in *Re-Reading José Martí (1853–1895) One Hundred Years Later*, ed. Julio Rodríguez-Luis, trans. Jorge Hernández Martín (Albany: State University of New York Press, 1999), 30.

7. La filosofía es la ciencia de las causas, de la causalidad (*Juicios filosofía, OC* 21:42).

8. John M. Kirk, *José Martí: Mentor of the Cuban Nation* (Tampa: University Presses of Florida, 1983), 153.

CHAPTER 1

Epigraph. No puede ser que Dios ponga en el hombre el pensamiento, y un arzobispo, que no es tanto como Dios, le prohíba expresarlo (*El Partido*, 16 January 1887, *OC* 11:147).

1. Ni la originalidad literaria cabe, ni la libertad política subsiste mientras no se asegure la libertad espiritual (*OC* 7:230).

2. Rufino Modesto Pavón Torres, *La relación ético-estética en el pensamiento martiano* (Holguín, Cuba: Ediciones Holguín, 2009), 12.

3. La metafísica es el conjunto de verdades absolutas que sirven de leyes explicativas y fundamentales a todos los conocimientos humanos (Notebook #2, *OC* 21:48).

4. Novoa, "'Transpensar'" (2017), 5.

5. La doctrina de la evolución, impotente aún para explicar todo el misterio de la vida, no se opone a la existencia de un poder supremo, sino que se limita a enseñar que obra por leyes naturales y no por milagros (*OC* 13:442).

6. El mundo no fue producido por creación, sino por continuado desenvolvimiento (*La Opinión Nacional*, 8 March 1882, *OC* 14:398).

7. Todas las escuelas filosóficas pueden concretarse en estas dos. Aristóteles dio el medio científico que ha elevado tanto, dos veces ya en la gran historia del mundo, a la escuela física. Platón, y el divino Jesús, tuvieron el purísimo espíritu y fe en otra vida que hacen tan poética, durable, la

escuela metafísica. Las dos unidas son la verdad: cada una aislada es sólo una parte de la verdad, que cae cuando no se ayuda de la otra (*Juicios filosofía*, *OC* 19:361).

8. El alma es la facultad de observar, juzgar y transmitir (Notebook #1, *OC* 21:17).

9. La naturaleza observable es la única fuente filosófica. El hombre observador es el único agente de la Filosofía (*Juicios filosofía*, *OC* 19:360).

10. El hombre por los sentidos recibe impresiones, —y la razón— que lo comunica con el mundo real (notes for his debate on *El idealismo y el realismo en el arte*, *OC* 19:418).

11. Platón-soñador-no filósofo: —quimérico.—Heredero de los faquires (ibid.).

12. Cuando el ciclo de las ciencias esté completo, y sepan cuanto hay que saber, no sabrán más que lo que sabe hoy el espíritu. (Emerson's eulogy, *La Opinión Nacional*, 19 May 1882, *OC* 13:25).

13. Pero hay dos clases de seres: los que se tocan y los que no se pueden tocar (*Juicios filosofía*, *OC* 19:360).

14. Por medio de la ciencia se llega a Dios. —No Dios, como hombre productor; sino Dios como inmenso mar de espíritus, adonde han de ir a confundirse, ya resueltas, todas las soberbias inconformidades de los hombres (*OC* 19:361).

15. ¡Verdad es! De mi vil carne la mano / ¡impotente verdad! —no llega al cielo; / ¡pero dentro del ser medido humano / hay otro ser sin forma y sin medida / que toca y ve, post-vida y ante-vida! ("Síntesis," *Versos varios*, 1873, *OC* 17:105).

16. Todo, en lo térreo, si cenizas se hace, / Más lozano y vivífico renace: / Y el alma resucita: yo la he visto / Clavada en la Cruz como el Inmenso Cristo, / Y luego, al sol de plácidos amores, / ¡Batir las alas y libar las flores! ("María," *Versos varios*, 1888, *OC* 17:129).

17. Miguel A. De La Torre, *Embracing Hopelessness* (Minneapolis: Fortress Press, 2017), ix.

18. El bárbaro opresor ("¡10 de octubre!" *Versos varios*, 1869, *OC* 17:20).

19. Compañero: ¿Has soñado tú alguna vez con la gloria de los apóstatas? ¿Sabes tú cómo se castigaba en la antigüedad la apostasía? Esperamos que un discípulo del Sr. Rafael María de Mendive no ha de dejar sin contestación esta carta (*OC* 1:39).

20. Carlos Alberto Montaner, *El pensamiento de Martí* (Madrid: Plaza Mayor Ediciones, 1971), 10.

21. *El presidio político*, *OC* 1:58.

22. Lomas, *Translating Empire*, 47.

23. Alfred J. López, *José Martí: A Revolutionary Life* (Austin: University of Texas Press, 2014), 72, 80, 128.

24. *El presidio político en Cuba*, 1871, *OC* 1:64–65.

25. Ibid., *OC* 1:66, 69, 56–57, 71.

26. Presidio era el presidio de Cuba, la institución del Gobierno, el acto mil veces repetido del Gobierno que sancionaron aquí los representantes del país (ibid., *OC* 1:61).

27. ¡Oh! No es tan bello ni tan heroico vuestro sueño, porque sin duda soñáis. Mirad, mirad hacia este cuadro que os voy a pintar, y si no tembláis de espanto ante el mal que habéis hecho, y no maldecís horrorizados esta faz de la integridad nacional que os presento, yo apartaré con vergüenza los ojos de esta España que no tiene corazón (ibid., *OC* 1:49).

28. Y yo todavía no sé odiar (ibid., *OC* 1:45).

29. Yo siento en mí a este Dios, yo tengo en mi a este Dios; este Dios en mí os tiene lástima, más lástima que horror y que desprecio (ibid., *OC* 1:61).

30. Dios existe, sin embargo, en la idea del bien, que vela el nacimiento de cada ser, y deja en el alma que se encama en él una lágrima pura. El bien es Dios. La lágrima es la fuente de sentimiento eterno (ibid., *OC* 1:45).

31. Ibid., *OC* 1:57.

32. El bochorno / Del hombre es mi bochorno: mis mejillas / Sufren de la maldad del Universo ("Vino de Chianti," *Flores del destierro*, *OC* 16:242).

33. Dios existe, y yo vengo en su nombre a romper en las almas españolas el vaso frío que encierra en ellas la lágrima (*El presidio político en Cuba*, 1871, *OC* 1:45).

34. Friedrich Wilhelm Nietzsche, *Die fröhliche Wissenschaft* (Chemnitz: Verlag von Ernst Schmeitzner, 1882), 3:125.

35. ¡Cuán desventurados son los pueblos cuando matan a Dios! . . . Y ¡cuánto han de llorar los pueblos cuando hacen llorar a Dios! (*El presidio político en Cuba*, 1871, *OC* 1:73).

36. El mundo es religioso (*La Opinión Pública*, 1889, *OC* 12:306).

37. Todo pueblo necesita ser religioso. No sólo lo es esencialmente, sino que por su propia utilidad debe serlo. Es innata la reflexión del espíritu en un ser superior; aunque no hubiera ninguna religión todo hombre sería capaz de inventar una, porque todo hombre la siente. Es útil concebir un gran ser alto . . . La moral es la base de una buena religión. La religión es la forma de la creencia natural en Dios y la tendencia natural a investigarlo y reverenciarlo. El ser religioso está entrañado en el ser humano. Un pueblo irreligioso morirá, porque nada en él alimenta la virtud. Las injusticias humanas disgustan de ella; es necesario que la justicia celeste la garantice (fragments of essay "Hay en el hombre," *OC* 19:392).

38. Las exageraciones cometidas cuando la religión cristiana, que como todas las religiones, se ha desfigurado por sus malos sectarios . . . El fundador de la familia no es responsable de los delitos que cometen los hijos de sus hijos (ibid., *OC* 19:391–92).

39. Hay en el hombre un conocimiento íntimo, vago, pero constante e imponente, de un gran ser creador: Este conocimiento es el sentimiento religioso, y su forma, su expresión, la manera con que cada agrupación de hombres concibe este Dios y lo adora, es lo que se llama religión. Por eso, en lo antiguo, hubo tantas religiones como pueblos originales hubo; pero ni un sólo pueblo dejó de sentir a Dios y tributarle culto. La religión está, pues, en la esencia de nuestra naturaleza. Aunque las formas varíen, el gran sentimiento de amor, de firme creencia y de respeto, es siempre el mismo. Dios existe y se le adora. Entre las numerosas religiones, la de Cristo ha ocupado más tiempo que otra alguna los pueblos y los siglos: esto se explica por la pureza de su doctrina moral, por el desprendimiento de sus evangelistas de los cinco primeros siglos, por la entereza de sus mártires, por la extraordinaria superioridad del hombre celestial que la fundó. Pero la razón primera está en la sencillez de su predicación que tanto contrastaba con las indignas argucias, nimios dioses y pueriles argumentos con que se entretenía la razón pagana de aquel tiempo, y a más de esto, en la pura severidad de su moral tan olvidada ya y tan necesaria para contener los indignos desenfrenos a que se habían entregado las pasiones en Roma y sus dominios (ibid., *OC* 19:391).

40. La vida espiritual es una ciencia, como la vida física (*La América*, May 1884, *OC* 15:396).

41. El culto es una necesidad para los pueblos. El amor no es más qua la necesidad de la creencia: hay una fuerza secreta que anhela siempre algo que respetar y en qué creer. Extinguido por ventura el culto irracional, el culto de la razón comienza ahora. No se cree ya en las imágenes de la religión, y el pueblo cree ahora en las imágenes de la patria (*Revista Universal*, 11 May 1875, *OC* 6:195).

42. Asesino alevoso, ingrato a Dios y enemigo de los hombres, es el que, so pretexto de dirigir a las generaciones nuevas, les enseña un cúmulo aislado y absoluto de doctrinas, y les predica al oído, antes que la dulce plática de amor, el evangelio bárbaro del odio (prologue to Pérez Bonalde's *Poema del Niágara*, 1882, *OC* 7:220).

43. Son simplemente convenciones religiosas, convenciones católicas. Acato el Matrimonio porque lo comprendo en el orden natural como justa ley moral, y en el orden civil como precisa institución social. Respeto la Extrema-unción, porque en la esfera humana de la caridad, es la compasión hacia el enfermo, y el respeto a la muerte, que tantas cosas bellas encierra para mí (Notebook #1, *OC* 21:18).

44. Y sigo a mi labor como creyente / A quien unge en la sien el sacerdote / De rostro liso y vestiduras blancas / Practico: en el divino altar comulgo / De la naturaleza: es mi hostia el alma humana ("Cuentan que antaño," *Versos libres*, *OC* 16:217).

45. Carolina Gutiérrez Marroquín, *Ética cristiana en la poesía de José Martí* (Holguín, Cuba: Ediciones Holguín, 2014), 19–20.

46. Las religiones todas son iguales: puestas una sobre otra, no se llevan un codo ni una punta: se necesita ser un ignorante cabal, como salen tantos de universidades y academias, para no reconocer la identidad del mundo. Las religiones todas han nacido de las mismas raíces, han adorado las mismas imágenes, han prosperado por las mismas virtudes y se han corrompido por los mismos vicios. Las religiones, que en su primer estado son una necesidad de los pueblos débiles, perduran luego como anticipo, en que el hombre se goza, del bienestar final poético que confusa y tenazmente desea. Las religiones, en lo que tienen de durable y puro, son formas de la poesía que el hombre presiente; fuera de la vida, son la poesía del mundo venidero: ¡por sueños y por alas los mundos se enlazan! giran los mundos en el espacio unidos, como un coro de doncellas, por estos lazos de alas. Por eso, la religión no muere, sino se ensancha y acrisola, se engrandece y explica con la verdad de la naturaleza y tiende a su estado definitivo de colosal poesía ("La excomunión del padre McGlynn," *El Partido Liberal*, 1887, *OC* 11:242–43).

47. ¡Ah! la religión, falsa siempre como dogma a la luz de un alto juicio, es eternamente verdadera como poesía ("El cisma de los Católicos en Nueva York," *El Partido Liberal*, 16 January 1887, *OC* 11:139–40).

48. El respecto a la libertad y al pensamiento ajenos, aun del ente más infeliz es mi fanatismo; si muero, o me matan, será por eso (*OC* 3:166).

49. En religión —lo que hay de esencial en todos, sin oprimir a ninguna. Nadie tiene el derecho de compeler a nadie. Ni librepensadores a católicos, ni católicos a librepensadores (undated fragments, *OC* 22:75).

50. Como en lo humano todo el progreso consiste acaso en volver al punto de que se partió, se está volviendo al Cristo, el Cristo crucificado, perdonador, cautivador, el de los pies desnudos y los brazos abiertos, no un Cristo nefando y satánico, malevolente, odiador, enconado, fustigante, ajusticiado, impío (prologue to Pérez Bonalde's *Poema del Niágara*, 1882, *OC* 7:226).

51. ¡Y el producto del imperio de los Césares, es el cristianismo! (Notebook #2, *OC* 22:96).

52. Entre los poderosos por la alianza que les ofrecía para la protección de los bienes mundanos, y entre los políticos por la necesidad que éstos tienen del voto católico ("El cisma de los Católicos en Nueva York," *El Partido Liberal*, 16 January 1887, *OC* 11:143).

53. El cristianismo ha muerto a manos del catolicismo. Para amar a Cristo, es necesario arrancarlo a las manos torpes de sus hijos. Se le extrae de la forma grosera en que la ambición de los pósteros convirtió las apologías y vaguedades que necesitaron para hablar a una época mitológica Jesús y los propagaron su doctrina (*Revista Universal*, 26 August 1875, *OC* 6:313).

54. Marcos Antonio Ramos, *Protestantism and Revolution in Cuba* (Coral Gables, FL: University of Miami, 1989), 21.
55. Calixto C. Masó y Vazquez, *Historia de Cuba: La lucha de un pueblo por cumplir su destino histórico y su vocación de libertad* (Miami: Ediciones Universal, 1998), 467.
56. Emilio Roig de Leuchsenring, *Martí y las religiones* (La Habana: Publicaciones de Accion, 1941), 7.
57. Al fin se esté librando la batalla. La libertad está frente a la Iglesia. No combaten la Iglesia sus enemigos, sino sus mejores hijos. ¿Se puede ser hombre y católico, o para ser católico se ha de tener alma de lacayo? Si el sol no peca con lucir ¿cómo he de pecar yo con pensar? ("La excomunión del padre McGlynn," *El Partido Liberal*, 1887, *OC* 11:243).
58. Manuel P. Maza, *The Cuban Catholic Church: True Struggles and False Dilemmas* (master's thesis, Georgetown University, 1982), 6–7, 13.
59. Los E.U. son más religiosos porque son más libres; por eso no ha aparecido aquí el poeta ateo. En los pueblos donde la religión se ha mostrado siempre hostil al ejercicio natural y amplio de las facultades del hombre, el odio a la religión ha sido una de las formas naturales del amor a la libertad (undated fragments, *OC* 22:77).
60. Pablo Richard, *Death of Christendoms, Birth of the Church: Historical Analysis and Theological Interpretation of the Church in Latin America* (Maryknoll, NY: Orbis Books, 1987), i.
61. El catolicismo fue una razón social-Aniquilada aquella sociedad, creada otra sociedad nueva, la razón social ha de ser distinta, el catolicismo ha de morir . . . El catolicismo muere, como murió la mitología, como murió el paganismo, como muere lo que un genio humano crea, o halla y la razón de otro genio destruye, o reemplaza (Notebook #1, *OC* 21:28–29).
62. Y como los hombres son soberbios, y no quieren confesar que otro hombre sea más fuerte o más inteligente que ellos, cuando había un hombre fuerte o inteligente que se hacía rey por su poder, decían que era hijo de los dioses. Y los reyes se alegraban de que los pueblos creyesen esto; y los sacerdotes decían que era verdad, para que los reyes les estuvieran agradecidos y los ayudaran. Y así mandaban juntos los sacerdotes y los reyes (*La edad de oro*, 1889, *OC* 18:328–29).
63. Leslie Dewart, *Christianity and Revolution: The Lesson of Cuba* (New York: Herder and Herder, 1963), 93.
64. La religión católica tiene dos fases que merecen cada una peculiar consideración. Es doctrina religiosa, y es forma de gobierno; si aquélla es errónea, no es necesario combatirla; cuando el error no está sostenido por la fuerza y la ignorancia dominantes, el error por sí propio se deshace y cae (*Revista Universal*, 8 June 1875, *OC* 6:226).
65. El doctor, el marqués, el padre Antonio aire tienen de gente recelosa; el aire de los buitres de la noche cuando en el claro oriente el sol asoma.

Noble, cura y doctor: las tres serpientes Que anidó en nuestro seno la colonia. Mata la ley astuta la justicia, los que a Jesús predican, lo deshonran, y esa raza de siervos con casaca con nuestra infamia un pergamino compra (*OC* 18:166).

66. ¿Quién puede desconocer cuántas heridas están abiertas, cuántos males están palpitantes, cuántos elementos dañosos hay en la constitución de nuestro pueblo por el dominio y afán absorbente de la doctrina católica? (*Revista Universal*, 7 August 1875, *OC* 6:297).

67. Y bien hace la doctrina muerta en temer a la patria viva (*Revista Universal*, 8 June 1875, *OC* 6:225).

68. Rafael Cepeda, *José Martí: Perspectivas éticas de la fe cristiana* (San José, Costa Rica: Editorial Departamento Ecuménico de Investigaciones, 1991), 140.

69. Cintio Vitier, "Imagen de Martí," *Anuario Martiano* 3 (1971): 238.

70. Gutiérrez Marroquín, *Ética cristiana en la poesía de José Martí*, 66.

71. Y como él te cobra por echar agua en la cabeza de tu hijo, por decir que eres el marido de tu mujer, cosa que ya tú sabes desde que la quieres y te quiere ella; como él te cobra por nacer, por darte la unción, por casarte, por rogar por tu alma, por morir; como te niega hasta el derecho de sepultura si no le das dinero por él, él no querrá nunca que tú sepas que todo eso que has hecho hasta aquí es innecesario, porque ese día dejará él de cobrar dinero por todo eso. Y como es una injusticia que se explote así tu ignorancia, yo, que no te cobro nada por mi libro, quiero, hombre del campo, hablar contigo para decirte la verdad. No te exijo que creas como yo creo. Lee lo que digo, y créelo si te parece justo. El primer deber de un hombre es pensar por sí mismo. Por eso no quiero que quieras al cura; porque él no te deja pensar (undated essay "Hombre de campo," *OC* 19:381).

72. Lo degradante en el catolicismo es el abuso que hacen de su autoridad los jerarcas de la Iglesia, y la confusión en que mezclan a sabiendas los consejos maliciosos de sus intereses y los mandatos sencillos de la fe ("El cisma de los Católicos en Nueva York," *El Partido Liberal*, 16 January 1887, *OC* 11:139).

73. Un casi siempre vicioso, que te obliga a tener mujer teniendo él querida, que quiere que tus hijos sean legítimos teniéndolos él naturales, que te dice que debes dar tu nombre a tus hijos y no da él su nombre a los suyos ("Hombre de campo," *OC* 19:382).

74. ¡Qué hacen los periódicos católicos? —Lo que hacen en todos los tiempos; vestirse con el manto de piedad; bajar a tierra estos ojos humanos que se han hecho para mirar de frente a todo; disimular bajo sus vestiduras negras las iracundas palpitaciones de su corazón, y ocultar con la sombra de sus hábitos la sonrisa que, ante los malvados que desolan una comarca fertilísima, se dibuja con regocijo en sus labios contraídos por la satisfacción y silencios (*Revista Universal*, 2 June 1875, *OC* 6:220).

75. Arce, *Religión poesía del mundo venidero*, 101–2.
76. El Sacerdocio católico es necesariamente inmoral (Notebook #1, *OC* 21:16).
77. Yo quiero educar a un pueblo que salve al que va a abogarse y que no vaya nunca a misa (ibid.).
78. Hay en el ser humano una invisible y extraordinaria fuerza de secretos, buen sentido y razón, y si la religión católica desconfía de su fuerza, a pesar de su sobrenatural origen; sí, a pesar de ser divina, tiene miedo de los hombres; si para dar al hombre la conciencia de sí mismo, quiere quitarle los medios de conciencia; si la religión de la dulzura se convierte en la cortesana de la ambición y de la fuerza, —este ser propio de que se nos quiere desposeer se levanta herido este ser que tiene libre el pensamiento no quiere que se haga hipócrita su voluntad (*Revista Universal*, 8 June 1875, *OC* 6:226).
79. Porque ha dicho lo que dijo Jesús ("El cisma de los Católicos en Nueva York," *El Partido Liberal*, 16 January 1887, *OC* 11:140–41).
80. "Cura de los pobres", al que los aconseja sin empequeñecerlos desde hace veintidós años, al que ha repartido entre los infelices su herencia y su sueldo, al que no les ha seducido sus mujeres ni iniciado en torpezas a sus hijas, al que les ha alzado en su barrio de pobres una iglesia que tiene siempre los brazos abiertos, al que jamás aprovechó el influjo de la fe para intimidar las almas, ni oscurecer los pensamientos, ni reducir su libre espíritu al servicio ciego de los intereses mundanos e impuros de la Iglesia ("El cisma de los Católicos en Nueva York," *El Partido Liberal*, 16 January 1887, *OC* 11:142–43).
81. Pues eso (curas en política) de meterse en las casas con la autoridad indiscutible e infalible de las cosas de Dios, esenciales y eternas, para influir en las cosas políticas . . . es un robo peor que cualquiera otro, y usurpación de almas (Notebook #18, 1894, *OC* 21:409).
82. ¿Dónde tienes tú escrita, Arzobispo: Papa, dónde tienes tú escrita la credencial que te da derecho a un alma? ¡Ya no vestimos sayo de cutí, ya leemos historia, ya tenemos curas buenos que nos expliquen la verdadera teología, ya sabemos que los obispos no vienen del cielo, ya sabernos por qué medios humanos, por qué conveniencias de mera administración, por qué ligas culpables con los príncipes, por qué contratos inmundos e indulgencias vergonzosas se ha ido levantando, todo de manos de hombres, todo como simple forma de gobierno, ese edificio impuro del Papado! ("La excomunión del padre McGlynn," *El Partido Liberal*, 1887, *OC* 11:243).
83. ¿Se puede ser hombre y católico, o para ser católico se ha de tener alma de lacayo? (ibid.).
84. Medardo Vitier, *Las ideas y la filosofía en Cuba* (La Habana: Editorial de Ciencias Sociales, 1970), 77.
85. Ibid., 71.

86. Jorge Juan Lozano Ros, "Fundamentación de la obra de José Martí," *Historia Gráfica*, 6 (February 2012): 327.

87. Maza, *The Cuban Catholic Church*, 25–26, 33, 35.

88. Ibid., 25–26.

89. Ibid.

90. John M. Kirk, *Between God and the Party: Religion and Politics in Revolutionary Cuba*. (Tampa: University Presses of Florida, 1988), 20.

91. Medardo Vitier, *Las ideas y la filosofía en Cuba*, 203.

92. Joseph J. McCadden, "The New York-to-Cuba Axis of Father Varela," *The Americas* 20, no. 4 (April 1964): 376–77.

93. A aquel obispo español, que llevamos en el corazón todos los cubanos (letter to the historian and bibliographer Antonio Bachiller y Morales, *El Avisador Hispano-Americano*, 24 January 1889, *OC* 5:145).

94. Padre de los pobres y de nuestra filosofía, había declarado, más por consejo de su mente que por el ejemplo de los enciclopedistas, campo propio y cimiento de la ciencia del mundo el estudio de las leyes naturales (ibid.).

95. Edelberto Leyva, *José Agustín Caballero: Obras* (La Habana: Ediciones Imagen Contemporánea, 1999), 9.

96. Medardo Vitier, *Las ideas y la filosofía en Cuba*, 192.

97. José Agustín Caballero, *Philosophia Electiva*, in *Obras de José Agustín Caballero*, trans. Jenaro Artiles (La Habana: Editorial de la Universidad de la Habana, 1944), 1:171.

98. Isabel Monal, "Tres filósofos del centenario," in *Filosofía e ideología de Cuba siglo XIX*, ed. Isabel Monal and Olivia Miranda (Mexico City: Universidad Nacional Autónoma de México, 1994), 82.

99. Caballero, *Philosophia Electiva*, 267.

100. Medardo Vitier, *Las ideas y la filosofía en Cuba*, 18.

101. John Nichol, *Francis Bacon: His Life and Philosophy, Part II* (Philadelphia: J. B. Lippincott Co., 1889), 47.

102. José de la Luz y Caballero, "A la memoria del doctor don José Agustín Caballero," in *Obras IV* (1835; Barcelona: Linkgua Ediciones, 2019), 257.

103. Monal, "Tres filósofos del centenario," 84.

104. Roberto Agramonte, "Estudio preliminar," in José Agustín Caballero, *Philosophia Electiva. Obras de José Agustín Caballero, Vol 1.* (La Habana: Editorial de la Universidad de la Habana, 1944), xcvii.

105. Isabel Monal and Olivia Miranda, "Bosquejo de las ideas en Cuba hasta finales del siglo XIX," in *Filosofía e ideología de Cuba siglo XIX*, ed. Isabel Monal and Olivia Miranda (Mexico City: Universidad Nacional Autónoma de México, 1994), 19.

106. Although Caballero was eclectic, he was not part of the French eclectic school. As Buch Sánchez reminds us, we should not confuse Caballero's

philosophia electiva with the French philosopher Víctor Cousin's *filosofía ecléctica* that circulated in Europe in 1815, arriving in La Habana at the earliest in the 1830s—some three decades after Caballero was chair of philosophy. See Rita M. Buch Sánchez, "De Caballero a Martí: Trayectoria de la filosofía cubana electiva en el siglo XIX," *Honda*, no. 25 (2009): 4–5. Both Luz and Varela criticized and denounced Cousinian thought for its Hegelian reduction of philosophy to dialectic salvation history that serves to justify current oppressive social and political structures.

107. Félix Lizaso, *Panorama de la cultura cubana* (Mexico City: Fondo de Cultura Económica, 1949), 18.

108. Miguel A. De La Torre, *The Quest for the Cuban Christ: A Historical Search* (Gainesville: University Press of Florida, 2002), 22–23.

109. Christian Smith, *The Emergence of Liberation Theology: Radical Religion and Social Movement Theory* (Chicago: University of Chicago Press, 1991), 13.

110. Monal and Miranda, "Bosquejo de las ideas en Cuba," 22.

111. Marcos Antonio Ramos, *Panorama del protestantismo en Cuba: La presencia de los protestantes o evangélicos en la historia de Cuba desde la colonización Española hasta la revolución* (San José, Costa Rica: Editorial Caribe, 1986), 51.

112. Medardo Vitier, *Las ideas y la filosofía en Cuba*, 195.

113. Pope John Paul II, "Address of John Paul II," Apostolic Journey of His Holiness John Paul II to Cuba, 23 January 1998, https://w2.vatican.va/content/john-paul-ii/en/travels/1998/documents/hf_jp-ii_spe_23011998_lahavana-culture.html.

114. McCadden, "The New York-to-Cuba Axis of Father Varela," 376.

115. Ibid., 380.

116. Los restos de aquel patriota entero, que cuando vio incompatible el gobierno de España con el carácter y las necesidades criollas, dijo sin miedo lo que vio (reflection on visiting Varela's tomb, *Patria*, 6 August 1892, *OC* 2:96–97).

117. McCadden, "The New York-to-Cuba Axis of Father Varela," 389.

118. Félix Varela, "Elenco de 1816," in *Obras I* (1861; Barcelona: Linkgua Ediciones, 2014), 80.

119. Que el hombre viva en analogía con el universo, y con su época; para lo cual no le sirven el Latín y el Griego (*La América*, 1884, *OC* 8:430).

120. Varela, "Elenco de 1816," 82–83.

121. McCadden, "The New York-to-Cuba Axis of Father Varela," 377.

122. Medardo Vitier, *Las ideas y la filosofía en Cuba*, 195.

123. La experiencia es la base más firme del conocimiento . . . no tengo el derecho de asentar un sistema metafísico sobre imaginaciones (*Revista Universal*, 21 September 1875, *OC* 6:333).

124. Varela, "Elenco de 1816," 103–4.

125. Varela, "Proyecto para el gobierno de las provincias de Ultramar: Preámbulo de la instrucción para el gobierno de Ultramar," in *Obras II* (1823; Barcelona: Linkgua Ediciones, 2015), 115.
126. Monal and Miranda, "Bosquejo de las ideas en Cuba," 25.
127. John Farina, "General Introduction," in *Félix Varela: Letters to Elpido*, ed. Felipe J. Estévez (New York: Paulist Press, 1989), xiii, xv.
128. Alfredo José Estrada, *Havana: Autobiography of a City* (New York: Palgrave Macmillan, 2007), 104–5.
129. Félix Varela, "Carta a los habitantes de la Habana despidiéndose para ir a ejercer el cargo de diputado en las Cortes de 1822–1823," in *Obras II* (1821; Barcelona: Linkgua Ediciones, 2015), 91.
130. Varela, "Carta a redactor de Diario de la Habana," *El Habanero: Papel político, científico y literario*, no. 2, in *Obras II* (1826; Barcelona: Linkgua Ediciones, 2015), 2:344.
131. Varela, "Estado eclesiástico en la isla de Cuba," *El Habanero: Papel político, científico y literario*, no. 2, in *Obras II* (1824; Barcelona: Linkgua Ediciones, 2015), 1:217.
132. Olivia Miranda, "El hombre en la teoría revolucionaria de Félix Varela," in *Filosofía e ideología de Cuba siglo XIX*, ed. Isabel Monal and Olivia Miranda (Mexico City: Universidad Nacional Autónoma de México, 1994), 118.
133. Félix Varela "Cartas a Elpidio: sobre la impiedad la superstición y el fanatismo en sus relaciones con la sociedad," in *Obras III* (1835; Barcelona: Linkgua Ediciones, 2019), 10.
134. Varela, "Carta a redactor de Diario de la Habana," 344.
135. Varela, "Diálogo que han tenido en esta ciudad un español partidario de la independencia de la isla de Cuba y un paisano suyo antiindependiente," *El Habanero: Papel político, científico y literario*, no. 3. In *Obras II* (1824; Barcelona: Linkgua Ediciones, 2015), 1:250.
136. Al padre amoroso del alma cubana (*Patria*, 11 June 1892, *OC* 4:418).
137. Cintio Vitier, *Ese sol del mundo moral: Para una historia de la eticidad cubana* (Mexico City: Siglo Veintiuno, 1975), 36.
138. Por dos hombres temblé y lloré al saber de su muerte, sin conocerlos, sin conocer un ápice de su vida: por Don José de la Luz y por Lincoln (*OC* 1:297).
139. Sembró hombres (*El Economista Americano*, March 1888, *OC* 5:249).
140. Cintio Vitier and Daisaku Ikeda, *José Martí Cuban Apostle: A Dialogue*, ed. and trans. Richard L. Gage (2001; London: I. B. Tauris, 2013), 18.
141. Ramos, *Protestantism and Revolution in Cuba*, 21.
142. José de la Luz y Caballero, "Doctrinas de psicología, lógica y moral, expuestas en la clase de filosofía del Colegio de San Cristóbal," in *Obras III* (1835; Barcelona: Linkgua Ediciones, 2015), 86.
143. Cintio Vitier, *Lecciones cubanas* (La Habana: Editorial Pueblo y Educación, 1996), 30.

144. Monal, "Tres filósofos del centenario," 94.
145. José de la Luz y Caballero, "Discurso en los exámenes generales del Colegio del Salvador, pronunciado el 16 de diciembre de 1858," in *Obras III* (1858; Barcelona: Linkgua Ediciones, 2015), 483.
146. Monal and Miranda. "Bosquejo de las ideas en Cuba," 27.
147. José de la Luz y Caballero, "Dos discursos leídos en los exámenes del Colegio del Salvador," in *Obras III* (1861; Barcelona: Linkgua Ediciones, 2015), 602.
148. Por medio de la ciencia se llega a Dios (*Juicios filosofía*, *OC* 19:361).
149. Guillermo de Zéndegui, *Ámbito de Martí* (Madrid: Escuela Gráfica Salesiana, 1954), 49; Gutiérrez Marroquín, *Ética cristiana en la poesía de José Martí*, 26.
150. Ramos, *Protestantism and Revolution in Cuba*, 21.
151. ¡Qué Hermosa poesías tiene la Biblia! (*La América*, May 1884, *OC* 8:290).
152. Rudimentario y erróneo (*La Nación*, 21 October 1883, *OC* 9:466).
153. Que en verdad es libro que, en cosas de alma, dijo todo (*La Nación*, 20 June 1883, *OC* 9:412).
154. *OC* 6:133.
155. *OC* 7:197.
156. Tras las épocas de fe vienen las de crítica. Tras las de síntesis caprichosa, las de análisis escrupuloso. Mientras más confiada fue la fe, más desconfiado es el análisis (undated fragments, *OC* 22:199).
157. El único medio de salvar todavía a la Religión, es aplicar la razón a la Biblia (*La América*, April 1884, *OC* 13:439).
158. La única autoridad legítima y definitiva para el establecimiento de la verdad es la razón (ibid., *OC* 13:440).
159. Pero las Iglesias se irritan contra ese examen da la Biblia, porque él requiere lo que a ellas no agrada, el ejercicio de la libertad. Ese es el secreto de la ira que levanta el descubrimiento de que el libro que se suponía haber caído de los cielos como un meteorito, pertenece en realidad a las "letras humanas"; y no es, por tanto, el "déspota infalible del entendimiento y la conciencia" (ibid., *OC* 13:440).

CHAPTER 2

Epigraph. El ejercicio de la libertad conduce a la religión nueva (Beecher's eulogy, 1887, *OC* 13:33).

1. Jack Beatty, *Age of Betrayal: The Triumph of Money in America, 1865–1900* (New York: Vintage Books, 2007), xi.
2. González, *José Martí*, 49.
3. Gigantes que llevan siete leguas en las botas y le pueden poner la bota encima (opening lines to "Nuestra América," *El Partido Liberal*, 30 January 1891, *OC* 6:15).

4. Herbert Spencer, *The Coming Slavery and Other Essays* (New York: Humboldt Publishing, 1888), 1.

5. Herbert Spencer, *The Man versus the State* (London: Williams & Norgate, 1894), 34.

6. Los pueblos que no creen en la perpetuación y universal sentido, en el sacerdocio y glorioso ascenso de la vida humana, se desmigajan como un mendrugo roído de ratones (*OC* 15:388).

7. ¿Cómo vendrá a ser el socialismo, ni cómo éste ha de ser una nueva esclavitud? Juzga Spencer como victorias crecientes de la idea socialista, y concesiones débiles de los buscadores de popularidad, esa nobilísima tendencia, precisamente para hacer innecesario el socialismo, nacida de todos los pensadores generosos que ven como el justo descontento de las clases llanas les lleva a desear mejoras radicales y violentas, y no hallan más modo natural de curar el daño de raíz que quitar motivo al descontento. Pero esto ha de hacerse de manera que no se trueque el alivio de los pobres en fomento de los holgazanes; y a esto sí hay que encaminar las leyes que tratan del alivio, y no a dejar a la gente humilde con todas sus razones de revuelta (*OC* 15:389).

8. Si los pobres se habitúan a pedirlo todo al Estado, cesaran a poco de hacer esfuerzo alguno por su subsistencia . . . Y todas esas intervenciones del Estado las juzga Herbert Spencer como causadas por la marea que sube, e impuestas por la gentualla que las pide, como si el loabilísimo y sensato deseo de dar a los pobres casa limpia, que sanea a la par el cuerpo y la mente, no hubiera nacido en los rangos mismos de la gente culta, sin la idea indigna de cortejar voluntades populares; y como si esa otra tentativa de dar los ferrocarriles al Estado no tuviera, con varios inconvenientes, altos fines moralizadores; tales como el de ir dando de baja los juegos corruptores de la bolsa, y no fuese alimentada en diversos países, a un mismo tiempo, entre gentes que no andan por cierto en tabernas ni tugurios (*OC* 15:389–90).

9. Dos peligros tiene la idea socialista, como tantas otras: —el de las lecturas extranjerizas, confusas e incompletas: —y el de la soberbia y rabia disimulada de los ambiciosos, que para ir levantándose en el mundo empiezan por fingirse, para tener hombros en que alzarse, frenéticos defensores de los desamparados. Pero en nuestro pueblo no es tanto el riesgo, como en sociedades más iracundas, y de menos claridad natural (*OC* 3:168).

10. La república, en Puerto Rico como en Cuba, no será el predominio injusto de una clase de cubanos sobre las demás, sino el equilibrio abierto y sincero de todas las fuerzas reales del país, y del pensamiento y deseo libres de los cubanos todos (*Patria*, 14 March 1893, *OC* 2:255).

11. La libertad política no estará asegurada, mientras no se asegure la libertad espiritual (undated notes, *OC* 18:290)

12. "El teísmo científico" —los contornos, cada día más claros . . . cada vez con más bríos del conocimiento científico del mundo (*La Nación*, 1 April 1886, *OC* 10:387–88).

13. Religión —lo que hay de esencial en todas, sin oprimir a ninguna (undated fragment, *OC* 22:75).

14. La libertad es la religión definitiva. Y la poesía de la libertad el culto nuevo (review of a presentation given by Walt Whitman, *La Nación*, 19 April 1887, *OC* 13:135).

15. Cepeda, *José Martí*, 154.

16. La nueva religión: no la virtud por el castigo y por el deber; la virtud por el patriotismo, el convencimiento y el trabajo (*Guatemala*, published by the Mexican newspaper *El Siglo XIX*, 1878, *OC* 7:120).

17. Nada ayuda más eficazmente que la libertad a la verdadera religión (undated essay "La libertad religiosa en los Estados Unidos," *OC* 19:397).

18. ¡Pues nada menos proponemos que la religión nueva y los sacerdotes nuevos! ¡Nada menos vamos pintando que las misiones con que comenzará a esparcir pronto su religión la época nueva! El mundo está de cambio; y las púrpuras y las casullas, necesarias en los tiempos místicos del hombre, están tendidas en el lecho de la agonía. La religión no ha desaparecido, sino que se ha transformado. Por encima del desconsuelo en que sume a los observadores el estudio de los detalles y envolvimiento despacioso de la historia humana, se ve que los hombres crecen, y que ya tienen andada la mitad de la escala de Jacob: ¡qué hermosas poesías tiene la Biblia! Si acurrucado en una cumbre se echan los ojos de repente por sobre la marcha humana, se verá que jamás se amaron tanto los pueblos como se aman ahora, y que a pesar del doloroso desbarajuste y abominable egoísmo en que la ausencia momentánea de creencias finales y fe en la verdad de lo Eterno trae a los habitantes de esta época transitoria, jamás preocupó como hoy a los seres humanos la benevolencia y el ímpetu de expansión que ahora abrasa a todos los hombres. Se han puesto en pie, como amigos que sabían uno de otro, y deseaban conocerse; y marchan todos mutuamente a un dichoso encuentro (*La América*, May 1894, *OC* 8:290).

19. No sé si soy un loco, puesto que soy un idealista tan completo. El realismo santo maravilloso, milagroso, es la lógica de la naturaleza (notes for his debate on *El idealismo y el realismo en el arte*, *OC* 19:429).

20. Yo sueño con los ojos / Abiertos (*OC* 16:22).

21. *OC* 21:29.

22. ¿Templos? ahora se necesitan más que nunca templos de amor y humanidad que desaten todo lo que hay en el hombre de generoso y sujeten todo lo que hay en él, de crudo y vil (*La Nación*, 5 September 1884, *OC* 10:80).

23. Montaner, *El pensamiento de Martí*, 9.

24. Patria es algo más que opresión, algo más que pedazos de terreno sin libertad y sin vida, algo más que derecho de posesión a la fuerza. Patria es comunidad de intereses, unidad de tradiciones, unidad de fines, fusión dulcísima y consoladora de amores y esperanzas (*La república española ante la revolución cubana*, 1873, *OC* 1:93).

25. Aquella apretadísima comunión de los espíritus, por largas raíces, por el enlace de las gentes, por el óleo penetrante de los dolores comunes, por el gustosísimo vino dc las glorias patrias, por aquella alma nacional que se cierne en el aire, y con él se respira, y se va aposentando en las entrañas, por todos los sutiles y formidables hilos de la historia atados, como la epidermis a la carne (*La Nación*, 20 March 1885, *OC* 10:157).

26. Patria es humanidad (*Patria*, 26 January 1895, *OC* 5:468).

27. El patriotismo es un deber santo, cuando se lucha por poner la patria en condición de que vivan en ella más felices los hombres (*Patria*, 14 March 1892, *OC* 1:320).

28. Un día que es, para los cubanos, religioso (*OC* 1:199).

29. ¡Clubs de espíritus es lo que queremos[!] (*OC* 4:263).

30. El catolicismo muere, como murió la mitología, como murió el paganismo, como muere lo que un genio humano crea, o halla y la razón de otro genio destruye, o reemplaza. Una sola cosa no ha de morir. —El Dios Conciencia, la dualidad sublime del amor y del honor, el pensamiento inspirador de todas las religiones, el germen eterno de todas las creencias, la ley irreformable, la ley fija, siempre soberana de las almas, siempre obedecida con placer, siempre noble, siempre igual; —he aquí la Idea Poderosa y fecunda que no ha de perecer, porque renace idéntica con cada alma que surge a la luz; —he aquí la única cosa verdadera porque es la única cosa por todos reconocida; —he aquí el eje del mundo moral; —he aquí a nuestro Dios omnipotente y sapientísimo. El Dios Conciencia, que es el hijo del Dios que creó, que es el único lazo visible unánimemente recibido, unánimemente adorado, que une a la humanidad impulsada con la divinidad impulsadora. —Adorado, y no parezca esto reminiscencia de educación católica. —Este Dios, y el Dios Patria, son en nuestra sociedad y en nuestra vida las únicas cosas adorables (Notebook #1, *OC* 21:29).

31. Armando García de la Torre, *José Martí and the Global Origins of Cuban Independence* (Kingston, Jamaica: University of the West Indies Press, 2015), 14.

32. C. Neale Ronning, *José Martí and the Émigré Colony in Key West* (New York: Praeger Publishers, 1990), 32.

33. Para la guerra democrática y juiciosa de la independencia fue creado el Partido Revolucionario, y no se desviará de su objeto, que es hacer con democracia y con juicio la guerra de independencia (*Patria*, 19 August 1893, *OC* 2:369).

34. Leonardo Griñán Peralta, *Martí: Líder político* (La Habana: Editorial de Ciencias Sociales, 1970), 89.

35. Unir, con propósito y fuerza bastante, a todos los elementos necesarios para acelerar, por una organización revolucionaria de espíritu y métodos democráticos, el establecimiento de una república donde todo ciudadano, cubano o español, blanco o negro, americano o europeo, pueda gozar, en el trabajo y en la paz, de su derecho entero de hombre (*Patria*, 20 August 1892, *OC* 2:139).

36. Ronning, *José Martí and the Émigré Colony in Key West*, 68–69.

37. Carlos Márquez Sterling, *Martí: Ciudadano de América* (New York: Las Americas Publishing, 1965), 301–4.

38. Porque el cristianismo se siente como al morir, en los umbrales de la Iglesia nueva donde, con el cielo por techo, se sentará el Cristo católico junto al Cristo hindú, con Confucio de un lado y Wotan de otro, sin más clérigo que el sentimiento del deber, ni más candelabros que los rayos del sol, ni más incensarios que los cálices de las flores (*El Partido Liberal*, March 1890, *OC* 12:418).

39. Contestaré acabando de limpiar mi vida, si no está bien limpia ya, de todo pensamiento o culpa que me impidan el servicio absoluto de mi patria (letter to José Dolores Poyo, a fellow organizer in Florida for the Cuban Revolution, 20 April 1892, *OC* 1:405).

40. Los artículos de la fe no han desaparecido: han cambiado de forma. A los del dogma católico han sustituido las enseñanzas de la razón. La enseñanza obligatoria es un artículo de fe del nuevo dogma (*Revista Universal*, 26 October 1875, *OC* 6:352).

41. La religión, en suma, de los hombres libres nuevos, vasta, grandiosa, fraternal, humana, libre como ellos (undated fragment, *OC* 22:307).

42. Una fe que ha de sustituir a la que ha muerto y surge con un claror radioso de la arrogante paz del hombre redimido ("El poeta Walt Whitman," *La Nación*, 19 April 1887, *OC* 13:140).

43. Así hablaba la Iglesia: . . . Al rico: "Las masas se están echando encima: sólo la Iglesia prometiéndoles justicia en el cielo, puede contenerlas: es necesario hacer frente a las masas." Al pobre: "La pobreza es divina: ¿qué cosa más bella que un alma fortificada por la resignación?: allá en el cielo se encuentra luego el premio y el descanso!" ("La excomunión del padre McGlynn," *El Partido Liberal*, 1887, *OC* 11:245).

44. *OC* 19:103.

45. Rafael Cepeda "José Martí profeta de la teología de la liberación," *Paso*, no. 16 (March–April 1988): 1. It should be noted that for Cepeda, Martí is a liberation theologian because of his propensity to the ideas of love and justice manifested in the political process while in solidarity with workers committed to change social economic structures. See Rafael

Cepeda, "José Martí: Praxis del evangelio," *Anuario del Centro de Estudios Martianos*, no. 16 (1993): 43–49, in *En el ala de un colibrí: Esencia del pensamiento martiano Rafael Cepeda*, ed. Carlos R. Molina Rodríguez (1993; La Habana: Editorial Caminos, 2008), 176. Although I am in total agreement with Martí's commitment to implementing the ideas of love and justice in the political process, I find his solidarity not necessarily with the worker but with the poor and oppressed. There are numerous times that Martí supports and/or praises employers over and against employees. The addition of solidarity with workers committed to economic change might have more to do with the political milieu in which Cepeda found himself than Martí's actual writings.

46. Arce, *Religión poesía del mundo venidero*, 135.

47. La libertad cuesta muy cara, y es necesario, o resignarse a vivir sin ella, o decidirse a comprarla por su precio (*OC* 4:193).

48. ¿Conque el que sirve a la libertad, no puede servir a la Iglesia? . . . ¿Conque la Iglesia se vuelve contra los pobres que la sustentan y los sacerdotes que estudian sus males . . . ? ¿Conque la Iglesia no aprende historia, no aprende libertad, no aprende economía política? ("La excomunión del padre McGlynn," *El Partido Liberal*, 1887, *OC* 11:241).

49. ¿Conque la Iglesia compra influjo y vende voto? ¿Conque la santidad la encoleriza? ¿Conque es la aliada de los ricos de las sectas enemigas? ¿Conque prohíbe a sus párrocos el ejercicio de sus derechos políticos; a no ser que los ejerzan en pro de los que trafican en votos con la Iglesia? ¿Conque intenta arruinar y degrada a los que ofenden su política autoritaria, y siguen mansamente lo que enseñó el dulcísimo Jesús? ¿Conque no se puede ser hombre y católico? ¿Véase como se puede, según nos lo enseñan estos nuevos pescadores! ¡Oh Jesús! ¿Dónde hubieras estado en esta lucha? ("El cisma de los Católicos en Nueva York," *El Partido Liberal*, 16 January 1887, *OC* 11:150).

50. Una iglesia sin credo dogmático, sino con ese grande y firme credo que la majestad del Universo y la del alma buena e inmortal inspiran ¡qué gran iglesia fuera! ¡y cómo dignificaría a la religión desacreditada! (*La América*, June 1884, *OC* 8:440).

51. Ser caballero de los hombres, obrero del mundo futuro, cantor de alba, y sacerdote de la Iglesia nueva (prologue to Rafael De Castro Palomino's *Cuentos de hoy y de mañana*, 1883, *OC* 5:103).

52. Un cura de pueblo que quería mucho a los indios (*La edad de oro*, 1889, *OC* 18:306).

53. Astros tienen los cielos, y la tierra: como un astro refulgente el cadalso de John Brown. Jesús murió en la cruz y éste en la horca. Luego de muertos los hombres, vacíanse, sin carne y sin conciencia de su memoria, en la existencia universal: en remolinos suben; camino al Sol caminan; dicho-

samente bogan; mas si se hallaran los hombres después de muertos, que no han de hallarse, andarían de la mano Jesús y John Brown (*La Nación*, 9 May 1886, *OC* 10:191).

54. Rafael Cepeda, "La Biblia en Martí," in *En el ala de un colibrí: Esencia del pensamiento martiano Rafael Cepeda*, ed. Carlos R. Molina Rodríguez (1964; La Habana: Editorial Caminos, 2008), 70.

55. Ramos, *Protestantism and Revolution in Cuba*, 20.

56. Ibid.

57. Louis A. Pérez Jr., *Essays on Cuban History: Historiography and Research* (Gainesville: University Press of Florida, 1995), 54–55, 59.

58. Ramos, *Protestantism and Revolution in Cuba*, 22.

59. Ramos, *Panorama del protestantismo en Cuba*, 91–104.

60. Rafael Cepeda, "Martí y los protestantes cubanos," *Caminos*, no. 9 (January–March 1988): 57–61, in *En el ala de un colibrí: Esencia del pensamiento martiano Rafael Cepeda*, ed. Carlos R. Molina Rodríguez (1988; La Habana: Editorial Caminos, 2008), 185.

61. Cepeda, *José Martí*, 145.

62. Se levantó primero Brooklyn, hogar de la Iglesia Protestante, que guarda a pesar de sus estrecheces —¿por qué no decirlo?— la semilla de la libertad humana (*La Nación*, 9 May 1885, *OC* 10:204).

63. Todo hombre libre debía colgar en sus muros, como el de un redentor, el retrato de Lutero (*La Nación*, April 1884, *OC* 13:442).

64. Que no quiere saber de este dogma ni aquél; sino de lo esencial de la fe en Dios (*El Partido Liberal*, March 1890, *OC* 12:419).

65. Comenzó su discurso lento y grave, con palabras que involuntariamente recordaban los martillazos con que clavó Lutero su tesis en la puerta de la iglesia de Wittenberg (*El Partido Liberal*, 1887, *OC* 11:247).

66. Lleno de fuego criollo, con su alma rica de bondad (*Patria*, 7 May 1892, *OC* 4:399).

67. Ramos, *Panorama del protestantismo en Cuba*, 148.

68. *OC* 5:160–61.

69. *OC* 19:397–98.

70. Con su carga de arados, de escopetas y de Biblias: en busca de ese puerto venían cuando a bordo de la "Flor" reconocieron y firmaron que en las cosas del alma no hay mas guía ni autoridad que la razón . . . puritanos de quijada fuerte y de mosquete al hombro que quemaban brujas y acribillaban a balazos a los cuáqueros (*El Partido Liberal*, 6 October 1889, *OC* 12:289).

71. La Iglesia Metodista, que por otras partes cae, en Chantanqua florece, porque allí tomó fila con los humildes, y abrió sus flancos a los tiempos, que no quieren férula dominical ni puerta cerrada, ni están por guerras de topo, por credo más o credo menos, sino que piden a la naturaleza el

secreto de ella; y hallan en la comunión inteligente y libre un placer más digno y penetrante, más humano y religioso que el que, porque la iglesia tenga un pico o tenga tres, echa a aborrecerse y destruirse a los hombres. Las Iglesias acá, para no perecer en el mundo, andan con él (*La Nación*, 22 October 1890, *OC* 12:438).

72. Y el pueblo de las ciudades, si religioso, es ultramontano, y si no religioso, ha ido demasiado adelante en su fe en la libre razón para volver a las negaciones tímidas y concepciones incompletas del protestantismo (*La Opinión Nacional*, 12 January 1882, *OC* 23:149).

73. Moody, otro evangelista, está en una iglesia menor, poniendo la Biblia en chistes, y convirtiendo con anécdotas a los reacios: los convida con la llaneza, los retiene con la amenidad, los conmueve de súbito con una exhortación vehemente y desesperada, les enjuga con un cuento las lágrimas de los ojos (*El Partido Liberal*, 4 March 1890, *OC* 12:416).

74. Unos predicadores grotescos y frenéticos (*La Opinión Nacional*, 10 December 1881, *OC* 9:173).

75. *OC* 10:204.

76. No un cerdo que engendra churches, como el protestantismo (undated fragments, *OC* 22:307).

77. ¡Porque la enseñanza es falsa, el carácter duro, el rico soberbio, el pobre desconfiado, y la época de vuelco y reencarnación, que pide para guía del juicio y consuelo del alma algo más que Iglesias ligadas en pro de los pudientes contra los míseros, y que se rebajan al empleo de instrumentos de gobierno, y defensa de castas, y caen al suelo de una embestida de uñas! (*La Nación*, 7 February 1889, *OC* 12:117).

78. Nueva York va desfilando por allí: Vanderbilt y Roosevelt, Stebbins y Schuylers, Ceiton Sweets y Van Santvoorts, todas las familias, todas las noblezas, los obispos protestantes de alzacuello y levita, el ejército en plaza: con botones de oro y entorchados, el almirantazgo con charreteras de oro (*La Nación*, 7 February 1888, *OC* 11:394).

79. Y puede decirse a boca llena que el clero oficial, que muestra hoy en servir a los ricos (*La Nación*, 8 April 1888, *OC* 11:426).

80. ¡De ese modo se ve que en esta fortaleza del protestantismo, los protestantes, que aún representan aquí la clase rica y culta, son los amigos tácitos y tenaces, los cómplices agradecidos de la religión que los tostó en la hoguera, y a quien hoy acarician porque les ayuda a salvar su exceso injusto de bienes de fortuna! ¡Fariseos todos, y augures! ("El cisma de los Católicos en Nueva York," *El Partido Liberal*, 16 January 1887, *OC* 11:143).

81. El obispo de la Iglesia Metodista, una Iglesia robusta y protegida por gente de caudales, envía a los templos de su credo una pastoral que causa en el país una emoción profunda: "Basta —dice: este edificio donde vivimos es un edificio de injusticia: esto no es lo que enseñó Jesús, ni lo

que debemos hacer los hombres: nuestra civilización es injusta: nuestro sistema de salarios, asilos y hospitales ha sido sometido A prueba y ha fracasado. "Repugna al orden de la razón que unos tengan demasiado y otros no tengan lo indispensable. Lo que está hecho así, debe deshacerse, porque no está bien hecho. Salgamos amistosamente al encuentro de la justicia, si no queremos que la justicia se desplome sobre nosotros. "Por Cristo y por la razón: esta fábrica injusta ha de cambiarse. "¡Rico, tú tienes mucha tierra! ¡Pobre, tú debes tener tu parte de tierra!" Esas palabras: que condensan las de la pastoral, han sacudido la atención, porque no vienen de filántropos desacreditados, ni de gente de odas y de libros, sino de un gran sacerdote, de mucho seso y pensamiento, que tiene una iglesia de granito con ventanas de suaves colores, y ha pasado una vida majestuosa en el trato y cariño de los ricos. ¡Bendita sea la mano que se baja a los pobres! (*La Nación*, 16 May 1886, *OC* 10:448).

82. Esas ligas de los ricos de todas las sectas, esa osadía de hablar de la pobreza de Jesús y vivir de faisán con vino de oro en pompa de palacio, deslizando la púrpura, suave entre altas damas, que gusten de los clérigos blandílocuos ("La excomunión del padre McGlynn," *El Partido Liberal*, 1887, *OC* 11:245).

83. Pérez, *Essays on Cuban History*, 61.

84. "Shall Cuba Be Taken for Christ," *American Missionary* 52, no. 3 (September 1898): 106.

85. Richard B. Kimball, *Cuba and the Cubans; Comprising a History of the Island of Cuba, Its Present Social, Political, and Domestic Condition; also, Its Relationship to England and the United States* (New York: Samuel Hueston, 1850), 157–58.

86. Louis A. Pérez Jr., *On Becoming Cuban: Identity, Nationality, and Culture* (Chapel Hill: University of North Carolina Press, 1999), 58, 248–51.

87. Ramos, *Protestantism and Revolution in Cuba*, 23, 29.

88. La esclavitud tuvo sus sacerdotes, así como más tarde había de tener sus mártires; tuvo sus salmos, sus oraciones y sus interpretadores de la Biblia. Al principio, los mismos hombres del Sur la llamaron un "mal necesario": arrastrados, después, por el vértigo de la polémica, levantóse a dogma la justificación de la trata . . . El hombre del Sur creía en la esclavitud como creía en Dios (6 November 1884, *OC* 10:95).

89. Rafael Cepeda, Elizabeth Carrillo, Rhode González, and Carlos E. Ham, "Changing Protestantism in a Changing Cuba," in *In the Power of the Spirit: The Pentecostal Challenge to Historical Churches in Latin America*, ed. Benjamin F. Gutiérrez and Dennis A. Smith (Louisville, KY: Presbyterian Church, 1996), 95.

90. Vicente Rodríguez Carro, "Krause y las raíces 'masónicas' del krausismo español," *Studia Zamorensia* 13 (2014): 277–78.

91. Benedikt Paul Göcke, *The Panentheism of Karl Christian Friedrich Krause (1781–1832): From Transcendental Philosophy to Metaphysics* (Berlin: Peter Lang, 2018), 44, 123, 161.

92. Rodríguez Carro, "Krause y las raíces 'masónicas' del krausismo español," 285.

93. Göcke, *The Panentheism of Karl Christian Friedrich Krause*, 41.

94. Rodríguez Carro, "Krause y las raíces 'masónicas' del krausismo español," 286.

95. Se ama a un Dios que lo penetra y lo prevale todo. Parece profanación dar al Creador de todos los seres y de todo lo que ha de ser, la forma de uno solo de los seres (prologue to Pérez Bonalde's *Poema del Niágara*, 1882, *OC* 7:226).

96. José Ferrater Mora, "Krause" and "Krausismo," in *Diccionario de filosofía* (Buenos Aires: Editorial Sudamericana, 1941), 1:1066.

97. B. R. Martin, *Karl Christian Friedrich Krause's Leben, Lehre und Bedeutung* (Leipzig: Verlag Von Otto Heinrichs, 1885), 33.

98. Ferrater Mora, "Krause" and "Krausismo," 1065.

99. Göcke, *The Panentheism of Karl Christian Friedrich Krause*, 33, 43, 181.

100. Para ser bueno no necesita más que ver lo bello . . . Ve que el espectáculo de la naturaleza inspira fe, amor y respeto . . . La naturaleza inspira, cura, consuela, fortalece y prepara para la virtud al hombre. Y el hombre no se halla completo, ni se revela a sí mismo, ni ve lo invisible, sino en su íntima relación con la naturaleza (Emerson's eulogy, *La Opinión Nacional*, 19 May 1882, *OC* 13:22–26).

101. Más grande, los estudia en el Sujeto, en el Objeto, y en la manera subjetiva individual a que la Relación lleva el sujeto que examina al objeto examinado. —Yo tuve gran placer cuando hallé en Krause esa filosofía intermedia, secreto de los dos extremos, que yo había pensado en llamar Filosofía de relación (*Juicios filosofía*, *OC* 19:367).

102. José Francisco Vales, "La influencia de la cultura alemana en la formación del pensamiento de José Martí," *Iberoamericana* 20, no. 1 (1996): 7–8.

103. Medardo Vitier, *Las ideas y la filosofía en Cuba*, 223–34.

104. Peter Turton, *José Martí: Architect of Cuba's Freedom* (London: Zed Books, 1986), 149.

105. Rodríguez Carro, "Krause y las raíces 'masónicas' del krausismo español," 281.

106. Ferrater Mora, "Krause" and "Krausismo," 1067–68.

107. Christopher Abel, "Martí, Latin America and Spain," in *José Martí: Revolutionary Democrat*, ed. Christopher Abel and Nissa Torrents (London: Athlone Press, 1986), 131–32.

108. Ellos alemanizan el espíritu; ellos explican a un pueblo de imaginación generalizadora abstractas durezas de inteligencia positiva: ellos krausi-

fican el derecho; pero ellos son espíritus severos, limpios, claros, e hijos en verdad legítimos de la grave madre ciencia (*Revista Universal*, 13 March 1875, *OC* 15:39).

109. Krause no es todo verdad. Este es simplemente lenguaje simplificador, divisor, castellano del que me valgo y uso porque me parece más adecuado para realizar en la expresión exterior (expresar) mis ideas (Notebook #2, *OC* 21:98).

110. Rodríguez Carro, "Krause y las raíces 'masónicas' del krausismo español," 280.

111. McCadden, "The New York-to-Cuba Axis of Father Varela," 379.

112. F. de P. Rodriguez, "Cuban Freemasonry," *Quarterly Bulletin: Iowa Masonic Library* 17, no. 3 (July 1916): 68–69.

113. Creyó en aquella primera masonería de Cuba, de hijos del muérdago inmortal, jurados a extinguir la servidumbre, ajena o propia (*Patria*, 2 October 1894, *OC* 5:445).

114. Rodriguez, "Cuban Freemasonry," 68–69.

115. Ted Henken, Miriam Celaya, and Dimas Castellanos, eds., *Cuba* (Santa Barbara, CA: ABC-CLIO, 2013), 197.

116. Mario J. Pentón, "La filiación masónica de Martí, historia de una polémica que marcó sus ideales," *El Nuevo Herald*, 27 January 2017, 1B.

117. Clara Emma Chávez Álvarez, *Hacedora de la bandera cubana: Emilia Margarita Teurbe Tolón y Otero* (La Habana: Publicaciones de la Oficina del Historiador de la Ciudad de la Habana, 2011), 67–68.

118. Henken, *Cuba*, 198.

119. Robert Freke Gould, *Gould's History of Freemasonry Throughout the World* (New York: Charles Scribner's Sons, 1936), 4:127.

120. Ibid., 128.

121. Lomas, *Translating Empire*, 15.

122. Lo que nace del fuego patriótico perdura (*Patria*, 21 May 1892, *OC* 5:50).

123. Todas las virtudes necesarias para el goce pacífico de la libertad (*Patria*, 3 April 1892, *OC* 5:347).

124. *OC* 12:234.

125. Sin el trato libre e indulgente de los que han de vivir en ella como hermanos, no cayó solo, ni entre pechos fríos, sino rodeado de cabezas descubiertas (*OC* 4:382).

126. Y allá en Cuba, ¿se verá al cubano como aquí, asociándose para crecer, defendiendo de la muerte la caza, enseñando de noche después de trabajar de día, creando desde el taburete del obrero una religión nueva de amor activo entre los hombres, el sábado en la logia, el domingo en su presidencia o en su tesorería, la noche entre el periódico y el libro? (*Patria*, 1 April 1893, *OC* 2:279).

127. De esa logia mayor y perfecta, la logia celestial (*Patria*, 21 May 1892, *OC* 5:50).

128. Jossianna Arroyo, *Writing Secrecy in Caribbean Freemasonry* (New York: Palgrave Macmillan, 2013), 103–4.
129. La masonería no puede ser una sociedad secreta en los países libres, porque su obra es la misma obra del adelanto general . . . La masonería no es más que una forma activa del pensamiento liberal. See José Martí, "Al federalista I," 1876, in *José Martí Obras completas: Edición crítica*, vol. 2, *1875–1876, México*, ed. Cintio Vitier (La Habana: Centro de Estudios Martianos, 2009), 270.
130. Pentón, "La filiación masónica de Martí," 1B.
131. López, *José Martí*, 74, 183.
132. Arroyo, *Writing Secrecy in Caribbean Freemasonry*, 106.
133. Pentón, "La filiación masónica de Martí," 1B.
134. Ezequiel Martínez Estrada, *Martí, Revolucionario* (La Habana: Casa de las Américas, 1967), 107.
135. Y masones, protestantes y católicos corearon juntos, al pie del monumento de la razón libre, el himno "América" (*La Nación*, August 1889, *OC* 12:289).
136. Roig de Leuchsenring, *Martí y las religiones*, 34.
137. See *OC* 1:136; *OC* 1:200; 4:215, 229.
138. Arroyo, *Writing Secrecy in Caribbean Freemasonry*, 71, 105, 107.
139. Gutiérrez Marroquín, *Ética cristiana en la poesía de José Martí*, 16.
140. Arroyo, *Writing Secrecy in Caribbean Freemasonry*, 106.

CHAPTER 3

Epigraph. El espíritu presente; las creencias ratifican (Emerson's eulogy, *La Opinión Nacional*, 19 May 1882, *OC* 13:25).

1. No soy bastante instruido en cada una de las religiones para poder decir con razón que pertenezco a una de ellas. Me basta —sí— un absurdo para alejar mi simpatía (Notebook #1, *OC* 21:42).
2. La única religión digna de los hombres es aquella que no excluye a hombre alguno de su seno (Cooper's eulogy, *La Nación*, 3 June 1883, *OC* 13:53).
3. Venérese a los hombres de religión, sean católicos o tarahumaras: todo el mundo, lacio o lanudo, tiene derecho a su plena conciencia: tirano es el católico que se pone sobre un hindú, y el metodista que silba a un católico . . . El hombre sincero tiene derecho al error (*Patria*, 8 September 1894, *OC* 8:257).
4. Adriana Novoa, "'Transpensar': Materialism, Spiritualism, and Race in José Martí's Philosophy," *Cuban Studies*, 47 (2019): 169–94.
5. Que cada grano de materia traiga en sí un grano de espíritu (*La Opinión Nacional*, 15 June 1882, *OC* 23:317).

6. Raquel Catalá, "Conceptos teosóficos de Martí," *Revista Teosófica Cubana* 34, no. 3 (March 1939): 25.

7. *OC* 12:501.

8. Edúquese lo superior del hombre, para que pueda, con ojos de más luz, entrar en el consuelo, adelantar en el misterio, explorar en la excelsitud del orbe espiritual (*El Partido Liberal*, 17 December 1891, *OC* 12:504).

9. Hay que descubrir y clasificar los hechos del espíritu: hechos del espíritu, científicos como cualesquiera otros, son todos los del hipnotismo y el mesmerismo, los sueños y la clarividencia, el genio y el poder de transferir el pensamiento, todo lo que está en los libros de Sínnett y en "La Doctrina Secreta" de la gran sacerdotisa que se les acaba de morir, la rusa Blavatsky (ibid., *OC* 12:503).

10. There is a difference in how I am using the words *spiritism* and *spiritualism*. The former refers to followers of Kardec's practices, specifically communication with the dead. The latter, spiritualism, is a belief in the metaphysical that includes the existence of the departed spirit with which we may or may not be able to communicate. Hence a spiritist is a spiritualist, but a spiritualist (like Martí) may not necessarily be a spiritist.

11. Allan Kardec, *Le livre des esprits*, 2nd ed. (Paris: Didier et Cie, Libraires-Éditeurs, 1860), 464.

12. Ibid.

13. Allan Kardec, *La genèse, les miracles et les predictions selon le spiritisme* (Paris: Librairie Internationale, 1868), 12.

14. Ibid.

15. Ibid., 188.

16. Ibid., 278–79.

17. Allan Kardec, "Les déserteurs," *Œuvres posthumes*, ed. P. Leymarie (1869; Paris: Librairie des Sciences Spirites et Psychiques, 1912), 290–91.

18. Allan Kardec, *Le livre des médiums: Ou guide des médiums et des évocateurs* (Paris: Didier et Cie, Libraires-Éditeurs, 1861), 132.

19. Miguel A. De La Torre, *Santería: The Beliefs and Rituals of a Growing Religion in America* (Grand Rapids, MI: Wm. B. Eerdmans Publishing, 2004), 172–73.

20. Lia Theresa Schraeder, "The Spirits of the Times: The Mexican Spiritist Movement from Reform to Revolution" (PhD diss., University of California, Davis, 2009), 55.

21. De La Torre, *Santería*, 173.

22. El alma post-existe. Y si post-existe, y no nacemos iguales, pre-existe, ha pasado por distintas formas. —¿Aquí o allá?— Es inútil preguntarlo, pero ha pasado (Notebook #1, *OC* 21:43).

23. De La Torre, *Santería*, 173.

24. El espíritu fuera de la forma del hombre no es humano. El medium no habla por sí. ¿Cómo entonces ha de hablar un lenguaje humano el espíritu que no lo es? ¿Cómo habla siempre el lenguaje del medium? Dos mediums de idénticas condiciones consultan a un mismo espíritu sobre una misma materia. Y las dos respuestas son diferentes (Notebook #1, *OC* 21:43).

25. Un tamboril que suena por electricidad, invita a los desocupados de Broadway a entrar a ver en el teatro de los minstrels cómo el prestidigitador Kellar, el rival de Hernian, repite y explica todos los ruidos, escrituras y apariciones con que los espiritistas de profesión, como cierto doctor Slade, engañan a las almas tristes y finas a quienes saca de nivel el desconsuelo de lo terrestre y la necesidad de lo maravilloso (*La Nación*, 1 April 1889, *OC* 12:194).

26. Yo vengo a esta discusión con el espíritu de conciliación que norma todos los actos de mi vida. Yo estoy entre el materialismo que es la exageración de la materia, y el espiritismo que es la exageración del espíritu. (Sensación.) ¿Qué es el espíritu? nos pregunta el señor Baz. El espíritu es lo que en él piensa, lo que nos induce a actos independientes de nuestras necesidades corpóreas, es lo que nos fortalece, nos anima, nos agranda en la vida. (Aplausos.) ¿No recuerda el señor Baz cuando ha depositado un beso casto y puro en la frente de su madre, (bravo, bravo) cuando ha amado con la pasión del poeta, cuando ha escrito con miserable tinta y en miserable papel algo que no era miserable? (Bravo, bien, bien.) Ese algo nos da la propia convicción de nuestra inmortalidad, nos revela nuestra preexistencia y nuestra sobre existencia. (Aplausos estrepitosos.) Por otra parte, señores, creo que esta discusión será inútil, si no se reforma la proposición del señor Baz, porque si no averiguamos antes si es cierto o no el espiritismo, de una cosa falsa no puede resultar una verdad. (Aplausos.) . . . Con mi inconformidad en la vida, con mi necesidad de algo mejor, con la imposibilidad de lograrlo aquí, lo demuestro: lo abstracto se demuestra con lo abstracto, yo tengo un espíritu inmortal, porque lo siento, porque lo creo, porque lo quiero. (Grandes aplausos). See José Martí, *Debate en el Liceo Hidalgo*, ed. Pedro Pablo Rodríguez (1875; La Habana: Centro de Estudios Martianos, 2010), 240–41.

27. *OC* 13:25.

28. Divino Jesús (*OC* 19:361).

29. Rafael Rojas, *José Martí: La invención de Cuba* (Madrid: Editorial Colibrí, 2000), 30.

30. Ralph Waldo Emerson, "October 4, 1844 Letter to William Emerson," in *The Letters of Ralph Waldon Emerson*, ed. Ralph L. Rusk (New York: Columbia University Press, 1939), 3:262.

31. El grandioso Emerson, tenido como uno de los más potentes y originales pensadores de estos tiempos, como varón excelso, y como el más grande

de los poetas de América (*La Opinión Nacional*, 23 May 1882, *OC* 23:305).

32. *OC* 13:132.

33. Ya he andado bastante por la vida, y probado sus varios manjares. Pues el placer más grande, el único placer absolutamente puro que hasta hoy he gozado fue el de aquella tarde —en que desde mi cuarto medio desnudo vi a la ciudad postrada, y entreví lo futuro pensando en Emerson (undated fragment, *OC* 22:323).

34. Escribir: Los momentos supremos: . . . La tarde de Emerson (undated note, *OC* 18:288).

35. Lo imperfecto de esta existencia se conoce en que en toda ella apenas hay unos cuantos momentos de dicha absoluta, dicha pura, que son los de pleno desinterés, los de confusión del hombre con la naturaleza. (Emerson. La tarde de Emerson: cuando pierde el hombre el sentido de sí, y se transfunde en el mundo.) (*Juicios filosofía*, *OC* 19:369–70).

36. *OC* 11:164; *OC* 5:190.

37. Él era un sacerdote de la naturaleza . . . El veía detrás de sí al Espíritu creador que a través de él hablaba a la naturaleza (Emerson's eulogy, *La Opinión Nacional*, 19 May 1882, *OC* 13:19).

38. Fue uno de aquellos a quienes la naturaleza se revela, y se abre, y extiende los múltiples brazos, como para cubrir con ellos el cuerpo todo de su hijo (ibid., *OC* 13:18).

39. Emerson, un Dante amoroso, que vivió sobre la tierra, más que en ella, —por lo que la vio con toda holgura y certidumbre, y escribió Biblia humana (*La América*, January 1884, *OC* 8:427).

40. *OC* 17:329.

41. Cada uno a su oficio: Fábula nueva del filósofo norteamericano Emerson (*OC* 17:154).

42. Ralph Waldo Emerson, "The Over-Soul," in *The Prose Works of Ralph Waldo Emerson*, rev. ed. (1841; Boston: Fields, Osgood, & Co., 1870), 358.

43. Que todo en ella es símbolo del hombre, y todo lo que hay en el hombre lo hay en ella (Emerson's eulogy, *La Opinión Nacional*, 19 May 1882, *OC* 13:23).

44. A Dios no es menester defenderlo; la naturaleza lo defiende (*La América*, October 1883, *OC* 7:326).

45. Ese hombre anda pisoteando en el fango de la dialéctica (Emerson's eulogy, *La Opinión Nacional*, 19 May 1882, *OC* 13:30).

46. La naturaleza inspira fe, amor y respeto (ibid., *OC* 13:24).

47. La naturaleza inspira, cura, consuela, fortalece, prepara la virtud al hombre. Y el hombre no se halla completo, ni se revela a sí mismo, ni ve lo invisible, sino en su íntima relación con la naturaleza (ibid., *OC* 13:25–26).

48. Emerson no discute: establece. Lo que le enseña la naturaleza le parece preferible a lo que le enseña el hombre. Para él un árbol sabe más que un

libro; y una estrella enseña más que una universidad; y una hacienda es un evangelio; y un niño de la hacienda está más cerca de la verdad universal que un anticuario. Para él no hay cirios como los astros, ni altares como los montes, ni predicadores como las noches palpitantes y profundas (ibid., *OC* 13:22).

49. ¿Qué es la Naturaleza? El pino agreste, el viejo roble, el bravo mar, los ríos que van al mar como a la Eternidad vamos los hombres: la Naturaleza es el rayo de luz que penetra las nubes y se hace arco iris; el espíritu humano que se acerca y eleva con las [palabra ininteligible] nubes del alma, y se hace bienaventurado. Naturaleza es todo lo que existe, en toda forma, —espíritus y cuerpos; corrientes esclavas en su cauce; raíces esclavas en la tierra; pies, esclavos como las raíces; almas, menos esclavas que los pies. El misterioso mundo íntimo, el maravilloso mundo externo, cuanto es, deforme o luminoso u oscuro, cercano o lejano, vasto— o raquítico, licuoso o terroso, regular todo, medido todo menos el cielo y el alma de los hombres [illegible] es Naturaleza (*Juicios filosofía*, *OC* 19:364).

50. ¿Qué son en suma los dogmas religiosos, sino la infancia de las verdades naturales? "El cisma de los Católicos en Nueva York," *El Partido Liberal*, 14 April 1887, *OC* 11:140).

51. Las contradicciones no están en la naturaleza, sino en que los hombres no saben descubrir sus analogías. No desdeña la ciencia por falsa, sino por lenta. Abrense sus libros, y rebosan verdades científicas (Emerson's eulogy, *La Opinión Nacional*, 19 May 1882, *OC* 13:29).

52. La naturaleza ha prescrito una ley, ineludible, como todas las suyas. —La Religión católica impone a sus apóstoles la inobservancia preciso de cata ley. Si Religión es la manifestación clara de Dios en la tierra, si es Dios que crea y que manda y hombre que adora y que obedece, ¿cómo es natural, cómo es legítima religión que manda al hombre que se rebele contra el precepto de su Dios? Más claro: ¡Cómo es natural religión que se rebela contra la naturaleza? ¡Cómo es legitima religión que se alza contra la Ley? (Notebook #1, *OC* 21:16–17).

53. Lizaso, *Posibilidades filosóficas en Martí*, 21

54. *OC* 22:316.

55. Jerome Schwartz, *Diderot and Montaigne: The Essais and the Shaping of Diderot's Humanism* (Geneva: Librairie Droz, 1966), 88.

56. Ralph Waldo Emerson, *English Traits* (1856; Boston: Houghton, Mifflin and Co., 1883), 65–67, 71.

57. El Oriente invade el Occidente (opening line of *Juicios filosofía*, *OC* 19:359).

58. *OC* 18:461–70

59. ¡Qué método tan cierto, tan racional, de dar con la verdad! fijar la atención sobre un objeto, de modo de investigar plenamente las partes que lo constituyen, el principio y el origen, la existencia y la destrucción

final; la naturaleza de las partes que lo componen, —lo que hay en él de esencial y de accidental (*OC* 21:260).

60. Que el dulce nirvana, que es la hermosura como de luz que le da al alma el desinterés, no se logra viviendo, como loco o glotón, para los gustos de lo material, y para amontonar a fuerza de odio y humillaciones el mando y la fortuna, sino entendiendo que no se ha de vivir para la vanidad, ni se ha de querer lo de otros y guardar rencor, ni se ha de dudar de la armonía del mundo o ignorar nada de él o mortificarse con la ofensa y la envidia, ni se ha de reposar hasta que el alma sea como una luz de aurora, que llena de claridad y hermosura al mundo, y llore y padezca por todo lo triste que hay en él, y se vea como médico y padre de todos los que tienen razón de dolor: es como vivir en un azul que no se acaba? con un gusto tan puro que debe ser lo que se llama gloria, y con los brazos siempre abiertos. Así vivió Buda (*OC* 18:466).

61. *OC* 18:467.

62. *Hay alma en los animales* (Notebook #1, undated, *OC* 21:16).

63. García de la Torre, *José Martí and the Global Origins of Cuban Independence*, 70–72.

64. A veces deslumbrado por esos libros resplandecientes de los hindús para los que la criatura humana, luego de purificada por la virtud, vuela como mariposa de fuego, de su escoria terrenal al seno de Brahma siéntase a hacer lo que censura, y a ver la naturaleza a través de ojos ajenos, porque ha hallado esos ojos conformes a los propios, y ve oscuramente y desluce sus propias visiones. Y es que aquella filosofía india embriaga como un bosque de azahares, y acontece con ella como con ver volar aves, que enciende ansias de volar (*La Opinión Nacional*, 19 May 1882, *OC* 13:27).

65. Cuando nací, sin sol, mi madre dijo: / "Flor de mi seno, Homagno generoso, / De mí y de la Creación suma y reflejo, / Pez que en ave y corcel y hombre se torna" (*OC* 16:161).

66. Realmente, el cuerpo no es más que un siervo del espíritu (undated fragments, *OC* 22:221).

67. La muerte es una victoria, y cuando se ha vivido bien, el féretro es un carro de triunfo . . . La muerte de un justo es una fiesta, en que la tierra toda se sienta a ver como se abre el cielo . . . Va a reposar, el que lo dio todo de si, e hizo bien a los otros. Va a trabajar de nuevo, el que hizo mal su trabajo en esta vida . . . será inmortal el que merezca serlo: morir es volver lo finito a lo infinito (Emerson's eulogy, *La Opinión Nacional*, 19 May 1882, *OC* 13:17–18, 24).

68. El que más trabaja es el que es menos vicioso, el que vive amorosamente con su mujer y sus hijos. Porque un hombre no es una bestia hecha para gozar, como el toro y el cerdo; sino una criatura de naturaleza superior, que si no cultiva la tierra, ama a su esposa, y educa a su hijuelos, volverá

a vivir indudablemente como el cerdo y como el toro (*Hombre del campo*, *OC* 19:383).

69. Allá en otros mundos, en tierras anteriores, en que firmemente creo, como creo en las tierras venideras, —porque de aquéllas tenemos la intuición pasmosa que puesto que es conocimiento previo de la vida revela vida previa . . . allá, en tierras anteriores, he debido cometer para con la que fue entonces mi patria alguna falta grave, por cuanto está siendo desde que vivo mi castigo, vivir perpetuamente desterrado de mi natural país, que no sé dónde está, —del muy bello en que nací, donde no hay más que flores venenosas (Notebook #8, 1880–1882, *OC* 21:246).

70. Los hombres van en: los que aman y fundan, los que odian y deshacen. Y la pelea del mundo viene a ser la de la dualidad hindú: bien contra mal (*Patria*, 21 May 1892, *OC* 4:413).

71. Y la pelea del mundo viene a ser la de la dualidad hindú: bien contra mal (ibid.).

72. García de la Torre, *José Martí and the Global Origins of Cuban Independence*, 73–75.

73. *OC* 12:77–83.

74. yo: esto es: Una personalidad briosa e impotente, libérrima y esclava, nobilísima y miserable, —divina y humanísima, delicada y grosera, noche y luz. Esto soy yo. Esto es cada alma. Esto es cada hombre (Notebook #2, *OC* 21:68).

75. *OC* 18:459–70; he was also critical of their colonial venture in Tunisia (*OC* 14:127–30).

76. *OC* 14:115. He also critiqued the English for their ventures in Egypt (*OC* 14:115) and Ireland (*OC* 8:383).

77. García de la Torre, *José Martí and the Global Origins of Cuban Independence*, 35.

78. Usamos moño, y sombrero de pico, y calzones anchos, y blusón de color, y somos amarillos, chatos, canijos y feos; pero trabajamos a la vez el bronce y la seda: y cuando loa franceses nos han venido a quitar nuestro Hanoi, nuestro Hue, nuestras ciudades de palacios de madera, nuestros puertos llenos de casas de bambú y de barcos de junco, nuestros almacenes de pescado y arroz, todavía, con estos ojos de almendra, hemos sabido morir, miles sobre miles, para cerrarles el camino. Ahora son nuestras amos; pero mañana ¡quién sabe! (*La edad de oro*, 1889, *OC* 18:461–62).

79. Alexander Welsh, *Strong Representations: Narrative and Circumstantial Evidence in England* (Baltimore: Johns Hopkins University Press, 1992), ix.

80. De La Torre, *Santería*, 165.

81. Escribo cada día sobre lo que cada día veo (OC 7:97).

82. *OC* 22:63–64.

83. *OC* 21:195–205.

84. Tiene el negro una gran bondad nativa, que ni el martirio de la esclavitud pervierte, ni se oscurece con su varonil bravura. Pero tiene, más que otra raza alguna, tan íntima comunión con la naturaleza, que parece más apto que los demás hombres a estremecerse y regocijarse con sus cambios. Hay en su espanto y alegría algo de sobrenatural y maravilloso que no existe en las demás razas primitivas, y recuerda en sus movimientos y miradas la majestad del león: hay en su afecto una lealtad tan dulce que no hace pensar en los perros, sino en las palomas: y hay en sus pasiones tal claridad, tenacidad, intensidad, que se parecen a las de los rayos del sol (*La Nación*, 14 October 1886, *OC* 11:73).

85. *OC* 3:105.

86. Fiestas bárbaras de África (*La Opinión*, April 15, 1882, *OC* 9:294).

87. Philip D. Curtin and Jan Vansina, "Sources of the Nineteenth Century Atlantic Slave Trade," *Journal of African History* 5 (1964): 185–208.

88. Albert J. Raboteau, *Slave Religion: The "Invisible Institution" in the Antebellum South* (Oxford: Oxford University Press, 1978), 90; Hugh Thomas, *Cuba; or, The Pursuit of Freedom*, 1971 (New York: Da Capo Press, 1998), 1546–47.

89. Guadalupe García, *Beyond the Walled City: Colonial Exclusion in Havana* (Oakland: University of California Press, 2016), 129–30.

90. de Zéndegui, *Ámbito de Martí*, 24; Ferrer, *Insurgent Cuba*, 2.

91. de Zéndegui, *Ámbito de Martí*, 21–23.

92. García, *Beyond the Walled City*, 130.

93. López, *José Martí*, 11, 15.

94. de Zéndegui, *Ámbito de Martí*, 22.

95. Jorge Mañach, *Martí el Apóstol* (1933; Madrid: Espasa-Calpe, 1942), 60.

96. Pedro Pablo Rodríguez, "José Martí: Cubanos es más que blanco, más que mulato, más que negro" (unpublished, undated article), 2.

97. De La Torre, *Santería*, 4–5.

98. Hay en la armonía de las obras bellas algo de sagrado (*La Opinión Nacional*, 1 April 1882, *OC* 14:448).

99. *OC* 8:189.

100. Es un mundo lo que estamos equilibrando: no son sólo dos islas las que vamos a libertar (*Patria*, 17 April 1894, *OC* 3:142).

101. El mundo es equilibrio, y hay que poner en paz a tiempo las dos pesas de la balanza (*Patria*, 14 March 1893, *OC* 2:251).

102. Buscará el hombre fuera de los dogmas históricos y puramente humanos, aquella armonía del espíritu de religión con el juicio libre, que es la forma religiosa del mundo moderno, adonde ha de venir a parar, como el río al mar, la idea cristiana (*El Partido Liberal*, 4 March 1890, *OC* 12:419).

103. Hay carácter moral en todos los elementos de la naturaleza: puesto que todos avivan este carácter en el hombre (*OC* 13:25).

104. Naturaleza es todo lo que existe, en toda forma (*OC* 19:364).

105. Que todo da en el hombre, que lo embellece con su mente todo, que a través de cada criatura pasan todas las corrientes de la naturaleza, que cada hombre tiene en sí al Creador, y cada cosa creada tiene algo del Creador en sí, y todo irá a dar al cabo en el seno del Espíritu creador (Emerson's eulogy, *La Opinión Nacional*, 19 May 1882, *OC* 13:24).

106. *OC* 5:324–25.

107. Patria es humanidad (*OC* 5:468).

108. En la guerra, ante la muerte, descalzos todos y desnudos todos, se igualaron los negros y los blancos: se abrazaron, y no se han vuelto a separar (5 January 1894, *OC* 3:27).

109. *OC* 2:299.

110. Alejandro de la Fuente, *A Nation for All: Race, Inequality, and Politics in Twentieth-Century Cuba* (Chapel Hill: University of North Carolina Press, 2001), 33.

111. *OC* 6:359.

112. *OC* 20:16.

113. De aquí en canoa a Isla de Mujeres; luego, en cayuco, a Belice; en lancha a Izabal; a caballo, a Guatemala (*OC* 20:26).

114. *OC* 19:113.

115. ¿Cómo podemos andar, historia adelante, con ese crimen a la espalda, con esa impedimenta? (*La Nación*, 20 August 1885, *OC* 10:273).

116. ¡Estos nacidos en América, que se avergüenzan porque llevan delantal indio, de la madre que los crio, y reniegan. ¡bribones!, de la madre enferma, y la dejan sola en el lecho de tas enfermedades! (*El Partido Liberal*, 30 January 1891, *OC* 6:16).

117. Que el indio de la reserva de los pueblos, que apenas tiene carne que comer y algo que vestir, tiene razón para resistirse a pagar las cargas públicas de una ciudadanía de que no goza, y de unas leyes escritas en una lengua que no entiende (*La Nación*, 16 January 1886, *OC* 10:374).

118. Susan Gillman, "*Ramona* on 'Our America,'" in *José Martí's "Our America": From National to Hemisphere*, ed. Jeffrey Belnap and Raúl Fernández (Durham, NC: Duke University Press, 1998), 96.

119. El indio es discreto, imaginativo, inteligente, dispuesto por naturaleza a la elegancia y a la cultura. De todos los hombres primitivos es el más bello y el menos repugnante. Ningún pueblo salvaje se da tanta prisa a embellecerse, ni lo hace con tanta gracia, corrección y lujo de colores (*La América*, January 1884, *OC* 8:329).

120. Era raza noble e impaciente, como esa de hombres que comienzan a leer los libros por el fin. Lo pequeño no conocían y ya se iban a lo grande. Siempre fue el amor al adorno dote de los hijos de América, y por ella lucen, y por ella pecan el carácter movible, la política prematura y la literatura hojosa de los países americanos (*La América*, April 1884, *OC* 8:334).

121. La raza indígena, habituada, por imperdonable y bárbara enseñanza, a la pereza inaspiradora y a la egoísta posesión, ni siembra, ni deja sembrar, y enérgico y patriótico, el Gobierno a sembrar la obliga, o permitir que siembren. Y lo que ellos, perezosos, no utilizan, él, ansioso de vida para la patria, quiebra en lotes y lo da. Porque sólo para hacer el bien, la fuerza es justa. Para esto solo; siempre lo pensé (*OC* 7:134).

122. El ahorro es inútil para quien no conoce los placeres que produce el capital, el ahorro inteligente, honrado y acumulado. Nada tiene porque nada desea. No trabaja por su bienestar porque no quiere hogar más amoroso, lecho más blando, vestido más valioso, mesa mejor provista que los que tiene ya. El hombre inteligente está dormido en el fondo de otro hombre bestial. La raza no ve más que hoy: nada más que para hoy trabaja; trabaja lo que necesita, hace producir lo que cree que consumirá: su inteligencia es estrecha, estrecho es todo lo que concibe y lo que hace. La raza imbécil: he aquí a nuestro juicio la explicación de la raza miserable (*Revista Universal*, 29 July 1875, *OC* 6:281).

123. La inteligencia americana es un penacho indígena. ¿No se ve cómo del mismo golpe que paralizó al indio, se paralizó a América? Y hasta que no se haga andar al indio, no comenzará a andar bien la América (*La América*, April 1884, *OC* 8:336–37).

124. Jeffrey Belnap, "Headbands, Hemp Sandals, and Headdresses," in *José Martí's "Our America": From National to Hemisphere*, ed. Jeffrey Belnap and Raúl Fernández (Durham, NC: Duke University Press, 1998), 194.

125. Larry Catá Backer, "Hatuey to Che: Indigenous Cuba without Indians and the U.N. Declaration on the Rights of Indigenous Peoples," *American Indian Law Review* 33, no. 1 (2008–2009): 203–4.

126. ¿Qué importa que vengamos de padres de sangre mora y cutis blanco? El espíritu de los hombres flota sobre la tierra en que vivieron, y se le respira. ¡Se viene de padres de Valencia y madres de Canarias, y se siente correr por las venas la sangre enardecida de Tamanaco y Paracamoni y se ve como propia . . . los desnudos y heroicos caracas! (*La América*, April 1884, *OC* 8:336).

127. Belnap, "Headbands, Hemp Sandals, and Headdresses," 205.

128. Que vagaban como hombres malditos por la tierra cristiana (*La Opinión Nacional*, 1 March 1882, *OC* 23:222). See also *OC* 23:149, 159.

129. *OC* 2:379; *OC* 11:183; *OC* 23:240.

130. *OC* 15:401.

131. Acaudalan, como los judíos (*La Nación*, 16 August 1887, *OC* 11:238).

132. Con los ojos y el ademán, al que se acerca a la garita, con la misma expresión y gesto con que los judíos del Bowery, apostados en la puerta de sus tiendas, se disputan al comprador rural, incierto y aturdido (*La Nación*, 29 December 1887, *OC* 11:328).

133. Que vendió un Cuadro suyo en más de lo que dio por él, como mercader judío (*La Opinión Nacional*, 6 May 1882, *OC* 15:276).

134. *OC* 23:133.

135. Que no se ha de pensar tan mal de los judíos, aunque en lo hondo del más generoso se vea la angustia y miseria de la raza, porque hay entre los hebreos mucha nobleza natural, por más que el vivir sin patria los haga interesados y egoístas (*La Nación*, 15 July 1888, *OC* 12:16).

136. Judíos: perseguidos spre., oprimidos siempre, . . . La implacabilidad y la venganza, lo que habían menester los judíos para la satisfacción tremenda de sus iras . . . Después, el Judío se hace rico y se corrompe. — Déspota, educa por medio del terror.— "No sonrías a tu hija". Eclesiastés. Bestias. —Sometían a la mujer a indecente prueba. ¡Hacían consistir la grandeza de la mujer y la nobleza del matrimonio, en el vigor de la tela himénica! (*OC* 22:45).

137. *OC* 10:120; *OC* 9:424.

138. Como en toda sociedad hay el visionario y el incrédulo, el poeta y el vulgo, el Mesías y los hebreos, el que anuncia lo venidero y el que no cree sino en lo visible (*Revista Universal*, 7 March 1876, *OC* 7:347).

139. Al cabo de diecinueve siglos que el mundo adoraba la divina inocencia de Jesús, ha habido hombres bastante soberbios y extraviados para formular de nuevo contra su Divina Majestad las acusaciones que presentaron los judíos (*La Opinión Nacional*, 4 April 1882, *OC* 23:253).

140. Este cargo sólo prueba la confusión y perversidad de los judíos (ibid.).

141. Erasmo puso el huevo y lo empolló Lutero (*La América*, April 1884, *OC* 13:445).

142. Cristiano, pura y simplemente Cristiano —Observancia rígida de la moral,— mejoramiento mío, ansia por el mejoramiento de todos, vida por el bien, mi sangre por la sangre de los demás; he aquí la única religión (Notebook #1, *OC* 21:18).

143. Alberto Entralgo Cancio, *Martí ante el proceso de Jesús* (La Habana: Ediciones La Verdad, 1956), 34–35.

144. *OC* 19:361.

145. ¿A quién preguntaremos? ¿A la fe? —¡Ay! No basta. En nombre de la fe se ha mentido mucho. Se debe tener fe en la existencia superior, conforme a nuestras soberbias agitaciones internas, —en el inmenso poder creador, que consuela, —en amor, que salva y une, —en la vida que empieza con la muerte. Una voz interior y natural, la primera voz que los pueblos primitivos oyeron, y el hombre de siempre oye, clama por todo esto. —Pero la fe mística, la fe en la palabra cósmica de los Brahmanes, en la palabra exclusivista de los Magos, en la palabra tradicional, metafísica e inmóvil de los Sacerdotes, la fe, que enfrente del movimiento en la tierra, dice que se mueve de otra manera; la fe, que enfrente del mecánico de Valen-

cia, lo aherroja y lo ciega; la fe, que condena por brujos al Marqués de Villena, a Bacon y Galileo; la fe, que niega primero lo que luego se ha visto obligada a aceptar; —esa fe no es un medio para llegar a la verdad, sino para oscurecerla y detenerla; no ayuda al hombre, sino que lo detiene; no le responde, sino que lo castiga; no le satisface, sino que lo irrita. —Los hombres libres tenemos ya una fe diversa. Su fe es la eterna sabiduría (*Juicios filosofía, OC* 19:363).

146. Julio Ramón Pita, "Explorando la religiosidad martiana." *Palabra Nueva* 7, no. 72 (January 1999), 15.

147. El espíritu percibe y siente, y con ello alcanza la verdad (Notebook #2, *OC* 21:62).

148. Contra la razón augusta nada (*La Nación*, 24 July 1885, *OC* 10:262).

149. Martínez Estrada, *Martí, revolucionario*, 107.

CHAPTER 4

Epigraph. De vez en cuando es necesario sacudir el mundo, para que lo podrido caiga a tierra (*El Partido Liberal*, 1887, *OC* 11:242).

1. Paul W. Borgeson, *Hacia el hombre nuevo: Poesia y pensamiento de Ernesto Cardenal* (London: Tamesis Books, 1984), 68, 76, 144; *OC* 16:131.

2. Luis N. Rivera-Pagan, "Theology and Literature in Latin America: John A. Mackay and *The Other Spanish Christ." Journal of Hispanic/Latino Theology* 7, no. 4 (May 2000): 18.

3. Miguel A. De La Torre, "Constructing a Cuban-Centric Christ," in *Jesus in the Hispanic Community: Images of Christ from Theology to Popular Religion*, ed. Harold J. Recinos and Hugo Magallanes (Louisville, KY: Westminster John Knox Press, 2009), 71.

4. In previous writings, I have argued for a nuance between liberation theology and liberative theologies. Liberation theology is rooted in the Christian faith (originally Catholic) as manifested in Latinoamérica during the 1960s, although liberative theologies need not be Christian. Liberative religious movements can be Muslim, Hindu, humanist, or even atheist. See Miguel A. De La Torre, introduction to *Ethics: A Liberative Approach*, ed. Miguel A. De La Torre (Minneapolis: Fortress Press, 2013), 3. Because Martí's writings are rooted in a Christian context, I focus on the classical understand of liberation theology in Latinoamérica.

5. Pope Paul VI, *Gaudium et spes*, Pastoral Constitution on the Church in the Modern World, December 7, 1965, Preface 1, https://www.vatican.va/archive/hist_councils/ii_vatican_council/ documents/vat-ii_const_19651207_gaudium-et-spes_en.html.

6. Camilo Torres, *Revolutionary Priest: The Complete Writings and Messages of Camilo Torres*, ed. John Gerassi (London: Jonathan Cape, 1971), xiii.

7. Emilio Antonio Núñez, *Liberation Theology* (Chicago: Moody Publishers, 1985), 116.

8. Although a detailed exploration of the rise of liberation theology is beyond the scope of this book, those interested can find a synopsis of the global movement in my book *Liberation Theologies for Armchair Theologians* (Louisville, KY: Westminster John Knox Press, 2013) or a more detailed analysis in my edited book *Introducing Liberative Theologies* (Maryknoll, NY: Orbis Books, 2015).

9. Gustavo Gutiérrez, *A Theology of Liberation: History, Politics, and Salvation*, rev. ed., trans. Sister Caridad Inda and John Eagleson (1971; Maryknoll, NY: Orbis Books, 1993), xxxv.

10. Vitier and Ikeda, *José Martí Cuban Apostle*, 59.

11. Cepeda, *José Martí*, 33.

12. Abrácense los vivos en amor inefable; amen la yerba, el animal, el aire, el mar, el dolor, la muerte; el sufrimiento es menos para las almas que el amor posee ("El poeta Walt Whitman," *La Nación*, 19 April 1887, *OC* 13:134).

13. La única verdad de esta vida, y la única fuerza, es el amor. En él esta la salvación, y en él está el mando. El patriotismo no es más que amor. La amistad no es más que amor (*Patria*, 29 April 1893, *OC* 5:21).

14. Arce, *Religión poesía del mundo venidero*, 91.

15. Es necesario, para ser servido de todos, servir a todos (*Patria*, 19 March 1892, *OC* 1:337).

16. Servir es nuestra gloria, y no servirnos (letter to General José Miró, 7 May 1896, *OC* 4:163).

17. Los que no saben amar (*Patria*, 31 March 1894, *OC* 3:105).

18. Yo sólo sé de amor. Tiemblo espantado / Cuando, como culebras, las pasiones / Del hombre envuelven tercas mi rodilla ("Vino de Chianti," *Flores del destierro, OC* 16:241).

19. Gutiérrez Marroquín, *Ética cristiana en la poesía de José Martí*, 34–35. It should be noted that this prophet of unconditional love, at one point appears to reserve love for those who resist oppression, offering instead tolerance for those do not (see *OC* 3:119).

20. Ni odio contra los que no piensan como nosotros. Cualidad mezquina, fatal en las masa, y raquítica e increíble en verdaderos hombres de Estado, ésta de no conocer a tiempo y constantemente la obra e intención de los que con buen espíritu se diferencian en métodos de ellos! (undated fragments, *OC* 22:58).

21. ¡Olvidaban que en aquel hombre iba Dios! (*El presidio político en Cuba*, 1871, *OC* 1:61).

22. Tiene a Dios en sí (*Revista Universal*, 31 July 1875, *OC* 6:286).

23. El amor es el lazo de los hombres, el modo de enseñar y el centro del mundo (tribute to the transcendentalist Bronson Alcott, *La Nación*, 29 April 1883, *OC* 13:188).

24. Soy pecador; pero no en mi manera de amar a los hombres (*OC* 20:373).

25. No se canse de amar (*OC* 20:474).

26. ¡Ellos son! ¡Ellos son! Ellos me dicen / Que mi furor colérico suspenda, / Y me enseñan sus pechos traspasados, / Y sus heridas con amor bendicen, / Y sus cuerpos estrechan abrazados, / ¡Y favor por los déspotas imploran! . . . / —¡Perdón!— ¡Así dijeron / Para los que en la tierra abandonada / Sus restos esparcieron! ("A mis hermanos muertos el 27 de noviembre," *Versos varios*, 1872, *OC* 17:39–40).

27. Sólo el amór construye (*Patria*, 8 September 1894, *OC* 5:241).

28. Mi deber será entonces muy sencillo: morir por lo que amo. See Gonzalo de Quesada y Miranda, *Así fue Martí* (La Habana: Gente Nueva, 1977), 68.

29. Sólo en el cumplimiento triste y áspero del deber está la verdadera gloria. Y aun ha de ser el deber cumplido en beneficio ajeno, porque si va con él alguna esperanza de bien propio, por legítimo que parezca, o sea, ya se empaña y pierde fuerza moral. La fuerza está en el sacrificio (*Patria*, 22 September 1894, *OC* 3:266).

30. Sea nuestro lema: libertad sin ira (*Patria*, 17 April 1894, *OC* 3:141).

31. La guerra no es contra el español, que, en el seguro de sus hijos y en el acatamiento a la patria que se ganen podrá[n] gozar respetado[s], y aun amado[s], de la libertad que sólo arrollará a los que le salgan, imprevisores, al camino (*OC* 4:94).

32. Los cubanos empezamos la guerra, y los cubanos y los españoles la terminaremos. No (los) nos maltraten, y no se les maltratará. Respeten, y se les respetará. Al acero responda el acero, y la amistad a la amistad, En el pecho antillano no hay odio; y el cubano saluda en la muerte al (bravo) español a quien la crueldad del ejercicio forzoso arrancó de su (hogar) casa y su terruño para venir a asesinar en pechos de hombre la libertad que él mismo ansía (*OC* 4:97).

33. Y si a los esp., por ser españoles, los ataco, mi padre saldría de la tumba, y me diría: parricida. —Pero el mal gobierno, la opresión, la ignorancia en q. vivimos, la miseria moral a q. se nos condena, esto ¡padre mío! no eres tú, eso no es España, sino otro país; eso es infamia y abominación, y dondequiera que lo encontraras lo has de acabar (undated fragments, *OC* 22:11).

34. Conozco el hombre, y lo he encontrado malo. / ¡Así, para nutrir el fuego eterno / Perecen en la hoguera los mejores! / ¡Los menos por los más! ¡los crucifixos / Por los crucificantes! En maderos / Clavaron a Jesús: sobre sí mismos / Los hombres de estos tiempos van clavados ("Yo sacré lo que en el pecho tengo," *Versos libres*, OC 16:224).

35. Por Dios que esta es guerra legítima, —la última acaso esencial y definitiva que han de librar los hombres: la guerra contra el odio (undated fragment, *OC* 22:210).

36. *OC* 9:388–89.

37. Agnes I. Lugo-Ortiz, "En un rincón de la Florida: Exile and Nationality in José Martí's Biographical Chronicles in Patria," in *José Martí in the United States: The Florida Experience*, ed. Louis A. Pérez (Tempe: Arizona State University Center for Latin American Studies, 1995), 10.

38. Este deseo triste y firme de la guerra inevitable (*OC* 4:278).

39. Revolución santa (*OC* 4:277).

40. Por las puertas que abramos los desterrados . . . entrarán con el alma radical de la patria nueva los cubanos . . . La guerra se prepara en el extranjero para la redención y beneficio de todos los cubanos (*Patria*, 14 March 1892, *OC* 1:319).

41. La tiranía es una misma en sus varias formas, aun cuando se vista en algunas de ellas de nombres hermosos y de hechos grandes (*OC* 1:185).

42. Louis A. Pérez Jr., introduction to *José Martí in the United States: The Florida Experience*, ed. Louis A. Pérez Jr. (Tempe: Arizona State University, 1995), 2.

43. Máximo Gómez, *Diario de Campaña 1868–1899* (1895; La Habana: Instituto del Libro, 1968), 192.

44. Philip S. Foner, *Antonio Maceo: The "Bronze Titan" of Cuba's Struggle for Independence* (New York: Monthly Review Press, 1977), 121.

45. Es mi determinación de no contribuir en un ápice, por amor ciego a una idea en que me está yendo la vida, a traer a mi tierra a un régimen de despotismo personal, que sería más vergonzoso y funesto que el despotismo político que ahora soporta, y más grave y difícil de desarraigar, porque vendría excusado por algunas virtudes, establecido por la idea encarnada en él, y legitimado por el triunfo. Un pueblo no se funda, General, como se manda un campamento (*OC* 1:177).

46. ¡Qué hermoso! Solo entran en el cielo, y se sientan al lado de Dios los que han batallado! (undated fragment, *OC* 22:63).

47. Los derechos se toman, no se piden; se arrancan, no se mendigan (toast given in La Habana at a banquet in honor of journalist Adolfo Márquez Sterling, 21 April 1879, *OC* 4:177).

48. Los derechos se conquistan con sacrificios (letter circulated widely, 28 April 1880, *OC* 1:146).

49. Los grandes derechos no se compran con lágrimas, —sino con sangre (lecture at Steck Hall, New York City, at a meeting of Cuban immigrants, 24 January 1880, *OC* 4:207).

50. Todo hombre de justicia y honor pelea por la libertad dondequiera que la vea ofendida, porque eso es pelear por su entereza de hombre; y el que ve

la libertad ofendida, y no pelea por ella, o ayuda a los que la ofenden, — no es hombre entero (*Patria*, 16 April 1892, *OC* 4:391).

51. El mejor modo de servir a Dios es ser hombre libre y cuidar de que no se menoscabe la libertad (Beecher's eulogy, 1887, *OC* 13:39).

52. En la piedra en bruto trabajan a la vez las dos manos, la blanca y la negra: ¡seque Dios la primera mano que se levante contra la otra! (*El Avisador Cubano*, 10 October 1888, *OC* 4:359).

53. Rafael E. Tarragó, "'Rights are Taken, Not Pleaded': José Martí and the Cult of the Recourse to Violence in Cuba," in *The Cuban Republic and José Martí: Reception and Use of a National Symbol*, ed. Mauricio A. Font and Alfonso W. Quiroz (Lanham, MD: Lexington Books, 2006), 69.

54. Antes todo se hacía con los puños: ahora, la fuerza está en el saber, más que en los puñetazos; aunque es bueno aprender a defenderse, porque siempre hay gente bestial en el mundo, y porque la fuerza da salud, y porque se ha de estar pronto a pelear, para cuando un pueblo ladrón quiera venir a robarnos nuestro pueblo (*La edad de oro*, 1889, *OC* 18:349).

55. Se cede en lo justo y lo injusto cae solo (*OC* 1:253).

56. Para verdades trabajamos, y no para sueños (*OC* 4:270).

57. Los tiempos son para Sísifo, y no para Jeremías; para empujar rocas hasta la cima de la montaña; no para llorar sobre exánimes ruinas (*La Opinión Nacional*, 26 October 1881, *OC* 9:63).

58. Si mi vida me defiende, nada puedo alegar que me ampare más que ella. Y si mi vida me acusa, nada podré decir que la abone. Defiéndame mi vida (*OC* 1:292).

59. Cuando el libro de los hebreos quería dar nombre a un varón admirable, lo llamaba, un justo (*La América*, December 1883, *OC* 9:479).

60. No en nombre de esa integridad de tierra que no cabe en un cerebro bien organizado; no en nombre de esa visión que se ha trocado en gigante; en nombre de la integridad de la honra verdadera, la integridad de los lazos de protección y de amor que nunca debisteis romper; en nombre del bien, supremo Dios; en nombre de la justicia, suprema verdad (*El presidio político en Cuba*, 1871, *OC* 1:50).

61. Y eso quiere, y es, la justicia; la acomodación del Derecho positivo al natural (*OC* 7:101).

62. ¡Es el sueño mío, es el sueño de todos; las palmas son novias que esperan; y hemos de poner la justicia tan alta como las palmas! (*OC* 4:273).

63. Se pelea mientras hay por qué, ya que puso la Naturaleza la necesidad de justicia en unas almas, y en otras las de desconocerla y obedecerla. Mientras la justicia no esté conseguida, se pelea (eulogy for Ulysses S. Grant, *La Nación*, 27 September 1885, *OC* 13:83).

64. Hacer justicia es hacérnosla (*La Opinión Nacional*, 1881, *OC* 8:167).

65. La libertad no es placer propio: es deber extenderla a los demás (*Revista Universal*, 10 July 1875, *OC* 6:266).

66. El Dios Conciencia (Notebook #1, *OC* 21:29).

67. Cuando los aranceles son injustos, o rencorosa la ley fronteriza, el contrabando es el derecho de insurrección. En el contrabandista se ve al valiente, que se arriesga; al astuto, que engaña al poderoso; al rebelde, en quien los demás se ven y admiran. El contrabando viene a ser amado y defendido, como la verdadera justicia (war diary entry, 2 March 1895, *OC* 19:200).

68. Todos juntos, podremos . . . Estando todos juntos, como que somos más, venceremos; pero no venceremos si no tenemos de nuestro lado la justicia, porque un solo hombre con ella es más fuerte que una muchedumbre sin ella. Para vencer en la realidad a nuestros enemigos debemos haberlos vencido moralmente. El que convence a su enemigo de que no tiene razón, ya lo tiene vencido. Nada se hace sin el dios de adentro. José Martí, "Letter to 'El Partido Liberal,'" 1886, in *Nuevas Cartas de Nueva York*, ed. Ernesto Mejía Sánchez (Mexico City: Siglo Veintiuno Editores, 1980), 28.

69. William D. P. Bliss, Rudolph M. Binder, and Edward Page Gaston, eds., "Currency," in *The New Encyclopedia of Social Reform* (New York: Funk & Wagnalls Co., 1909), 344.

70. Blaine, que con el rufián habla en su jerga, y con el irlandés contra Inglaterra, y con el inglés contra Irlanda . . . que abusaba del gran nombre de su pueblo para que los beligerantes reconociesen la impura obligación; Blaine, móvil e indómito, perspicacísimo y temible, nunca grande; . . . Blaine, mercadeable, que a semejanza de sí propio, -en el mercado de hombres compra y vende (*OC* 10:199).

71. Enrico Mario Santí, "'Our America,' the Gilded Age, and the Crises of Latinamericanism," in *José Martí's "Our America": From National to Hemisphere*, ed. Jeffrey Belnap and Raúl Fernández (Durham, NC: Duke University Press, 1998), 181.

72. Sobre nuestra tierra, Gonzalo, hay otro plan más tenebroso que lo que hasta ahora conocemos y es el inicuo de forzar a la Isla, de precipitarla, a la guerra, para tener pretexto de intervenir en ella, y con el crédito de mediador y de garantizador, quedarse con ella. Cosa más cobarde no hay en los anales de los pueblos libres: Ni maldad más fría (*OC* 6:128).

73. Santí, "'Our America,' the Gilded Age, and the Crises of Latinamericanism," 182.

74. Jamás hubo en América, de la independencia acá, asunto que requiera más sensatez, ni obligue a más vigilancia, ni pida examen más claro y minucioso, que el convite que los Estados Unidos potentes, repletos de productos invendibles: y determinados a extender sus dominios en América, hacen a las naciones americanas de menos poder, ligadas por el comercio libre y útil con los pueblos europeos, para ajustar una liga contra Europa, y cerrar tratos con el resto del mundo. De la tiranía de España supo salvarse la América española; y ahora, después de ver con

ojos judiciales los antecedentes, causas y factores del convite, urge decir, porque es la verdad, que ha llegado para la América española la hora de declarar su segunda independencia (*OC* 6:46).

75. Fue aquel invierno de angustia, en que por ignorancia, o por fe fanática, o por miedo, o por cortesía, se reunieron en Washington, bajo el águila temible, los pueblos hispanoamericanos. ¿Cuál de nosotros ha olvidado aquel escudo, el escudo en que el águila de Monterrey y de Chapultepec, el águila de López y de Walker, apretaba en sus garras los pabellones todos de la América? Y la agonía en que viví, hasta que pude confirmar la cautela y el brío de nuestros pueblos; y el horro y vergüenza en que me tuvo el temor legítimo de que pudiéramos los cubanos, con manos parri-cidas, ayudar el plan insensato de aparta a Cuba, para bien único de un Nuevo amo disimulado, de la patria que la reclama y en ella se complete, de la patria hispanoamericana, —que quitaron las fuerzas mermadas por dolores injustos (*OC* 6:143).

76. Manuel Pedro González, *Fuentes para el studio de José Martí* (La Habana: Ministerio de Educación, 1950), 399.

77. José Martí, "Committee Report to the International American Monetary Commission," in *Minutes of the International American Monetary Commission* (Washington, DC: U.S. Printing Office, 1891), 44, 48.

78. de Quesada y Miranda, *Así fue Martí*, 14.

79. Gusanos me parecen todos esos despreciadores de los pobres (26 October 1884, *OC* 10:77).

80. Con los oprimidos había que hacer causa común, para afianzar el sistema opuesto a los intereses y hábitos de mando de los opresores ("Nuestra América," *El Partido Liberal*, 30 January 1891, *OC* 6:19).

81. Con los pobres de la tierra / Quiero yo mi suerte echar: / El arroyo de la sierra / Me complace más que el mar. / Denle al vano el oro tierno / Que arde y brilla en el crisol: / A mí denme el bosque eterno / Cuando rompe en él el sol (*Versos sencillos*, 1891, *OC* 16:67).

82. ¡Mientras haya un hombre infeliz, hay algún hombre culpable! (*El Partido Liberal*, 21 May 1887, *OC* 11:191).

83. ¡Oh Jesús! ¿Dónde hubieras estado en esta lucha? ¿acompañado al Canadá al ladrón rico, o en la casita pobre en que el padre McGlynn espera y sufre? ("El cisma de los Católicos en Nueva York," *El Partido Liberal*, 16 January 1887, *OC* 11:150).

84. ¿Quién peca, el que abusa de su autoridad en las cosas del dogma para favorecer inmoralmente desde la cátedra sagrada a los que venden la ley en pago del Voto que les pone en condición de dictarla, o el que sabiendo que al lado del pobre no hay más que amargura, lo consuela en el templo como sacerdote, y le ayuda fuera del templo como ciudadano? (ibid., *OC* 11:147–48).

85. *OC* 19:392.
86. La vanidad y la pompa continuaron la obra iniciada por la fe; desdeñando a la gente humilde, a quien debía su establecimiento y abundancia, levantó reales la Iglesia en la calle de los ricos . . . para presentarse ante los ricos alarmados como el único poder que con su sutil influjo en los espíritus podía refrenar la marcha temible de los pobres ("El cisma de los Católicos en Nueva York," *El Partido Liberal*, 16 January 1887, *OC* 11:142).
87. No vayas a enseñar este libro al cura de tu pueblo: porque a él le interesa mantenerte en la oscuridad; para que todo tengas que ir a preguntárselo a él ("Hombre de campo," *OC* 19:381).
88. Ese Dios [de la Iglesia católica] que regatea, que vende la salvación, que todo lo hace a cambio de dinero, que manda las gentes al infierno si no pagan, y si les pagan las manda al cielo, ese Dios es una especie de prestamista, de usurero, de tender. ¡No, amigo mío, hay otro Dios! (ibid., *OC* 19:383).
89. Más, más cien veces que entrar en un templo, mueve el alma el entrar, en una madrugadita de este frío de febrero, en uno de los carros que llevan, de los barrios pobres a las fábricas, artesanos de vestidos timados, rostro sano y curtido y manos montuosas, —donde, ya a aquella hora briba un periódico. —He ahí un gran sacerdote, un sacerdote vivo: el trabajador (*La América*, February 1884, *OC* 8:285).
90. ¡Y son como siempre los humildes, los descalzos, los desamparados, los pescadores, los que se juntan frente a la iniquidad hombro a hombro, y echan a volar, con sus alas de plata encendida, el Evangelio! ¡La verdad se revela mejor a los pobres y a los que padecen! ¡Un pedazo de pan y un vaso de agua no engañan nunca! ("El cisma de los Católicos en Nueva York," *El Partido Liberal*, 16 January 1887, *OC* 11:139).
91. Cuando el pobre exagera sus derechos rebánesele sus pretensiones y en buena hora, que nadie tenga un derecho que lastime el de otro; pero repudiar como criaturas que manchan y avergüenzan a aquellos cuyas virtudes pacientes y admirables ni por un solo día serían capaces de imitar los que la repudian, es una vileza digna de un castigo público (*La Nación*, 26 October 1884, *OC* 10:77–78).
92. Cuanto rebaje a un hombre me rebaja (*El Yara*, 19 May 1894, *OC* 4:337).
93. Si la república no abre los brazos a todos y adelanta con todos, muere la república ("Nuestra América," *El Partido Liberal*, 30 January 1891, *OC* 6:21).
94. En América, la revolución está en su período de iniciación —Hay que cumplirlo. Se ha hecho la revolución intelectual de la clase alta: helo aquí todo. Y de esto han venido más males que bienes (Notebook #6, 1881, *OC* 21:178).
95. José Martí, "The Truth about the United States," 1894, in *José Martí Reader: Writings on the Americas*, ed. Deborah Shnookal and Mirta Muñiz (New York: Ocean Press, 1999), 175.

96. *OC* 17:159–64.

97. ¿No estarían mejor los fieles de las iglesias levantando estas almas, y calzando a estos desnudos, y apartando estas botellas de los labios, que oyendo comentarios sobre la bestia del Apocalipsis, y regocijándose en los picotazos que se dan los pastores de los templos rivales del distrito? (*La Nación*, 16 July 1884, *OC* 10:60).

98. Esteban Montejo, *The Autobiography of a Runaway Slave*, ed. Miguel Barnet, trans. Jocasta Innes (New York: Pantheon Books, 1968), 118.

99. El árbol debe venir sano desde la raíz. See de Quesada y Miranda, *Así fue Martí*, 86.

   Martí might have dismissed García's offer; but General Antonio Maceo did not. As early as 1890, the general met with the bandit to obtain a commitment to support the independence cause, leading the bandit to increase his "criminal" activities against the Spanish authorities. In 1894, he ransomed off a kidnapped plantation owner and a politician for fifteen thousand pesos, of which more than half made its way to the Partido Revolucionaro Cubano's cell in La Habana, and on the eve of the outbreak of the war of independence, he donated $75,000 to the PRC junta in New York City. See Louis A. Pérez Jr., *Cuba Between Empires: 1878–1902* (Pittsburgh, PA: University of Pittsburgh Press, 1983), 35–36.

100. *OC* 15:409.

101. Hacer, es la mejor manera de decir. (*Revista Venezolana*, 1 July 1881, *OC* 7:197).

102. Ya usted sabe que servir es mi mejor manera de hablar (*OC* 1:16).

103. En mi estante tengo amontonada hace meses toda la edición, —porque como la vida no me ha dado hasta ahora ocasión suficiente para mostrar que soy poeta en actos, tengo miedo de que por ir mis versos a ser conocidos antes que mis acciones, vayan las gentes a creer que sólo soy, como tantos otros, poeta en versos (letter to Mercado, 11 August 1882, *OC* 20:64).

104. Renace el fuego de los mártires y los apóstoles. Cunde entre los apáticos el ardor de los generosos. John Brown se ofrece en sacrificio, y convierte la idea en acción (eulogy for Ulysses S. Grant, *La Nación*, 27 September 1885, *OC* 13:91).

105. José Martí, "Final Correspondence: Letter to His Mother," 1895, in *José Martí: Selected Writings*, ed. and trans. Esther Allen (New York: Penguin Books, 2002), 346.

106. La Justicia misma no da hijos, ¡sino es el amor quien los engendra! (*La Nación*, 13 and 16 May 1883, *OC* 9:387).

107. Amar con explosiones, no con palabras (*Revista Universal*, 29 April 1876, *OC* 6:432).

108. Antes de hacer colección de mis versos me gustaría hacer colección de mis acciones (undated fragment, *OC* 22:129).

109. Carlos Ripoll, *José Martí, The United States, and the Marxist Interpretation of Cuban History* (New Brunswick, NJ: Transaction Books, 1984), 2.

110. Un hombre es el instrumento del deber: así se es hombre (*Revista Universal*, 11 May 1875, *OC* 6:198).

111. El verdadero hombre no mira de qué lado se vive mejor, sino de qué lado está el deber (*OC* 4:247).

112. Es un ladrón el hombre egoísta. Es un ladrón el político interesado (*La Nación*, 11 October 1888, *OC* 12:44).

113. Para mí la patria, no será nunca triunfo, sino agonía y deber (*OC* 4:111).

114. Callo, y entiendo, y me quito / La pompa del rimador: / Cuelgo de un árbol marchito / Mi muceta de doctor (*Versos sencillos*, 1891, *OC* 16:65).

115. Pensar es servir (*El Partido Liberal*, 30 January 1891, *OC* 6:22).

116. Un orador brilla por lo que habla; pero definitivamente queda por lo que hace. Si no sustenta con sus actos sus frases, aun antes de morir viene a tierra, porque ha estado de pie sobre columnas de humo (*La América*, May 1884, *OC* 13:55).

117. Es crimen (*La América*, January 1884, *OC* 8:430).

118. Eso es mejor que ser príncipe: ser útil. Los niños debían echarse a llorar, cuando ha pasado el día sin que aprendan algo nuevo, sin que sirvan de algo (*La edad de oro*, 1889, *OC* 18:455).

119. Conciencia.— Ciencia de nosotros mismos. Sabemos por conciencia todo aquello que experimentamos. Conocimiento de todo lo que en nosotros pasa. Ella conoce todo lo del individuo-individuad todo lo que puede sucederle-contingente —En el margen dice: Individual y contingente— (Notebook #2, *OC* 21:63).

120. ¿Taberna nada más ha de ser Cuba, u holgazana cervecería de San Jerónimo, y fonda de las Cuatro Naciones? ¿O pueblo propio, trabajador, y americano? Esta, y no menos, es la obra de Cuba (*Patria*, 10 November 1894, *OC* 3:359).

121. Pan no se puede dar a todos los que lo han menester . . . en cada calle, un kindergarten . . . una ciudad es culpable mientras no es toda ella una escuela: la calle que no lo es, es una mancha en la frente de la ciudad (*El Partido Liberal*, March 1890, *OC* 12:414).

122. I.— Instrucción no es lo mismo que educación . . . II.— Educación popular no quiere decir exclusivamente educación de la clase pobre; sino que todas las clases de la nación, que es lo mismo que el pueblo, sean bien educadas . . . Todos son iguales. III.— El que sabe más, vale más. Saber es tener. La moneda se funde, y el saber no . . . Un rico necesita de sus monedas para vivir, y pueden perdérsele, y ya no tiene modos de vida. Un hombre instruido vive de su ciencia, y como la lleva en sí, no se le pierde, y su existencia es fácil y segura. IV.— El pueblo más feliz es el que tenga mejor educados a sus hijos, en la instrucción del pensamiento, y en la dirección de los sentimientos. Un pueblo instruido ama el trabajo y sabe sacar provecho de él. Un pueblo virtuoso vivirá más feliz y más rico que otro lleno de vicios, y se defenderá mejor de todo ataque. V.-Al venir a la

tierra, todo hombre tiene derecho a que se le eduque, y después, en pago, el deber de contribuir a la educación de los demás. VI.— A un pueblo ignorante puede engañársele con la superstición, y hacérsele servil. Un pueblo instruido será siempre fuerte y libre. Un hombre ignorante está en camino de ser bestia, y un hombre instruido en la ciencia y en la con- ciencia, ya está en camino de ser Dios. No hay que dudar entre un pueblo de Dioses y un pueblo de bestias. El mejor modo de defender nuestros derechos . . . Un pueblo de hombres educados será siempre un pueblo de hombres libres. —La educación es el único medio de salvarse de la esclavitud (undated essay on popular education, *OC* 19:375).

123. Lo imposible, es posible. —Los locos, somos cuerdos (*OC* 20:285).

124. El que se cree con derecho a dar una razón, tiene el deber de oír la que le dan a él en respuesta (*La Nación*, 9 September 1888, *OC* 13:354).

125. Los pueblos fanáticos son malos. Todo tiene en lo vida su cantor y su poema. —Pero el poema del fanatismo es terrible. —El Circo en Roma, la Saint-Barthèlemy en Francia, la Inquisición en España— horrorosos cantos. —Nerón. Catalina de Médicis, Torquemada, —bárbaros cantores (Notebook #1, *OC* 21:17).

126. La primera libertad, base de todas, es la de la mente (*La Nación*, 22 November 1889, *OC* 12:348).

127. No hay deleite mayor que el de ver a los hombres batallar con libertad y fe, por lo que les parece verdadero, así como no hay espectáculo más doloroso que el de los hombres sumisos, por la ignorancia o la pasión o el interés, a la voluntad ajena (Notebook #18, 1894, *OC* 21:380).

128. La educación del hijo de estos pueblos menores en un pueblo de carácter opuesto y de riqueza superior, pudiera llevar al educando a una oposición fatal al país nativo donde ha de servirse de su educación, —o a la peor y más vergonzosa de las desdichas humanas, al desdén de su pueblo (*Patria*, 2 July 1892, *OC* 5:262).

129. Ni la originalidad literaria cabe, ni la libertad política subsiste mientras no se asegure la libertad espiritual. El primer trabajo del hombre es reconquistarse (prologue to Pérez Bonalde's *Poema del Niágara*, 1882, *OC* 7:230).

130. El vino, de plátano; y si sale agrio, ¡es nuestro vino! ("Nuestra América," *El Partido Liberal*, 30 January 1891, *OC* 6:20).

131. Publiquen, publiquen. A Cuba por todos los agujeros. Las guerras van sobre caminos de papeles. Que no nos tengan miedo y que nos deseen. Que lleguen a tener confianza en nosotros. Es más fácil invadir un país que nos tiende los brazos, que un país que nos vuelve la espalda. Abrirle los brazos a fuerza de amor. Y a fuerza de razón abrirles el juicio (*OC* 1:297).

132. Leer es trabajar (prologue to Rafael De Castro Palomino's *Cuentos de hoy y de mañana*, 1883, *OC* 5:104).

133. La inteligencia da bondad, justicia y hermosura: como un ala, levanta el espíritu; como una corona, hace monarca al que la ostenta (ibid., *OC* 5:108).
134. Pensar es prever (*La América*, October 1883, *OC* 7:325).
135. Hasta que los obreros no sean hombres cultos no serán felices. La pasión hace a veces odiosa la misma justicia. La razón es como un brazo colosal, que levanta a la Justicia donde no pueden alcanzarla las avaricias de los hombres. —A los obreros ignorantes, que quieren poner remedios bruscos a un mal que sienten, pero cuyos elementos no conocen, los vencerá siempre el interés de los capitalistas, disfrazados, como de piel de cordero una zorra, de conveniencias y prudencias sociales (*La América*, September 1883, *OC* 8:352).
136. Ha sido poner los ojos limpios de prejuicios en todos los campos (*OC* 9:17).
137. No se puede ver una cosa sin mirarla. No se puede entender una cosa sin examinarla. El examen es el ojo de la razón.— Luego nosotros mismos somos el primer medio del conocimiento de las cosas, el medio natural de investigación, el medio natural filosófico (*Juicios filosofía*, *OC* 19:364).
138. Paulo Freire, *Pedagogy of the Oppressed*, trans. Myra Bergman Ramos (1970; New York: Continuum, 1994), 55–57.
139. El profesor no ha de ser un molde donde los alumnos echan la inteligencia y el carácter, para salir con sus lobanillos y jorobas, sino un guía honrado, que enseña de buena fe lo que hay que ver, y explica su pro lo mismo que el de sus enemigos, para que se le fortalezca el carácter de hombre al alumno, que es la flor que no se ha de secar en el herbario de las universidades (*La Nación*, 22 November 1889, *OC* 12:348).
140. Toda semilla que se echa en el alma florece y fructifica (Notebook #5, 1881, *OC* 21:159).
141. *OC* 12:459.
142. El mejor entretenimiento, es sembrar almas (*Patria*, 30 April 1892, *OC* 5:357).
143. *OC* 12:414.
144. Cuerpo de maestros viajeros (*La América*, June 1884, *OC* 8:16).
145. *OC* 8:288.
146. Las ciudades son la mente de las naciones; pero su corazón, donde se agolpa, y de donde se reparte la sangre, está en los campos. Los hombres son todavía máquinas de comer, y relicarios de preocupaciones. Es necesario hacer de cada hombre una antorcha ("Maestros Ambulantes," *La América*, May 1884, *OC* 8:290).
147. *OC* 12:414–15.
148. Alfonso W. Quiroz, "Martí in Cuban Schools," in *The Cuban Republic and José Martí: Reception and Use of a National Symbol*, ed. Mauricio A. Font and Alfonso W. Quiroz (Lanham, MD: Lexington Books, 2006), 79.

149. Leslie Bethell, ed., *Cuba: A Short History* (Cambridge: Cambridge University Press, 1993), 89–90.

CHAPTER 5

Epigraph. Morir no es nada, morir es vivir, morir es sembrar. El q. muere, si muere donde debe, sirve (Notebook #6, 1881, *OC* 21:370).

1. López, *José Martí*, 318.
2. Gómez, *Diario de Campaña*, 284–85.
3. Enrico Mario Santí, "Thinking through Martí," in *Re-Reading José Martí (1853–1895) One Hundred Years Later*, ed. Julio Rodríguez-Luis (Albany: State University of New York Press, 1999), 71–72.
4. Quería el editor que yo hablase del "temor de Dios," y que el nombre de Dios, y no la tolerancia y el espíritu divino estuvieran en todos los artículos e historias (*OC* 20:153).
5. ¡Raza humana amante de lo servil! —Yo concibo bien a Dios sin sentir la necesidad de ser su esclavo (Notebook #2, *OC* 21:60).
6. ¿A quién lo podemos preguntar? ¿A Dios? —¡Ay! No responde, porque nos han enseñado a creer en un Dios que no es el verdadero. —El verdadero impone el trabajo como medio de llegar al reposo, la investigación como medio de llegar a la verdad, la honradez como medio de llegar a la pureza (*Juicios filosofía*, *OC* 19:363).
7. No es necesario fingir a Dios desde que se le puede probar. —Por medio de la ciencia se llega a Dios.— No Dios, como hombre productor; sino Dios como inmenso mar de espíritus, adonde han de ir a confundirse, ya resueltas, todas las soberbias inconformidades de los hombres (ibid., *OC* 19:361).
8. La única autoridad legítima y definitiva para el establecimiento de la verdad es la razón (*La América*, April 1884, *OC* 13:440).
9. Y con esta fe científica, se puede ser un excelente cristiano, un deísta amante, un perfecto espiritualista (*Juicios filosofía*, *OC* 19:363).
10. Antonio Iraizoz y de Villar, *Las ideas pedagógicas de Martí* (La Habana: Imprenta El Siglo XX, 1920), 21.
11. Arce, *Religión poesía del mundo venidero*, 53.
12. No hay Providencia. La Providencia no es más que el resultado lógico y preciso de nuestras acciones, favorecido o estorbado por las acciones de los demás. Si aceptáramos la Providencia católica, Dios sería un atareadísimo Tenedor de Libros (Notebook #1, *OC* 21:17).
13. Creo en Dios, porque comprendo a Dios. No creo en la Providencia, porque mi razón no me hace ver sus efectos, ni sentir su necesidad (ibid., *OC* 21:35).

14. Es fatal el progreso, —pero está en nosotros mismos; nosotros somos nuestro criterio; nosotros somos nuestras leyes, todo depende de nosotros: —el hombre es la lógica y la Providencia de la humanidad (*Revista Universal*, 8 June 1875, *OC* 6:226).

15. La Providencia para los hombres no es más que el resultado de sus obras mismas: no vivimos a la merced de una fuerza extraña (*Revista Universal*, 31 July 1875, *OC* 6:286).

16. Y vuelve los ojos a un Padre que no ve, pero de cuya presencia ésta seguro (*La Opinión Nacional*, 19 May 1882, *OC* 13:26).

17. Y así revuelve este hombre gigantesco la poderosa mente, y busca con los ojos abiertos en la sombra el cerebro divino, y lo halla próvido, invisible, uniforme y palpitante en la luz, en la tierra, en las aguas y en sí mismo, y siente que sabe lo que no puede decir, y que el hombre pasará eternamente la vida tocando con sus manos, sin llegar a palparlos jamás, los bordes de las alas del águila de oro, en que al fin ha de sentarse. Este hombre se ha erguido frente al Universo, y no se ha desvanecido. Ha osado analizar la síntesis, y no se ha extraviado (ibid., *OC* 13:27).

18. Y en el cielo suceden las cosas lo mismo que en la tierra; como que son los hombres los que inventan los dioses a su semejanza, y cada pueblo imagina un cielo diferente, con divinidades que viven y piensan lo mismo que el pueblo que las ha creado y las adora en los templos: porque el hombre se ve pequeño ante la naturaleza que lo crea y lo mata, y siente la necesidad de creer en algo poderoso, y de rogarle, para que lo trate bien en el mundo, y para que no le quite la vida (*La edad de oro*, 1889, *OC* 18:330).

19. Cree que el espíritu eterno adivina lo que la ciencia humana rastrea. Esta, husmea como un can; aquél, salva el abismo, en que el naturalista anda entretenido, como enérgico cóndor (Emerson's eulogy, *La Opinión Nacional*, 19 May 1882, *OC* 13:29).

20. Si mi Dios maldijera, yo negaría por ello a mi Dios (*El presidio político en Cuba*, 1871, *OC* 1:45).

21. Perseguidos spre., oprimidos siempre, por el poder, no podían esperar su redención sino de otro poder superior a aquél. Por eso el Dios de los Judíos es potente. Sus atributos son el temor. La implacabilidad y la venganza, lo que habían menester los judíos para la satisfacción tremenda de sus iras; no perdona, sino castiga, se anuncia entre truenos y relámpagos. Como todos los pueblos, los judíos admiten por Dios aquello que les hace falta. Les hace falta un libertador, un vengador fortísimo, para que sea más grande que sus opresores; terrible como su rencor. —Viene Jeremías, hombre amoroso, y llora. Desde entonces lloró el Dios Judío, que como todos los dioses se desarrolla y cambia de forma a medida que se desenvuelve su pueblo. —Deducción: Dios cambia con los cambios de los

hombres— Luego vino Jesús, el hombre del perdón, y perdonó. —Pues, si fuera Dios, debió ser siempre un Dios mismo. Y hay algo de revolución en Jeremías, contra algo de casta. Dice lo mismo que yo he dicho: La redención vendrá a los hombres por los hombres: —Todos me conocerán, sin ser Doctores (undated fragments, *OC* 22:45).

22. Dios es la idea de sustancia creada envuelve en sí la idea de esencia creadora. Y sustancia creada como somos, nos rige un algo que llamamos conciencia dirige otro algo que llamamos razón, disponemos de otro algo que llamamos voluntad.— Voluntad, razón, conciencia, —la esencia en tres formas. —Si nosotros, vida creada, tenemos esto,— Dios, ser creador, vida creadora, lo ha de tener. —Y quien a tantos da, mucho tiene. Dios es, pues. Y es la suprema conciencia, la suprema voluntad, y la suprema razón (Notebook #1, *OC* 21:18).

23. Diego Jorge González Serra, "Martí: Sus ideas filosóficas," *Varona: Revista Científico-Metodológica*, no. 63 (July–December 2016): 7–8.

24. Y mantiene que todo se parece a todo, que todo tiene el mismo objeto, que todo da en el hombre, que lo embellece con su mente todo, que a través de cada criatura pasan todas las corrientes de la naturaleza, que cada hombre tiene en sí al Creador, y cada cosa creada tiene algo del Creador en sí, y todo irá a dar al cabo en el seno del Espíritu creador, que hay una unidad central en los hechos, —en los pensamientos, y en las acciones; que el alma humana, al viajar por toda la naturaleza, se halla a sí misma en toda ella; que la hermosura del Universo fue creada para inspirarse el deseo, y consolarse los dolores de la virtud, y estimular al hombre a buscarse y hallarse; que "dentro del hombre está el alma del conjunto, la del sabio silencio, la hermosura universal a la que toda parte y partícula está igualmente relacionada: el Uno Eterno" (Emerson's eulogy, *La Opinión Nacional*, 19 May 1882, *OC* 13:24).

25. Yo quiero que la ley primera de nuestra república sea el culto de los cubanos a la dignidad plena del hombre (speech in Tampa, 26 November 1891, *OC* 4:270).

26. De gusano a hombre (Notebook #18, 1894, *OC* 21:409).

27. Y que si Buda hubiera vivido, habría dicho la verdad, que él no vino del cielo sino como vienen los hombres todos, que traen el cielo en sí mismos (*La edad de oro*, 1889, *OC* 18:467).

28. El mejor modo de servir a Dios es ser hombre libre y cuidar de que no se menoscabe la libertad (Beecher's eulogy, 1887, *OC* 13:39).

29. Con ser hombres, traemos a la vida el principio de la libertad; y con ser inteligentes, tenemos el deber de realizarla (*Revista Universal*, 7 March 1876, *OC* 7:349).

30. El hombre inteligente esta dormido en el fondo de otro hombre bestial (29 July 1875, *OC* 6:283).

31. So pretexto de completar el ser humano, lo interrumpen. No bien nace, ya están en pie, junto a su cuna con grandes y fuertes vendas preparadas

en las manos, las filosofías, las religiones, las pasiones de los padres, los sistemas políticos. Y lo atan; y lo enfajan; y el hombre es ya, por toda su vida en la tierra, un caballo embridado (prologue to Pérez Bonalde's *Poema del Niágara*, 1882, *OC* 7:230).

32. Pues ¿qué es el hombre, sino vaso quebrable del que se desbordan, fragantes y humeantes, esencias muy ricas? Cada hombre es la cárcel de un águila: se siente el golpe de sus alas, los quejidos que le arranca su cautividad, el dolor que en el seno y en el cráneo nos causan sus garras. La naturaleza no ha podido formular una pregunta a la que no haya de dar al fin respuesta (*La Opinión National*, 1882, *OC* 9:304).

33. Todos los pueblos tienen algo inmenso de majestuoso y de común, más vasto que el cielo, más grande que la tierra, más luminoso que las estrellas, más ancho que el mar: el espíritu humano; esta espiritual fuerza simpática, que aprieta y une los pechos honrados de los hombres, buenos en esencia, hermanos intuitivos, generosos innatos, que más se aman cuando más se compadecen (*El Federalista*, 16 December 1876, *OC* 6:361–62).

34. La vida es indudablemente una contradicción. Deseamos lo que no podemos obtener; queremos lo que no tendremos; y no podría existir contradicción si no existieran dos fuerzas distintas y contrarias (Note-book #2, *OC* 21:68).

35. Nada es un hombre en sí, y lo que es, lo pone en él su pueblo. En vano concede la Naturaleza a algunos de sus hijos cualidades privilegiadas; porque serán polvo y azote si no se hacen carne de su pueblo (Beecher's eulogy, 1887, *OC* 13:34).

36. Pero los pueblos no están hechos de los hombres como debieran ser, sino de los hombres como son. Y las revoluciones no triunfan, y los pueblos no se mejoran si aguardan a que la naturaleza humana cambie; sino que han de obrar conforme a la naturaleza humana y de batallar con los hombres como son, —o contra ellos (*Patria*, 9 July 1892, *OC* 2:62).

37. Con todos, y para el bien de todos (speech in Tampa, 26 November 1891, *OC* 4:279).

38. Esta es en todas partes época de reenquiciamiento y de remolde. El siglo pasado aventó, con ira siniestra y pujante, los elementos de la vida vieja. Estorbado en su paso por las ruinas, que a cada instante, con vida galvánica amenazan y se animan, este siglo, que es de detalle y preparación, acumula los elementos durables de la vida nueva (*La Nación*, 13 September 1882, *OC* 9:325).

39. Patria es humanidad, es aquella porción de la humanidad que vemos más de cerca, y en que nos tocó nacer (*Patria*, 26 January 1895, *OC* 5:468).

40. Sin aire, la tierra muere. Sin libertad, como sin aire propio y esencial, nada vive . . . Como el hueso al cuerpo humano, y el eje a una rueda, y el ala a un pájaro, y el aire al ala, —así es la Libertad la esencia de la vida. Cuanto sin ella se hace es imperfecto, mientras en mayor grado se la goce,

con más flor y más fruto se vive. Es la condición ineludible de toda obra útil (*La América*, September 1883, *OC* 9:451).

41. El Universo es siervo y rey el ser humano. El Universo ha sido creado para la enseñanza, alimento, placer y educación del hombre . . . Como en un eje, giran en esta verdad todas sus leyes para la vida: "toda la naturaleza tiembla ante la conciencia de un niño". El culto, el destino, el poder, la riqueza, las ilusiones, la grandeza, fueron por él, como por mano de químico, descompuestos y analizados (Emerson's eulogy, *La Opinión Nacional*, 19 May 1882, *OC* 13:26).

42. De nuestro bien o mal autores somos, / Y cada cual autor de sí; la queja ("Estrofa nueva," *Versos libres*, *OC* 16:175).

43. Desagrada (tener que) reconocer que el hombre de mayor idealidad del Universo, el Cristo, pueda tener el rostro deslustrado, cansado, caído, sin aquella beldad y aquella gloria que aún a los rostros sube de la inocencia y confianza del ama no probada, en la edad de la juventud, ignorante y fiera. Pero la verdad es que la vida come, y por donde pasa deja la huella de su diente; y en los que viven con más intensidad, ya por el amor de sí, o el de los demás, más la deja. La verdad es que los rostros de más belleza moral decaen y pierden gran luz conforme viven, y los ojos se fatigan y se apagan y la piel se decolora, y el cráneo se despuebla de cabello, y la frente se enjuta, y las mejillas se ahuecan, y solo en las divinas horas de la acción o el discurso supremo les sale al rostro la Gloria del alma (Notebook #14, 1886–1887, *OC* 21:344–45).

44. La mayor parte de los hombres ha pasado dormida sobre la tierra. Comieron y bebieron; pero no supieron de sí. La cruzada se ha de emprender ahora para revelar a los hombres su propia naturaleza, y para darles, con el conocimiento de la ciencia llana y práctica, la independencia personal que fortalece la bondad y fomenta el decoro y el orgullo de ser criatura amable y cosa viviente en el magno universo ("Maestros Ambulantes," *La América*, May 1884, *OC* 8:289).

45. C. Neale Ronning, "José Martí, Cuban Independence and the North American Economic, Political and Social Agenda," in *José Martí in the United States: The Florida Experience*, ed. Louis A. Pérez Jr. (Tempe: Arizona State University Center for Latin American Studies, 1995), 47.

46. Lo que tengo que decir, antes de que se me apague la voz y mi corazón cese de latir en este mundo, es que mi patria posee todas las virtudes necesarias para la conquista y el mantenimiento de la libertad (speech at Hardman Hall, New York, 17 February 1892, *OC* 4:293).

47. Se nace siempre bueno; el mal se hace después . . . Porque todo hombre es bueno: falta sólo producirle en medio de bondad (*Revista Universal*, 12 October 1876, *OC* 6:446, 449).

48. Tengo fe en el mejoramiento humano, en la vida futura, en la utilidad de la virtud, y en ti (*OC* 16:17).

49. El hombre es noble, y tiende a lo mejor: el que conoce lo bello, y la moral que viene de él, no pude vivir luego sin moral y belleza (*El Partido Liberal*, March 1890, *OC* 12:414).

50. No ha de volver a Dios los ojos: tiene a Dios en sí: hubo de la vida razón con que entenderse, inteligencia con que aplicarse, fuerza activa con que cumplir la honrada voluntad (*Revista Universal*, 31 July 1875, *OC* 6:286).

51. Hay un Dios: el hombre; —hay una fuerza divina: todo. El hombre es un pedazo del cuerpo infinito, que la creación ha enviado a la tierra vendado y atado en busca de su padre, cuerpo propio (*Revista Universal*, 8 June 1875, *OC* 6:226).

52. Don Juan, que simboliza para este poeta la poesía lánguida, el amor corruptor, el brillo falso, la pereza pervertidora, debe ser muerto. Don Juan debe morir, y Jesús debe vivir: Jesús, fuerza. trabajo, verdad, libertad, igualdad, justicia, amor casto (*La Opinión Nacional*, 17 November 1881, *OC* 23:83).

53. Con las palabras del rebelde sublime que con la fuerza de su patriotismo, dio empuje de humanidad, y alcance de Universo (undated notes, *OC* 19:455).

54. Si Jesús era Dios, ¿por qué ese vacío de unción evangélica desde la creación hasta él? O no era Dios, o Dios es caprichoso (Notebook #1, *OC* 21:16).

55. Fue un hombre sumamente pobre, que quería que los hombres se quisiesen entre sí, que el que tuviera ayudara al que no tuviera, que los hijos respetasen a los padres, siempre que los padres cuidasen a los hijos; que cada uno trabajase, porque nadie tiene derecho a lo que no trabaja; que se hiciese bien a todo el mundo y que no se quisiera mal a nadie. Cristo estaba lleno de amor para los hombres. Y como él venía a decir a los esclavos que debían ser más que esclavos de Dios, y como los pueblos le tomaron un gran cariño, y por donde iba diciendo estas cosas, se iban detrás de él, los déspotas que gobernaban entonces le tuvieron miedo y lo hicieron morir en una cruz (undated essay "Hombre de campo," *OC* 19:381–82).

56. Cepeda, *José Martí: Perspectivas éticas de la fe Cristiana*, 187.

57. Jesús no murió en Palestina, sino que está vivo en cada hombre . . . La cruzada se ha de emprender ahora para revelar a los hombres su propia naturaleza—naturaleza ética y moral ("Maestros ambulantes," *La América*, May 1884, *OC* 8:289).

58. Como en lo humano todo el progreso consiste acaso en volver al punto de que se partió, se está volviendo al Cristo, al Cristo crucificado, perdonador, cautivador, al de los pies desnudos y los brazos abierto, no a un Cristo nefando y satánico, malevolente, odiado, enconado, fustigante, ajusticiador, impío (prologue to Pérez Bonalde's *Poema del Niágara*, 1882, *OC* 7:226).

59. *OC* 19:383.

60. ¡El nombre del sublime Blasfemia me parece en vuestras bocas!- ¡El que esclavo mantiene, el sacerdote Que fingiendo doctrinas religiosas Desfigura a Jesús, el que menguado Un dueño busca en apartada zona; El que a los pobres toda ley deniega, El que a los ricos toda ley abona; El que, en vez de morir en su defensa, El sacrificio de una raza explota, Miente a Jesús, y al manso pueblo enseña Manchada y criminal su faz radiosa! (*OC* 18:171).

61. Rafael Cepeda, "El pensamiento religioso-contextual en la obra escrita de José Martí," in *En el ala de un colibrí: Esencia del pensamiento martiano Rafael Cepeda*, ed. Carlos R. Molina Rodríguez (1985; La Habana: Editorial Caminos, 2008), 80.

62. En la cruz murió el hombre en un día: pero se ha de aprender a morir en la cruz todos los días (*OC* 20:478).

63. Un Cristo roto ("¡No, música tenaz . . . !," *Versos libres*, *OC* 16:218).

64. Cristo sin cruz ("Isla famosa," *Versos libres*, *OC* 16:163).

65. Quiero que conste que por la causa de Cuba me dejo clavar en la cruz, y que iré al sacrificio sin exhalar una sola queja. See de Quesada y Miranda, *Así fue Martí*, 100.

66. Los hombres de corazón escriben en la primera página de la historia del sufrimiento humano: Jesús. Los hijos de Cuba deben escribir en las primeras páginas de su historia de dolores: Castillo. Todas las grandes ideas tienen su gran Nazareno, y don Nicolás del Castillo ha sido nuestro Nazareno infortunado. Para él, como para Jesús, hubo un Caifás. Para él, como para Jesús, hubo un Longinos. Desgraciadamente para España, ninguno ha tenido para él el triste valor de ser siquiera Pilatos (*El presidio político en Cuba*, 1871, *OC* 1:56).

67. La prensa es Vinci y Ángelo, creadora del nuevo templo magno e invisible, del que es el hombre puro y trabajador el bravo sacerdote (*La Nación*, September 13, 1882, *OC* 9:326).

68. Novoa, "'Transpensar,'" 2017, 33.

69. El arte es una forma de la armonía (*Revista Universal*, 31 December 1875, *OC* 6:390).

70. En toda palabra, ha de ir envuelto un acto. La palabra es una coqueta abominable, cuando no se pone al servicio del honor y del amor (prologue to Rafael De Castro Palomino's *Cuentos de hoy y de mañana*, 1883, *OC* 5:108).

71. Susana Rotker, *The American Chronicles of José Martí: Journalism and Modernity in Spanish America*, trans. Jennifer French and Katherine Semler (Hanover, NH: University Press of New England, 2000), 19.

72. Lo que ha de hacer el poeta de ahora es aconsejar a los hombres que se quieran bien, y pintar todo lo hermoso del mundo de manera que se vea en los versos como si estuviera pintado con colores, y castigar con la poesía, como con un látigo, a los que quieran quitar a los hombres su

libertad, o roben con leyes pícaras el dinero de los pueblos, o quieran que los hombres de su país les obedezcan como ovejas y les laman la mano como perros. Los versos no se han de hacer para decir que se está contento o se está triste, sino para ser útil al mundo, enseñándole que la naturaleza es hermosa, que la vida es un deber, que la muerte no es fea, que nadie debe estar triste ni acobardarse mientras haya libros en las librerías, y luz en el cielo, y amigos, y madres (*OC* 18:349).

73. Para ser bueno no necesita más que ver lo bello (Emerson's eulogy, *La Opinión Nacional*, 19 May 1882, *OC* 13:22).

74. El que conoce lo bello, y la moral que viene de él, no puede vivir luego sin moral y belleza (*El Partido Liberal*, March 1890, *OC* 12:414).

75. Abanicar como el pavón la enorme cola; sino para el bien del prójimo (*La Nación*, 11 January 1885, *OC* 10:135).

76. ¡Triste aquel que delante de un cuadro hermoso no haya sentido en sí como el crecimiento de una fuerza extraña, y en su garganta como amontonadas sin salida las palabras de contento y conmoción! Son las leyes de lo eterno, que escapan a los legisladores de lo físico (*Revista Universal*, 29 December 1875, *OC* 6:387–88).

77. Los pueblos inmorales tienen todavía una salvación: el arte. El arte es la forma de lo divino, la revelación de lo extraordinario. La venganza que el hombre tomó al cielo por haberlo hecho hombre, arrebatándole los sonidos de su arpa, desentrañando con luz de oro el seno de colores de sus nubes. El ritmo de la poesía, el eco de la música, el éxtasis beatífico que produce en el ánimo la contemplación de un cuadro bello, la suave melancolía que se adueña del espíritu después de estos contactos sobrehumanos, son vestimentos místicos, y apacibles augurios de un tiempo que será todo claridad. ¡Ay, que esta luz de siglos le ha sido negada al pueblo de la América del Norte! (travel notes from 1875 and 1877, *OC* 19:17).

78. ¿Quieren levantar templo? Que hagan casas para los pobres. ¿Salvar almas quieren? Pues bájense a este infierno, no con limosnas que envilecen, sino con las artes del ejemplo, puesto, que la naturaleza humana, esencialmente buena, apenas ve junto a sí modelo noble, se levanta hasta él (*La Nación*, 16 July 1884, *OC* 10:60).

79. El arte libre, el arte en todo y a todas horas, es tan necesario a los pueblos como el aire libre. Pueblo sin arte, sin mucho arte, es pueblo segundón. Los grandes educadores, y los grandes gobiernos, han hecho siempre obligatoria la enseñanza del arte (*Patria*, 7 May 1892, *OC* 4:399).

80. Bien es que en el teatro se enseñe; mas hay forma divina y humana; de enseñar; queda esta última encargada a la comedia, y aquella a las exaltaciones de la fantasía, locura para los que no la alcanzan, y revelación y religión pare los que en sí la acarician y la sienten. ¿Quién niega la cumbre de un monte porque sus ojos débiles no lleguen a la cumbre?

Belleza y bondad van en sus obras tan unidas, que nunca se realiza la una sin producir inmediatamente la otra. Y si no es esto lo cierto, ¿qué enseñanza ha habido que conmoviese nuestro espíritu tan hondamente como esas de éxtasis extraño, que nos dejan más grande el corazón y fatigado y abrumado nuestro cuerpo? Porque tanto fatiga a veces la alegría (*OC* 6:431).

81. *OC* 12:378.

82. Pertenece a la humanidad nueva, y a aquella legión de hombres estéticos y áticos ... escribe, como satisfacción de la dilatada injusticia a los que tanto hacen (*La Opinión Nacional*, January 1882, *OC* 14:303).

83. Pierre Bourdieu, *The Rules of Art: Genesis and Structure of the Literary Field*, trans. Susan Emanuel (Stanford, CA: Stanford University Press, 1995), 214.

84. Van escritos, no en tinta de academia, sino en mi propia sangre (*OC* 16:131).

85. ¿Con qué había de pintar Munkácsy sino con las tristezas de su alma, con sus recuerdos tétricos, con aquellas tintas propias de quien no ha conocido la alegría? ("El Cristo de Munkacsy," *La Nación*, 28 January 1887, *OC* 15:345).

86. Bourdieu, *The Rules of Art*, 32–34.

87. Clive W. Kronenberg, "The Power of Ideas: The Ethical-Aesthetic Dimension of José Martí's Humanist Tradition." *Hispanic Research Journal* 15, no. 4 (August 2014): 318.

88. Es preciso, para entender bien a Jesús, haber venido al mundo en pesebre oscuro, con el espíritu limpio y piadoso, y palpado en la vida la escasez del amor, el florecimiento de la codicia y la victoria del odio: es preciso haber aserrado la madera y amasado el pan entre el silencio y la ofensa de los hombres ("El Cristo de Munkacsy," *La Nación*, 28 January 1887, *OC* 15:343).

89. El ve a Jesús, como la encarnación más acabada del poder invencible de la idea. La idea consagra, enciende, adelgaza, sublima, purifica: da una estatura que no se ve y se siente: limpia el espíritu de escoria, como consume el fuego la maleza: esparce una beldad clara y segura que viene hacia las almas y se siente en ellas. El Jesús de Munkácsy es el poder de la idea pura (ibid., *OC* 15:346).

90. El hombre acrisolado que ama y muere, y el bestial que odia y mata (ibid., *OC* 15:347).

91. ¡Es ese rico odioso de todos los tiempos!: la fortuna le ha henchido de orgullo brutal: la humanidad le parece su escabel: se adora en su bolsa y en su plenitud (ibid., *OC* 15:348).

92. Es el Jesús sin halo, el hombre que se doma, el Cristo vivo, el Cristo humano, racional, y fiero (ibid., *OC* 15:349).

93. Cada ser humano lleva en sí un hombre ideal (*La edad de oro*, 1889, *OC* 18:390).

94. Pecadores somos todos, los de allá y los de acá, y todos somos héroes (*Patria*, May 1892, *OC* 4:415).

95. De odio y de amor, y de más odio que amor, están hechos los pueblos; sólo que el amor, como sol que es, todo lo abrasa y funde; y lo que por siglos enteros van la codicia y el privilegio acumulando, de una sacudida lo echa abajo con su séquito natural de almas oprimidas, la indignación de un alma piadosa (*Patria*, 17 April 1894, *OC* 3:139).

96. ¿Por qué han de ser enemigos el alma y el cuerpo, lo que tiende a escaparse y lo que tiende a retener? (undated fragment, *OC* 22:219).

97. Yo creo en la divinidad de mi esencia, toco y miro y creo en la miserabilidad da mi existencia —Y sin embargo a veces, involuntariamente como que transijo con mi miserabilidad (Notebook #2, *OC* 21:69).

98. Todos los crímenes, todas las brutalidades, todas las vilezas están en germen en el hombre más honrado. Lo más vil o bestial ha aparecido en algún instante posible o deseable al alma más limpia (*La Nación*, 2 August 1888, *OC* 11:478).

99. *OC* 11:278; *OC* 1:92.

100. Los hombres son productos, expresiones, reflejos (Beecher's eulogy, 1887, *OC* 13:34).

101. El hombre es feo; pero la humanidad es hermosa. La humanidad es alegre, paciente y buena (*La Nación*, 9 March 1888, *OC* 11:383).

102. Tienen hambre: redímaseles el hambre. No sea vana la enseñanza del demócrata romano; ábranse al pueblo los graneros, cuando el pueblo no tiene granos en su hogar. Piense cada Estado en la manera de remediar el grave daño en sus comarcas; cree trabajo para los que sin él perecerían; den los que tienen sobrado a los que tienen la mesa vacía y el lecho sobre la tierra (*Revista Universal*, 29 July 1875, *OC* 6:284).

103. Hoy que la virtud el sólo el cumplimiento del deber, no ya su exageración heroica (*La república española ante la revolución cubana*, 1873, *OC* 1:96).

104. Aquel que no hace todo lo que puede hacer, peca contra lo natural y paga la culpa de su pecado (*OC* 20:198).

105. Pero V. está hecho para algo más que para vivir en paz, V. está siendo un grandísimo pecador, con no sacar afuera todo lo que tiene en sí (*OC* 20:313).

106. A un vil se le conoce en que abusa de los débiles. Los débiles deben ser como los locos eran para los griegos: sagrados. Da prenda de infamia el hombre que se goza en abatir a otro. Tiene su aristocracia el espíritu: y la forman aquellos que se regocijan con el crecimiento y afirmación del hombre. El género humano no tiene más que una mejilla: ¡dondequiera que un hombre recibe un golpe en su mejilla, todos los demás hombres lo reciben! (*La Nación*, 3 October 1885, *OC* 10:288).

107. Por la piedad ha peleado el cubano [y] nunca por la venganza ("Manifesto de Montecristi," 25 March 1895, *OC* 22:348).

108. Cultivo una rosa blanca / En julio como en enero / Para el amigo sincero / Que me da su mano franca. / Y para el cruel que me arranca / El corazón con que vivo, / Cardo ni oruga cultivo: / Cultivo la rosa blanca (*Versos sencillos*, 1891, *OC* 16:117).

109. Las cosas buenas se deben hacer sin llamar al universo para que lo vea a uno pasar. Se es bueno porque sí; y porque allá adentro se siente como un gusto cuando se ha hecho un bien, o se ha dicho algo útil a los demás. Eso es mejor que ser príncipe: ser útil (*La edad de oro*, 1889, *OC* 18:455).

110. Yo os exijo compasión para los que sufren en presidio, alivio para su suerte inmerecida, escarnecida, ensangrentada, vilipendiada. Si la aliviáis, sois justos. Si no la aliviáis, sois infames. Si la aliviáis, os respeto. Si no la aliviáis, compadezco vuestro oprobio y vuestra desgarradora miseria (*El presidio político en Cuba*, 1871, *OC* 1:50).

111. ¡Debe andar triste por dentro, el corazón de quien ayuda a oprimir a los hombres! (*Patria*, 27 August 1892, *OC* 2:145).

112. Consentidores quieren los hombres, que les permitan ir viviendo con sus apetitos y vicios; y no denunciadores amorosos, que se los saquen a la faz, para que tengan vergüenza de ellos, que pudren, —y se los curen (*La Nación*, 6 June 1884, *OC* 10:53).

113. ¡Qué alegre muere un mártir! ¡Qué satisfecho vive un sabio! Cumple su deber, lo cual, si no es el fin, es el medio! (*Juicios filosofía*, *OC* 19:363).

114. ¡Oh! Jesús, los que te amamos, lo callamos como culpa; y sufrimos; ¡oh hermano! por lo que tú sufriste, y nos preguntamos a nuestra alma llagada y agotada como tu cuerpo, —cuál de entre nosotros ha sido más heroico, si tú, que llevado de un objeto, moriste como a ti cumplía, adorado y odiado,— o nosotros que sin objeto que no guíe, no tenemos el derecho de morir (undated essay "Los ruidos humanos," *OC* 19:387).

115. Muchas cosas andan. Todo anda, La eternal justicia, insondable cuando eternal, anda también, y ¡algún día parará! (*El presidio político en Cuba*, 1871, *OC* 1:66).

116. Se olvidó de que no puede haber perdón, cuando no ha habido justicia ("Pushkin," *The Sun*, 28 August 1880, *OC* 15:421).

117. La suerte me escatima mucho sus recompensas. —O hay un plan de justicia universal, que sólo se equilibra al final de los mundos, por lo que resulta justo lo que parece injusto en éste, o la vida humana es la obra de un loco maligno: lo que no-es posible que sea cosa tan augusta y maravillosa, tan rica en goces puros y en dolores profundos. Porque si la justicia se limitara a la vida en la tierra, habría razón para creer, a juzgar por la parte de premios que me toca, que yo soy un gran malvado (*OC* 20:487).

118. Para mí no hay derrota. Prudencia y sacrificio y martirio sí, derrota, no (*OC* 4:109).

119. El dolor es la única escuela que produce hombres. —¡Dichoso aquel que es desgraciado! (*OC* 21:17).

120. Al que peca se le olvida; se le deja caer; se le da tiempo a que vuelva en sí, se le tienen las puertas abierta para que vuelva sin bochorno al cariño y a la honra (*Patria*, 28 November 1893, *OC* 4:459).

121. Yo soy como aquellos llanos de Siberia, que dan fruto abundante en medio del frío. —Del dolor, flores (Notebook #6, 1881, *OC* 21:185).

122. Lizaso, *Posibilidades filosóficas en Martí*, 20; Cepeda, "La Biblia en Martí," 49.

123. Presidio, Dios: ideas para mí tan cercanas como el inmenso sufrimiento y el eterno bien. Sufrir es quizás gozar. Sufrir es morir para la torpe vida por nosotros creada, y nacer para la vida de lo bueno, única vida verdadera . . . Sufrir es más que gozar: es verdaderamente vivir (*El presidio político en Cuba*, 1871, *OC* 1:54).

124. Ya estoy todos los días en peligro de dar mi vida por mi país y por mi deber (*OC* 4:167).

125. López, *José Martí*, 318.

126. ¡Muerte! ¡Muerte generosa! ¡Muerte amiga . . . ! ¡Seno colosal donde todos los sublimes misterios se elaboran; miedo de los débiles; placer de los valerosos; satisfacción de mis deseos; paso oscuro a los restantes lances de la vida; madre inmensa, a cuyas plantas nos tendemos a cobrar fuerzas nuevas para la vía desconocida donde el cielo es más ancho, tasto el limite, polvo los pies innobles, verdad, al fin, las alas; simpático misterio, quebrantador de hierros poderosos; nuncio de libertad (tribute to the poet Alfredo Torroella, 1879, *OC* 5:88).

127. ¡Soy nublo! El pueblo entero Por defender su libertad me aguarda: Un pueblo extraño nuestras tierras huella: Con vil esclavitud nos amenaza; Audaz nos muestra sus potentes picas, Y nos manda el honor, y Dios nos manda Por la patria morir, ¡antes que verla Del bárbaro opresor cobarde esclava! (*OC* 18:18).

128. Morir sabremos: hijos de la patria, Por ella moriremos, y el suspiro Que de mis labios postrimeros salga, Para Nubia será, que para Nubia Nuestra fuerza y valor fueron creados (*OC* 18:14).

129. En ti encerré mis horas de alegría / Y de amargo dolor; / Permite al menos que en tus horas deje / Mi alma con mi adiós. / Voy a una casa inmensa en que me han dicho / Que es la vida expirar. / La patria allí me lleva. Por la patria, / Morir es gozar más (*OC* 17:27).

130. Luis García Pascual, *Destinatario José Martí* (La Habana: Casa Editora April, 2005), 93.

131. El que no sabe despreciar la vida, no la merece (undated fragments, *OC* 22:89).

132. Hasta muertos dan ciertos luz de aurora (letter to his friend Manuel Mercado, 16 June 1889, *OC* 20:145).

133. Arce, *Religión poesía del mundo venidero*, 56.

134. Piensa en más que en lo hermoso de morir a caballo, peleando por el país, al pie de una palma! (*OC* 4:273).

135. Yo, ya sé cómo voy a morir. Lo que quiero es prestar el servicio que puedo prestar ahora (*OC* 3:226).

136. La muerte es una victoria, y cuando se ha vivido bien, el féretro es un carro de triunfo. El llanto es de placer, y no de duelo, porque ya cubren hojas de rosas las heridas que en las manos y en los pies hizo la vida al muerto. La muerte de un justo es una fiesta, en que la tierra toda se sienta a ver como se abre el cielo (Emerson's eulogy, *La Opinión Nacional*, 19 May 1882, *OC* 13:17).

137. Sepa usted que no me expondré irreflexivamente a un peligro innecesario, pero tampoco consentiré que se desatienda cualquier necesidad o acción en el combate para cuidarme y resguardarme como si yo fuera una frágil reliquia. See de Quesada y Miranda, *Así fue Martí*, 87.

138. Esta mañana abrí un libro, un libro de una mente sana, y leí: Life is a humbug!: Pero vengo aquí y veo que no es verdad. La vida es inspiración, la vida es fraternidad, la vida es estimulo. la vida es virtud! (undated fragment, *OC* 22:81–82).

139. *OC* 6:420.

140. ¡Triste el que muere sin haber hecho obra! (*La Opinión Nacional*, 26 October 1881, *OC* 9:63).

141. Se anda, se llora, el pecho está oprimido; / Y la mirada al cielo se extravía: / La esperanza en la tierra se ha perdido / Y se espera en el ciclo todavía. / Pues qué ¿me muero yo? Si yo concibo / La inmensa eternidad que no perece, / No muero nunca: eternamente vivo: / Yo sé bien dónde el Sol nunca anochece ("Flor blanca," *Revista Universal*, 27 June 1875, *OC* 17:94).

142. Eternidades tiene la Pureza: / Ella eterna, yo eterno, eterno todo / Desde el rayo que enciendo en mi cabeza / ¡Hasta el átomo mísero de lodo! ("Sin amores," *Revista Universal*, 14 March 1875, *OC* 17:49).

143. Quien vive para todos, continúa viviendo en todos, ¡dulce premio! ("Garfield ha muerto," *La Opinión Nacional*, 19 October 1881, *OC* 13:202).

144. Yo quiero salir del mundo, / Por la puerta natural: / En un carro de hojas verdes / A morir me han de llevar. / ¡No me pongan en lo oscuro / A morir como un traidor: / Yo soy bueno, y como bueno / Moriré de cara al sol! (*Versos sencillos*, 1891, *OC* 16:99).

145. En la cruz murió el hombre un día: pero se ha de aprender a morir en la cruz todos los días (Letter to friend Gonzalo de Quesada y Aróstegui, 1 April 1895, *OC* 1:28).

146. La muerte no es verdad cuando se ha cumplido bien la obra de la vida (*El Federalista*, March 1876, *OC* 6:420).

147. ¡Feliz aquel que en bien del hombre muere! ("Yo sacaré lo que en el pecho tengo," *Versos libres*, *OC* 16:224).

148. El martirio por la patria es Dios mismo, como el bien, como las ideas de

espontánea generosidad universales. Apaleadle, heridle, magulladle. Sois demasiado viles para que os devuelva golpe por golpe y herida por herida. Yo siento en mí a este Dios, yo tengo en mí a este Dios; este Dios en mí os tiene lástima, más lástima que horror y que desprecio (*El presidio político en Cuba*, 1871, *OC* 1:61).

149. Morir bien es el único modo seguro de continuar viviendo (*Patria*, 30 April 1892, *OC* 1:427).

150. ¡No! ¡la vida humana no es toda la vida ! La tumba es vía y no término (prologue to Pérez Bonalde's *Poema del Niágara*, 1882, *OC* 7:236).

151. La muerte no debe ser penosa para los que han vivido bien, ni para los que les conocían de cerca las virtudes. Morir es seguir viaje (*Patria*, 2 January 1895, *OC* 5:464).

152. Morir es lo mismo que vivir y mejor, si se ha hecho ya lo que se debe (*La Nación*, 17 April 1884, *OC* 10:24).

153. Moriremos por la libertad verdadera; no por la libertad que sirve de pretextó para mantener a unos hombres en el gocé excesivo, y a otros en el dolor innecesario (*Patria*, 15 March 1893, *OC* 2:255).

154. El fin de la vida no es más que el logro difícil de la compensación y conciliación de las fuerzas vitales. Puesto que tenemos voluntad, criterio e imaginación, sírvannos los tres: la imaginación para crear, el criterio para discernir y para reprimir la voluntad. Los hombres son todavía águilas caídas, y ha de haber alguna razón para que aún no se nos devuelvan nuestras alas (*El Federalista*, 11 February 1876, *OC* 6:367).

155. Yo vivo para el estricto cumplimiento de mis deberes (undated fragments, *OC* 22:254)

156. Es ley maravillosa de la naturaleza que sólo esté completo el que se da; y no se empieza a poseer la vida hasta que no vaciamos sin reparo y sin tasa, en bien de los demás, la nuestra (*Revista Venezolana*, 15 July 1881, *OC* 8:153).

157. Cumpliera cada uno con su deber de hombre, y los gobiernos, donde sean malos, habrían de ser mejores. Dejen de vivir como lapas inmundas, pegadas a los oficios del Estado (Notebook #18, 1894, *OC* 21:385–86).

158. Para mí la patria, no será nunca triunfo, sino agonía y deber. Ya arde la sangre (Letter to Federico Henríquez y Carvajal, 25 March 1895, *OC* 4:111).

159. Carlos Prío Socarrás, *Oración del Presidente Prío ante la tumba del apóstol José Martí*, Cementerio Santa Ifigenia, Santiago de Cuba (30 Junio 1951): 2–3.

160. Yo quiero, cuando me muera, / Sin patria, pero sin amo, / Tener en mi losa un ramo / De flores, —¡y una bandera! (*Versos sencillos*, 1891, *OC* 16:100).

BIBLIOGRAPHY

Abel, Christopher. "Martí, Latin America and Spain." In *José Martí: Revolutionary Democrat*, edited by Christopher Abel and Nissa Torrents, 124–52. London: Athlone Press, 1986.

Agramonte, Roberto. "Estudio preliminar." In *Philosophia electiva: Obras de José Agustin Caballero, Vol 1*, by José Agustín Caballero, lv–c. La Habana: Editorial de la Universidad de La Habana, 1944.

Arce, Reinerio. *Religión poesía del mundo venidero: Implicaciones teológicas en la obra de José Martí*. La Habana: Ediciones CLAI, 1996.

Arroyo, Jossianna. *Writing Secrecy in Caribbean Freemasonry*. New York: Palgrave Macmillan, 2013.

Beatty, Jack. *Age of Betrayal: The Triumph of Money in America, 1865–1900*. New York: Vintage Books, 2007.

Belnap, Jeffrey. "Headbands, Hemp Sandals, and Headdresses." In *José Martí's "Our America": From National to Hemisphere*, edited by Jeffrey Belnap and Raúl Fernández, 191–209. Durham, NC: Duke University Press, 1998.

Bethell, Leslie, ed. *Cuba: A Short History*. Cambridge: Cambridge University Press, 1993.

Bliss, William D. P., Rudolph M. Binder, and Edward Page Gaston, eds. "Currency." In *The New Encyclopedia of Social Reform*, 344. New York: Funk & Wagnalls Co., 1909.

Borgeson, Paul W. *Hacia el hombre nuevo: Poesía y pensamiento de Ernesto Cardenal*. London: Tamesis Books, 1984.

Bourdieu, Pierre. *The Rules of Art: Genesis and Structure of the Literary Field*. Translated by Susan Emanuel. Stanford, CA: Stanford University Press, 1995.

Buch Sánchez, Rita M. "De Caballero a Martí: Trayectoria de la filosofía cuba-na electiva en el siglo XIX." *Honda*, no. 25 (2009): 2–24.

Caballero, José Agustín. *Philosophia electiva*. In *Obras de José Agustín Caballero, Vol 1.*, translated from the Latin by Jenaro Artiles. La Habana: Editorial de la Universidad de la Habana, 1944.

Catá Backer, Larry. "Hatuey to Che: Indigenous Cuba without Indians and the U.N. Declaration on the Rights of Indigenous Peoples." *American Indian Law Review* 33, no. 1 (2008–2009): 201–38.

Catalá, Raquel. "Conceptos teosóficos de Martí." *Revista Teosófica Cubana* 34, no. 3 (March 1939): 24–30.

Cepeda, Rafael. "La Biblia en Martí." 1964. In *En el ala de un colibrí: Esencia del pensamiento martiano Rafael Cepeda*, edited by Carlos R. Molina Rodrí-guez, 48–51. La Habana: Editorial Caminos, 2008.

———. *José Martí: Perspectivas éticas de la fe cristiana*. San José, Costa Rica: Editorial Departamento Ecuménico de Investigaciones, 1991.

———. "José Martí: Praxis del Evangelio." *Anuario del Centro de Estudios Martianos*, no. 16 (1993): 43–49. In *En el ala de un colibrí: Esencia del pensa-miento martiano Rafael Cepeda*, edited by Carlos R. Molina Rodríguez, 171–84. La Habana: Editorial Caminos, 2008.

———. "José Martí profeta de la teología de la liberación." *Paso*, no. 16 (March–April 1988): 1–5.

———. "Martí y los protestantes cubanos." *Caminos*, no. 9 (January–March 1988): 57–61. In *En el ala de un colibrí: Esencia del pensamiento martiano Rafael Cepeda*, edited by Carlos R. Molina Rodríguez, 185–95. La Habana: Editorial Caminos, 2008.

———. "El pensamiento religioso-contextual en la obra escrita de José Martí." 1985. In *En el ala de un colibrí: Esencia del pensamiento martiano Rafael Cepeda*, edited by Carlos R. Molina Rodríguez, 73–103. La Habana: Edito-rial Caminos, 2008.

Cepeda, Rafael, Elizabeth Carrillo, Rhode González, and Carlos E. Ham. "Changing Protestantism in a Changing Cuba." In *In the Power of the Spirit: The Pentecostal Challenge to Historical Churches in Latin America*, edited by Benjamin F. Gutiérrez and Dennis A. Smith, 95–116. Louisville, KY: Presby-terian Church, 1996.

Chávez Álvarez, Clara Emma. *Hacedora de la bandera cubana: Emilia Margarita Teurbe Tolón y Otero*. La Habana: Publicaciones de la Oficina del Histori-ador de la Ciudad de la Habana, 2011.

Curtin, Philip D., and Jan Vansina. "Sources of the Nineteenth Century Atlan-tic Slave Trade." *Journal of African History* 5 (1964): 185–208.

de la Fuente, Alejandro. *A Nation for All: Race, Inequality, and Politics in Twentieth-Century Cuba*. Chapel Hill: University of North Carolina Press, 2001.

de la Luz y Caballero, José. "A la memoria del doctor don José Agustín Caballero." 1835. In *Obras IV*, 247–59. Barcelona: Linkgua Ediciones, 2019.

_____. "Discurso en los exámenes generales del Colegio del Salvador, pronunciado el 16 de diciembre de 1858." 1858. In *Obras III*, 377–92. Barcelona: Linkgua Ediciones, 2015.

_____. "Doctrinas de psicología, lógica y moral, expuestas en la clase de filosofía del Colegio de San Cristóbal." 1835. In *Obras III*, 71–87. Barcelona: Linkgua Ediciones, 2015.

_____. "Dos discursos leídos en los exámenes del Colegio del Salvador." 1861. In *Obras III*, 483–509. Barcelona: Linkgua Ediciones, 2015.

De La Torre, Miguel A. "Constructing a Cuban-Centric Christ." In *Jesus in the Hispanic Community: Images of Christ from Theology to Popular Religion*, edited by Harold J. Recinos and Hugo Magallanes, 58–73. Louisville, KY: Westminster John Knox Press, 2009.

_____. *Embracing Hopelessness*. Minneapolis: Fortress Press, 2017.

———, ed. *Introducing Liberative Theologies*. Maryknoll, NY: Orbis Books, 2015.

_____. Introduction to *Ethics: A Liberative Approach*, edited by Miguel A. De La Torre. Minneapolis: Fortress Press, 2013.

_____. *Liberation Theologies for Armchair Theologians*. Louisville, KY: Westminster John Knox Press, 2013.

_____. *The Quest for the Cuban Christ: A Historical Search*. Gainesville: University Press of Florida, 2002.

_____. *Santería: The Beliefs and Rituals of a Growing Religion in America*. Grand Rapids, MI: Wm. B. Eerdmans Publishing, 2004.

de Quesada y Miranda, Gonzalo. *Así fue Martí*. La Habana: Gente Nueva, 1977.

Dewart, Leslie. *Christianity and Revolution: The Lesson of Cuba*. New York: Herder and Herder, 1963.

de Zéndegui, Guillermo. *Ámbito de Martí*. Madrid: Escuela Gráfica Salesiana, 1954.

Eliade, Mircea. *Patterns in Comparative Religion*. Translated by Rosemary Sheed. New York: Meridian Books, 1963.

Emerson, Ralph Waldo. *English Traits*. 1856. Boston: Houghton, Mifflin and Co., 1883.

_____. "October 4, 1844 Letter to William Emerson." 1844. In *The Letters of Ralph Waldo Emerson, Vol. III*, edited by Ralph L. Rusk, 262–63. New York: Columbia University Press, 1939.

_____. "The Over-Soul." 1841. In *The Prose Works of Ralph Waldo Emerson: New and Revised Edition, Vol. I*, 355–71. Boston: Fields, Osgood, & Co., 1870.

Entralgo Cancio, Alberto. *Martí ante el proceso de Jesús*. La Habana: Ediciones La Verdad, 1956.

Estrada, Alfredo José. *Havana: Autobiography of a City*. New York: Palgrave Macmillan, 2007.

Farina, John. "General Introduction." In *Félix Varela: Letters to Elpido*, edited by Felipe J Estévez. New York: Paulist Press, 1989.

Ferrater Mora, José. "Krause" and "Krausismo." In *Diccionario de filosofía, tomo I, A–K*, 1065–68. Buenos Aires: Editorial Sudamericana, 1941.

Ferrer, Ada. *Insurgent Cuba: Race, Nation, and Revolution, 1868–1898*. Chapel Hill: University of North Carolina Press, 1999.

Freire, Paulo. *Pedagogy of the Oppressed*. 1970. Translated by Myra Bergman Ramos. New York: Continuum, 1994.

Foner, Philip S. *Antonio Maceo: The "Bronze Titan" of Cuba's Struggle for Independence*. New York: Monthly Review Press, 1977.

García, Guadalupe. *Beyond the Walled City: Colonial Exclusion in Havana*. Oakland: University of California Press, 2016.

García de la Torre, Armando. *José Martí and the Global Origins of Cuban Independence*. Kingston: University of the West Indies Press, 2015.

García Pascual, Luis. *Destinatario José Martí*. La Habana: Casa Editora April, 2005.

Gillman, Susan. "*Ramona* on 'Our America.'" In *José Martí's "Our America": From National to Hemisphere*, edited by Jeffrey Belnap and Raúl Fernández, 91–111. Durham, NC: Duke University Press, 1998.

Göcke, Benedikt Paul. *The Panentheism of Karl Christian Friedrich Krause (1781–1832): From Transcendental Philosophy to Metaphysics*. Berlin: Peter Lang, 2018.

Gómez, Máximo. *Diario de campaña 1868–1899*. La Habana: Instituto del Libro, 1968.

Gonçalves, João Felipe. "The 'Apostle' in Stone: Nationalism and Monuments in Honor of José Martí." In *The Cuban Republic and José Martí: Reception and Use of a National Symbol*, edited by Mauricio A. Font and Alfonso W. Quiroz, 18–33. Lanham, MD: Lexington Books, 2006.

González, Manuel Pedro. *Fuentes para el estudio de José Martí*. La Habana: Ministerio de Educación, 1950.

_____. *José Martí: Epic Chronicler of the United States in the Eighties*. 2nd ed. Chapel Hill: University of North Carolina, 1953.

González Serra, Diego Jorge. "Martí: Sus ideas filosóficas." *Varona: Revista Científico-Metodológica*, no. 63 (July–December 2016): 1–11.

Gould, Robert Freke. *Gould's History of Freemasonry Throughout the World, Vol. IV*. New York: Charles Scribner's Sons, 1936.

Griñán Peralta, Leonardo. *Martí: Líder político*. La Habana: Editorial de Ciencias Sociales, 1970.

Guerra, Lillian. *The Myth of José Martí: Conflicting Nationalism in Early Twentieth-Century Cuba*. Chapel Hill: University of North Carolina Press, 2005.

Gutiérrez, Gustavo. *A Theology of Liberation: History, Politics, and Salvation*. Rev. ed. 1971. Translated by Sister Caridad Inda and John Eagleson. Maryknoll, NY: Orbis Books, 1993.

Gutiérrez Marroquín, Carolina. *Ética cristiana en la poesía de José Martí*. Holguín, Cuba: Ediciones Holguín, 2014.

Henken, Ted, Miriam Celaya, and Dimas Castellanos, eds. *Cuba*. Santa Barbara, CA: ABC-CLIO, 2013.

Iraizoz y de Villar, Antonio. *Las ideas pedagógicas de Martí*. La Habana: Imprenta El Siglo XX, 1920.

John Paul II. "Address of John Paul II." Apostolic Journey of His Holiness John Paul II to Cuba, 23 January 1998. https://w2.vatican.va/content/john-paul-ii/en/travels/1998/documents/hf_jp-ii_spe_23011998_lahavana-culture.html.

Jrade, Cathy L. "Martí Confronts Modernity." In *Re-Reading José Martí (1853–1895) One Hundred Years Later*, edited by Julio Rodríguez-Luis, 1–16. Albany: State University of New York Press, 1999.

Kardec, Allan. *La genèse, les miracles et les predictions selon le spiritisme*. Paris: Librairie Internationale, 1868.

_____. *Le livre des esprits*. 2nd ed. Paris: Didier et Cie, Libraires-Éditeurs, 1860.

_____. *Le livre des médiums: Ou guide des médiums et des évocateurs*. Paris: Didier et Cie, Libraires-Éditeurs, 1861.

_____. "Les déserteurs." 1869. In *Œuvres posthumes*, edited by P. Leymarie, 283–92. Paris: Libraire des Sciences Spirites et Psychiques, 1912.

Kimball, Richard B. *Cuba and the Cubans; Comprising a History of the Island of Cuba, Its Present Social, Political, and Domestic Condition; also, Its Relationship to England and the United States*. New York: Samuel Hueston, 1850.

Kirk, John M. *Between God and the Party: Religion and Politics in Revolutionary Cuba*. Tampa: University Presses of Florida, 1988.

_____. *José Martí: Mentor of the Cuban Nation*. Tampa: University Presses of Florida, 1983.

Kronenberg, Clive W. "The Power of Ideas: The Ethical-Aesthetic Dimension of José Martí's Humanist Tradition." *Hispanic Research Journal* 15, no. 4 (August 2014): 318–31.

Leyva, Edelberto. *José Agustín Caballero: Obras*. La Habana: Ediciones Imagen

Contemporánea, 1999.

Lizaso, Félix. *Panorama de la cultura cubana*. Mexico City: Fondo de Cultura Económica, 1949.

_____. *Posibilidades filosóficas en Martí*. La Habana: Molina y Cía, 1935.

Lomas, Laura. *Translating Empire: José Martí, Migrant Latino Subjects, and American Modernities*. Durham, NC: Duke University Press, 2008.

López, Alfred J. *José Martí: A Revolutionary Life*. Austin: University of Texas Press, 2014.

Lozano Ros, Jorge Juan. "Fundamentación de la obra de José Martí." *Historia Gráfica* 6 (February 2012): 327–31.

Lugo-Ortiz, Agnes I. "*En un rincón de la Florida*: Exile and Nationality in José Martí's Biographical Chronicles in Patria." In *José Martí in the United States: The Florida Experience*, edited by Louis A. Pérez Jr., 9–22. Tempe: Arizona State University Center for Latin American Studies, 1995.

Mañach, Jorge. *Martí el Apóstol*. 1933. Madrid: Espasa-Calpe, 1942.

Márquez Sterling, Carlos. *Martí: Ciudadano de América*. New York: Las Americas Publishing Co., 1965.

Martí, José. "Al federalista I." 1876. In *José Martí Obras completas: Edición crítica: Tomo 2, 1875–1876, México*, edited by Cintio Vitier, 270–73. La Habana: Centro de Estudios Martianos, 2009.

_____. "Committee Report to the International American Monetary Commission." In *Minutes of the International American Monetary Commission*. Washington, DC, 1891.

_____. *Debate en el Liceo Hidalgo*. 1875. Edited by Pedro Pablo Rodríguez. La Habana: Centro de Estudios Martianos, 2010.

_____. "Final Correspondence: Letter to His Mother." 1895. In *Jose Martí: Selected Writings*, edited and translated by Esther Allen, 346. New York: Penguin Books, 2002.

_____. "Letter to 'El Partido Liberal.'" 1886. In *Nuevas cartas de Nueva York*, edited by Ernesto Mejía Sánchez, 19–30. Cerro del Agua: Siglo Veintiuno Editores, 1980.

_____. *Obras completas de José Martí*, 26 vols. La Habana: Centro de Estudios Martianos, 2001. (This work appears as *OC* in the notes.)

_____. "The Truth about the United States." 1894. In *José Martí Reader: Writings on the Americas*, edited by Deborah Shnookal and Mirta Muñiz, 184–89. New York: Ocean Press, 1999.

Martin, B. R. *Karl Christian Friedrich Krause's Leben, Lehre und Bedeutung*. Leipzig: Verlag Von Otto Heinrichs, 1885.

Martínez Estrada, Ezequiel. *Martí, revolucionario*. La Habana: Casa de las Américas, 1967.

Masó y Vázquez, Calixto C. *Historia de Cuba: La lucha de un pueblo por cumplir su destino histórico y su vocación de libertad*. Miami: Ediciones Universal, 1998.

Maza, Manuel P. "The Cuban Catholic Church: True Struggles and False Dilemmas." Master's thesis, Georgetown University, 1982.

Miranda, Olivia. "El hombre en la teoría revolucionaria de Félix Varela." In *Filosofía e ideología de Cuba siglo XIX*, edited by Isabel Monal and Olivia Miranda, 115–76. Mexico City: Universidad Nacional Autónoma de México, 1994.

McCadden, Joseph J. "The New York-to-Cuba Axis of Father Varela." *The Americas* 20, no. 4 (April 1964): 376–92.

Monal, Isabel. "Tres filósofos del centenario." In *Filosofía e ideología de Cuba Siglo XIX*, edited by Isabel Monal and Olivia Miranda, 79–98. Mexico City: Universidad Nacional Autónoma de México, 1994.

Monal, Isabel, and Olivia Miranda. "Bosquejo de las ideas en Cuba hasta finales del siglo XIX." In *Filosofía e ideología de Cuba siglo XIX*, edited by Isabel Monal and Olivia Miranda, 11–60. Mexico City: Universidad Nacional Autónoma de México, 1994.

Montaner, Carlos Alberto. *El pensamiento de Martí*. Madrid: Plaza Mayor Ediciones, 1971.

Montejo, Esteban. *The Autobiography of a Runaway Slave*. Edited by Miguel Barnet. Translated by Jocasta Innes. New York: Pantheon Books, 1968.

Nichol, John. *Francis Bacon: His Life and Philosophy, Part II*. Philadelphia: J. B. Lippincott Co., 1889.

Nietzsche, Friedrich Wilhelm. *Die fröhliche Wissenschaft*. Chemnitz: Verlag von Ernst Schmeitzner, 1882.

Novoa, Adriana. "'Transpensar': Materialism, Spiritualism, and Race in José Martí's Rejection of Socialism (1870–1890)." Paper presented at Cuban Research Institute, Florida International University, Miami, 23 February 2017.

———. "'Transpensar': Materialism, Spiritualism, and Race in José Martí's Philosophy." *Cuban Studies* 47 (2019): 169–94.

Núñez, Emilio Antonio. *Liberation Theology*. Chicago: Moody Publishers, 1985.

Paul VI. *Gaudium et spes, Pastoral Constitution on the Church in the Modern World*, December 7, 1965. https://www.vatican.va/archive/hist_councils/ii_vatican_council/documents/vat-ii_const_19651207_gaudium-et-spes_en.html.

Pavón Torres, Rufino Modesto. *La relación ético-estética en el pensamiento martiano*. Holguín, Cuba: Ediciones Holguín, 2009.

Pentón, Mario J. "La filiación masónica de Martí, historia de una polémica que marcó sus ideales." *El Nuevo Herald*, 27 January 2017.

Pérez, Louis A., Jr. *Cuba between Empires: 1878–1902*. Pittsburgh, PA: University of Pittsburgh Press, 1983.

_____. *Essays on Cuban History: Historiography and Research*. Gainesville: University Press of Florida, 1995.

_____. Introduction to *José Martí in the United States: The Florida Experience*, edited by Louis A. Pérez Jr. Tempe: Arizona State University, 1995.

_____. *On Becoming Cuban: Identity, Nationality, and Culture*. Chapel Hill: University of North Carolina Press, 1999.

Pita, Julio Ramón. "Explorando la religiosidad martiana." *Palabra Nueva* 7, no. 72 (January 1999): 14–15.

Prío Socarrás, Carlos. *Oración del Presidente Prío ante la tumba del apóstol José Martí*. Cementerio Santa Ifigenia, Santiago de Cuba (30 Junio 1951): 1–6.

Quiroz, Alfonso W. "Martí in Cuban Schools." In *The Cuban Republic and José Martí: Reception and Use of a National Symbol*, edited by Mauricio A. Font and Alfonso W. Quiroz, 71–81. Lanham, MD: Lexington Books, 2006.

Raboteau, Albert J. *Slave Religion: The "Invisible Institution" in the Antebellum South*. Oxford: Oxford University Press, 1978.

Ramos, Marcos Antonio. *Panorama del protestantismo en Cuba: La presencia de los protestantes o evangélicos en la historia de Cuba desde la colonización española hasta la Revolución*. San José, Costa Rica: Editorial Caribe, 1986.

_____. *Protestantism and Revolution in Cuba*. Coral Gables: University of Miami, 1989.

Richard, Pablo. *Death of Christendoms, Birth of the Church: Historical Analysis and Theological Interpretation of the Church in Latin America*. Maryknoll, NY: Orbis Books, 1987.

Ricoeur, Paul. *Interpretation Theory: Discourse and the Surplus of Meaning*. Fort Worth: Texas Christian University Press, 1976.

Ripoll, Carlos. *José Martí, The United States, and the Marxist Interpretation of Cuban History*. New Brunswick, NJ: Transaction Books, 1984.

Rivera-Pagan, Luis N. "Theology and Literature in Latin America: John A. Mackay and *The Other Spanish Christ*." *Journal of Hispanic/Latino Theology* 7, no. 4 (May 2000): 7–25.

Rodriguez, F. de P. "Cuban Freemasonry." *Quarterly Bulletin: Iowa Masonic Library* 17, no. 3 (July 1916): 68–72.

Rodríguez, Pedro Pablo. "José Martí: Cubanos es más que blanco, más que mulato, más que negro." La Habana: Unpublished article, undated.

Rodríguez Carro, Vicente. "Krause y las raíces 'masónicas' del krausismo español." *Studia Zamorensia* 13 (2014): 277–86.

Roig de Leuchsenring, Emilio. *Martí y las religiones*. La Habana: Publicaciones de Acción, 1941.

Rojas, Rafael. *José Martí: La invención de Cuba*. Madrid: Editorial Colibrí, 2000.

Ronning, C. Neale. *José Martí and the Émigré Colony in Key West*. New York: Praeger Publishers, 1990.

_____. "José Martí, Cuban Independence and the North American Economic, Political and Social Agenda." In *José Martí in the United States: The Florida Experience*, edited by Louis A. Pérez Jr., 43–56. Tempe: Arizona State University Center for Latin American Studies, 1995.

Rotker, Susana. *The American Chronicles of José Martí: Journalism and Modernity in Spanish America*. Translated by Jennifer French and Katherine Semler. Hanover, NH: University Press of New England, 2000.

_____. "José Martí and the United States: On the Margins of the Gaze." In *Re-Reading José Martí (1853–1895) One Hundred Years Later*, edited by Julio Rodríguez-Luis and translated by Jorge Hernández Martín, 17–34. Albany: State University of New York Press, 1999.

Santí, Enrico Mario. "'Our America,' the Gilded Age, and the Crises of Latinamericanism." In *José Martí's "Our America": From National to Hemisphere*, edited by Jeffrey Belnap and Raúl Fernández, 179–90. Durham, NC: Duke University Press, 1998.

_____. "Thinking through Martí." In *Re-Reading José Martí (1853–1895) One Hundred Years Later*, edited by Julio Rodríguez-Luis, 67–84. Albany: State University of New York Press, 1999.

Schraeder, Lia Theresa. "The Spirits of the Times: The Mexican Spiritist Movement from Reform to Revolution." PhD diss., University of California, Davis, 2009.

Schwartz, Jerome. *Diderot and Montaigne: The Essais and the Shaping of Diderot's Humanism*. Geneva: Librairie Droz, 1966.

"Shall Cuba Be Taken for Christ." *American Missionary* 52, no. 3 (September 1898): 106–7.

Smith, Christian. *The Emergence of Liberation Theology: Radical Religion and Social Movement Theory*. Chicago: University of Chicago Press, 1991.

Spencer, Herbert. *The Coming Slavery and Other Essays*. New York: Humboldt Publishing Co., 1888.

_____. *The Man versus the State*. London: Williams & Norgate, 1894.

Tarragó, Rafael E. "'Rights Are Taken, Not Pleaded': José Martí and the Cult of the Recourse to Violence in Cuba." In *The Cuban Republic and José Martí: Reception and Use of a National Symbol*, edited by Mauricio A. Font and Alfonso W. Quiroz, 53–70. Lanham, MD: Lexington Books, 2006.

Thomas, Hugh. *Cuba; or, The Pursuit of Freedom*. 1971. New York: Da Capo Press, 1998.

Tillich, Paul. *Dynamics of Faith*. New York: Harper Colophon Books, 1957.

Torres, Camilo. *Revolutionary Priest: The Complete Writings and Messages of Camilo Torres.* Edited by John Gerassi. London: Jonathan Cape, 1971.

Turton, Peter. *José Martí: Architect of Cuba's Freedom.* London: Zed Books, 1986.

Vales, José Francisco. "La influencia de la cultura alemana en la formación del pensamiento de José Martí." *Iberoamericana* 20, no. 1 (1996): 5–25.

Varela, Félix. "Carta a los habitantes de la Habana despidiéndose para ir a ejercer el cargo de diputado en las Cortes de 1822–1823." 1821. In *Obras II*, 91–92. Barcelona: Linkgua Ediciones, 2015.

_____. "Carta a redactor de Diario de la Habana." 1826. *El Habanero: Papel político, científico y literario* II, no. 2. In *Obras II*, 338–46. Barcelona: Linkgua Ediciones, 2015.

_____. "Cartas a Elpidio: Sobre la impiedad la superstición y el fanatismo en sus relaciones con la sociedad." 1835. In *Obras III*, 10. Barcelona: Linkgua Ediciones, 2019.

_____. "Diálogo que han tenido en esta ciudad un español partidario de la independencia de la isla de Cuba y un paisano suyo antiindependiente." 1824. *El Habanero: Papel político, científico y literario* I, no. 3. In *Obras II*, 250–53. Barcelona: Linkgua Ediciones, 2015.

_____. "Elenco de 1816." 1816. In *Obras I*, 77–97. Barcelona: Linkgua Ediciones, 2014.

_____. "Estado eclesiástico en la isla de Cuba." 1824. *El Habanero: Papel político, científico y literario* I, no. 2. In *Obras II*, 214–18. Barcelona: Linkgua Ediciones, 2015.

_____. "Proyecto para el gobierno de las provincias de Ultramar: Preámbulo de la instrucción para el gobierno de Ultramar." 1823. In *Obras II*, 112–16. Barcelona: Linkgua Ediciones, 2015.

Vitier, Cintio. *Ese sol del mundo moral: Para una historia de la eticidad cubana.* Mexico City: Siglo Veintiuno Editores, 1975.

_____. "Imagen de Martí." *Anuario Martiano* 3 (1971): 231–48.

_____. *Lecciones cubanas.* La Habana: Editorial Pueblo y Educación, 1996.

Vitier, Cintio, and Daisaku Ikeda. *José Martí Cuban Apostle: A Dialogue.* 2001. Edited and translated by Richard L. Gage. London: I. B. Tauris & Co., 2013.

Vitier, Medardo. *Las ideas y la filosofía en Cuba.* La Habana: Editorial de Ciencias Sociales, 1970.

Welsh, Alexander. *Strong Representations: Narrative and Circumstantial Evidence in England.* Baltimore: Johns Hopkins University Press, 1992.

INDEX

Garfield, James, 144
Gaudium et spes (Paul VI), 129
George, Henry, 30–31, 89
Germany, xix, 76, 79–80, 102, 116, 143, 147
Gillman, Susan, 117
Gnosticism, 89
God
  attributes of, xii, 10, 19, 28, 31, 43–44,
    47, 76–78, 81, 89, 99, 121–22, 141, 147,
    167, 190
  belief in and discipleship of, 16, 19, 43–
    44, 47, 71, 75, 77–78, 168–70, 173–74
  biblical, 23–24, 95–96, 113, 132–34, 141,
    165, 168, 173, 176
  Consciousness, 59–60, 78, 85, 142–43,
    166, 168
  as Creator, xii, 9, 17, 19, 43, 58–60, 77, 99,
    102, 114, 123, 165, 168–69, 172–73
  death of, 15, 60
  existence of, 14–15, 17, 28, 43, 67, 80, 90,
    98, 133, 165–68, 170, 194
  fear of, 164–65, 167–68
  as good, 14–15, 141, 168
  Holy Spirit, 24
  human as, 59, 166, 168–69, 175
  as human construct, 10, 15, 17, 85,
    165–67
  imago Dei, 18–19, 44, 59–60, 78, 131, 133
  incarnation in Jesus, 176, 184
  love for, 17, 44, 77, 132–33, 136, 141
  love of, 60, 95, 123, 132
  Martí understanding, 10, 14, 51, 67, 113,
    121, 123–24, 139, 141, 148, 156, 164–70,
    176, 194
  as nature, xiii, 42, 60, 62, 72, 78, 81, 88,
    98–99, 165, 169
  as *patria*, 58–63, 166, 169, 175, 194
  rejection of, 9, 15–18, 20, 28, 76, 80, 92,
    99, 148, 161–62, 164, 177
  revelation of, 15, 37, 42, 47, 76, 80, 85,
    92, 180–81
  solidarity with, 148–49, 177
  soul of, 77, 97
  worship of, 17, 59, 121, 148–49, 165, 177
  See also Jesus Christ; panentheism;
    pantheism

Gómez, Juan Gualberto, 83
Gómez, Máximo, 20, 83, 138–39, 161, 178, 190
Gonçalves, João Felipe, xiii
González, Manuel Pedro, xvii, 52
González Serra, Diego Jorge, 168–69
Grant, Ulysses S., 52, 142
Greek
  civilization, 9–10, 26, 46, 89, 122, 166,
    187
  language, xix, 41, 128, 135
Guerra, Lillian, xiii, xv
Gutiérrez, Gustavo, 126–27, 129–31
Gutiérrez Marroquín, Carolina, 86, 133

Habanero, El (Varela), 41, 43
Haiti, 82, 142
harmony
  Bible with nonsupernatural, 49
  ethics with aesthetics, 4, 112, 178–79
  humans with God, 77–78, 81, 97–99, 103,
    112, 169–75
  humans with nature, 77, 111–12, 172
  humans with social order, 171–72
  humans with themselves, 77
  with rationalism, 77, 81, 88, 113
  religious with political, 81, 101
  spiritual and material, 81, 99, 112–13,
    122–23, 172, 178–79
Harrison, Benjamin, 144
Hartmann, Eduard von, 89, 201n5
Hebrew language, xix, 128
Hechavarría, Santiago José de, 35
Hegel, Georg Wilhelm, 76–78, 98, 112,
  210n106
Henríquez y Carvajal, Federico, 153
hermeneutical suspicion, xv, 5, 158
Hidalgo, Miguel, 67
hija de rey, La (Peón Contreras), 180–81
Hinduism, 10, 62, 88, 101–3, 112–13, 123
History of Cuba at a Glance, The (Carrasco), 21
human
  depravity of, 27, 32, 36, 64, 103, 130–31,
    136, 170, 184–89
  duty of, 28, 35, 58, 133–35, 147, 152–53, 156,
    168, 170–73, 176, 179, 190–92, 194, 196

Printed in the USA
CPSIA information can be obtained
at www.ICGtesting.com
LVHW100328300823
756702LV00004B/331

9 780826 501677